P9-DWM-846

CALGARY PUBLIC LIBRARY

SEP - - 2005

DRAW YOUR OWN
MANGA
BEYOND THE BASICS

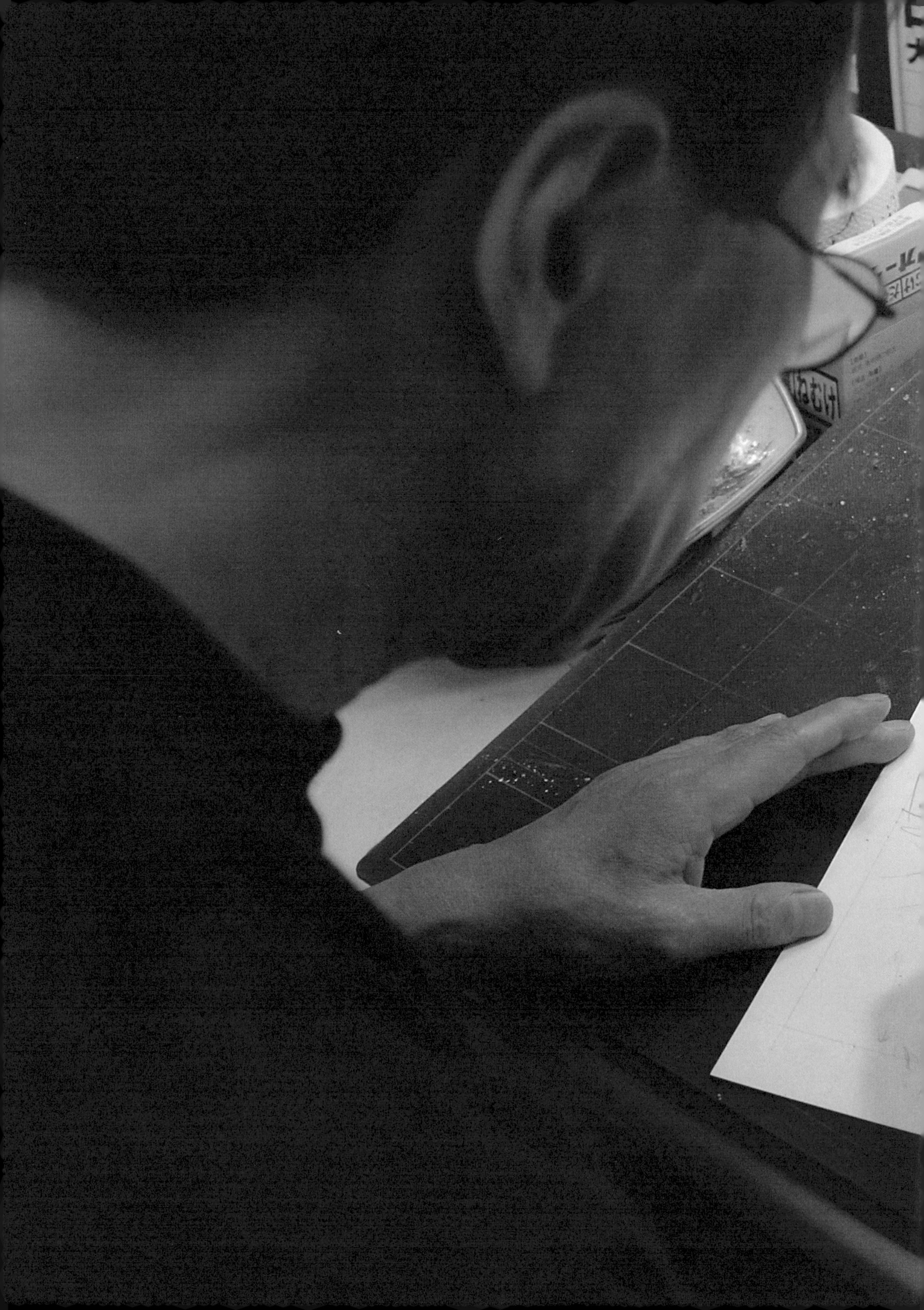

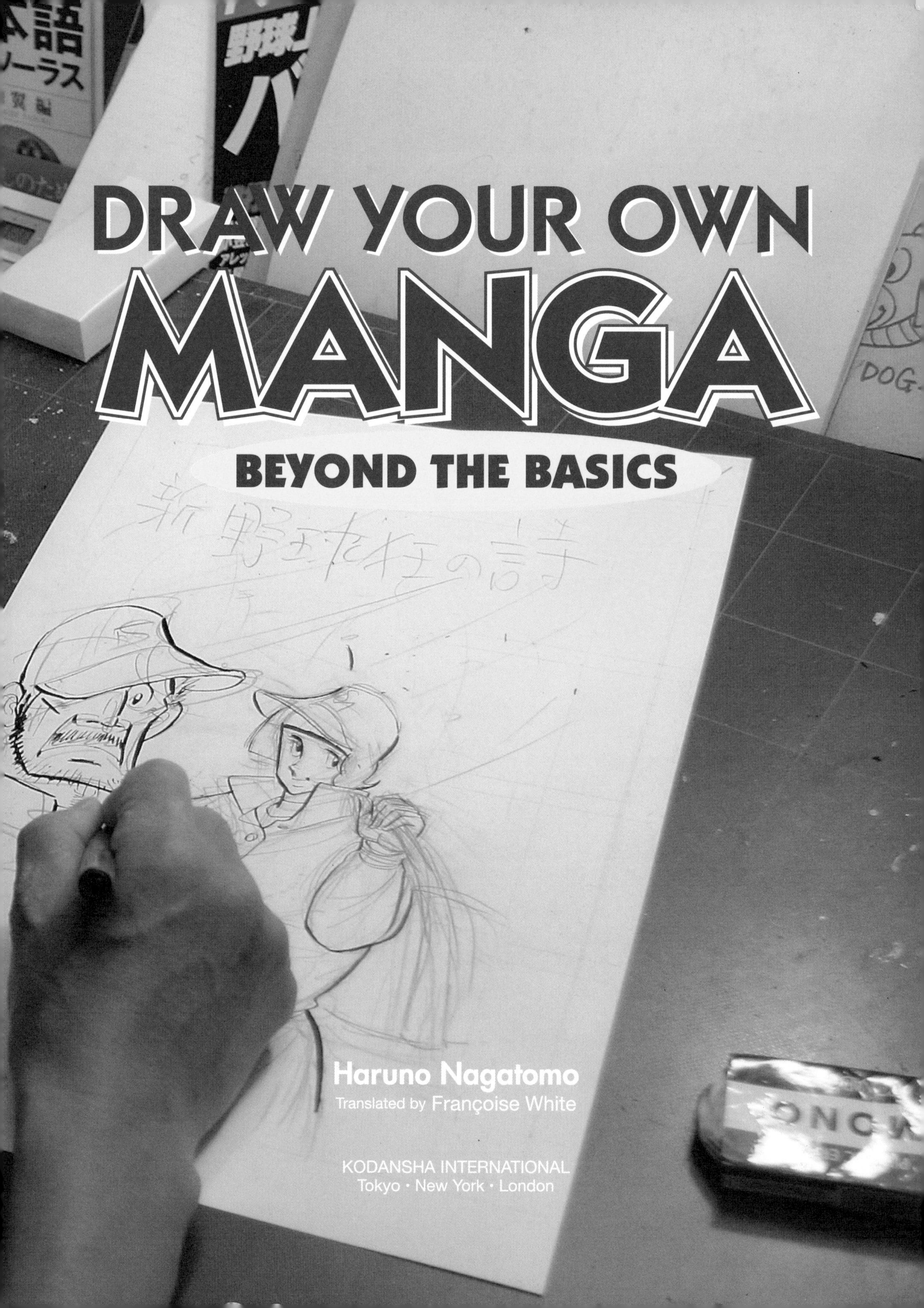

DRAW YOUR OWN MANGA

BEYOND THE BASICS

Haruno Nagatomo
Translated by Françoise White

KODANSHA INTERNATIONAL
Tokyo • New York • London

Photos of Shinji Mizushima by Kyūzō Akashi.

Pages 20–21, 23–38, 45–51, 54–70, 85–109
originally published in Japanese as *Manga,
irasto no kakikata suteppuappu hen*, edited by I.C. Inc.
and published by I.C. Inc. and Coade in 2003.

Distributed in the United States by Kodansha America, Inc.,
and in the United Kingdom and continental Europe by Kodansha Europe Ltd.

Published by Kodansha International Ltd.,
17–14 Otowa 1-chome, Bunkyo-ku, Tokyo 112–8652,
and Kodansha America, Inc.

Copyright © 2005 by I.C. Inc., Coade, and Kodansha International Ltd.
All rights reserved. Printed in Japan.
ISBN-13: 978-4-7700-2304-9
ISBN-10: 4-7700-2304-9

First edition, 2005
05 06 07 08 09 10 11 12   10 9 8 7 6 5 4 3 2 1

www. kodansha-intl.com

CONTENTS

"What's important in manga, and especially in sports manga, is that it should be powerful. To capture the sense of movement and speed, I redraw my manuscripts so many times they end up covered in black!"

Shinji Mizushima

Baseball is the most popular sport in Japan. Most kids here are familiar with a vocabulary used only in manga, so mentioning "baseball manga" to anyone will elicit an immediate response of "Shinji Mizushima." Likewise, mention "Shinji Mizushima" to anyone and they will say "baseball manga." Shinji Mizushima's best-known works are "Dokaben," "Abu-san" ("Mr. Abu"), and "Yakyūkyō no uta" ("Poem of the Baseball Craze"). These manga series lay claim to two generations of fans, adults and children, while the characters have come to be loved by all, even by female fans who have never played baseball. Their influence reaches not just the players in the Little League, High School League, and University League, but also a significant number in the professional leagues. Mizushima's work has also established a new style of drawing baseball in manga, from pitching and batting form to strategy and the playing field, and has influenced many manga artists.

Why did you choose baseball manga?

I was a big baseball fan to begin with, and thought it would be nice to draw pictures reflecting my passion. Unfortunately, though, my technique wasn't up to it. So whatever I tried to draw—pitching, batting, catching, running—didn't reflect how I understood baseball to be. So I continued to draw as much as possible, and accepted every offer of work except manga for young girls. That's why I've drawn historical and comic manga, too. Eventually, I became adept and could draw whatever I wanted to. I experimented more and more, and in 1970 I started "Otoko do aho Kōshien" ("Guys Crazy for Kōshien"). It was adapted to animation, and I worked on the series for five years. The ideas that came in during that time were all about baseball. I started the "Dokaben" series in 1972 and the "Mr. Abu" series in 1973. After that, I worked exclusively on baseball manga.

What is the most difficult thing about drawing baseball manga?

You must be able to draw a player doing a particular action in a particular position on a huge playing field. It's pointless if you can't express this on paper. Look at "Kyojin no hoshi" ("Star of the Giants," story by Ikki Kajiwara, drawn by Noboru Kawasaki): if you try to include everything you lose the sense of perspective. The second baseman is next to the first baseman, and the shortstop moves between them. This explains the scene well, but it holds no sense of reality for baseball fans. That's why I put a considerable amount of effort into the composition. Manga artists sometimes refer to film footage for the composition, but really we have more freedom. It's difficult for movie directors to turn manga into a movie. On the other hand, in manga we can't produce subtle perspectives that expand slowly, like in Akira Kurosawa's *Seven Samurai* or *Yojimbo the Bodyguard*.

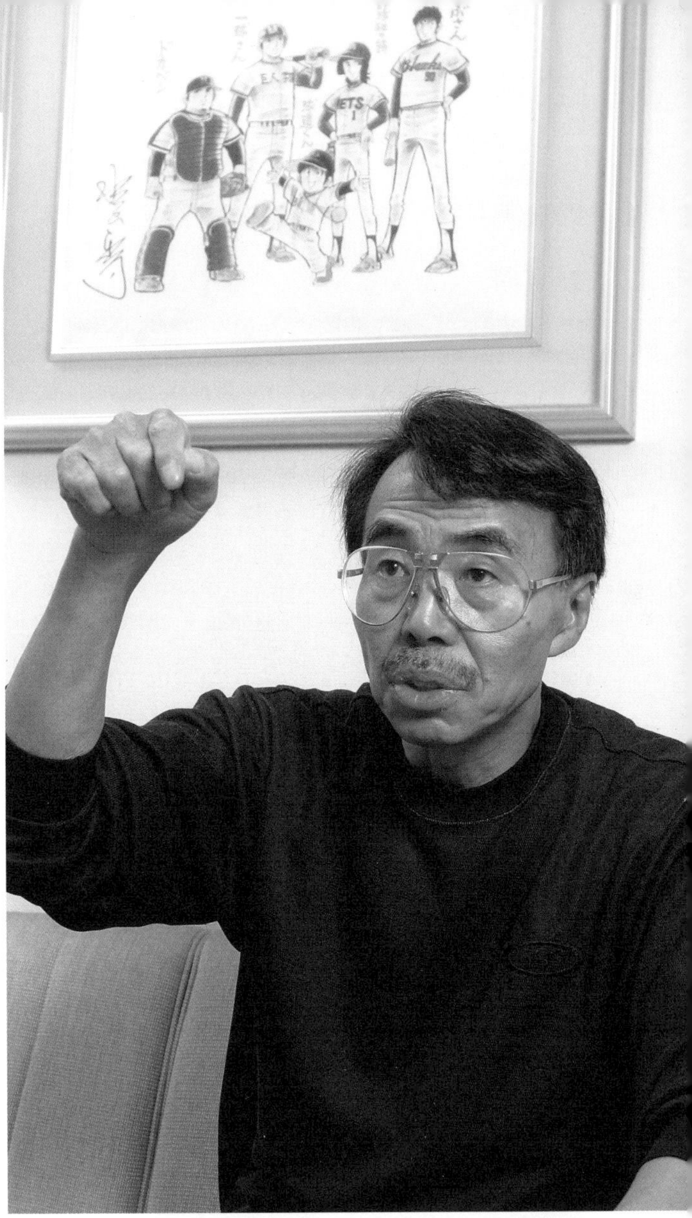

Your works have been animated for TV and cinema. How different is the animation from your original work?

I don't pay attention to television animation at all. One to two hundred animators draw picture cells based on my original pictures. They change it, resulting in a different flavor from that of the original, which is only natural. Once I was at an autograph session and had just drawn Dokaben when a child exclaimed, "That's not Dokaben!" When I heard that, it dawned on me that animation is a completely different genre. With its merchandise, theme songs, and so on, I think it possesses an awesome power.

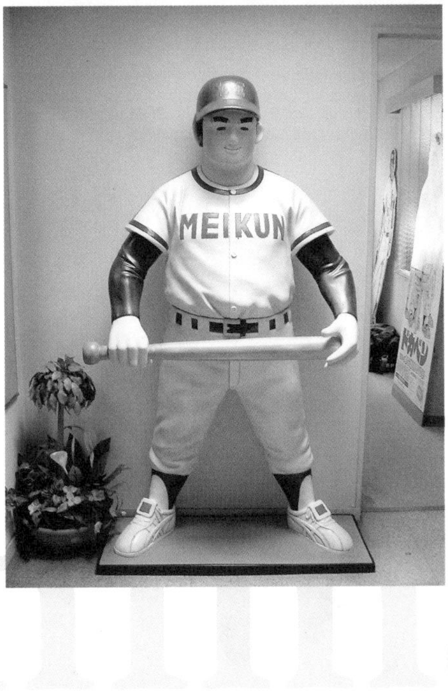
MEIKUN

How do you come up with your characters?

When I create a story, I start by deciding what kind of baseball team I want it to be about. Then I consider the kind of guy I want the pitcher to be. After finishing him, I give him a name to suit his face, and I decide everything from his height and weight, to his birth date and even his blood type! Then I do the same for the catcher. The catcher wears a face mask most of the time, so I have to create a face that will be instantly recognizable even through the mask. Take Tarō Yamada in "Dokaben," for example (Dokaben is Yamada's nickname). While other players perform amazing manga-style feats, I decided to portray Yamada as an average baseball kid. He's very determined, but he doesn't have any secret batting techniques, but neither is he particularly bad at pitching or batting. Kids who play baseball generally like complex characters, but I gave Yamada a rough and ready personality.

Anywhere in Japan, Tarō Yamada is recognizable as the most common name for a guy. The name Iwaki, on the other hand, is made up of the kanji for "rock" and "demon," and suits a tough and tenacious character. I got the name Satonaka from the one-time top artist in girls' manga, Machiko Satonaka. At that point, there weren't any female fans and I hoped the girls would relate to Satonaka. I also got the name Satoru from one of the kanji that make up the name Machiko.

Anyway, I think about the character first because his personality will naturally translate into his actions. Even the birth date is important! Yamada's birthday is May 5th, which is Children's Day in Japan—this confers on him a special privilege, so he only gets moving when he wants to. For example, I can make a story out of Iwaki going to see Yamada at the house where he lives with his sister, Sachiko. Sachiko's a tomboy, so she'd probably give Iwaki a hard time. Iwaki would probably react badly to this and call her ugly, even though she's actually quite cute. And it would develop from there.

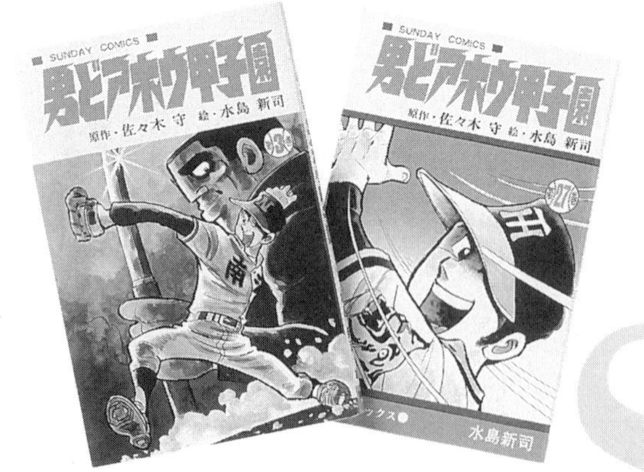
SUNDAY COMICS
男どアホウ甲子園
原作・佐々木守 絵・水島新司
SUNDAY COMICS
男どアホウ甲子園
原作・佐々木守 絵・水島新司
水島新司

The scriptwriter of TV's "Jūdō Icchokusen" ("Yawara! A Fashionable Judo Girl"), Mamoru Sasaki, was responsible for one of your works, wasn't he?

Yes, that was "Guys Crazy for Kōshien." I started it originally, but it was my first long-running serial and my stomach suffered badly from the stress. When it seemed like I couldn't carry on any longer, the editor in charge said we could get someone else to write the story, since the characters were already developed. So he talked with Mamoru Sasaki, who understood the situation and agreed to take over halfway through. But he didn't know the first thing about baseball, so when it came to scenes of the game, he stopped work and I developed that part instead. It was quite an unusual style of manga. Together we dreamed up ideas that would never have occurred to me by myself, like having a player wear drifter's clothing. We weren't just a good team, we were phenomenal.

What do you like drawing most of all in baseball manga?

When I read "Star of the Giants," I wonder whether baseball is really that heartbreaking! Will kids reading this even want to play baseball? It's a story of two generations aspiring to be the Giants' pitching ace. But baseball is really about the unity between the players—without this, they can never win, so naturally I like to portray cooperation in team sports. High school baseball is perfect for this, especially with the setting of the awe-inspiring Kōshien stadium (where the annual high school championship tournament is held). That's how I started "Dokaben."

You often base your stories on real-life characters and incidents, don't you?

"Dokaben" was originally just a story about high school, but when it became a pro-baseball series I started to incorporate real players. In "Mr. Abu," we used real baseball teams from the beginning, and as a result it was complicated from day one. It took about three years until the team let me have free rein with the story. At that time, the Pacific League was generally lacking in any sort of excitement, so they asked me to use manga to help spark interest in it and improve the stadium turnout. I said, "Okay, I'll do it for the Pacific League," and in that spirit continued for the next twenty-six years. Baseball is like that—you can play it, watch it, and even draw it, but you'll never tire of it. I'm lucky that even when I'm working it doesn't feel like work. It's a hobby and I draw for pleasure, so I usually end each year having worked solely on baseball. And because of that, I'm still able to draw actively at the age of sixty-five.

You're also well-known as a pitcher in amateur baseball. Do you think that playing baseball is useful for drawing baseball manga?

Not really, I don't want to obtain anything useful from playing amateur baseball. I do it only because I enjoy it. I wouldn't want to give up playing and just manage an amateur team either. That's why I'll keep doing my best as a player. My favorite team has turned out to be based in Kyushu and when I go to watch a game I take the bullet train, even though it takes five hours, because I hate planes. The best thing about going to a game, of course, is talking to the players, since I have free access to the locker rooms. If you only see the players on the field, you don't really get to appreciate their personalities.

Did you love baseball even as a child?

Yes I did, but I was so busy helping with the housework after school that I couldn't join a team even though I wanted to. And I longed to go to Meikun high school (which has a strong baseball team), but that was just a dream, too. When I was eighteen, I drew a manga called "Shinya no Kyaku" ("The Midnight Guest") and it won the Hinomaru manga prize. At the award ceremony, the company president observed, "So you're living at home, studying manga, and not working, is that it?" So I went to Osaka, despite my parents' opposition, and worked for him for six years drawing manga. When I was twenty-nine, I moved to Tokyo, and was invited to join Ikki Kajiwara's baseball team. It was the first time I had played in a team and I was surprised to find how good I was at playing. Until then, all I'd known about baseball was what I had seen on TV and heard on the radio. So I understood how it worked.

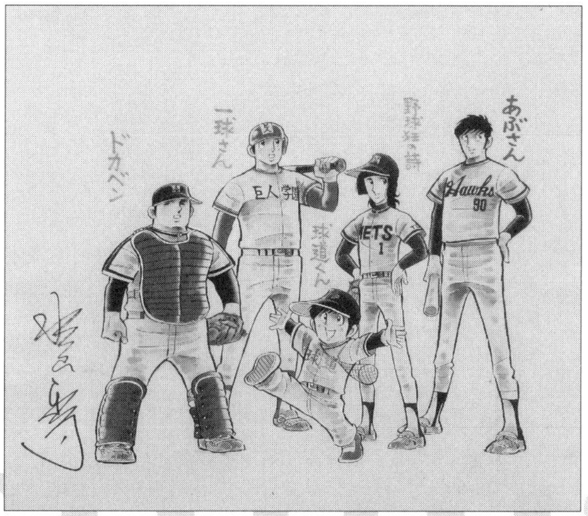

あぶさん
Hawks
90
野球狂の詩
METS
1
球道くん
一球さん
巨人学園
ドカベン

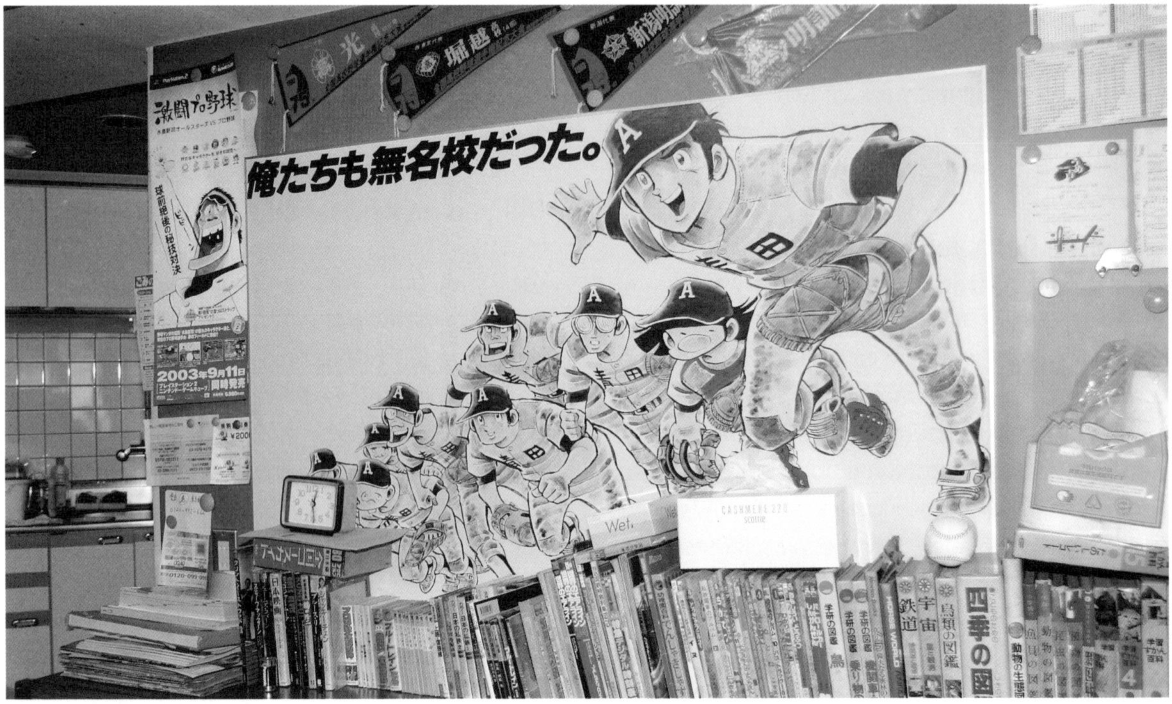
俺たちも無名校だった。
激闘プロ野球
2003年9月11日

Did you feel from early on that you would go into sports manga?

I've liked drawing since I was a child, especially manga—that might be why I came to create stories based around the characters. I used to imitate the manga of various artists. Osamu Tezuka was one, of course. And I copied various characters from "Donguri Tengu" (The Acorn-Faced, Long-Nosed Goblin) by Sōji Ushio to make my own playing cards. But more than Osamu Tezuka, I have been influenced by Takao Saitō of "Golgo 13" fame.

Moreover, I loved sports, but I left school after junior high and became a street hawker. Meikun and Niigata Shōgyō high schools were on our peddling route, and while my mom was doing the rounds I used to watch the baseball practice through the fence, although honestly speaking they weren't much good. One time I was watching a training session at the Niigata Shōgyō field and a player I'd been to school with was talking to the coach about something. He ran over to tell me, "We've been talking about you. The coach says he wants you do some catching practice." I was so happy! By the fifth ball, the coach said to the team, "Look, a boy who doesn't even play isn't scared of the ball, why can't you lot be like him?" I still clearly remember those words! They encouraged me to really dive to catch those balls. Later, I adapted this experience for a manga episode.

What are the key points for drawing sports manga?

There is always a particular fashion and style of the time. That's why my pictures also change. Baseball uniforms do, too. These days players wear something resembling longjohns, don't they? A long-running baseball manga series is like drawing a history of the fashion of players' pants!

The hardest thing to express in baseball and soccer manga is action and movement. For example, the batter skillfully slides to safety just before the fielder tags him because the fielder messes up somehow. It's this kind of stuff that you must be able to express in your drawing. A failed chase tag must be drawn accurately. I think young manga artists today don't have the patience to draw and redraw the manuscript until it's perfect. They just want to complete a commission, that's all. But if someone truly loves drawing, say, motorbikes, they'll pay infinite attention to getting just one wheel right. It's really hard to get that sense of speed when a wheel spins round. People who love cars will draw them in the manga style, while trying to make it as close as possible to the real thing to get that sense of speed too. In manga we can't depict the kind of speed seen in movies, so we write in sound effects like "whoosh" or "zip" for effect. I do this too for characters like Yamada and Iwaki when they hit a home run!

I racked my brains over how to depict Iwaki batting a really amazing ball that seems to fly forever. I drew the batting form first and then hit upon the idea of simply drawing a small ink dot in a blank white area to depict the ball. I was really excited when I thought of that!

Do you redraw your work a lot even now?

I probably redraw my work more than any other manga artist! Sometimes I look at a manuscript after redrawing it and wonder just what was so wrong with it. Even I'm not sure. It was probably something that I just felt was needed at that moment. For example, I get the feeling that the position of a player's feet is wrong, so I spread the legs a little wider. But then I realize that in that position, the hips are a bit tighter. So I say to myself, "That's the posture I wanted!" and set about redrawing that too. I mostly get absorbed in depicting the players' quirks when they step onto the plate. For example, I remember how the well-known pitcher Yutaka Enatsu goes to the mound and grasps the ball in a certain way on the first pitch. It's this sort of physical gesture that I really like.

Facial expressions and physical gestures are important in manga, aren't they?

I draw quite a few well-known players, but I'm not inclined to make the face resemble the actual person. Enatsu has square facial features and is slightly plump, so I use these features but only to the extent that it makes him recognizable. The rest is exaggerating the body type and gestures. From that point, the readers can expand the image by themselves. If Enatsu said to me, "I'm not this fat!" I'd reply that it was just an image. Actually he isn't fat at all, but anyone who sees that image will recognize it's him. And that's what manga is all about. Kazumi Saitō of the Daiei Hawks is very tall and lanky, while Kadokura's chin is long. I tell everyone that it's about exaggeration. The players' kids probably tell their dad, "That doesn't look anything like you!" If that happens, I hope they explain why.

So when you meet people, are you on the lookout for these features?

Yes, I am. Once I got the feeling that a player was telling me, "I throw with my left hand but I eat with my right." He didn't say this explicitly, but I could tell by watching him. But I sometimes get it wrong. Once a player told me, "You made

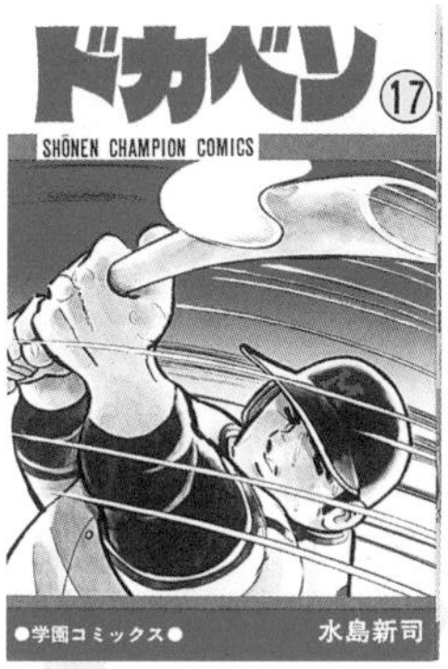
ドカベン
17
SHŌNEN CHAMPION COMICS
●学園コミックス●
水島新司

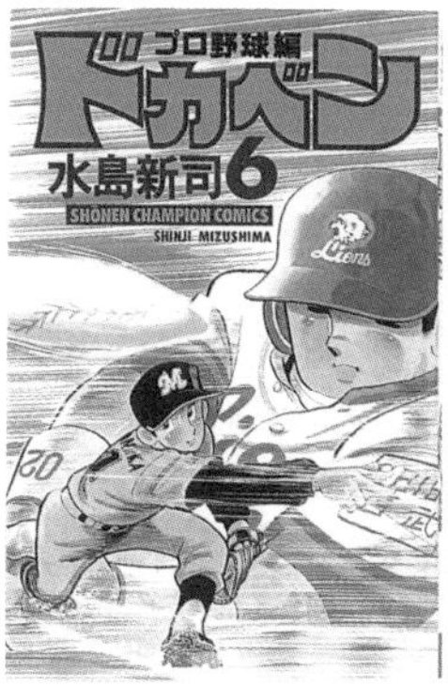
プロ野球編
ドカベン
水島新司6
SHŌNEN CHAMPION COMICS
SHINJI MIZUSHIMA

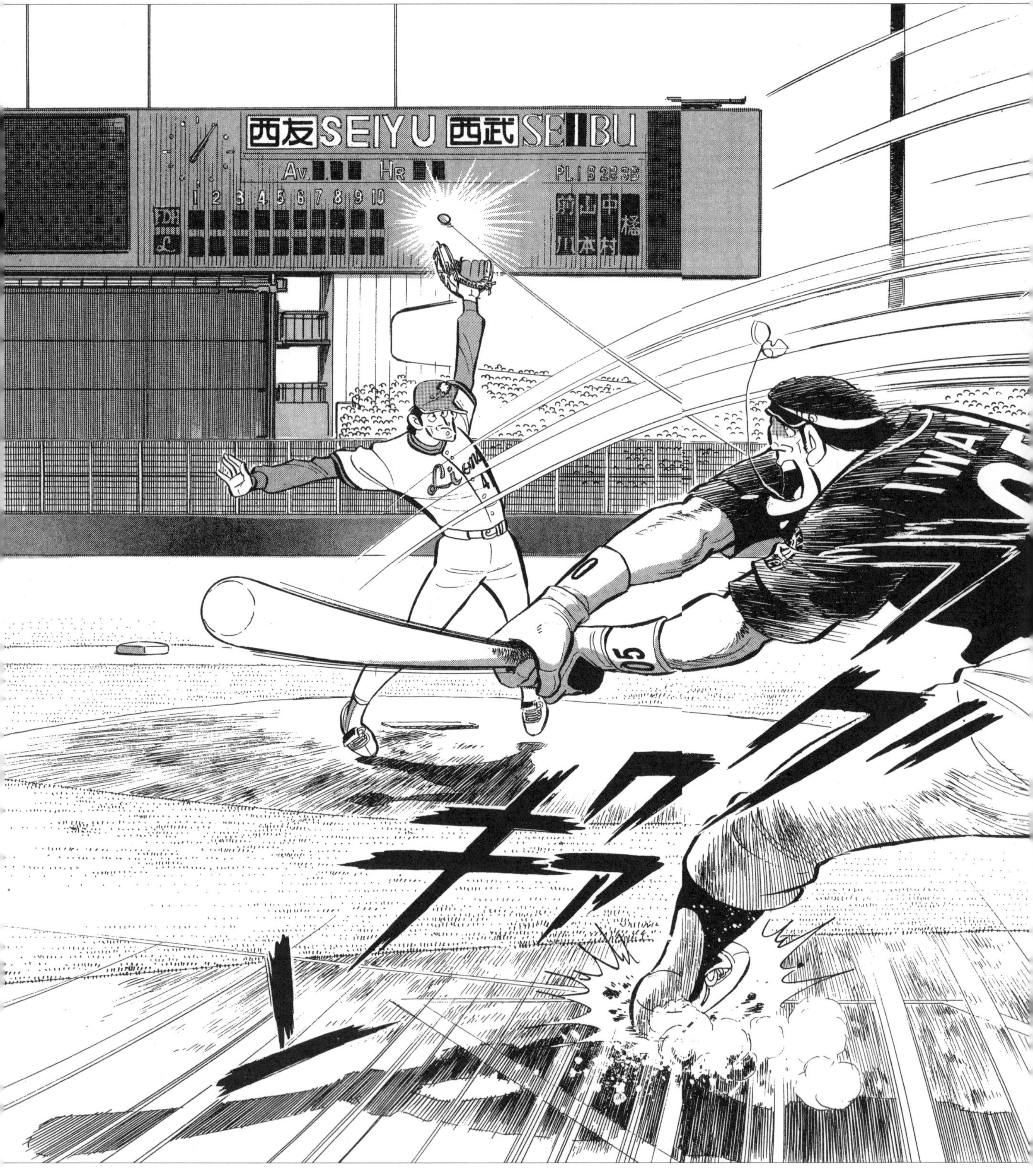
西友SEIYU 西武SEIBU
Av.
HR
PL 1B 2B 3B
カキ

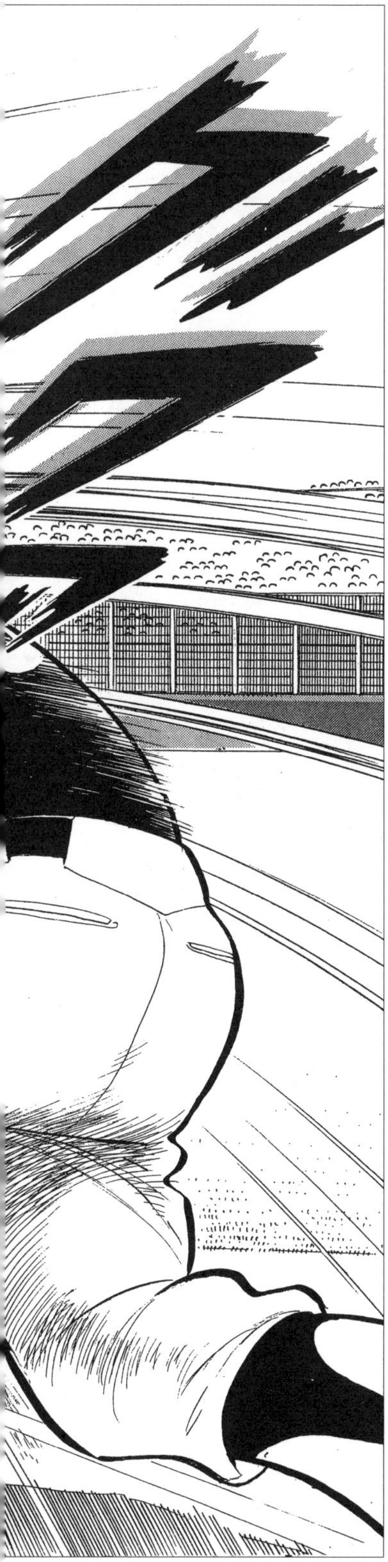

Left: Iwaki hits a home run. From the "Dokaben" series.

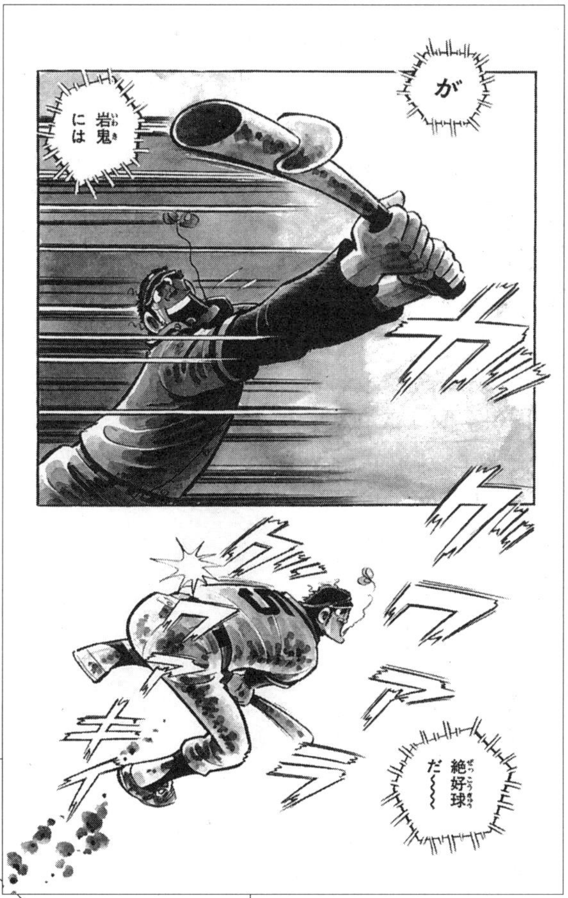
岩鬼には
が
絶好球だ〜〜

Right: Iwaki slugs the ball hard. From the "Dokaben" series.

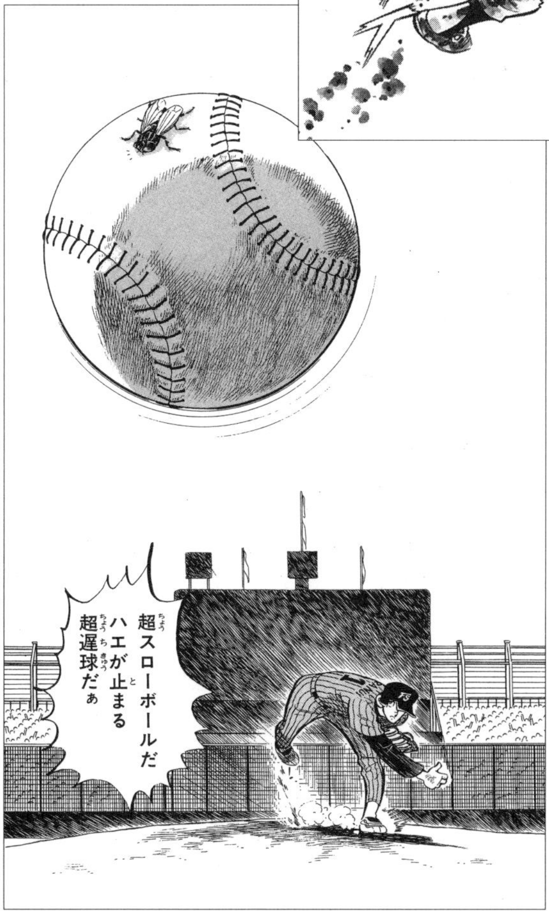
超スローボールだ
ハエが止まる
超遅球だぁ

Left: Shiranui's pitch is so slow that a fly lands on it! From the "Dokaben" series.

a mistake, didn't you? I write with my right hand and eat with my left, so actually I'm left handed." I replied, "Is that so? I'm sorry!" These gestures and habits come out in manga as the player's mood and character.

Do you have a message for other manga artists?

A work that bursts forth from your heart will reach every corner of the country. And nowadays your name and manga characters can reach a wider world through the Internet. Which leads me to think there is more to what I've always thought of as "just manga."

The Asian Manga Summit takes place in a different country each year and was held in Japan in 2002. I asked attendees what they thought about baseball manga, and the general consensus was that it's getting really popular. All the manga artists attending had heard of "Dokaben,"

and it's apparently popular in Taiwan, Korea, and China. I was a bit confused when they kept saying "suitō" to me, but I eventually realized this was the Chinese pronunciation for the kanji characters for "water" and "island" that make up my name! There may be fewer baseball fans than soccer fans around the world, but things like this make me glad that I've continued to draw baseball manga.

Lastly, can you offer any advice to people who can draw quite well but who want to improve their skills?

After becoming a professional, I just kept drawing and drawing. This is the only way to cultivate your abilities in drawing baseball manga. And then it was another nine years until I really took off. During that time, my perception gradually changed. What's important in manga, and especially in sports manga, is that it should be powerful. Action expressed in pictures. So there's no such thing as an advanced or intermediate level, is there? Personally, I can't really agree with schools teaching manga. We live in a world where drawing by yourself is really the only way to become good.

If there is any shortcut to getting good, it's to make up a story and draw your own pictures for it. There are no constraints, so you can cut out any bits you don't like. Start with drawing the things you like, that don't bore you, and keep drawing until you can draw anything. If you tend to draw certain things, then that's okay because they'll start to become part of your style.

At the Asian Manga Summit, pictures are brought together from all over the world. Seeing this display of manga is inspiring, and will lead to the art evolving. This is why I take part in the summit. Everyone who aspires to be a manga artist is talented, and I don't think I can teach them anything. There are schools where you can study manga, but I believe that doing it yourself like I did is really the only way. Takao Yaguchi, who is famous for "Tsurikichi Sanpei" ("Fishing-Mad Sanpei," see Draw Your Own Manga: All the Basics), couldn't very well teach his specific style of drawing grass and trees, could he? It'd be like, "You get the feel of grass like this" and "a sheet of spray is like this" or "you cast the line with a whip-like action." You only draw something if it interests you. And if you think, "No, it's not like this!" then you redraw it again and again. And eventually it starts to come together. When all is said and done, you've just got to draw a lot.

So it's about developing your good points and putting in a lot of effort, isn't it?

That's what all learning is about! It's similar to leaving high school and then going to college. Having drawn baseball manga for this long, I've thought about it a lot and decided that everyone has a particular ability. The world around us is really just a collection of skilled people. Many people don't know what to do after graduating from university, while some people are skilled in a trade by the time they leave high school. You sometimes see these experts on TV, and they excel in their own fields. I'd like to tell everybody to try to discover work that they like, and then to devote themselves to it no matter what it takes.

There are many genres within baseball manga, not just pro-baseball or teen stories. For example, there could be a sci-fi manga in which a player comes from the planet Mars … that'd be good! I couldn't do it, but there must someone out there with that sort of talent and I'd love to see people working on all different styles of baseball manga. Come to think of it, in Yasusuke Gomi's novel *Sportsman Ittōsai*, a samurai swordsman living in the present day appears at a stadium out of the blue and bats a home run! It's a rather bizarre story, but the author depicted Ittōsai with some distinct samurai-style features. Writers in the past were quite particular about this sort of thing.

I think that it will take time, but I'm hopeful that people from other countries will start drawing baseball manga from an original angle with their own unique perspective, in a style completely different to ours, because I too wish to be inspired.

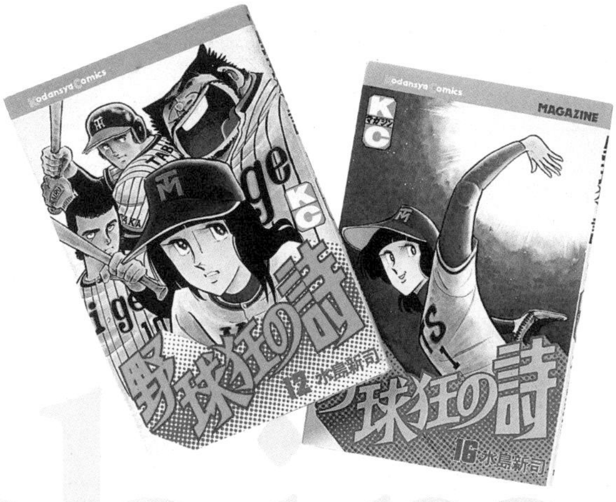

MAGAZINE
球狂の詩

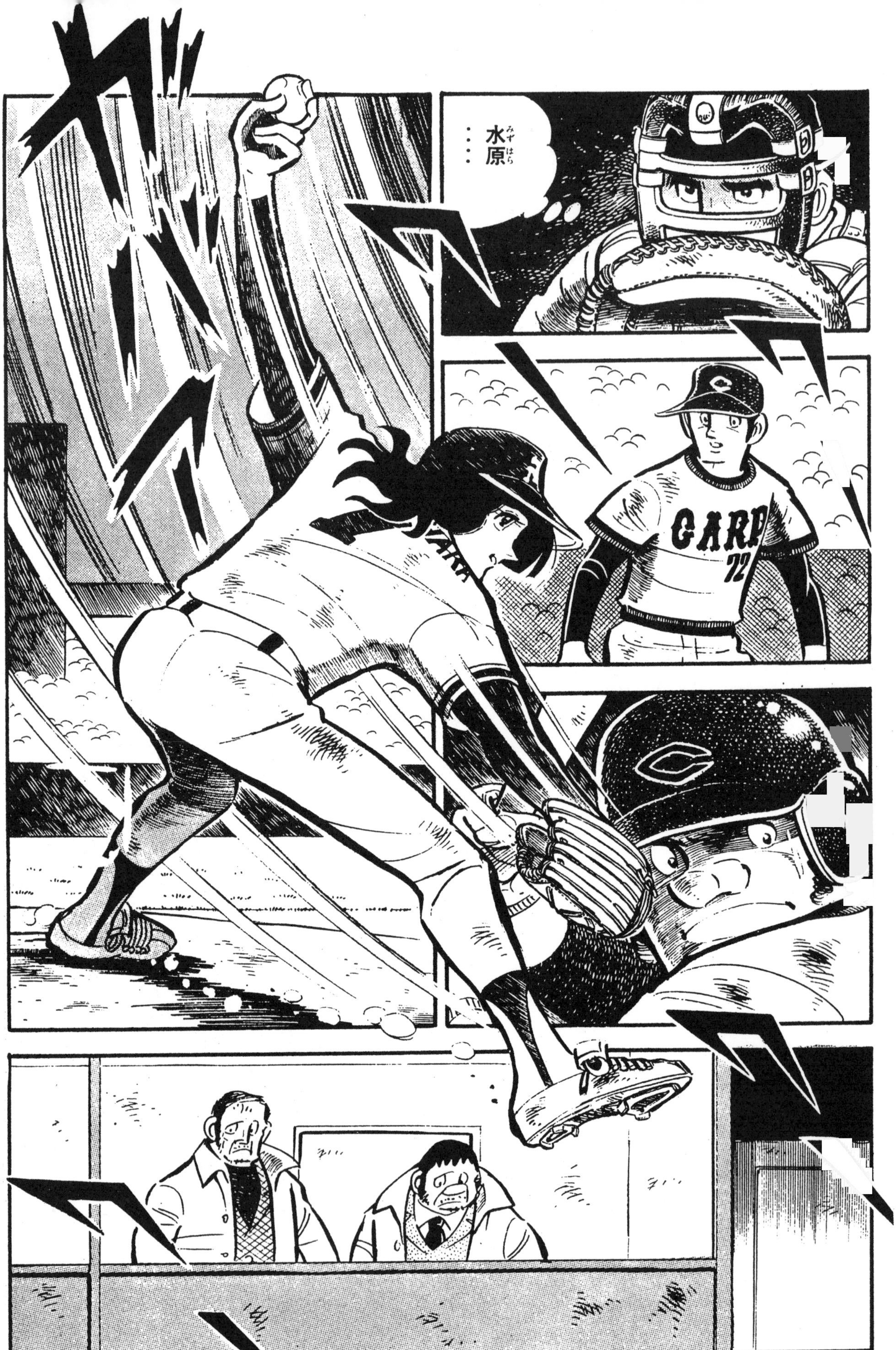
水原……
ガバッ

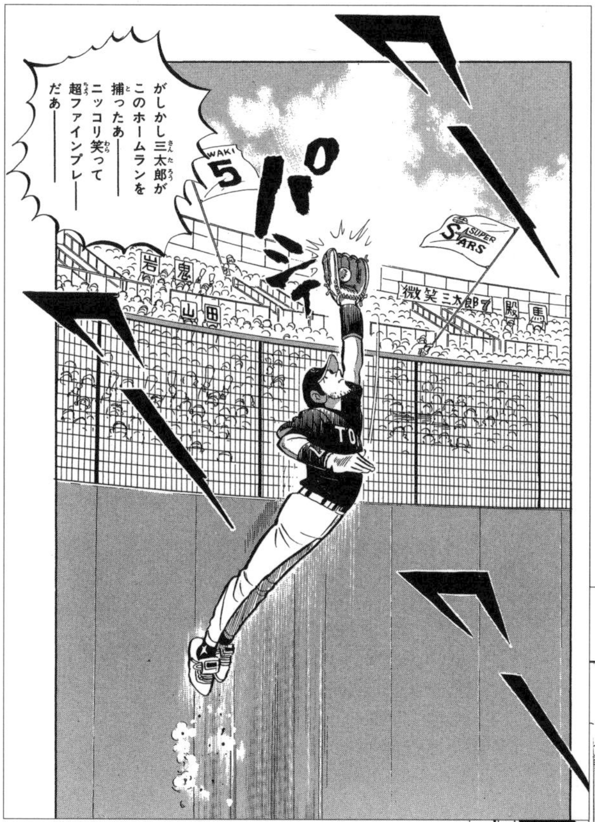
がしかし三太郎が このホームランを 捕ったあ―― ニッコリ笑って 超ファインプレ――だあ――
パシィ

Left: Santarō stops a home run with his catch. From the “Dokaben” series.

Below: And misses a catch to allow a two-run homer. From the “Dokaben” series.

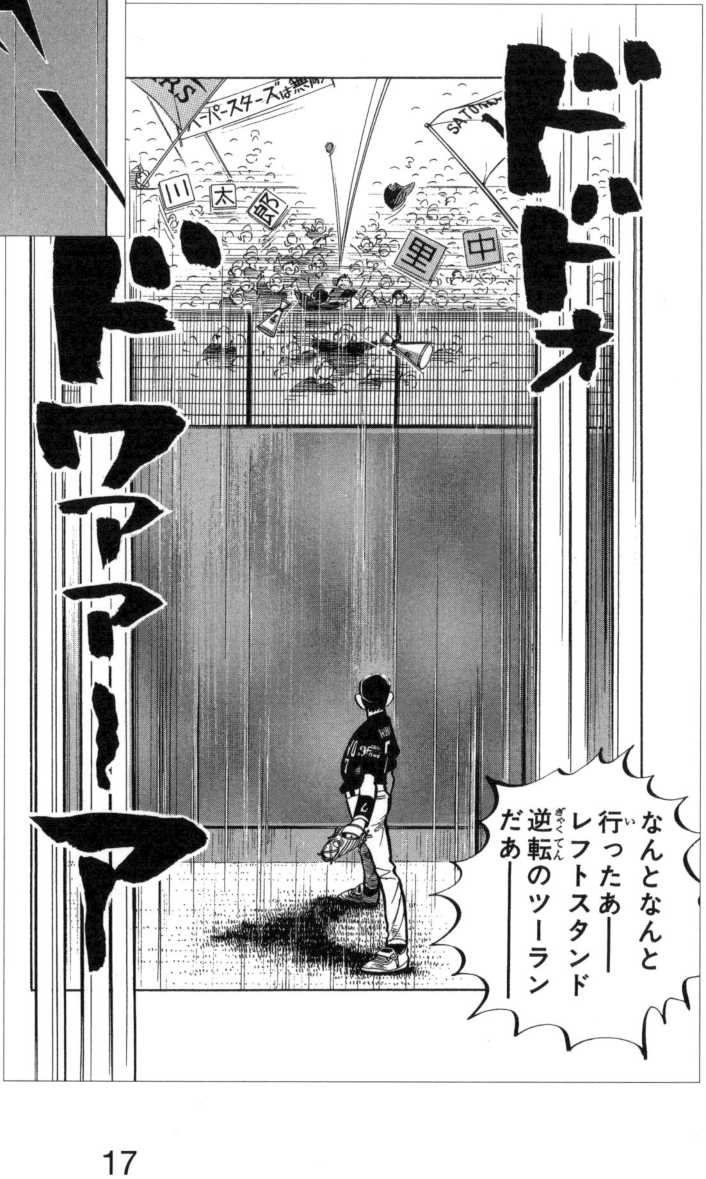
ドドオ
ドワアア―ア
なんとなんと 行ったあ―― レフトスタンド 逆転のツーラン だあ――

Left: The speed of Mizuhara’s pitch is emphasized by her stepping out of the frame. From the “Poem of the Baseball Craze” series.

The same scene created in tone (right) and ink (left) to different effect. From the “Dokaben” series.

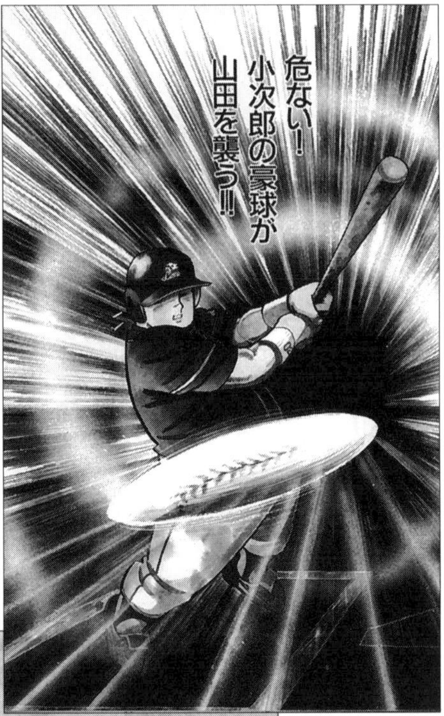
危ない!
小次郎の豪球が
山田を襲う!!

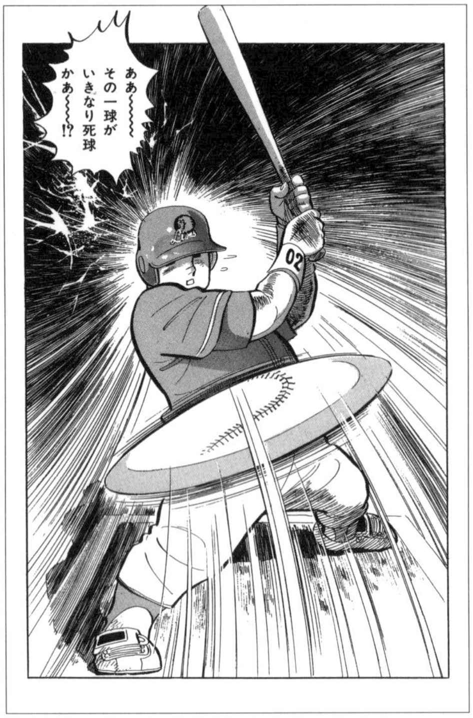
ああ〜〜〜
その一球が
いきなり死球
かあ〜〜〜!?

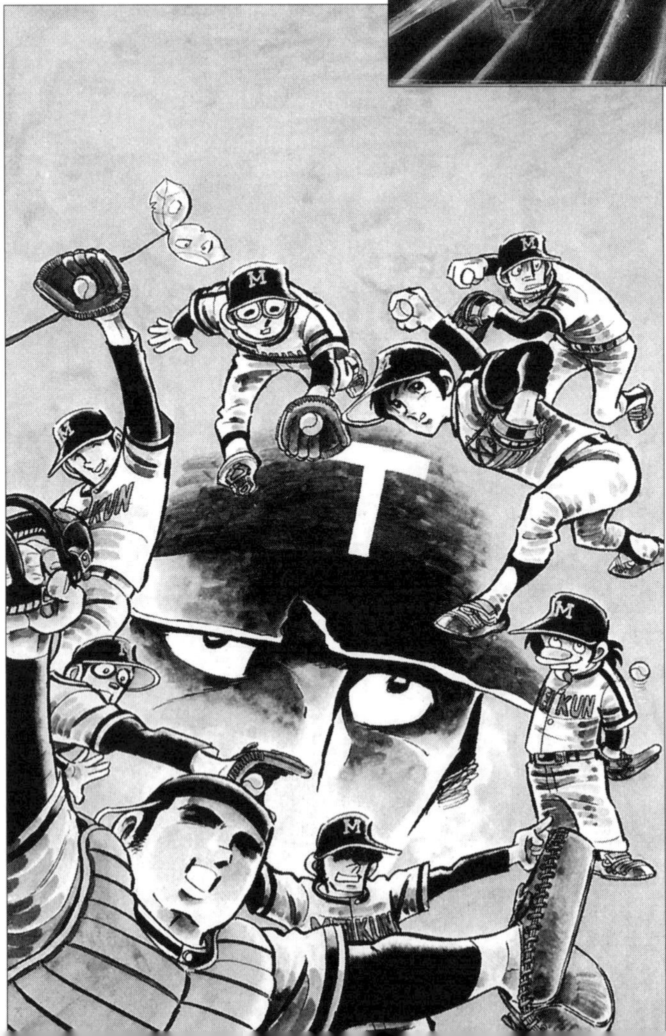

Right: Introducing the team! From the “Dokaben” series.

DRAW YOUR OWN
MANGA

BEYOND THE BASICS

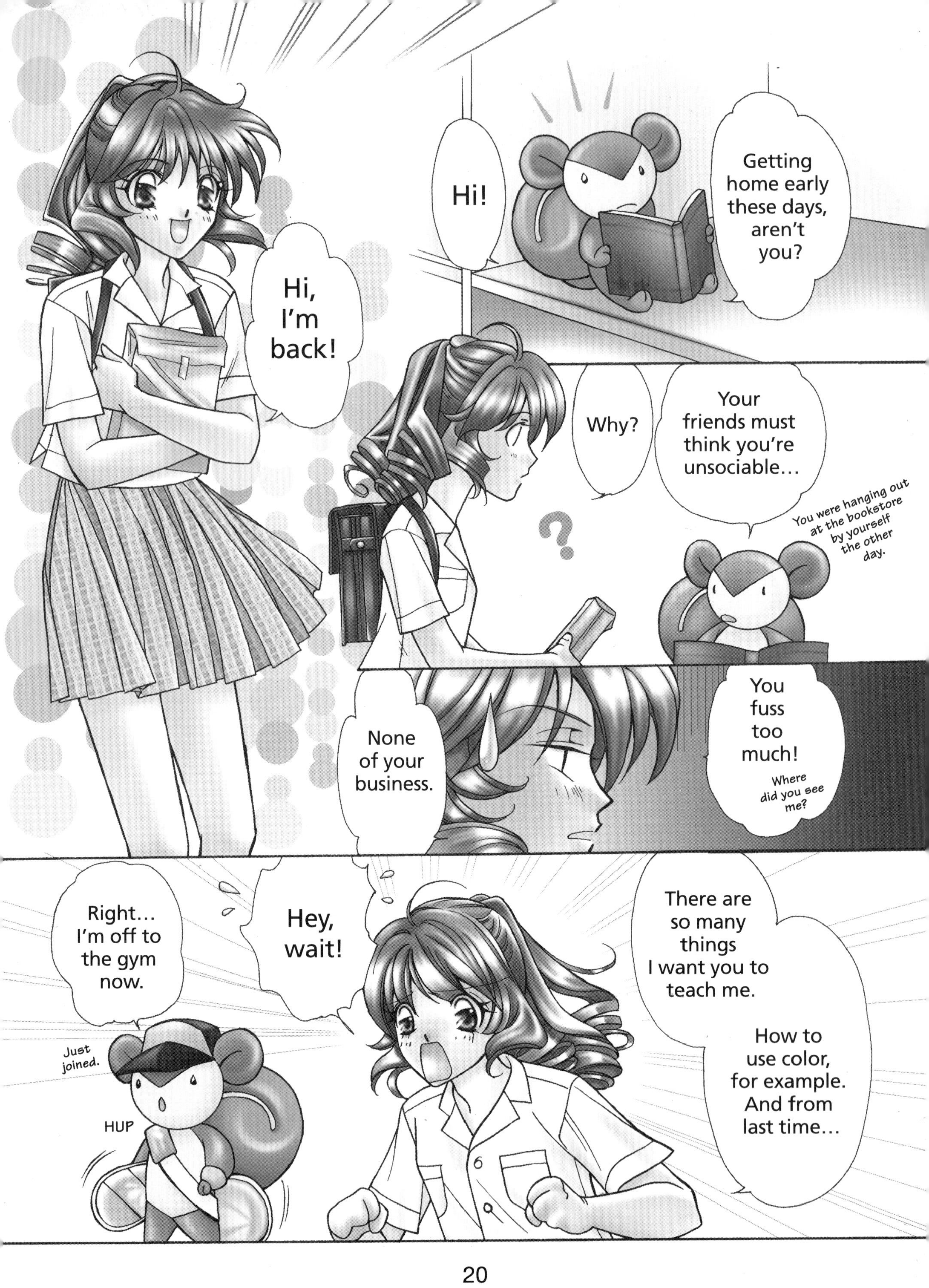
Hi, I'm back!
Hi!
Getting home early these days, aren't you?
Why?
Your friends must think you're unsociable…
You were hanging out at the bookstore by yourself the other day.
None of your business.
You fuss too much!
Where did you see me?
Right… I'm off to the gym now.
Just joined.
HUP
Hey, wait!
There are so many things I want you to teach me.
How to use color, for example. And from last time…

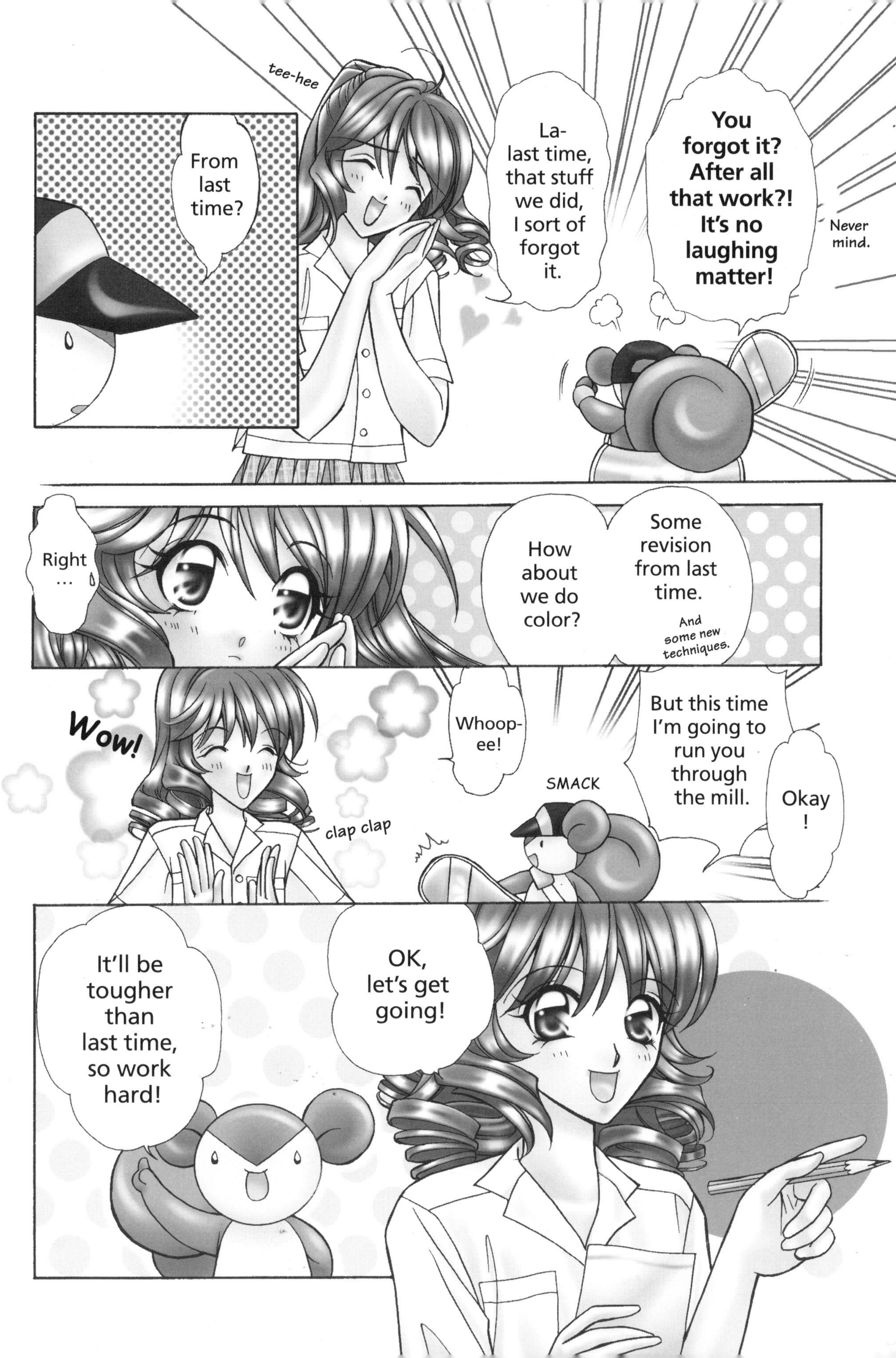

tee-hee
From last time?
La- last time, that stuff we did, I sort of forgot it.
You forgot it? After all that work?! It's no laughing matter!
Never mind.
Right …
How about we do color?
Some revision from last time.
And some new techniques.
Wow!
clap clap
Whoop-ee!
SMACK
But this time I'm going to run you through the mill.
Okay !
It'll be tougher than last time, so work hard!
OK, let's get going!

LESSON 1
CHARACTERS

It's fun drawing stuff like cute girls and cool guys,
but there's more to manga than that!
Male and female characteristics, hands and feet,
physical features at different ages,
clothes, and shading ... let's study these in detail!

CHARACTERS

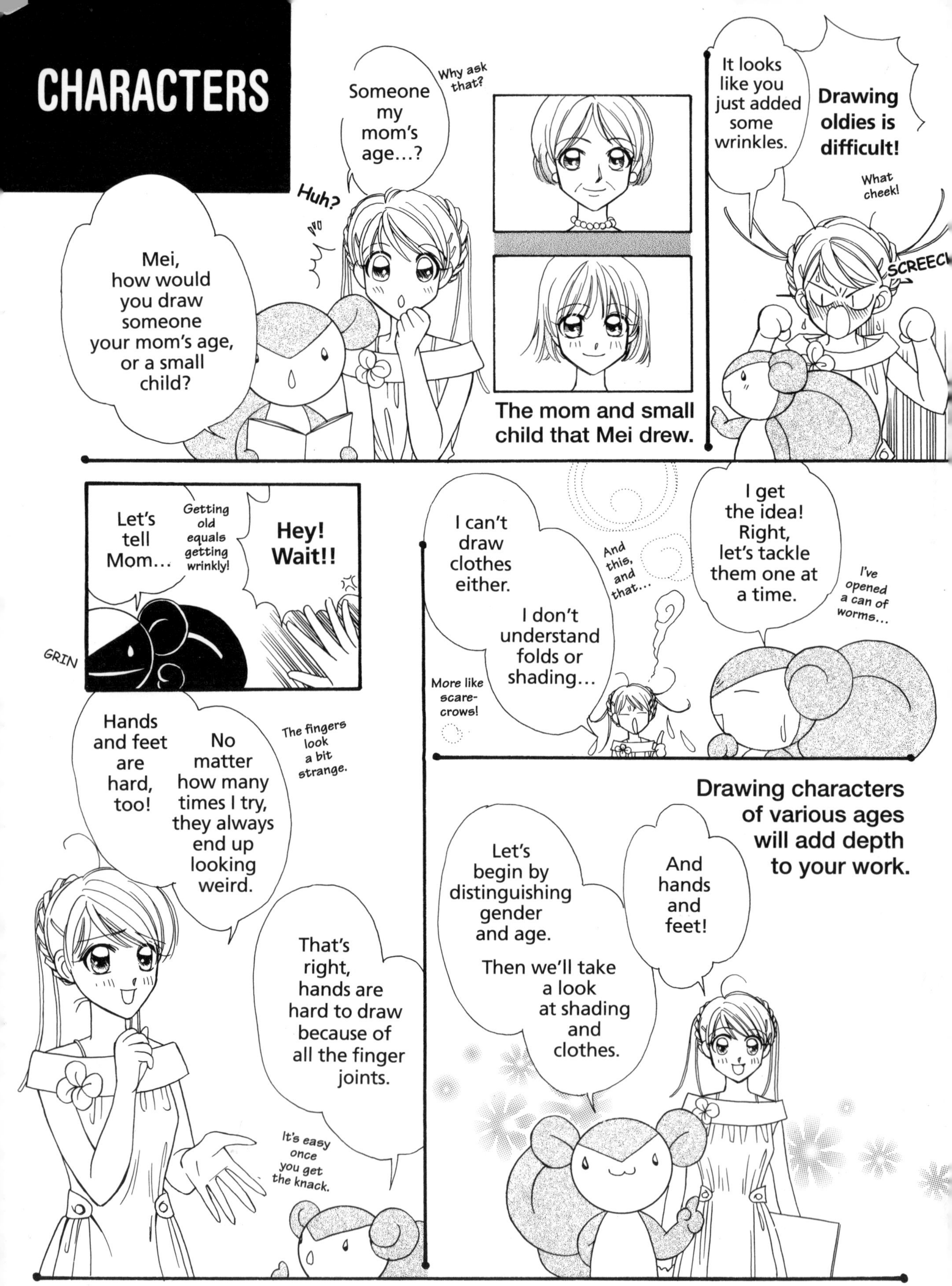

Mei, how would you draw someone your mom's age, or a small child?
Huh?
Someone my mom's age…?
Why ask that?
The mom and small child that Mei drew.
It looks like you just added some wrinkles.
Drawing oldies is difficult!
What cheek!
SCREECH
Let's tell Mom…
Getting old equals getting wrinkly!
Hey! Wait!!
GRIN
Hands and feet are hard, too!
No matter how many times I try, they always end up looking weird.
The fingers look a bit strange.
That's right, hands are hard to draw because of all the finger joints.
It's easy once you get the knack.
I can't draw clothes either.
I don't understand folds or shading…
And this, and that…
More like scare-crows!
I get the idea! Right, let's tackle them one at a time.
I've opened a can of worms…
Drawing characters of various ages will add depth to your work.
Let's begin by distinguishing gender and age.
Then we'll take a look at shading and clothes.
And hands and feet!

SMALL CHILD AGE 3

BOY

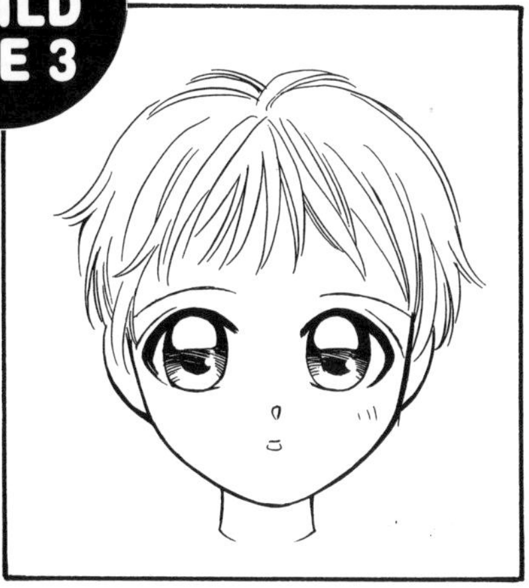

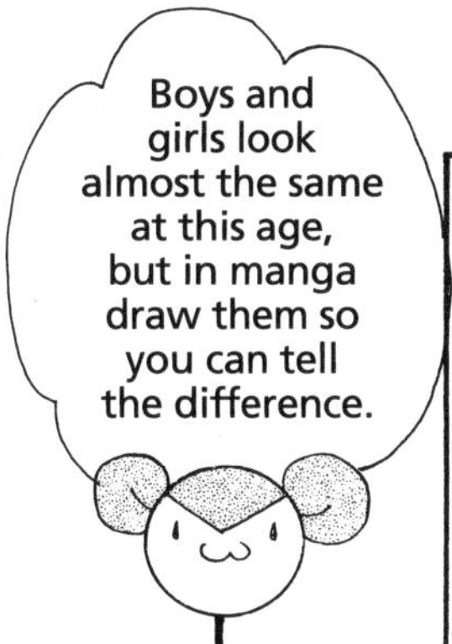
Boys and girls look almost the same at this age, but in manga draw them so you can tell the difference.

GIRL

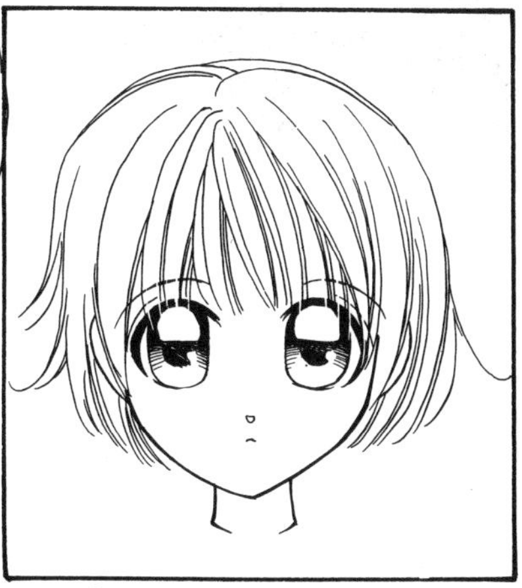

The boy-girl differences are few. They both have a rounded look, with a big head and relatively small face. Huge eyes and a small mouth give a childlike appearance.

The face is centered in the lower half of the head. The eyes are set slightly apart, and the nose is small.

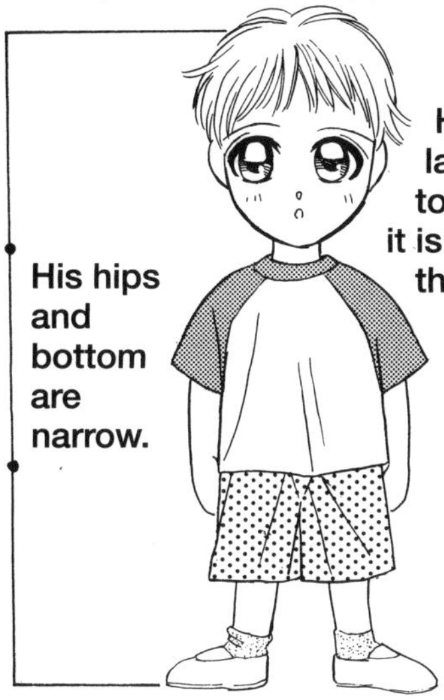

His head is large compared to his body, but it is still smaller than an adult's head.

His hips and bottom are narrow.

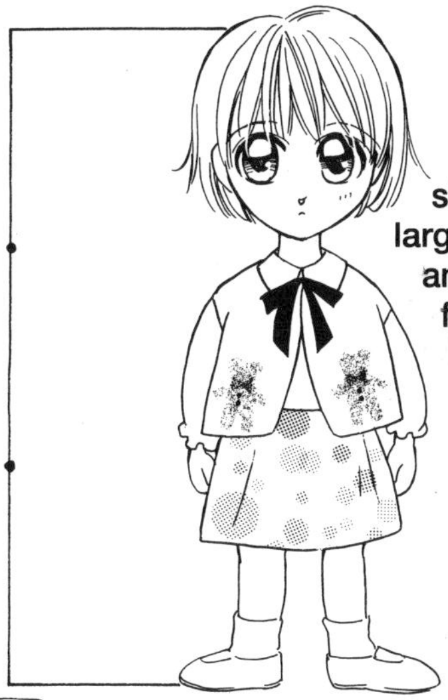

Compared to the boy, she has a larger bottom and is more fleshed out.

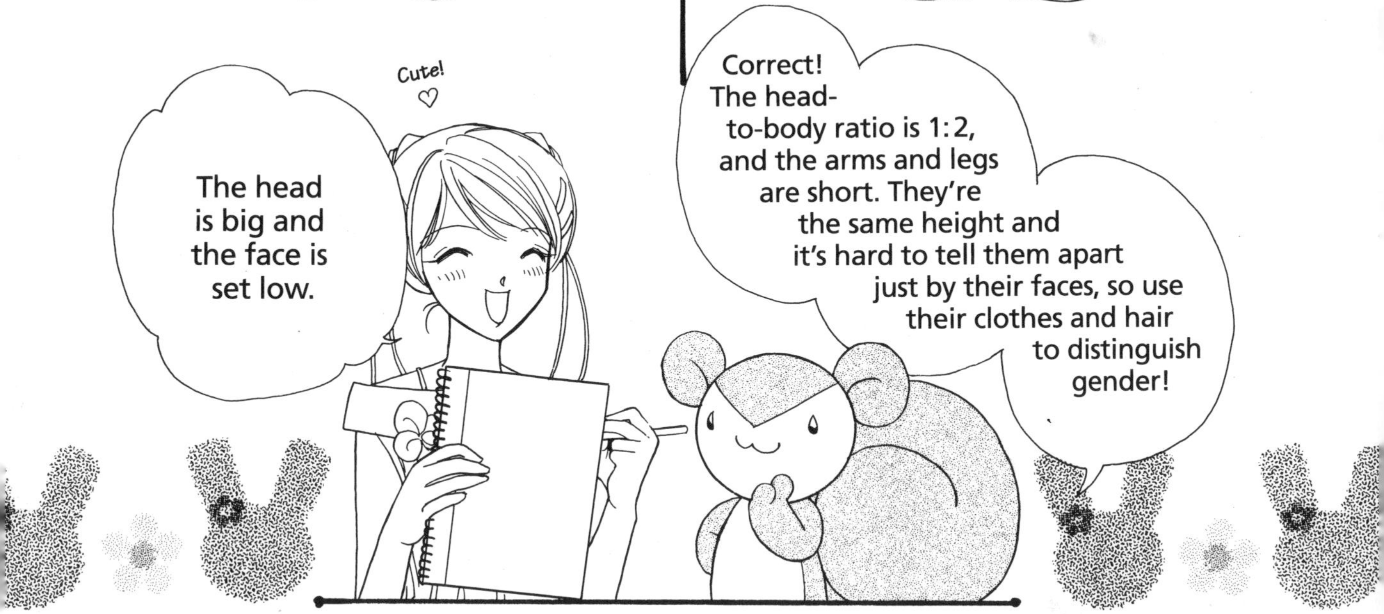
The head is big and the face is set low.
Cute!
Correct! The head-to-body ratio is 1:2, and the arms and legs are short. They're the same height and it's hard to tell them apart just by their faces, so use their clothes and hair to distinguish gender!

CHILD AGE 10

BOY

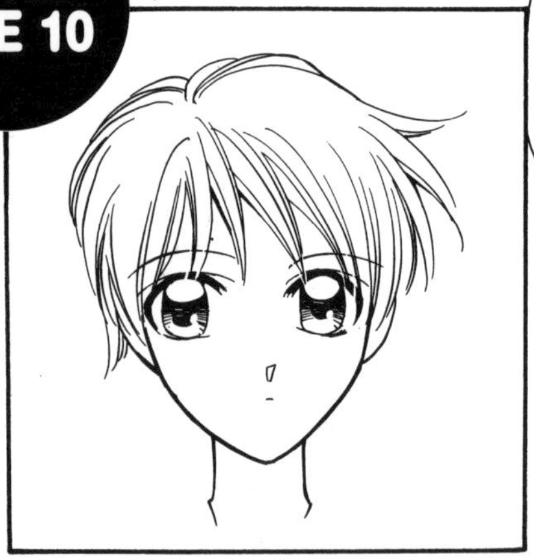

His nose is still small and his face is still round, with his chin tapering to a point. He looks younger than a girl of the same age.

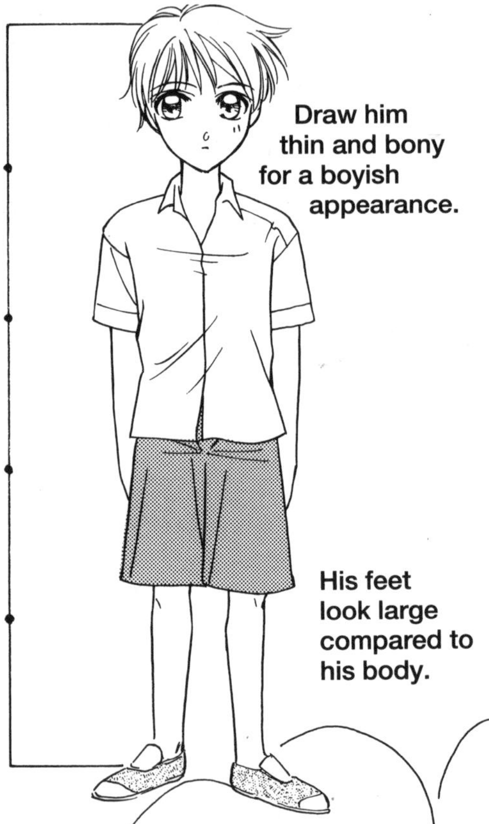
Draw him thin and bony for a boyish appearance.
His feet look large compared to his body.

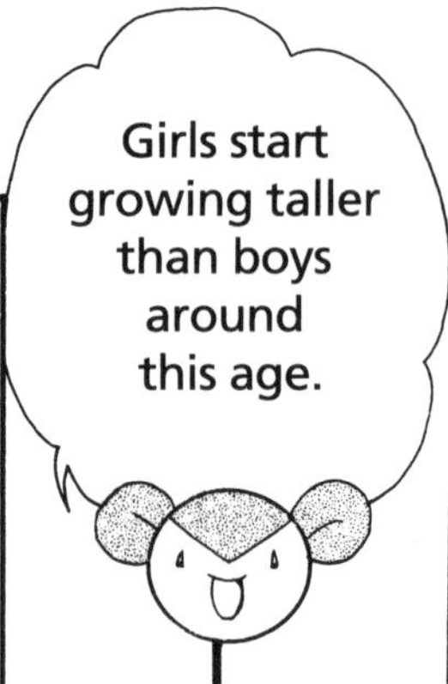
Girls start growing taller than boys around this age.

GIRL

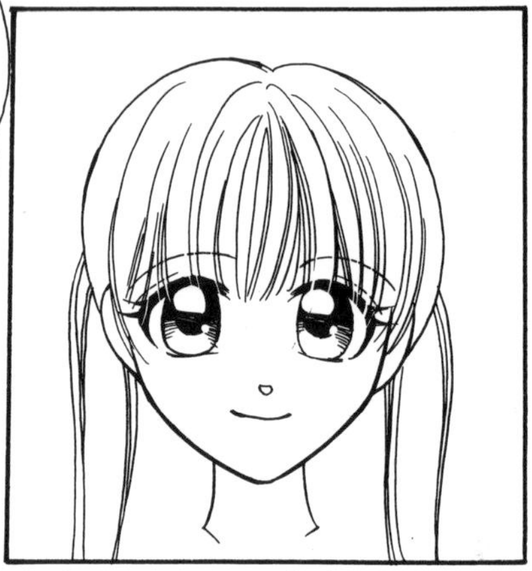

Draw her eyes exactly in the center of her face, between the crown and chin. She looks more mature than the boy.

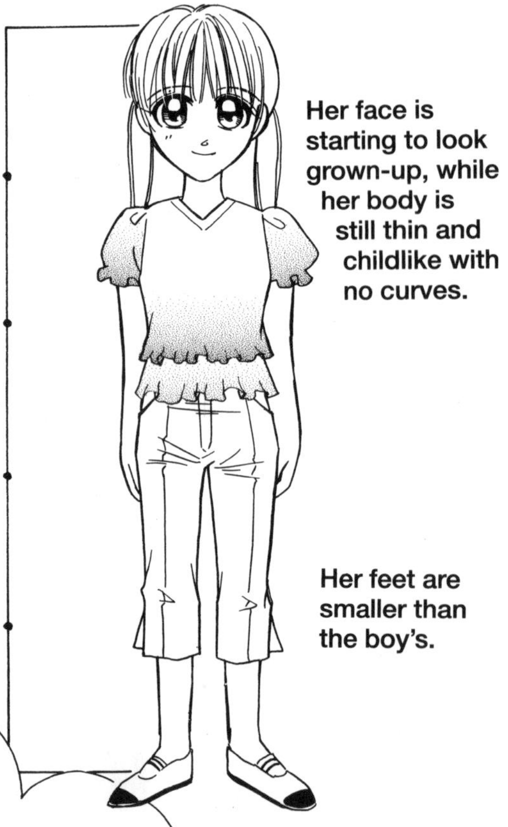
Her face is starting to look grown-up, while her body is still thin and childlike with no curves.
Her feet are smaller than the boy's.

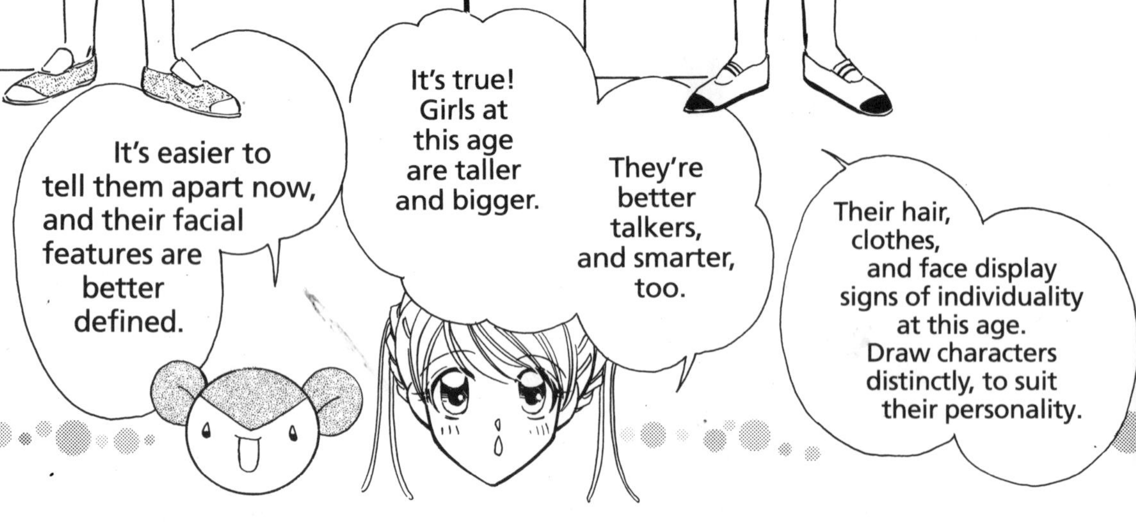
It's easier to tell them apart now, and their facial features are better defined.
It's true! Girls at this age are taller and bigger.
They're better talkers, and smarter, too.
Their hair, clothes, and face display signs of individuality at this age. Draw characters distinctly, to suit their personality.

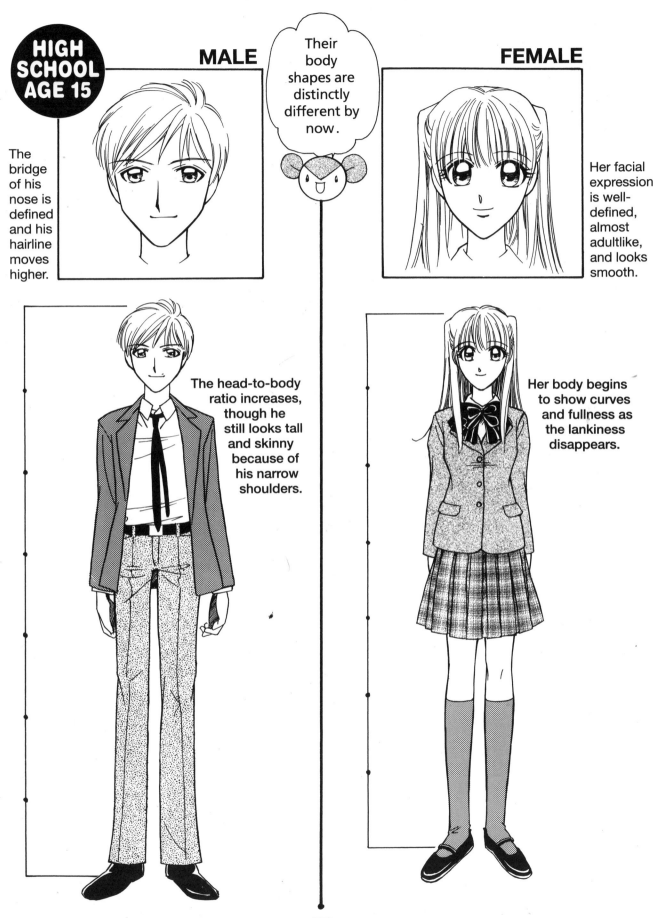

HIGH SCHOOL AGE 15

Their body shapes are distinctly different by now.

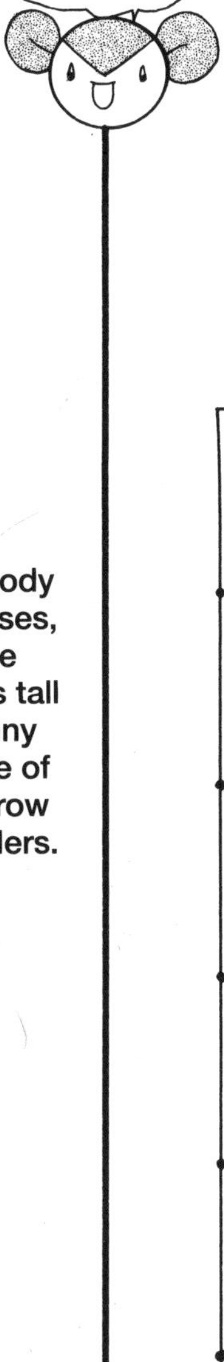

MALE

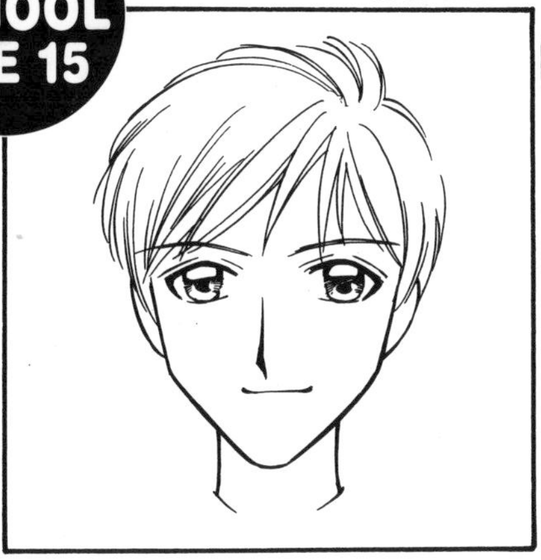

The bridge of his nose is defined and his hairline moves higher.

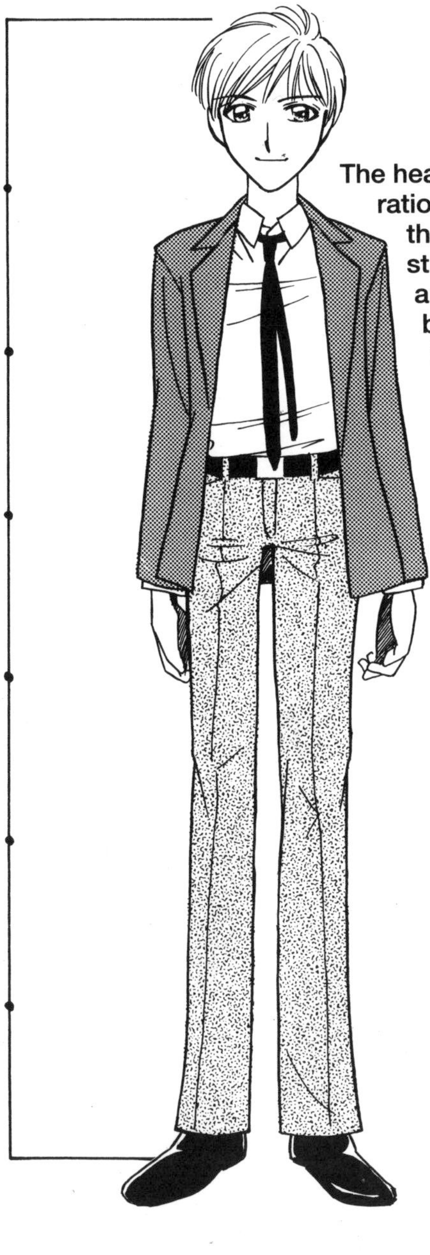

The head-to-body ratio increases, though he still looks tall and skinny because of his narrow shoulders.

FEMALE

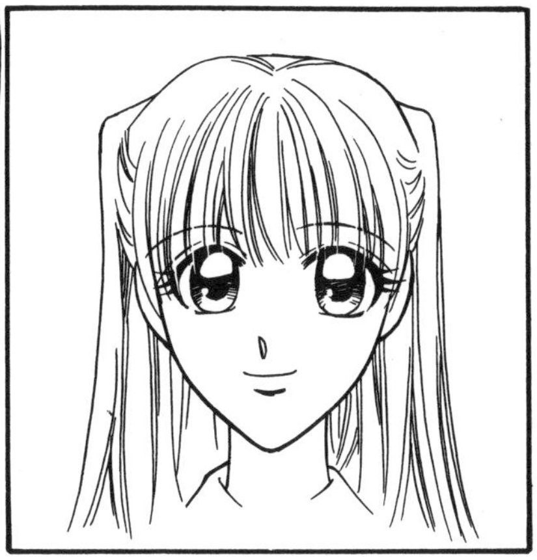

Her facial expression is well-defined, almost adultlike, and looks smooth.

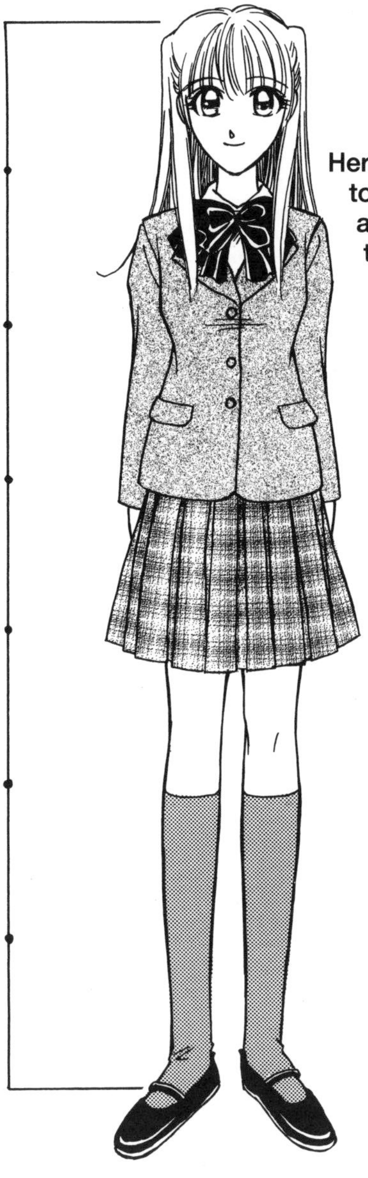

Her body begins to show curves and fullness as the lankiness disappears.

COLLEGE AGE 18

MALE

His facial structure is not so different from an adult's. Draw his chin and nose clearly for a mature appearance.

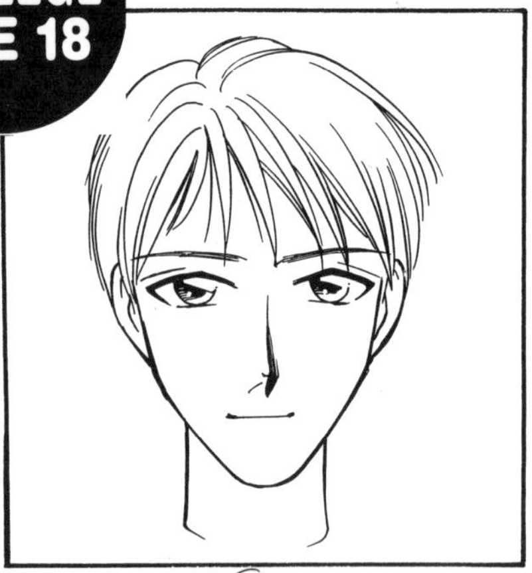

At this age, their bodies are very nearly fully adult.

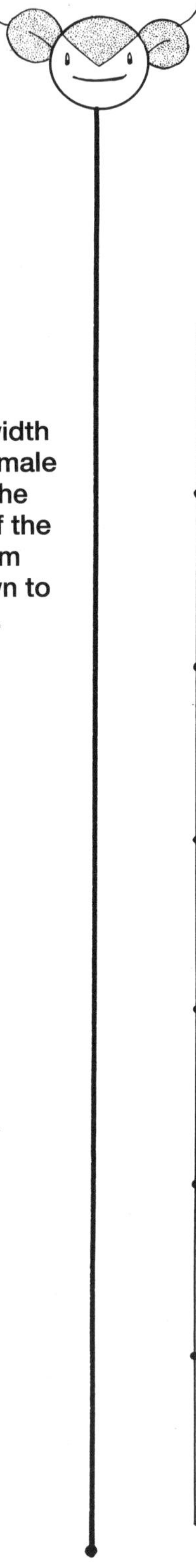

FEMALE

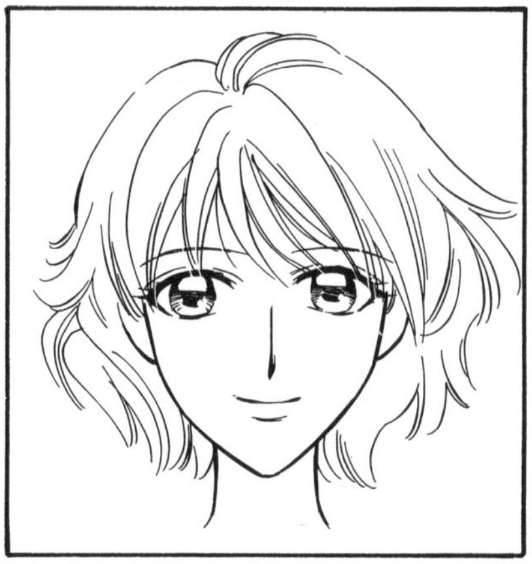

Female eyebrows are set high above the eyes. Her lips look fuller than his.

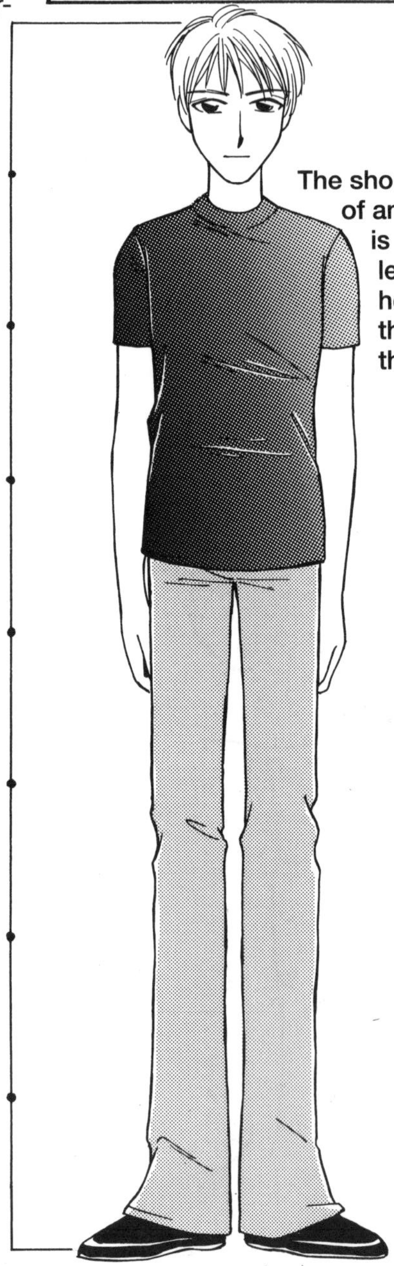

The shoulder width of an adult male is twice the length of the head from the crown to the chin.

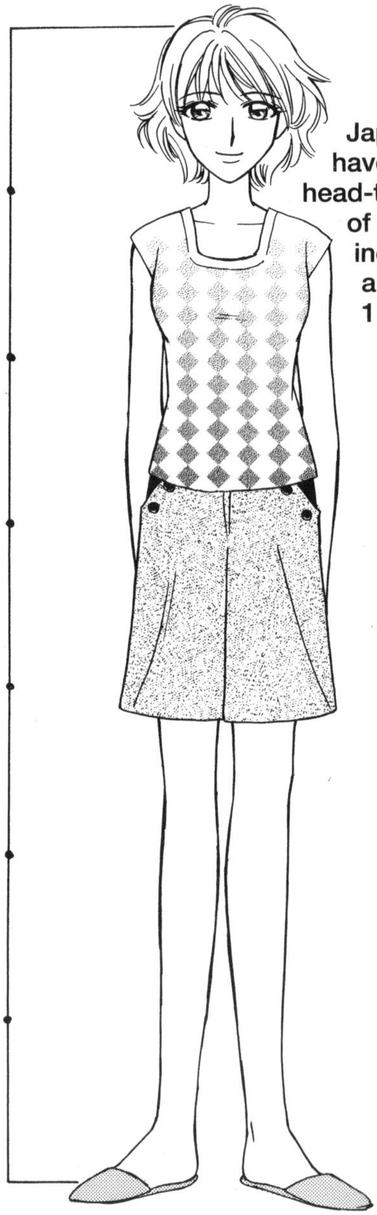

Japanese people have an average head-to-body ratio of 1: 6. You can increase this to a maximum of 1: 8 in manga.

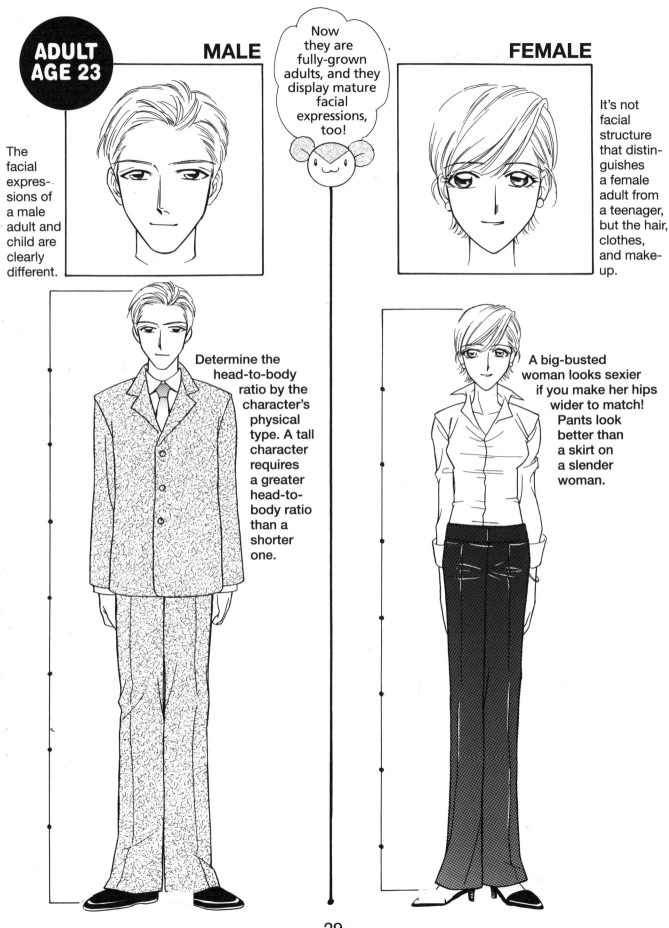

ADULT AGE 23

MALE

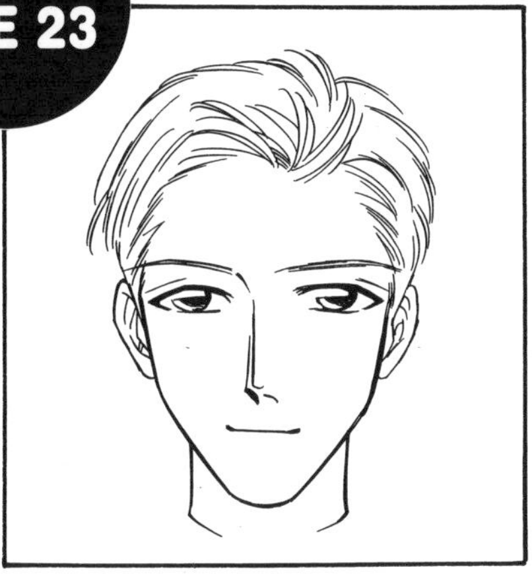

The facial expressions of a male adult and child are clearly different.

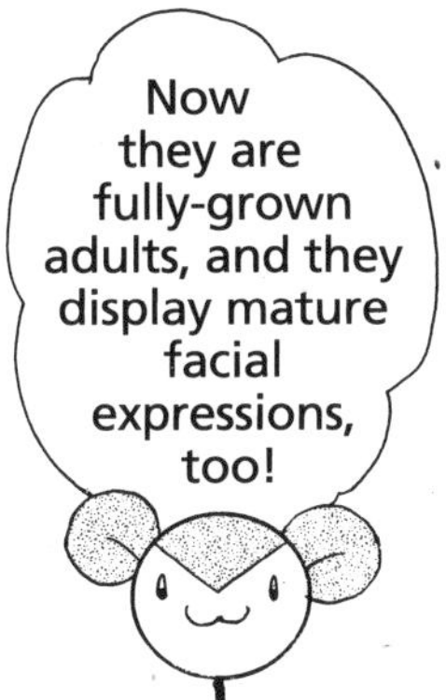
Now they are fully-grown adults, and they display mature facial expressions, too!

FEMALE

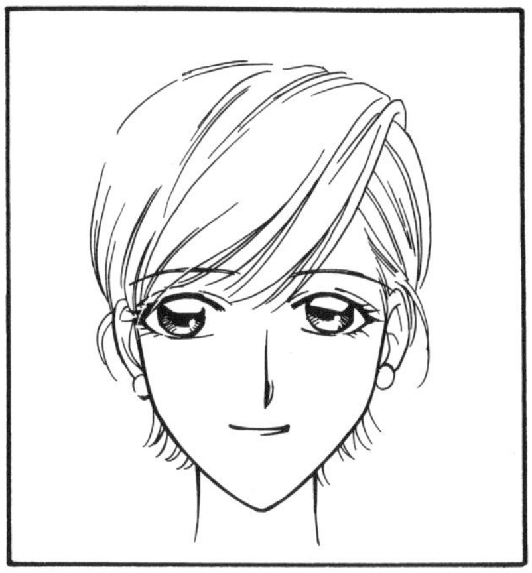

It's not facial structure that distinguishes a female adult from a teenager, but the hair, clothes, and make-up.

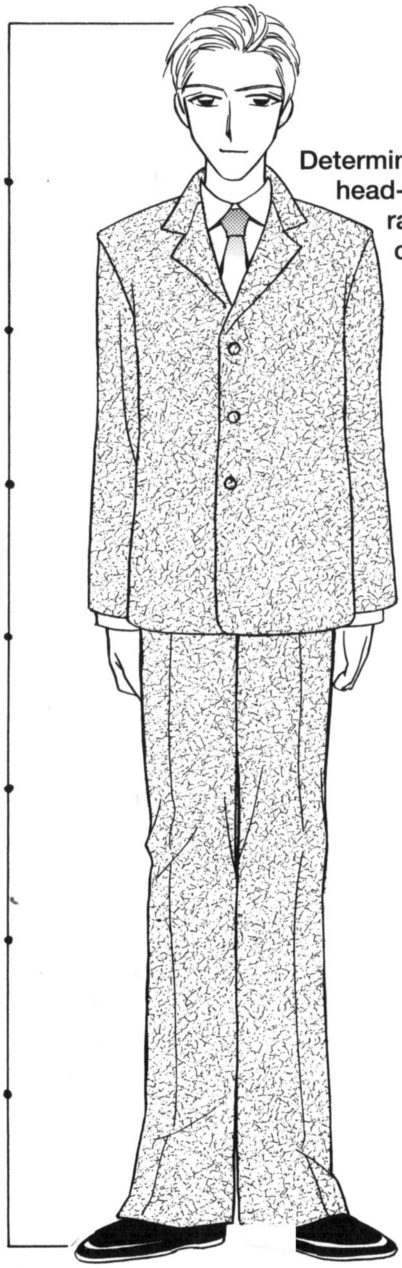

Determine the head-to-body ratio by the character's physical type. A tall character requires a greater head-to-body ratio than a shorter one.

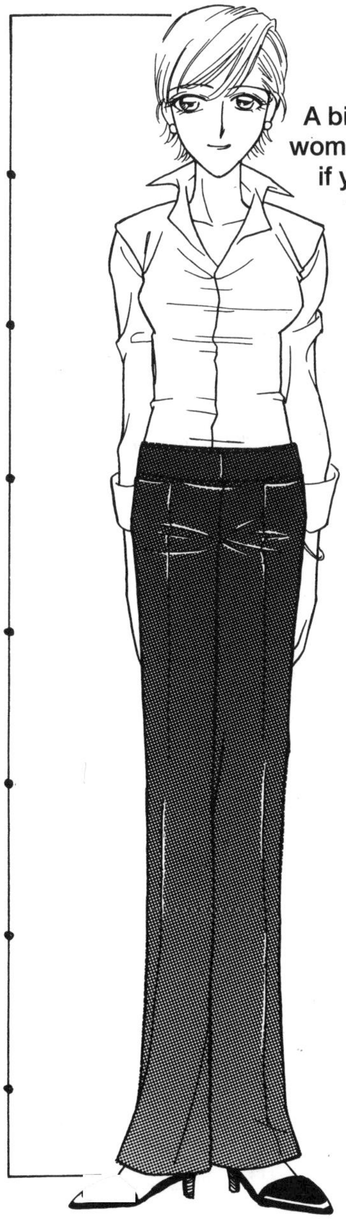

A big-busted woman looks sexier if you make her hips wider to match! Pants look better than a skirt on a slender woman.

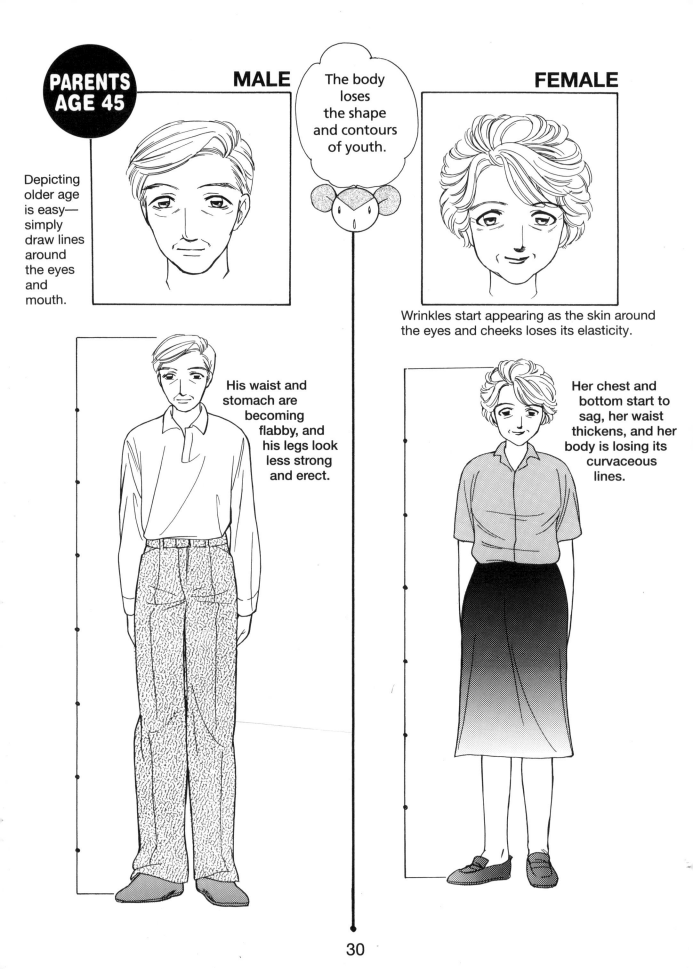

PARENTS AGE 45

The body loses the shape and contours of youth.

MALE

Depicting older age is easy—simply draw lines around the eyes and mouth.

His waist and stomach are becoming flabby, and his legs look less strong and erect.

FEMALE

Wrinkles start appearing as the skin around the eyes and cheeks loses its elasticity.

Her chest and bottom start to sag, her waist thickens, and her body is losing its curvaceous lines.

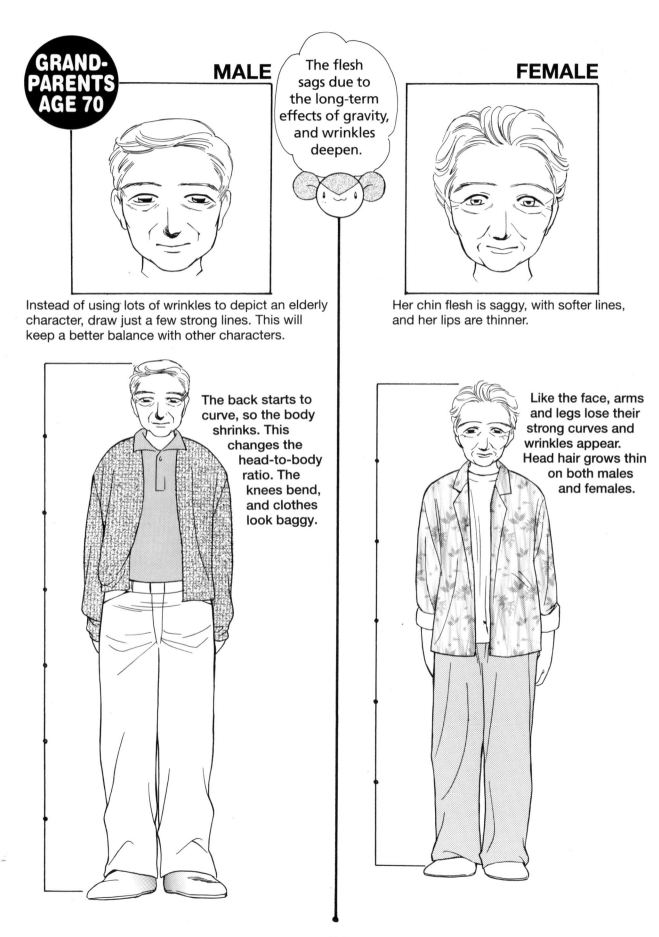

GRAND-PARENTS AGE 70

The flesh sags due to the long-term effects of gravity, and wrinkles deepen.

MALE

Instead of using lots of wrinkles to depict an elderly character, draw just a few strong lines. This will keep a better balance with other characters.

The back starts to curve, so the body shrinks. This changes the head-to-body ratio. The knees bend, and clothes look baggy.

FEMALE

Her chin flesh is saggy, with softer lines, and her lips are thinner.

Like the face, arms and legs lose their strong curves and wrinkles appear. Head hair grows thin on both males and females.

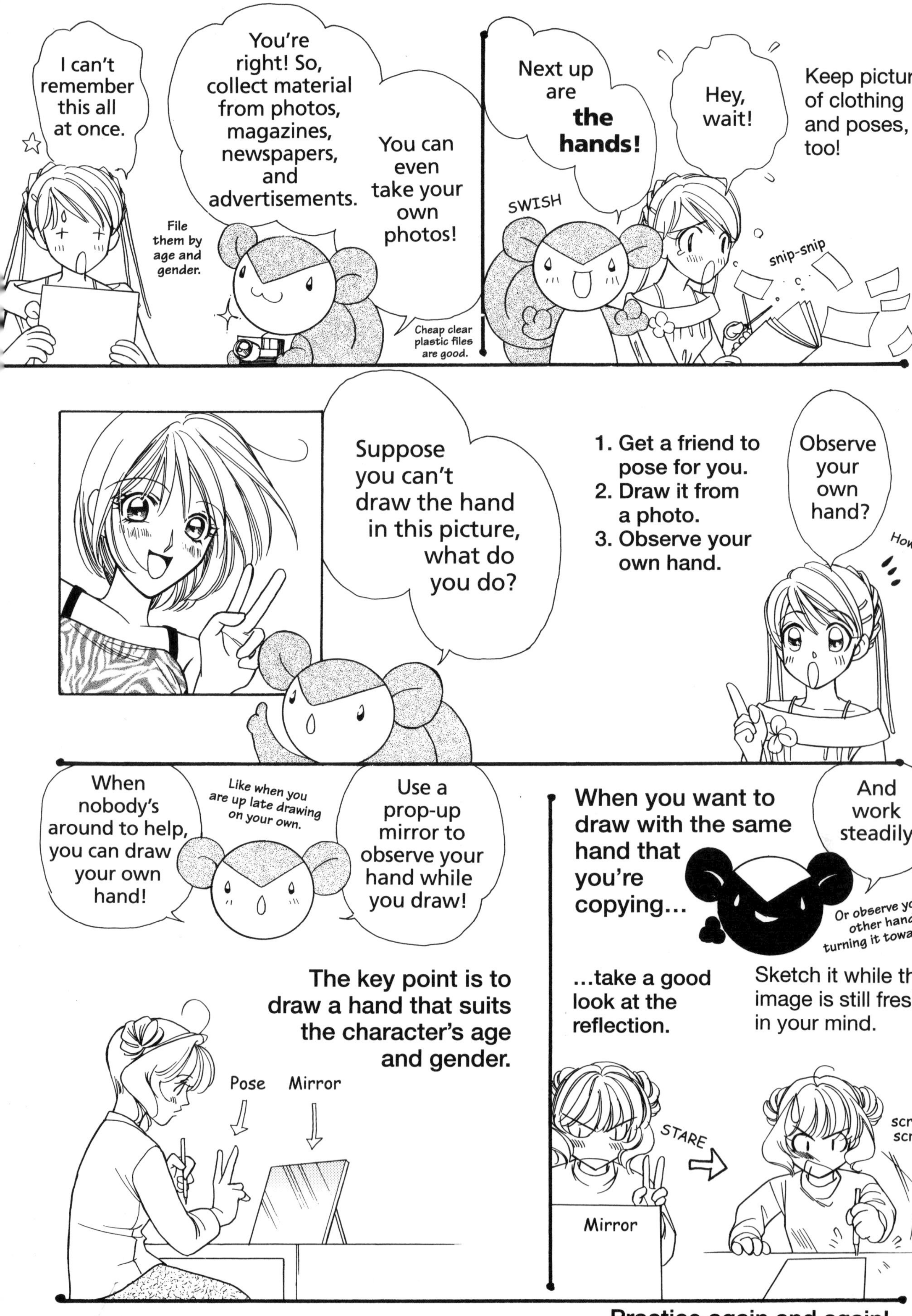
I can't remember this all at once.
You're right! So, collect material from photos, magazines, newspapers, and advertisements.
File them by age and gender.
You can even take your own photos!
Cheap clear plastic files are good.
Next up are **the hands!**
SWISH
Hey, wait!
Keep pictures of clothing and poses, too!
snip-snip
Suppose you can't draw the hand in this picture, what do you do?
1. Get a friend to pose for you.
2. Draw it from a photo.
3. Observe your own hand.
Observe your own hand?
How?
When nobody's around to help, you can draw your own hand!
Like when you are up late drawing on your own.
Use a prop-up mirror to observe your hand while you draw!
The key point is to draw a hand that suits the character's age and gender.
Pose
Mirror
When you want to draw with the same hand that you're copying...
And work steadily.
Or observe your other hand, turning it toward you.
...take a good look at the reflection.
Sketch it while the image is still fresh in your mind.
STARE
Mirror
scribble scribble

Practice again and again!

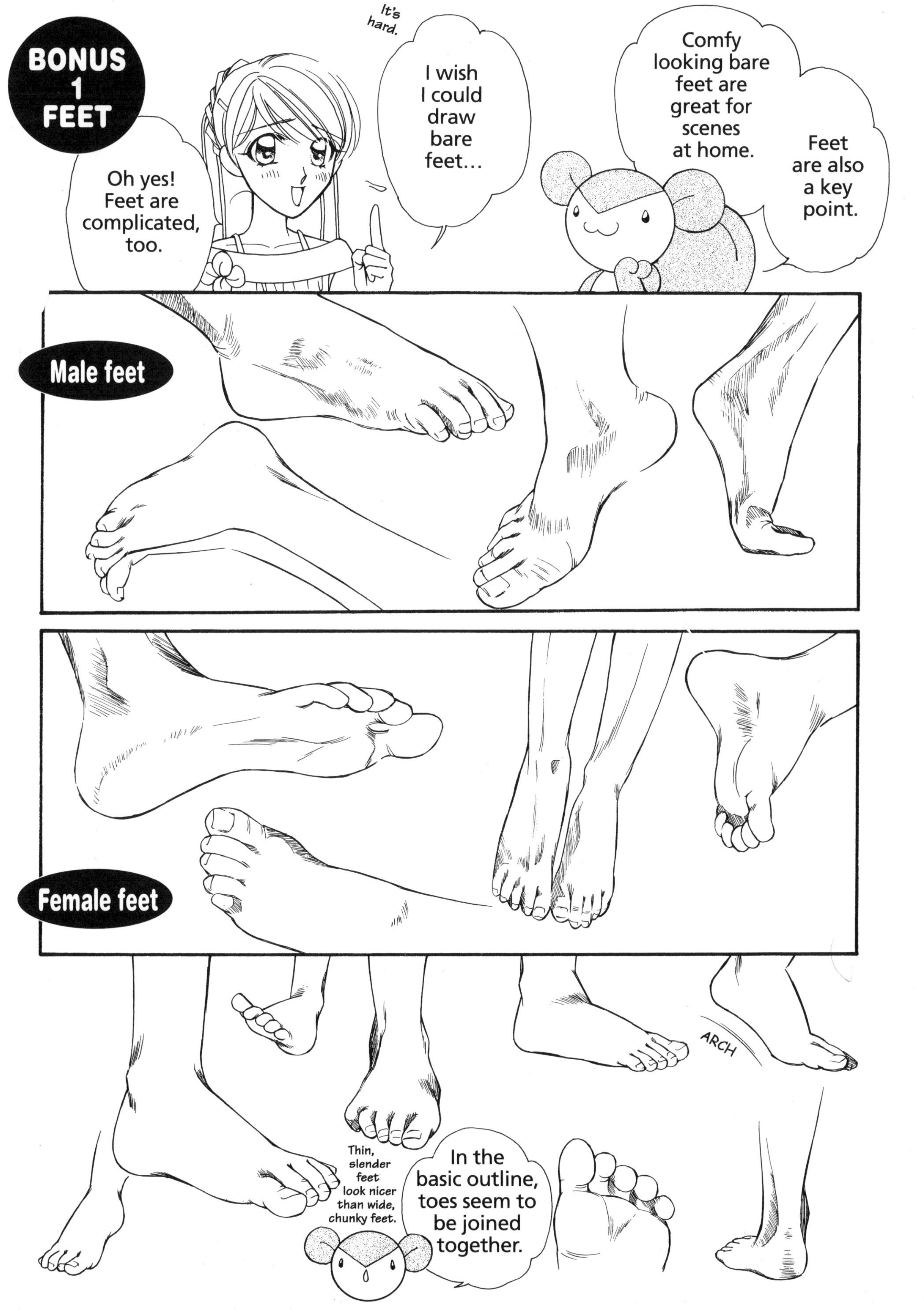
BONUS 1 FEET
Feet are also a key point.
Comfy looking bare feet are great for scenes at home.
I wish I could draw bare feet…
It's hard.
Oh yes! Feet are complicated, too.
Male feet
Female feet
ARCH
In the basic outline, toes seem to be joined together.
Thin, slender feet look nicer than wide, chunky feet.

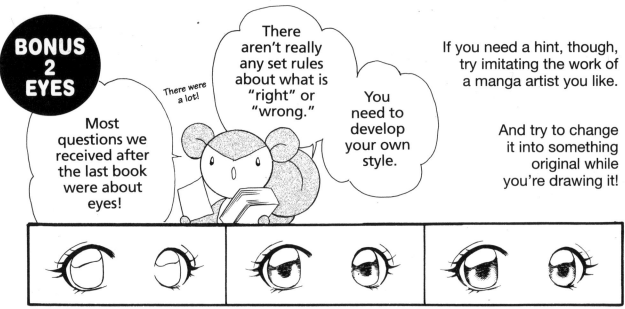

BONUS 2 EYES

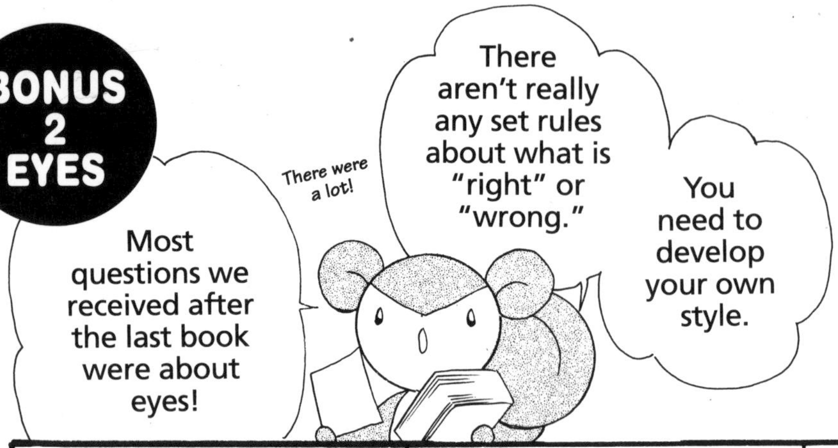
Most questions we received after the last book were about eyes!
There were a lot!
There aren't really any set rules about what is "right" or "wrong."
You need to develop your own style.

If you need a hint, though, try imitating the work of a manga artist you like.

And try to change it into something original while you're drawing it!

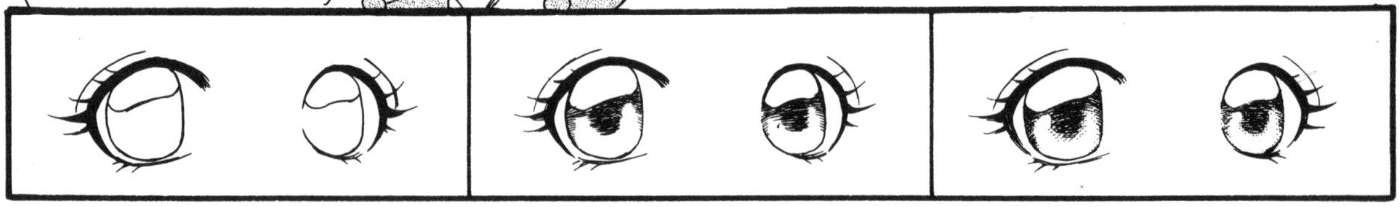

A cheerful, energetic character has clear eyes with lots of eyelashes.

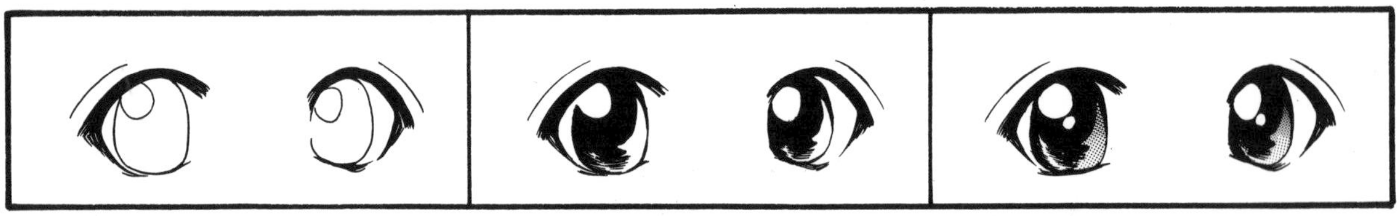

A child or a gentle person has round eyes with no lashes.

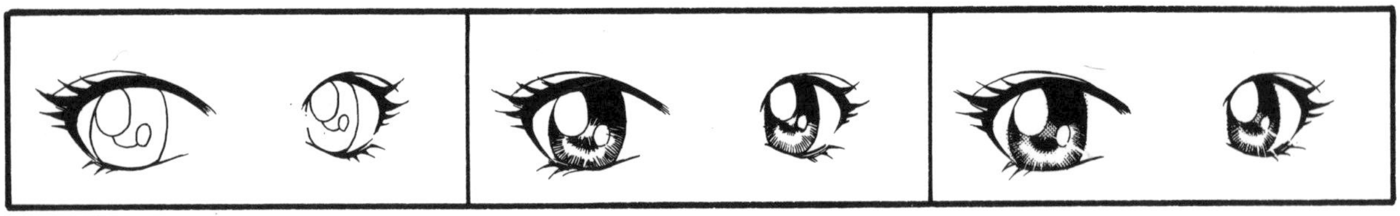

A character with slanted eyes seems strong-minded and alert.

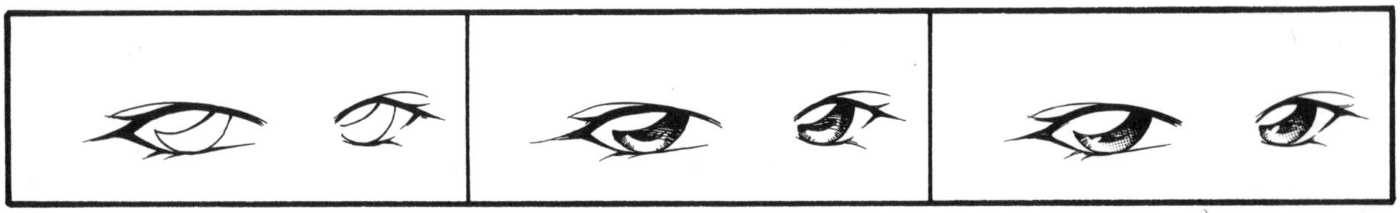

Narrow eyes suit a cool, intellectual character.

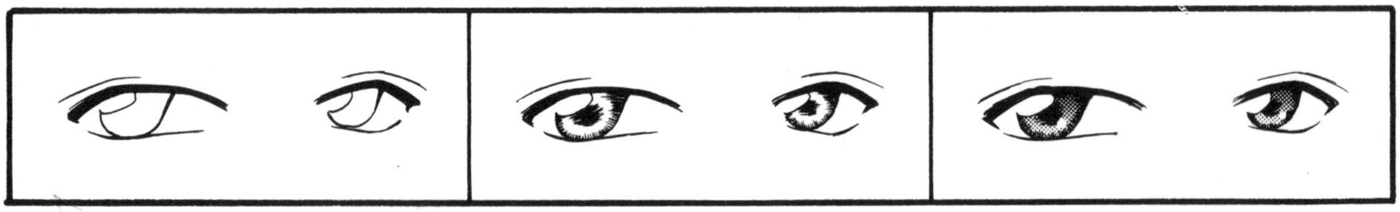

Elongate the eyes for adult males.

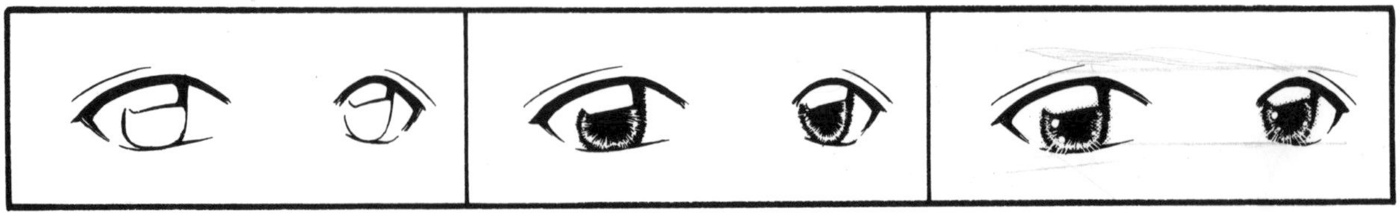

Round eyes on a boy lend character.

HAIR

MALE

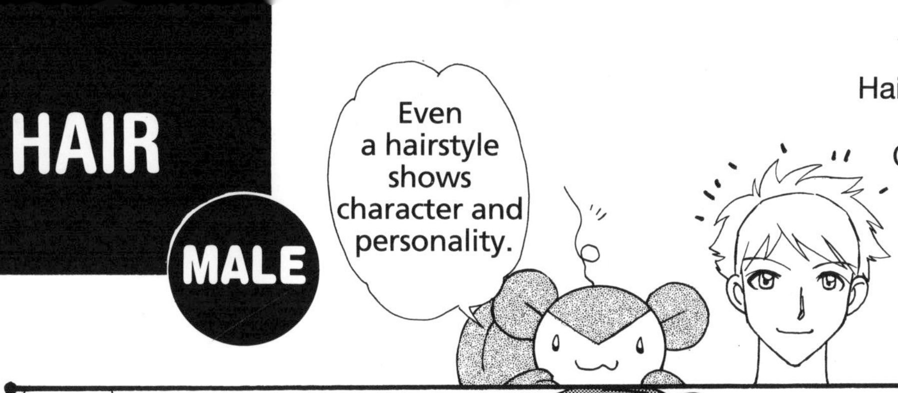

Even a hairstyle shows character and personality.

Hair grows on the head, which is round! Consider the balance of the hair and the head shape while drawing.

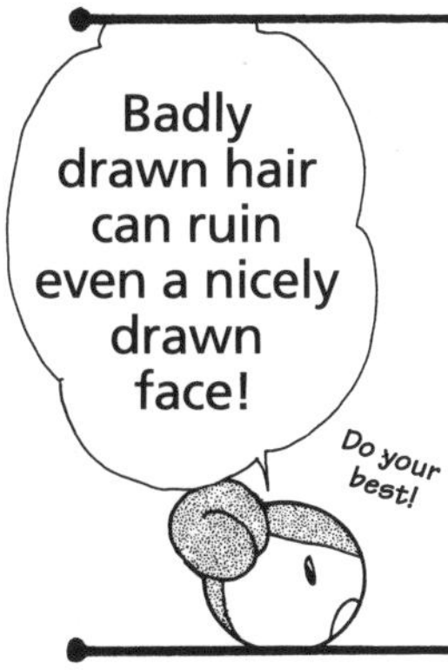

Badly drawn hair can ruin even a nicely drawn face!
Do your best!

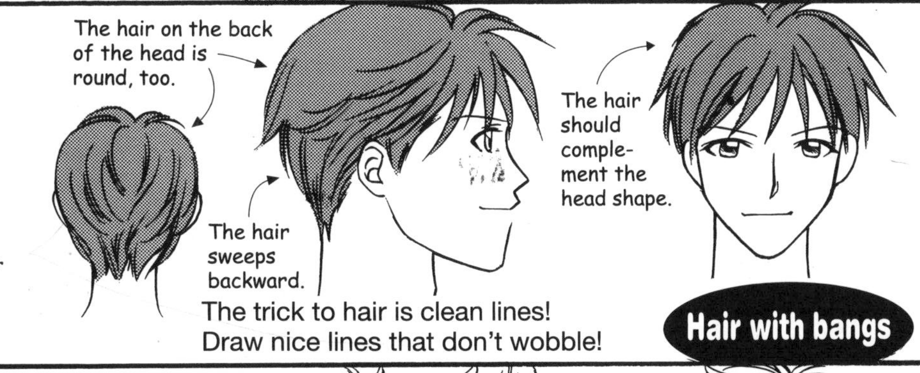

The hair on the back of the head is round, too.
The hair sweeps backward.
The hair should comple-ment the head shape.

The trick to hair is clean lines! Draw nice lines that don't wobble!

Hair with bangs

Draw long lines for long hair, short lines for short hair, soft lines for soft hair and coarse lines for coarse hair!

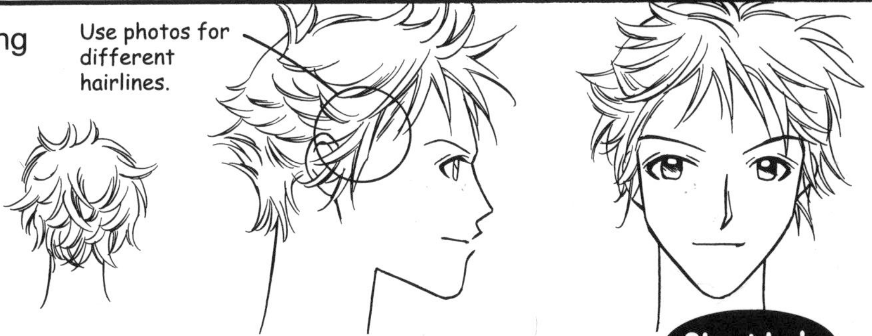

Use photos for different hairlines.

Short hair shows the shape of the head, too.

Short hair

When you have lots of characters, give them different hairstyles to help readers tell them apart.

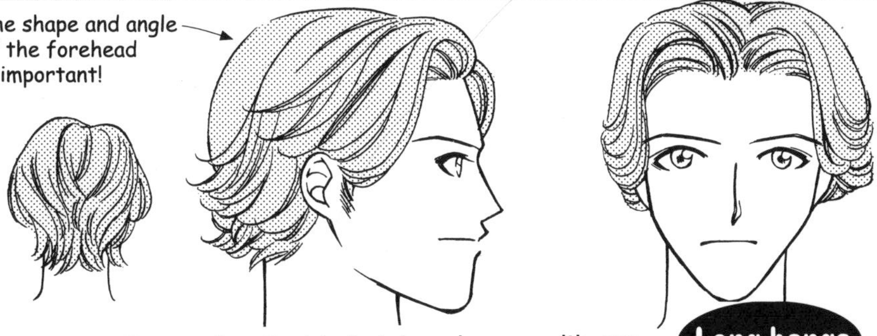

The shape and angle of the forehead is important!

Remember that hairstyles change with age.

Long bangs

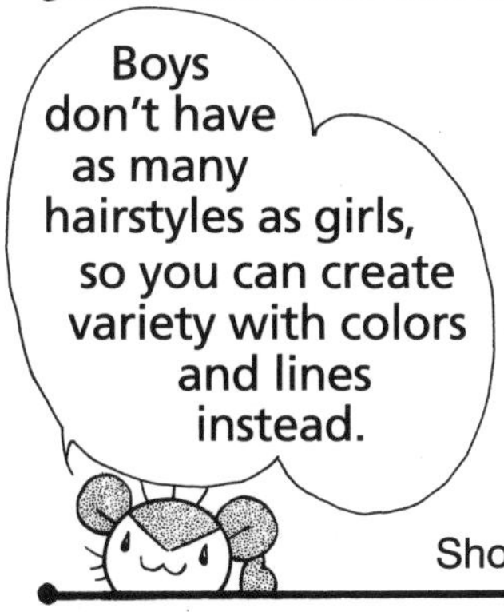

Boys don't have as many hairstyles as girls, so you can create variety with colors and lines instead.

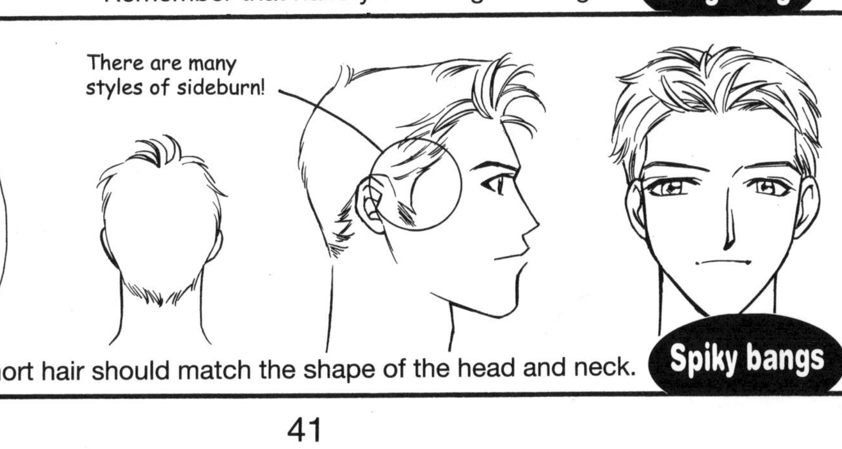

There are many styles of sideburn!

Short hair should match the shape of the head and neck.

Spiky bangs

FEMALE

Curve the strands of hair at the tips, so the hair looks soft. Completely straight hair looks coarse.

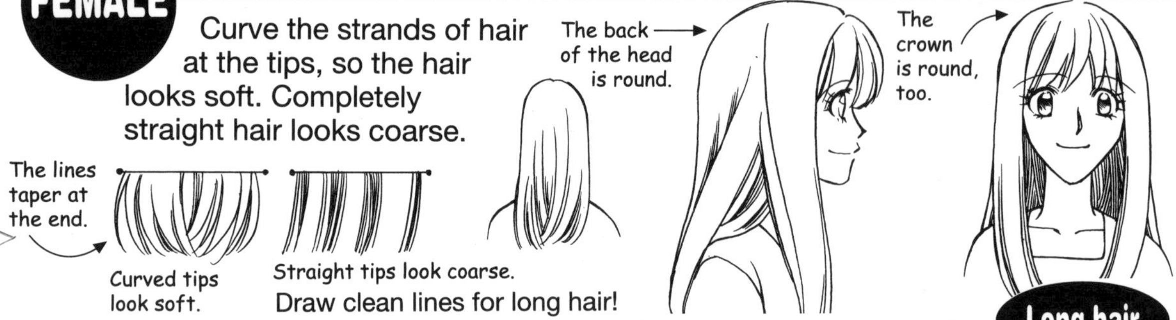

The lines taper at the end.
Curved tips look soft.
Straight tips look coarse.
The back of the head is round.
The crown is round, too.

Draw clean lines for long hair!
Draw a line in one stroke, and don't pause halfway through.

Long hair

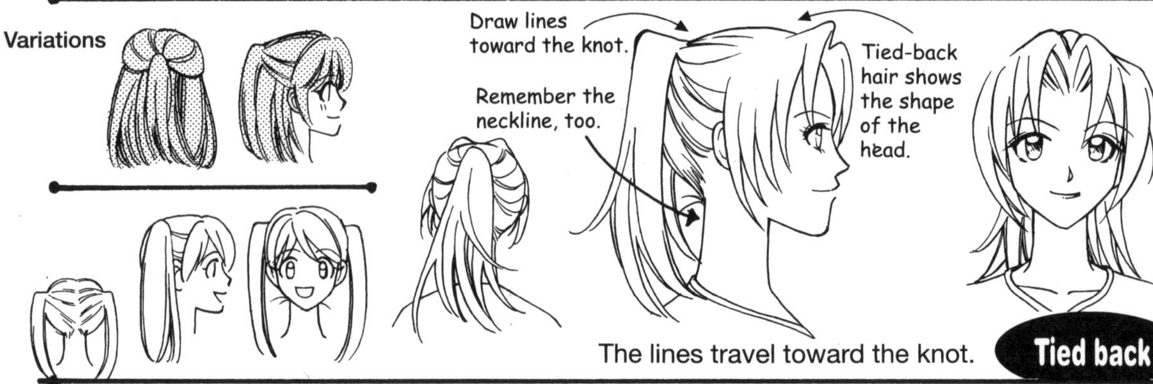

Variations
Draw lines toward the knot.
Remember the neckline, too.
Tied-back hair shows the shape of the head.

The lines travel toward the knot.

Tied back

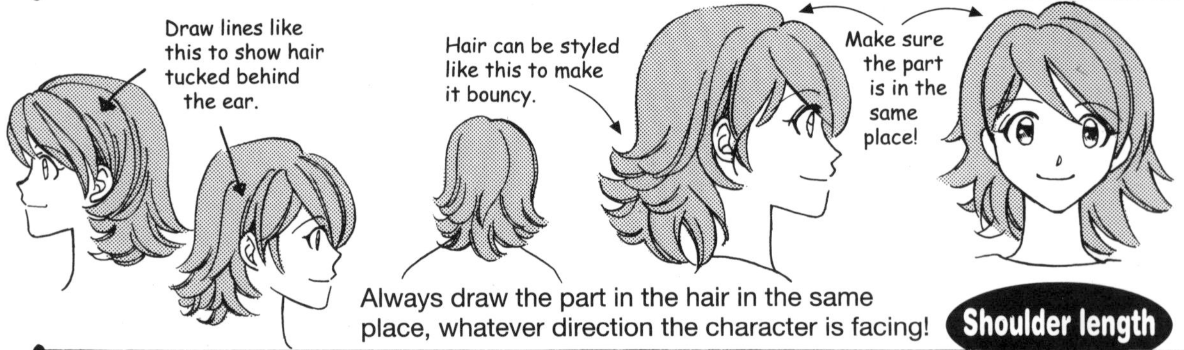

Draw lines like this to show hair tucked behind the ear.
Hair can be styled like this to make it bouncy.
Make sure the part is in the same place!

Always draw the part in the hair in the same place, whatever direction the character is facing!

Shoulder length

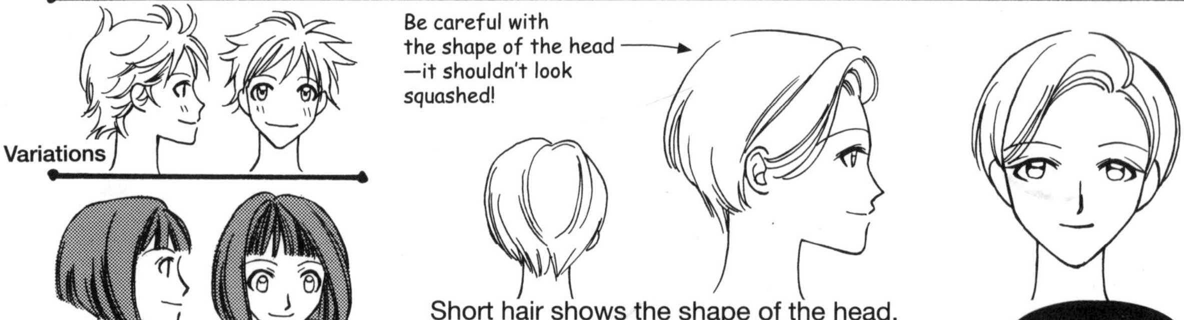

Variations
Be careful with the shape of the head—it shouldn't look squashed!

Short hair shows the shape of the head.
Be especially careful with the back of the head.

Short hair

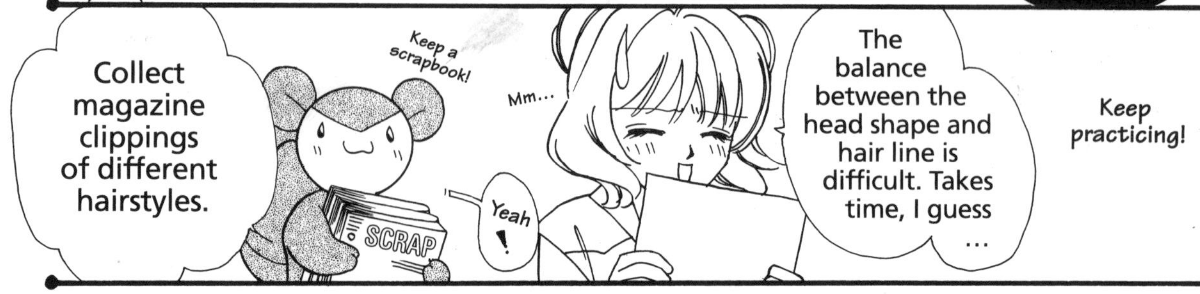

Collect magazine clippings of different hairstyles.
Keep a scrapbook!
SCRAP
Yeah!
Mm...
The balance between the head shape and hair line is difficult. Takes time, I guess ...
Keep practicing!

CLOTHING

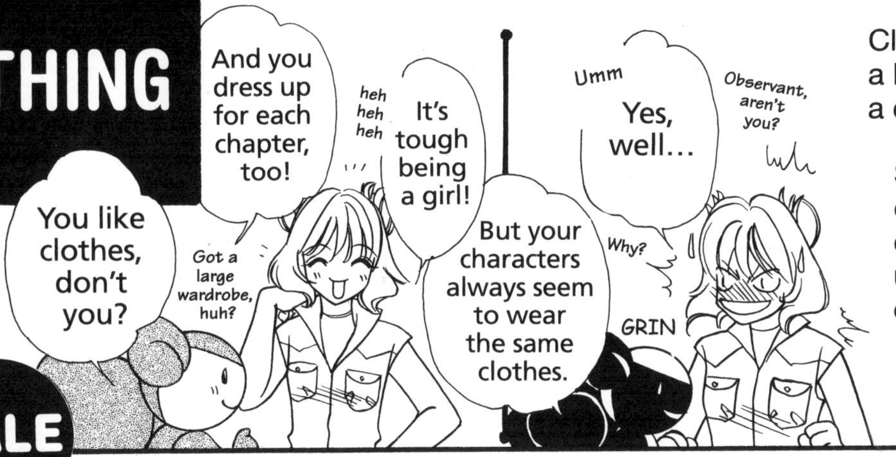
You like clothes, don't you?
Got a large wardrobe, huh?
And you dress up for each chapter, too!
heh heh heh
It's tough being a girl!
But your characters always seem to wear the same clothes.
GRIN
Why?
Umm
Yes, well…
Observant, aren't you?

Clothing can say a lot about a character too.

Suits, uniforms, dresses, scruffy clothes… use them for different scenes!

MALE

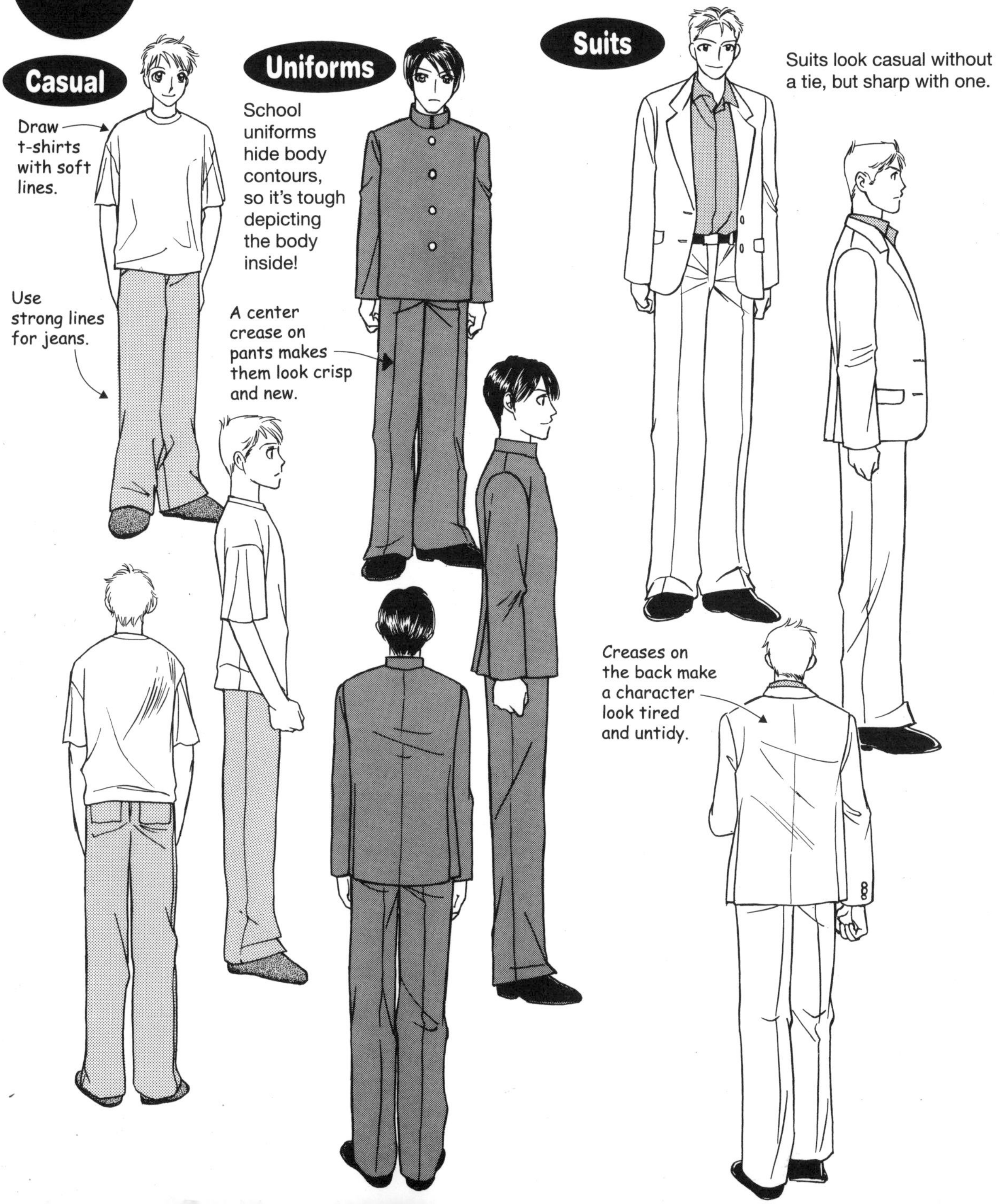
Casual
Draw t-shirts with soft lines.
Use strong lines for jeans.
Uniforms
School uniforms hide body contours, so it's tough depicting the body inside!
A center crease on pants makes them look crisp and new.
Suits
Suits look casual without a tie, but sharp with one.
Creases on the back make a character look tired and untidy.

FEMALE

Casual

Smart

Uniforms

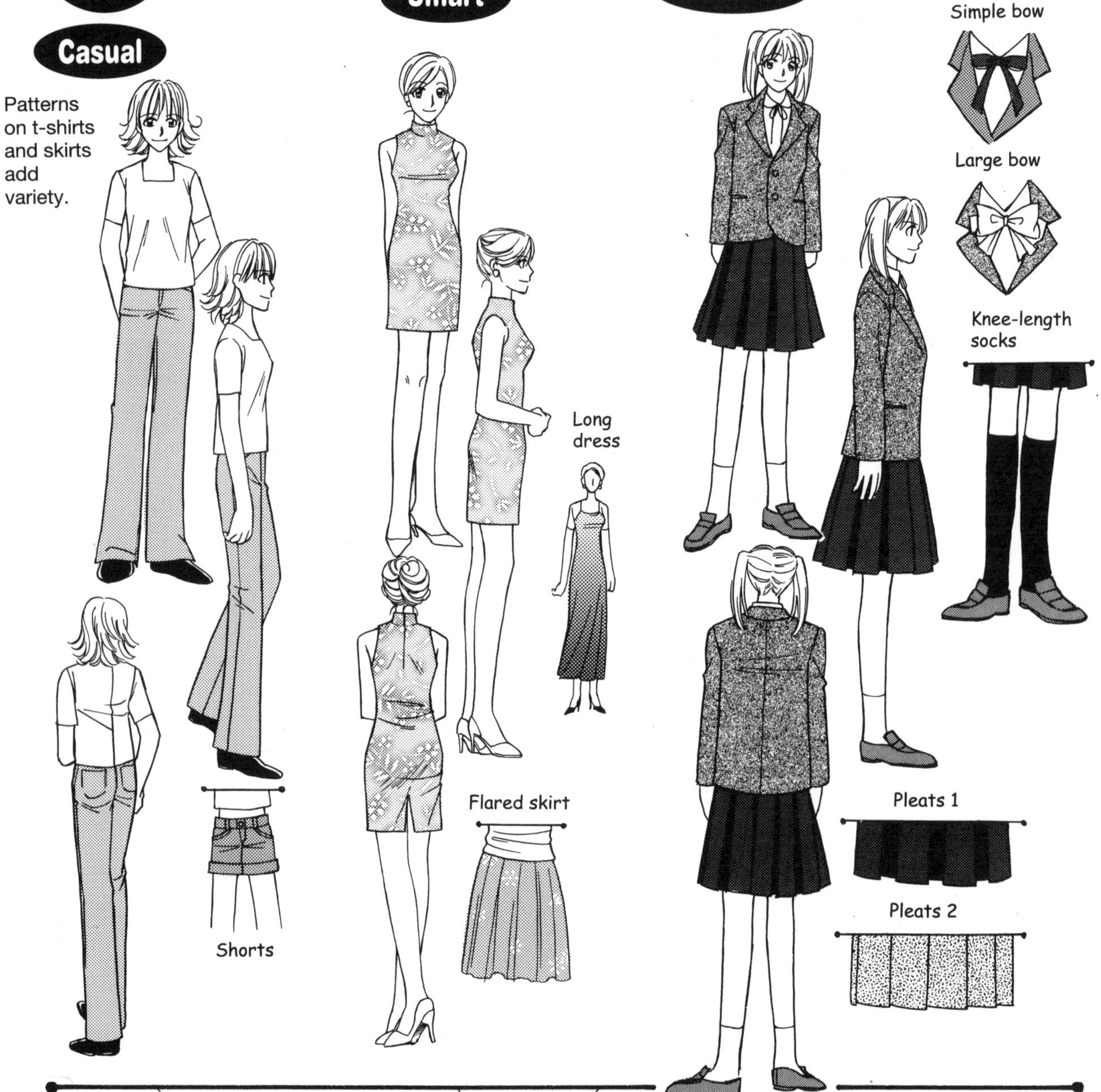

Patterns on t-shirts and skirts add variety.
Shorts
Long dress
Flared skirt
Simple bow
Large bow
Knee-length socks
Pleats 1
Pleats 2

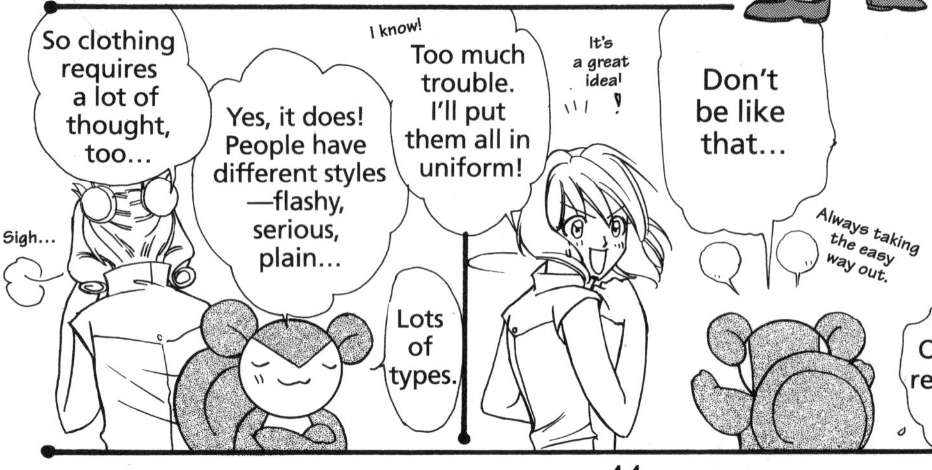

So clothing requires a lot of thought, too...
Sigh...
Yes, it does! People have different styles—flashy, serious, plain...
Lots of types.
I know!
Too much trouble. I'll put them all in uniform!
It's a great idea!
Don't be like that...
Always taking the easy way out.
Oh, really!!

Give careful thought to the clothing of the main characters.

Use magazines for reference material!

CLOTHING FOLDS

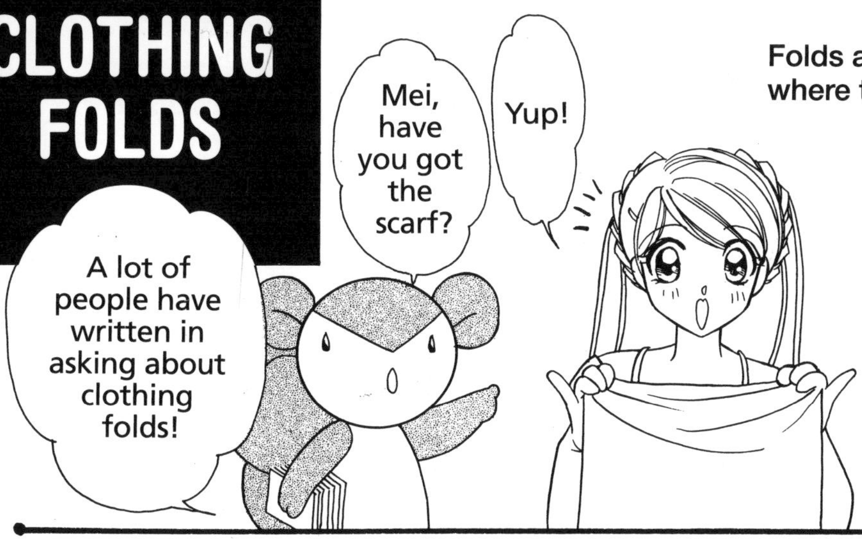
A lot of people have written in asking about clothing folds!
Mei, have you got the scarf?
Yup!

Folds appear from the point where the clothing is supported.

The type and softness of the fabric determines how and where the fold appears.

When just one side of the cloth is held up, the folds appear from that point.

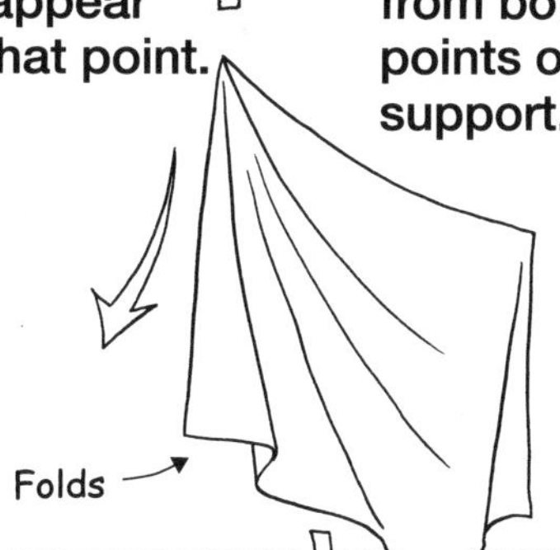
Folds

If the middle hangs down, folds appear from both points of support.

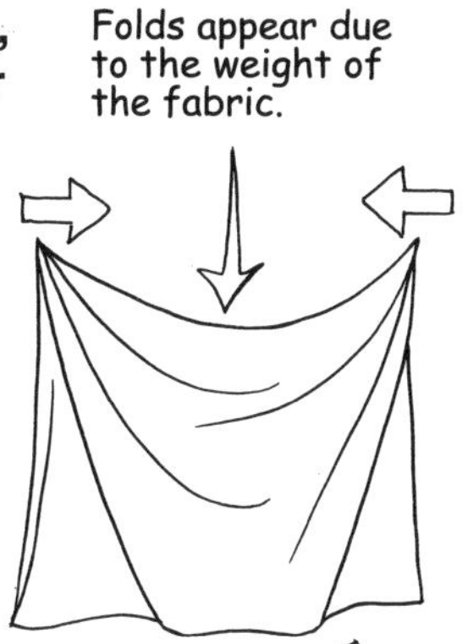
Folds appear due to the weight of the fabric.

Drape the center of the cloth over your hand, and see how the folds radiate from the center downwards.

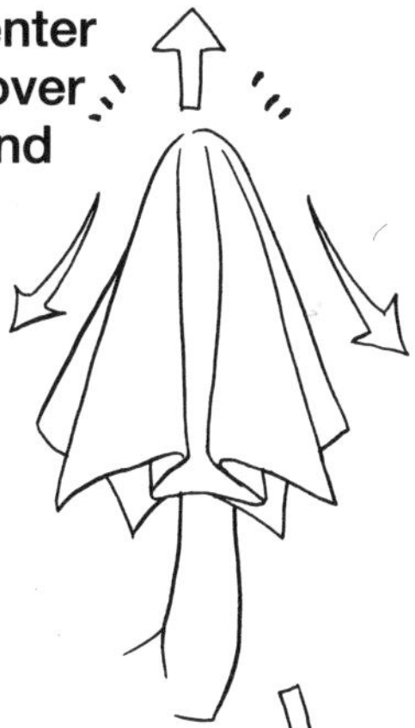

So let's use these principles for drawing clothing.

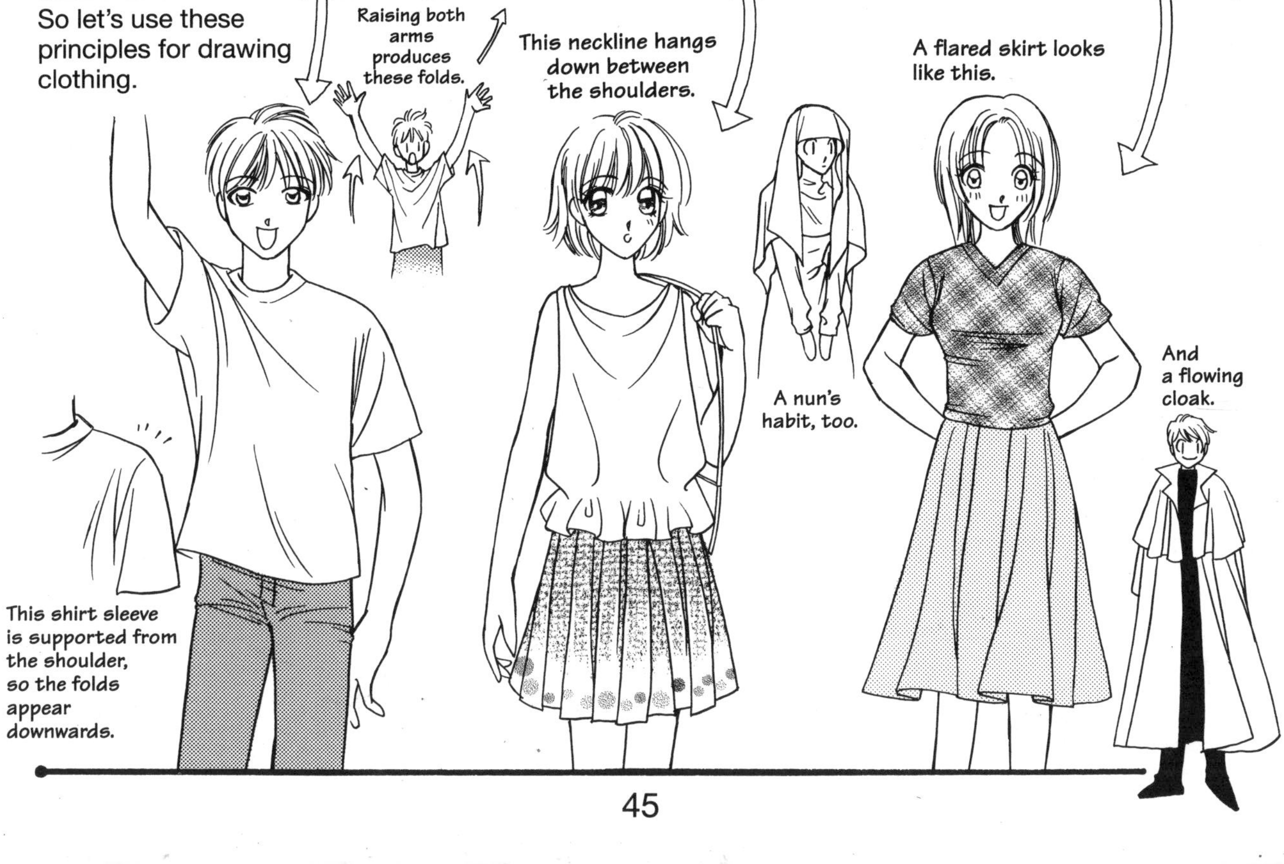
Raising both arms produces these folds.
This shirt sleeve is supported from the shoulder, so the folds appear downwards.
This neckline hangs down between the shoulders.
A nun's habit, too.
A flared skirt looks like this.
And a flowing cloak.

Female clothing

Male clothing

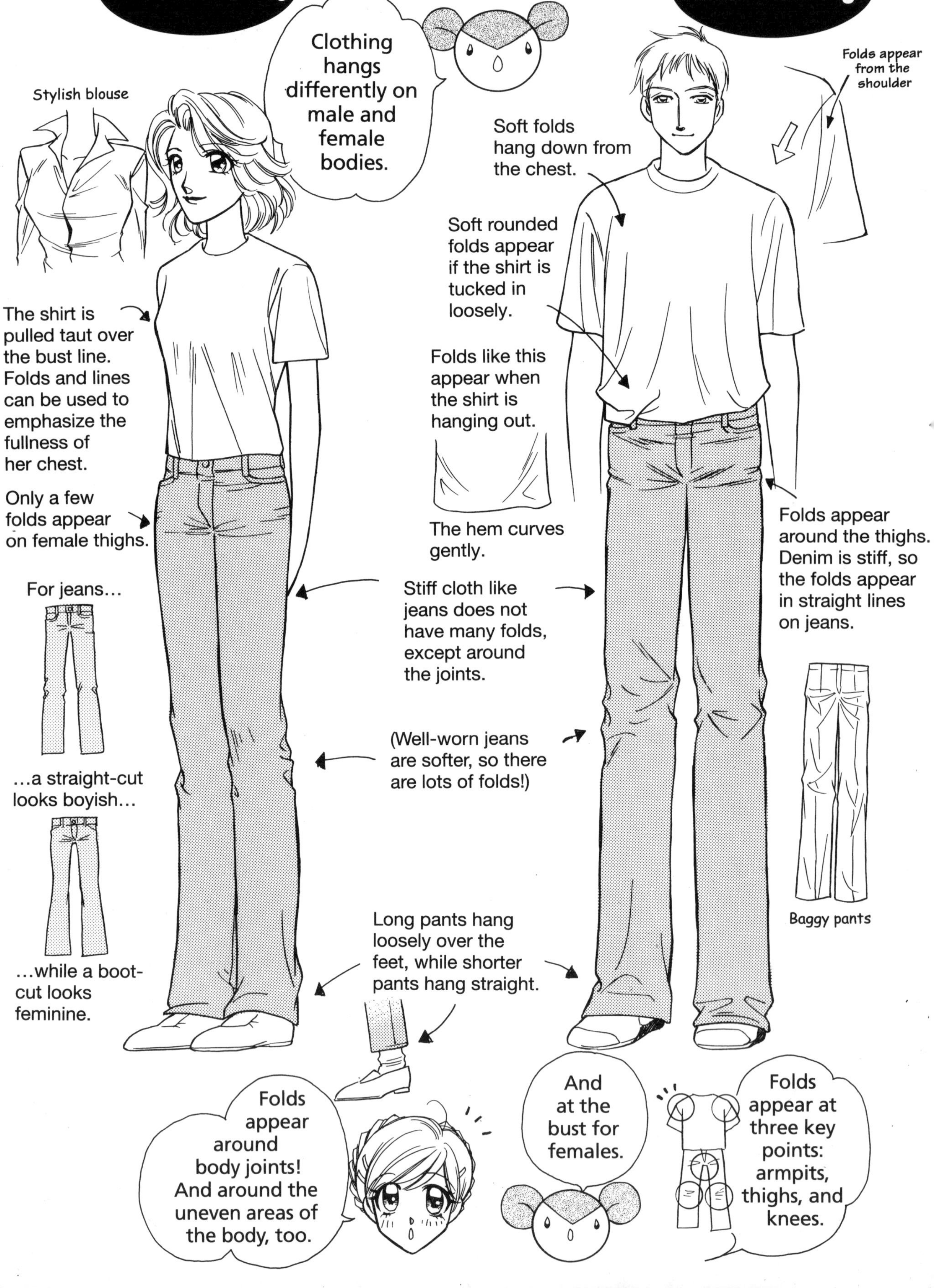

Clothing hangs differently on male and female bodies.
Stylish blouse
The shirt is pulled taut over the bust line. Folds and lines can be used to emphasize the fullness of her chest.
Only a few folds appear on female thighs.
For jeans…
…a straight-cut looks boyish…
…while a boot-cut looks feminine.
Soft folds hang down from the chest.
Soft rounded folds appear if the shirt is tucked in loosely.
Folds like this appear when the shirt is hanging out.
The hem curves gently.
Stiff cloth like jeans does not have many folds, except around the joints.
(Well-worn jeans are softer, so there are lots of folds!)
Long pants hang loosely over the feet, while shorter pants hang straight.
Folds appear from the shoulder
Folds appear around the thighs. Denim is stiff, so the folds appear in straight lines on jeans.
Baggy pants
Folds appear around body joints! And around the uneven areas of the body, too.
And at the bust for females.
Folds appear at three key points: armpits, thighs, and knees.

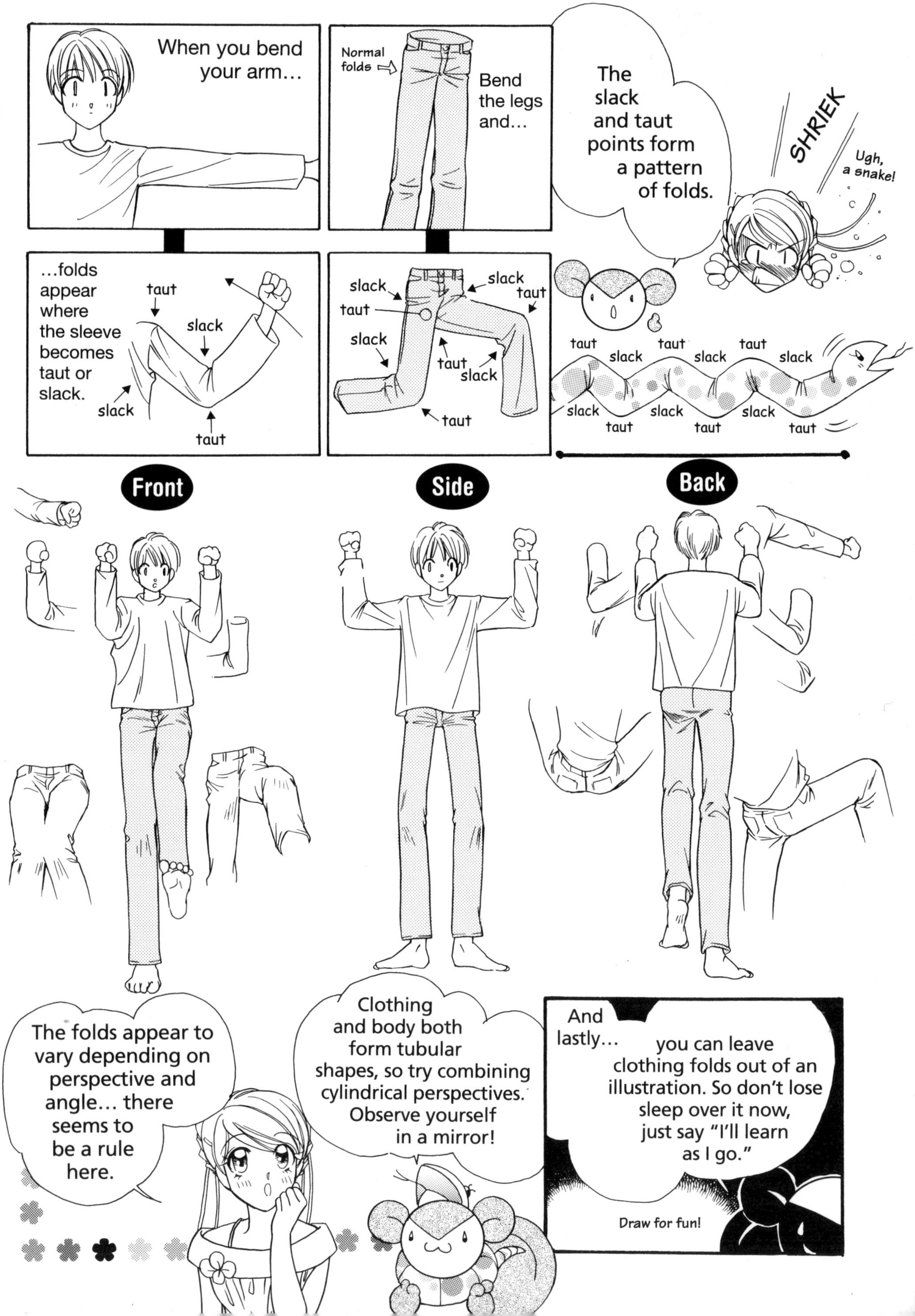
When you bend your arm…
…folds appear where the sleeve becomes taut or slack.
taut
slack
slack
taut
Normal folds
Bend the legs and…
slack
slack
taut
taut
slack
taut
slack
taut
The slack and taut points form a pattern of folds.
SHRIEK
Ugh, a snake!
taut
slack
taut
slack
taut
slack
slack
taut
slack
taut
slack
taut
Front
Side
Back
The folds appear to vary depending on perspective and angle… there seems to be a rule here.
Clothing and body both form tubular shapes, so try combining cylindrical perspectives. Observe yourself in a mirror!
And lastly…
you can leave clothing folds out of an illustration. So don't lose sleep over it now, just say "I'll learn as I go."
Draw for fun!

SHADING ON CHARACTERS

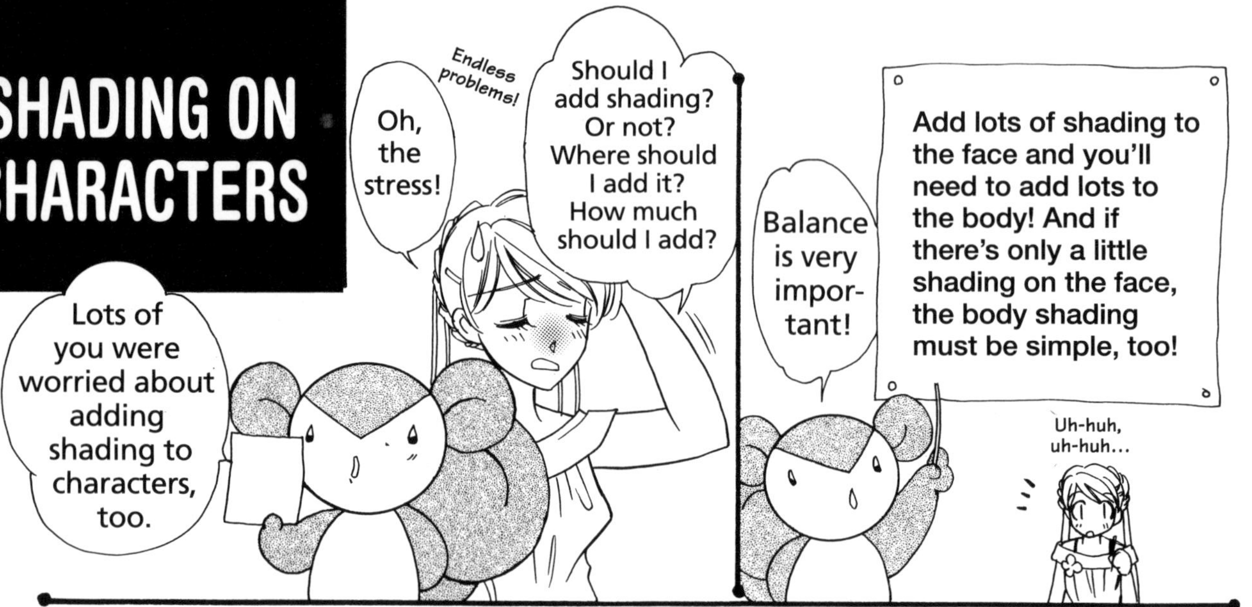
Lots of you were worried about adding shading to characters, too.
Oh, the stress!
Endless problems!
Should I add shading? Or not? Where should I add it? How much should I add?
Balance is very important!
Add lots of shading to the face and you'll need to add lots to the body! And if there's only a little shading on the face, the body shading must be simple, too!
Uh-huh, uh-huh...

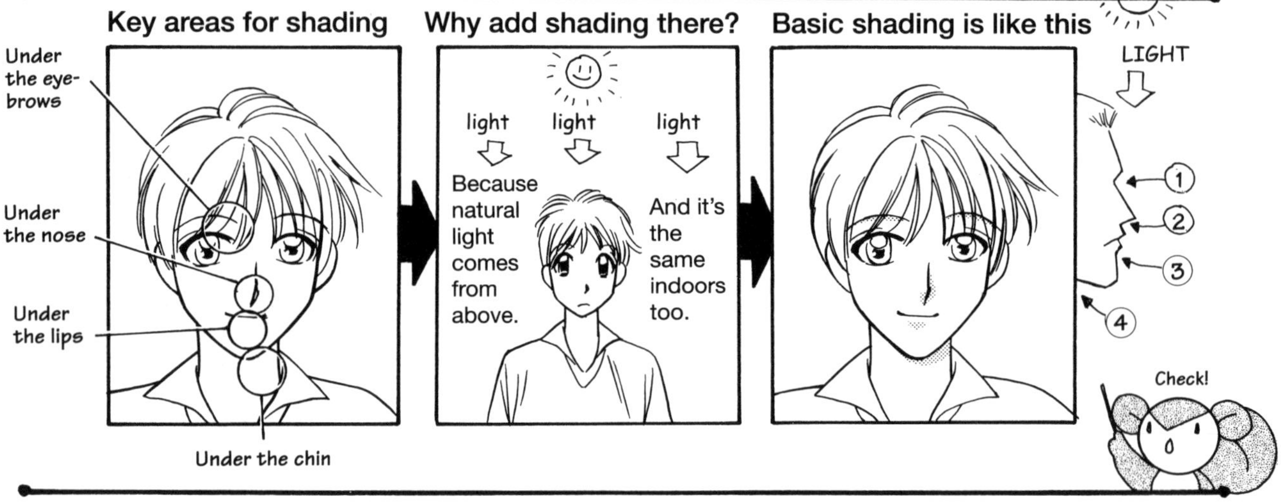
Key areas for shading
Under the eye-brows
Under the nose
Under the lips
Under the chin
Why add shading there?
light
light
light
Because natural light comes from above.
And it's the same indoors too.
Basic shading is like this
LIGHT
1
2
3
4
Check!

Light

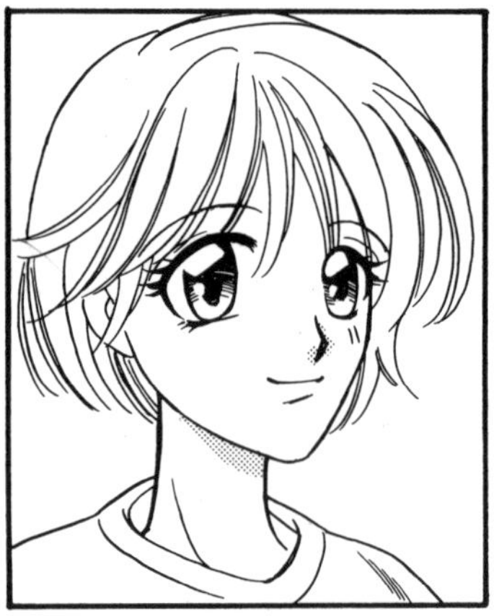

You can use very simple shading under the nose and chin only. This is suitable for pictures with simple or fine lines. Remember to match the shading on the body and clothes, too.

Basic

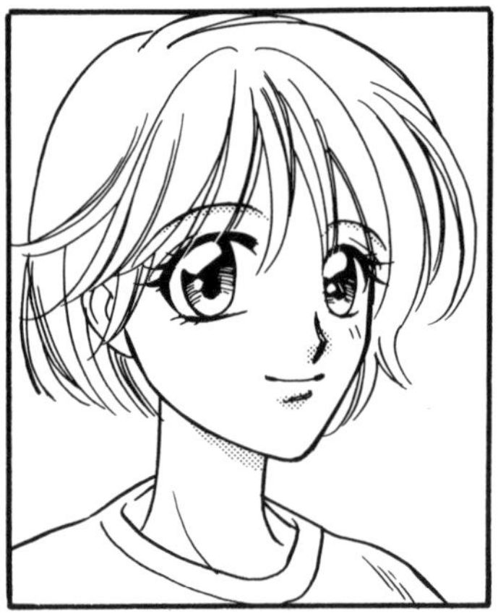

Standard shading. It's a lot of work to add shading to every character on every page, so either leave out shading on smaller characters or add it under the chin only.

Heavy

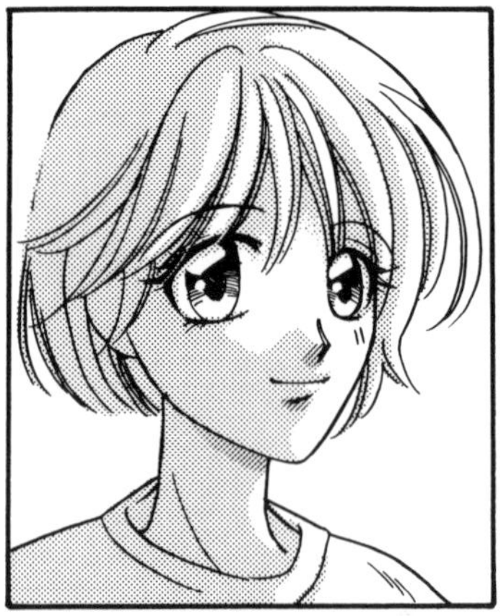

A lot of shading is added to the face. This image looks three-dimensional, but it also looks dark. Balancing the image is important, so you should add an equal amount of shading to the body and clothes.

Light

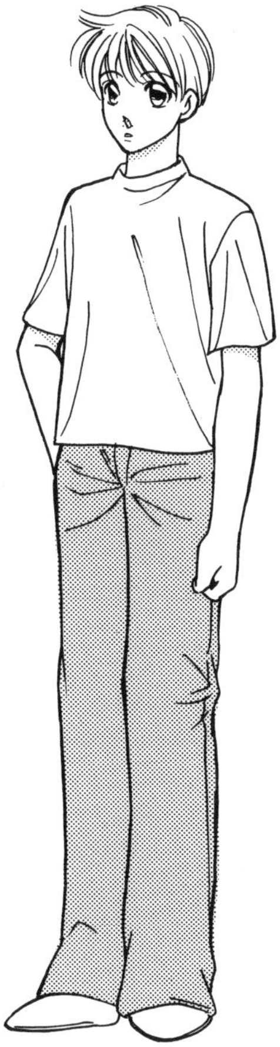

Add light shading to the clothing and body, too, for balance.

Basic

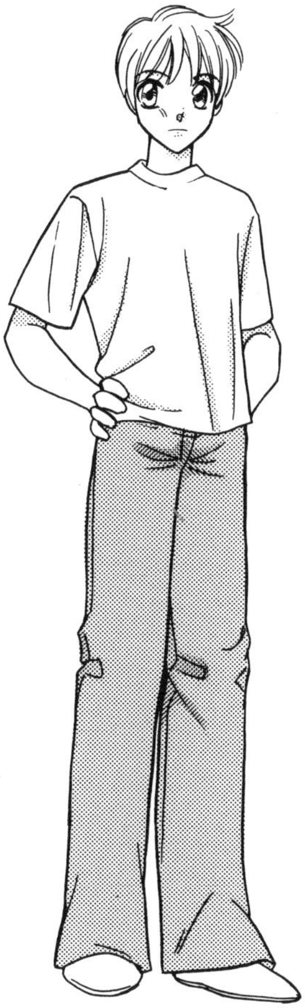

Shading on clothing is not especially needed here, though shading around large folds in the clothing and joints looks good.

Heavy

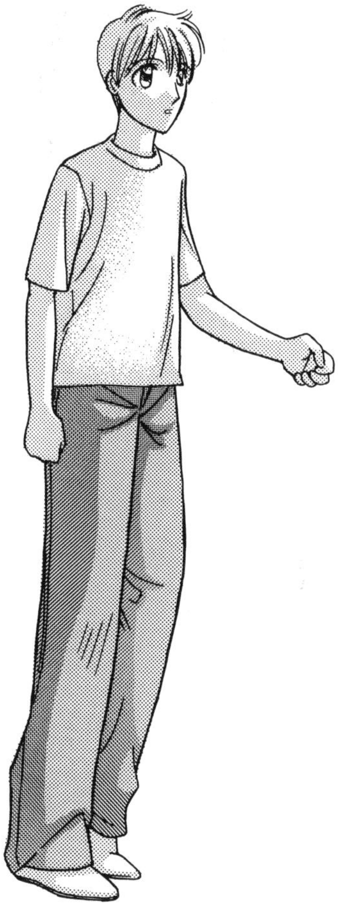

Add heavy shading to the clothing and limbs as well as the head, for balance. If you only shade the head, it well appear to sink and the clothing to float.

SHADING ACCORDING TO SCENE

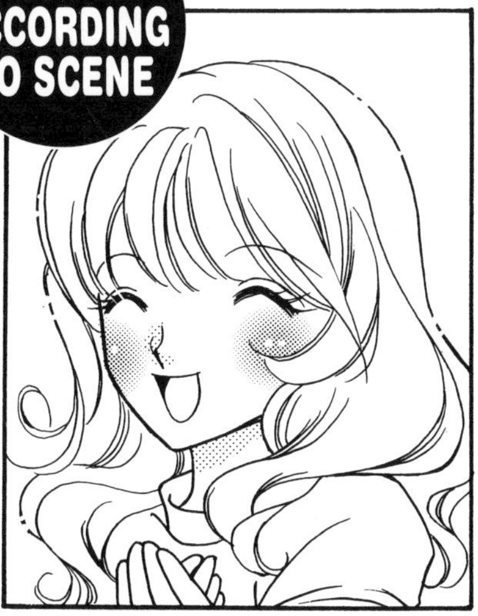

Light shading for a light-hearted scene.

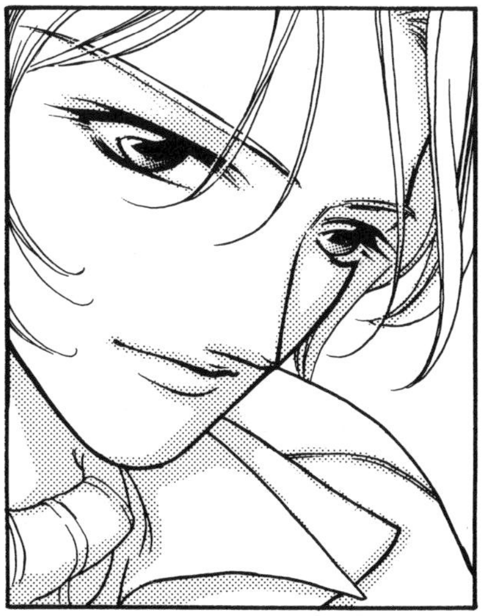

Basic shading for a close-up.

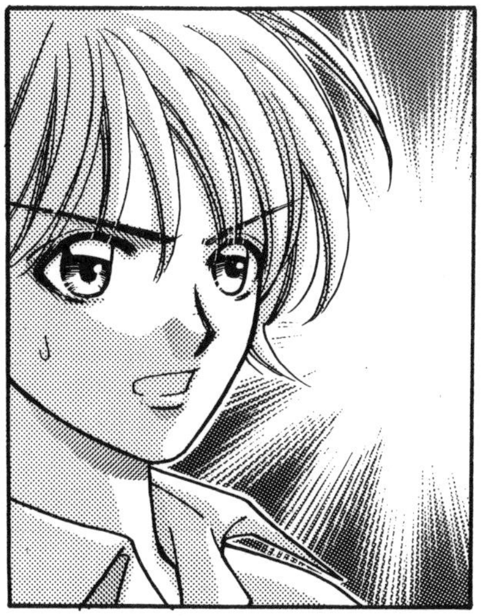

And heavy shading for impact.

SHADING ACCORDING TO SCENE 2

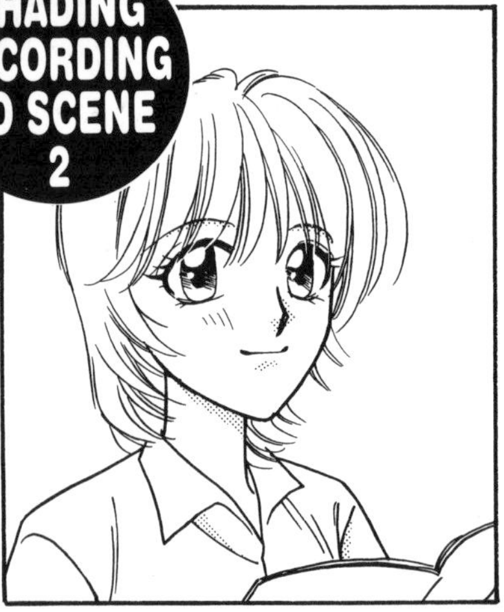

Use basic shading for a normal scene.

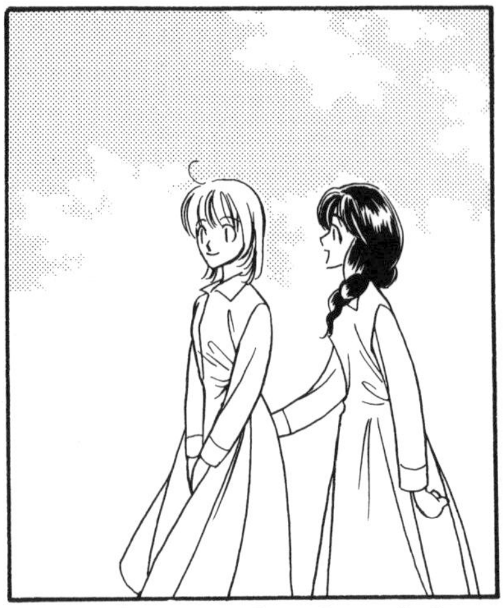

But don't use any for a long shot.

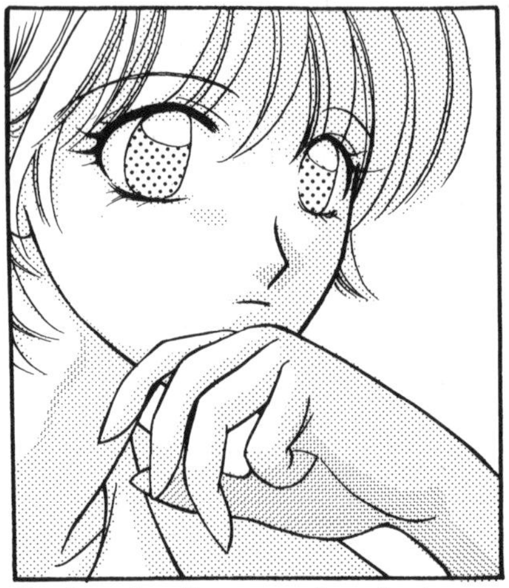

Use low-density screen tone for heavy shading in a close-up.

LAYERING SCREEN TONE

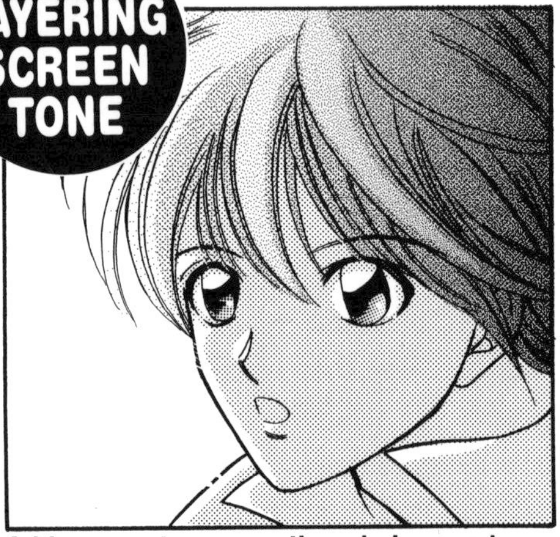

Add screen tone over the whole area to be shaded.

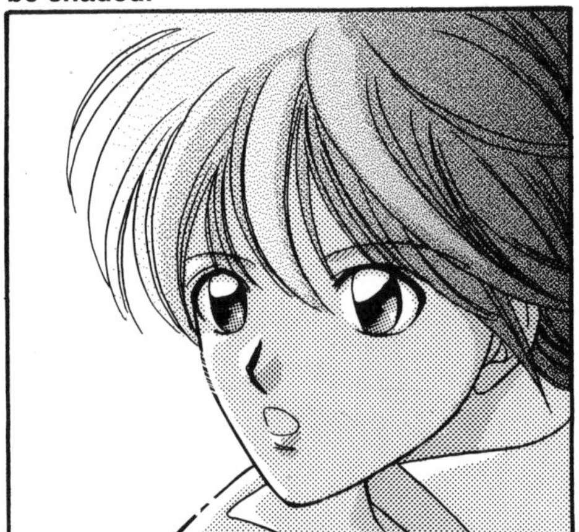

Layer more screen tone for extra shading, but take care to avoid the moiré effect.

It's best to add small details on top of a larger area of screen tone.

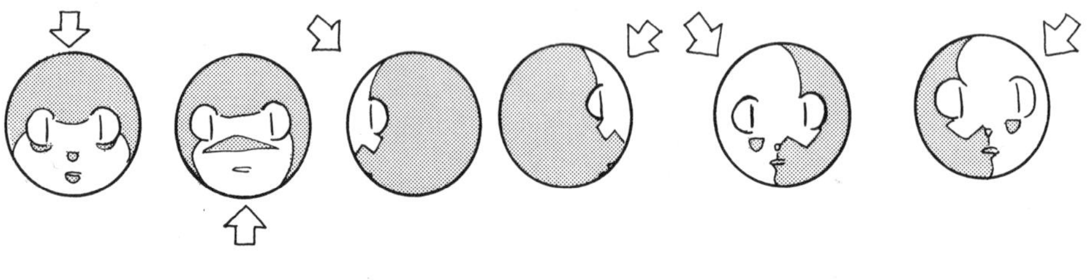

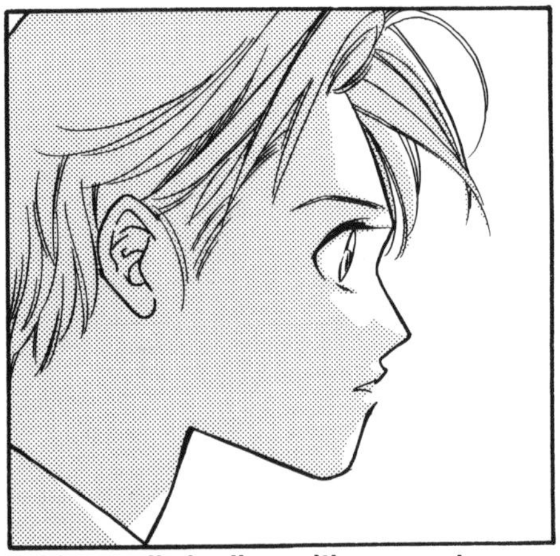

Add overall shading with screen tone.

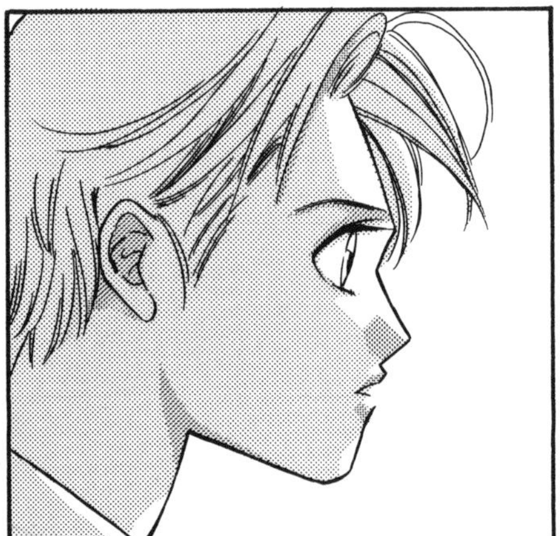

Then layer the areas you want darker with screen tone.

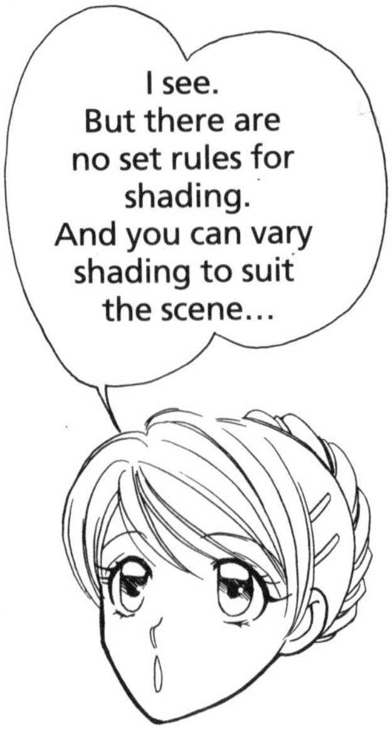
I see. But there are no set rules for shading. And you can vary shading to suit the scene...

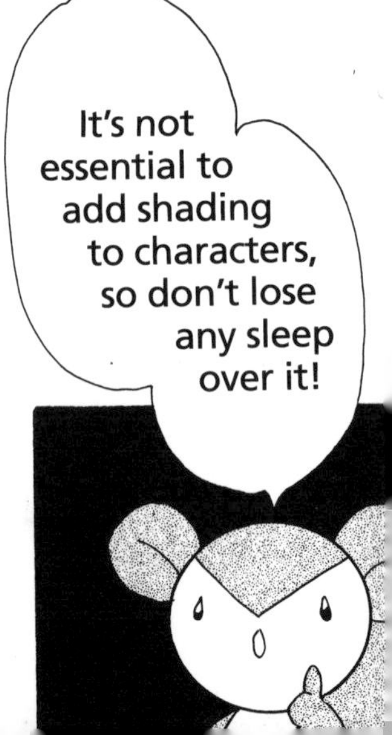
It's not essential to add shading to characters, so don't lose any sleep over it!

TEXTURES

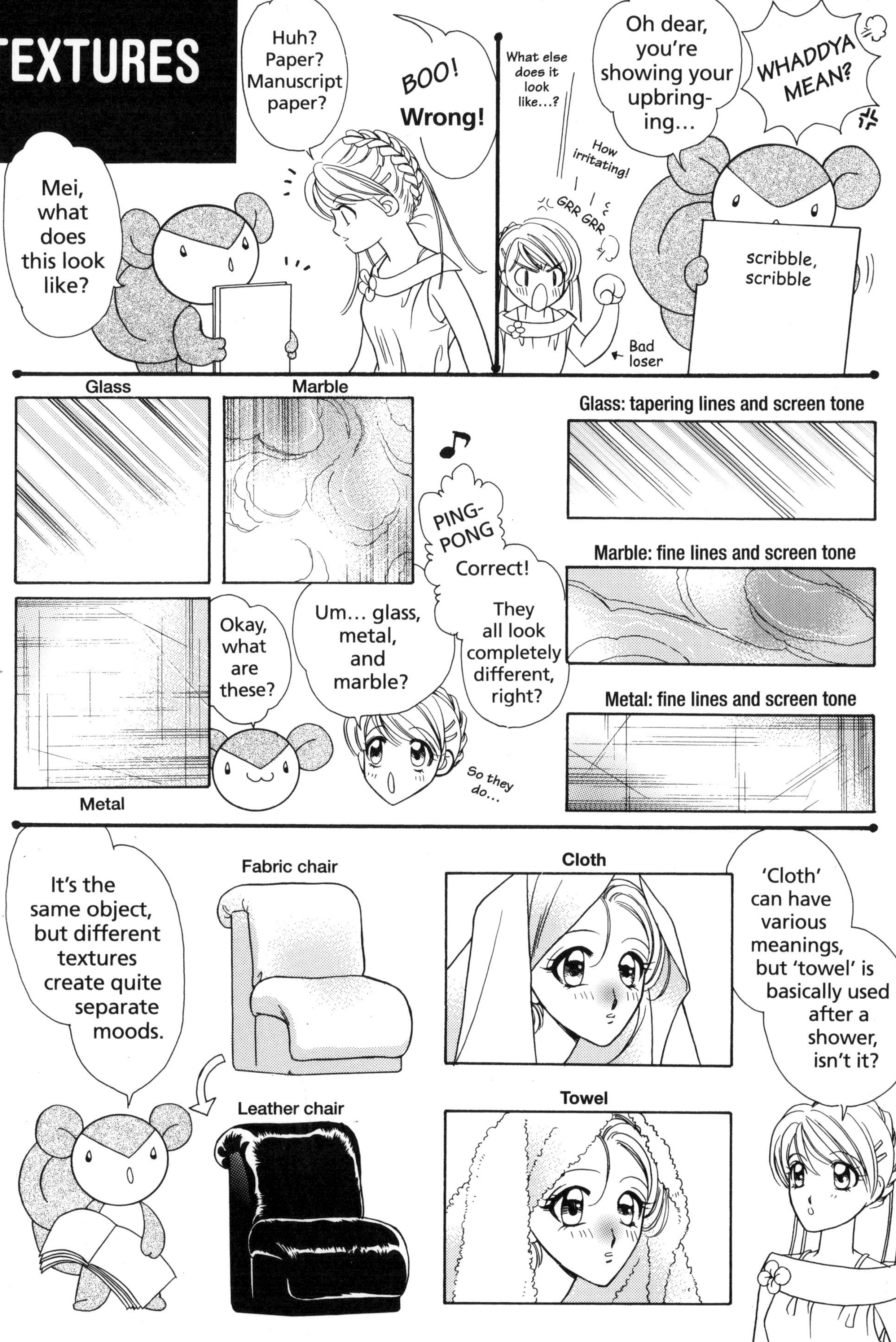
Mei, what does this look like?
Huh? Paper? Manuscript paper?
BOO! Wrong!
What else does it look like…?
How irritating!
GRR GRR
Bad loser
Oh dear, you're showing your upbringing…
WHADDYA MEAN?
scribble, scribble
Glass
Marble
Metal
Okay, what are these?
Um… glass, metal, and marble?
PING-PONG
Correct!
They all look completely different, right?
So they do…
Glass: tapering lines and screen tone
Marble: fine lines and screen tone
Metal: fine lines and screen tone
It's the same object, but different textures create quite separate moods.
Fabric chair
Leather chair
Cloth
Towel
'Cloth' can have various meanings, but 'towel' is basically used after a shower, isn't it?

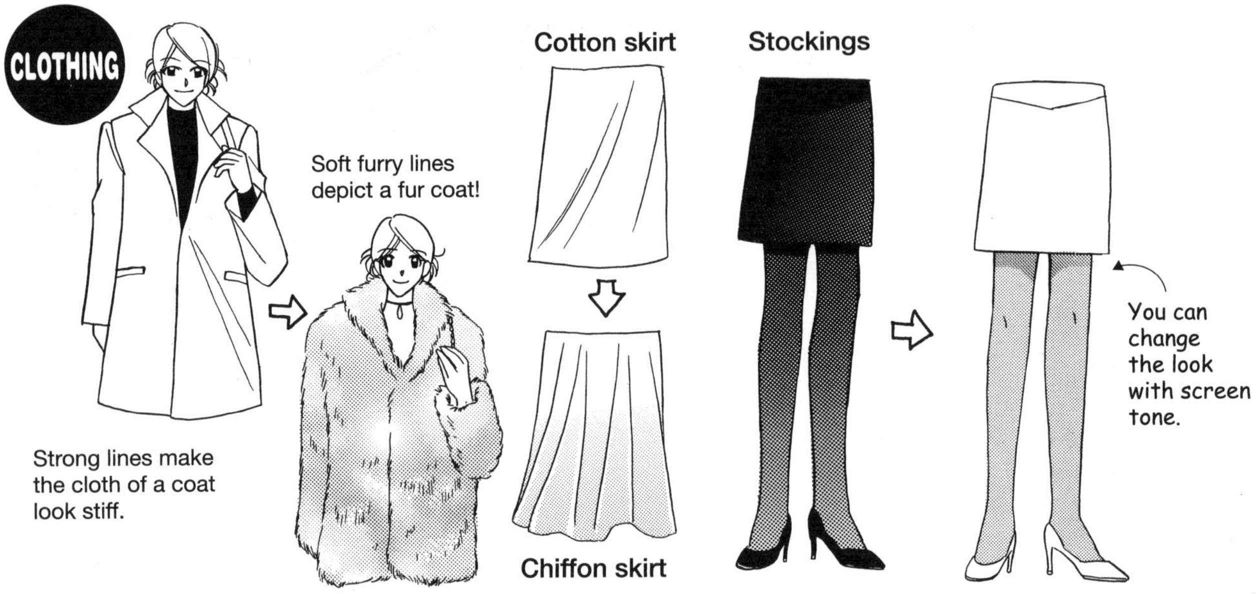
CLOTHING
Strong lines make the cloth of a coat look stiff.
Soft furry lines depict a fur coat!
Cotton skirt
Chiffon skirt
Stockings
You can change the look with screen tone.

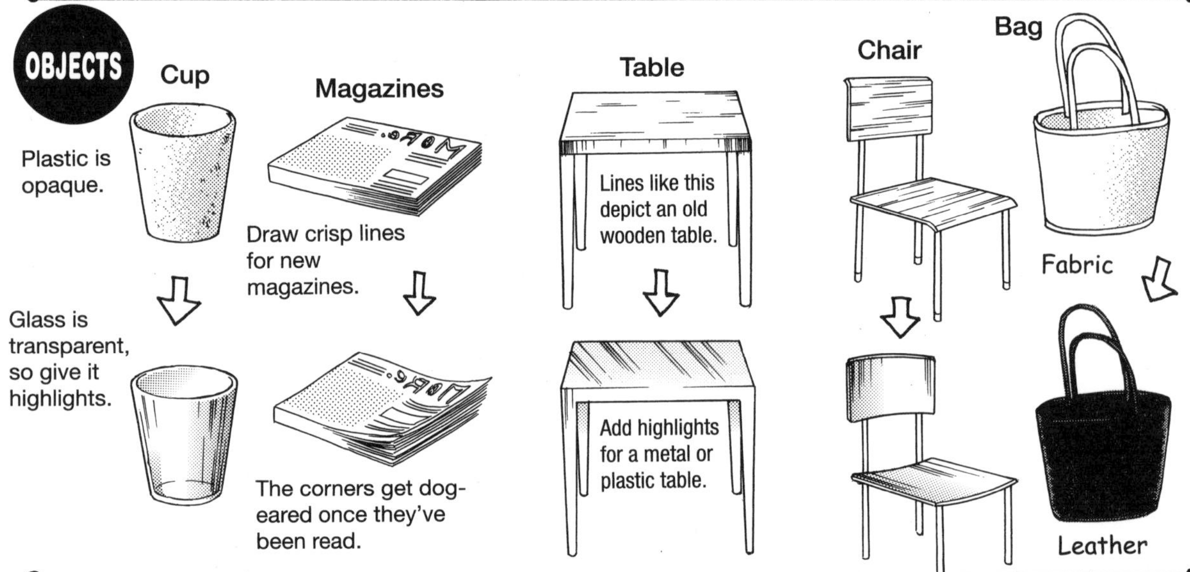
OBJECTS
Cup
Plastic is opaque.
Glass is transparent, so give it highlights.
Magazines
Draw crisp lines for new magazines.
The corners get dog-eared once they've been read.
Table
Lines like this depict an old wooden table.
Add highlights for a metal or plastic table.
Chair
Bag
Fabric
Leather

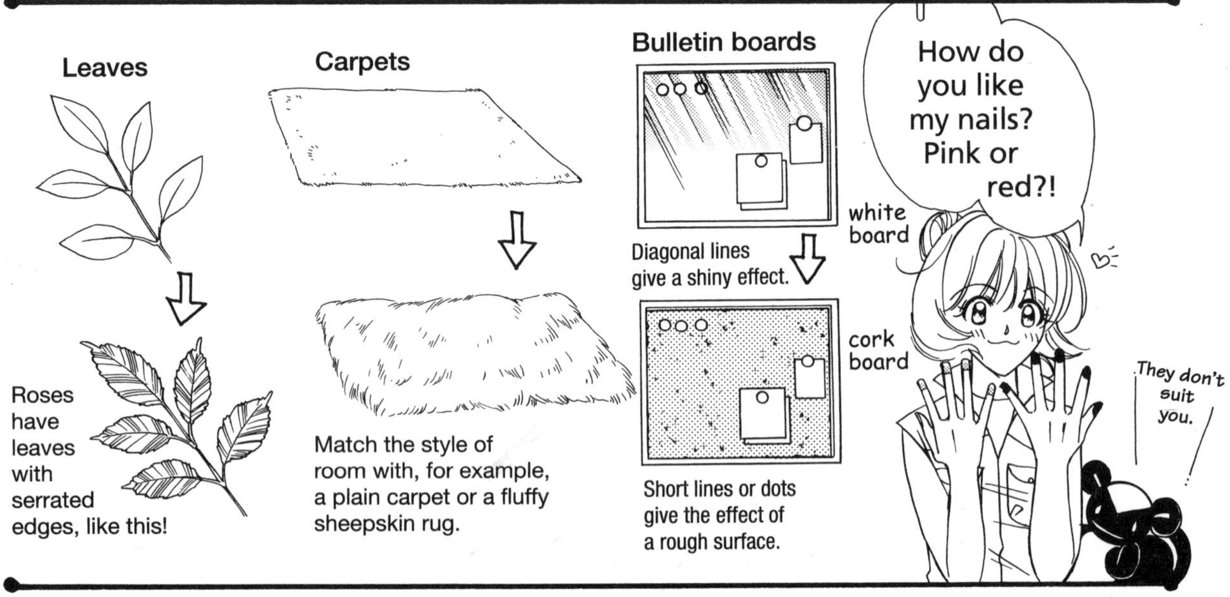
Leaves
Roses have leaves with serrated edges, like this!
Carpets
Match the style of room with, for example, a plain carpet or a fluffy sheepskin rug.
Bulletin boards
white board
Diagonal lines give a shiny effect.
cork board
Short lines or dots give the effect of a rough surface.
How do you like my nails? Pink or red?!
They don't suit you.

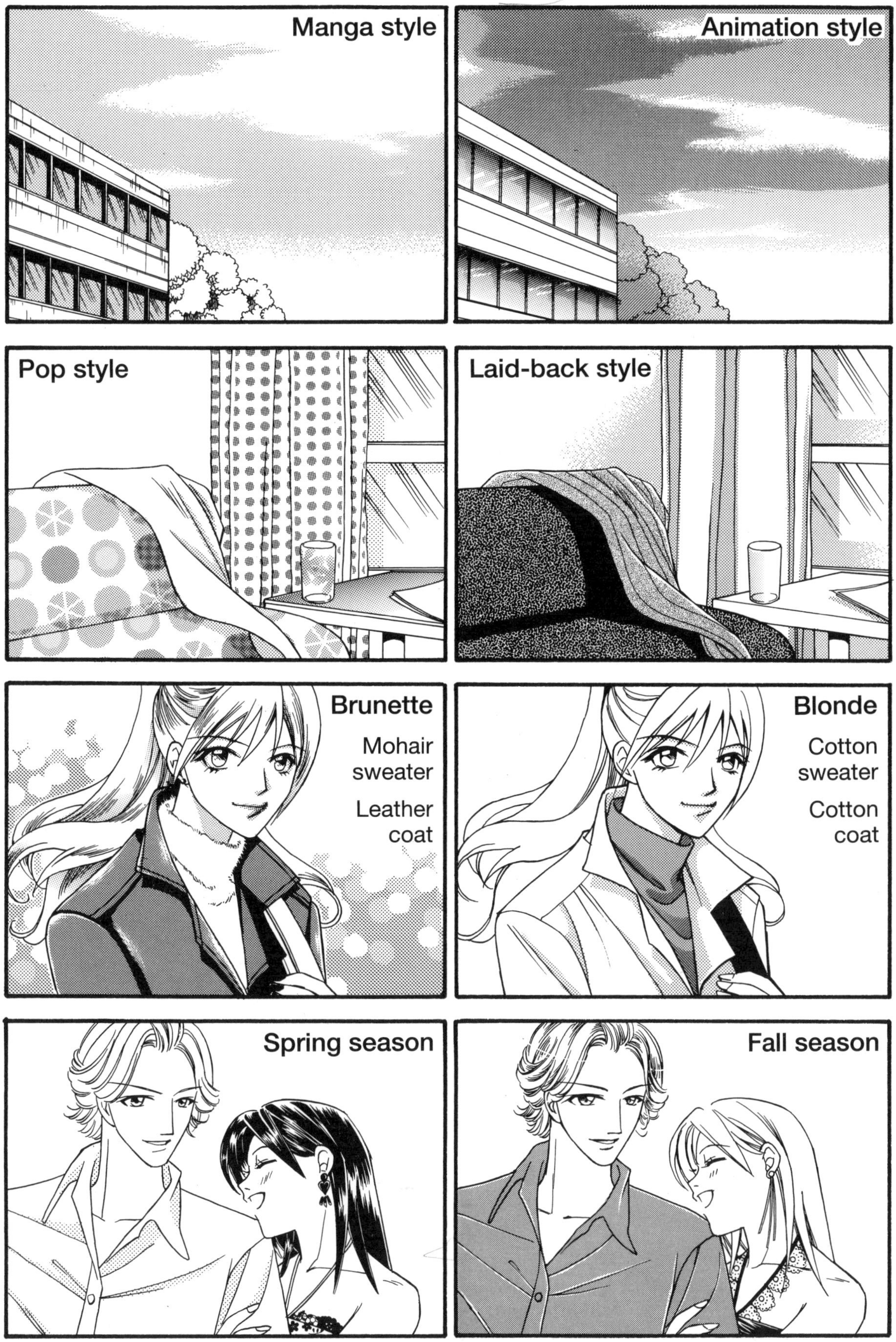
Manga style
Animation style
Pop style
Laid-back style
Brunette
Mohair sweater
Leather coat
Blonde
Cotton sweater
Cotton coat
Spring season
Fall season

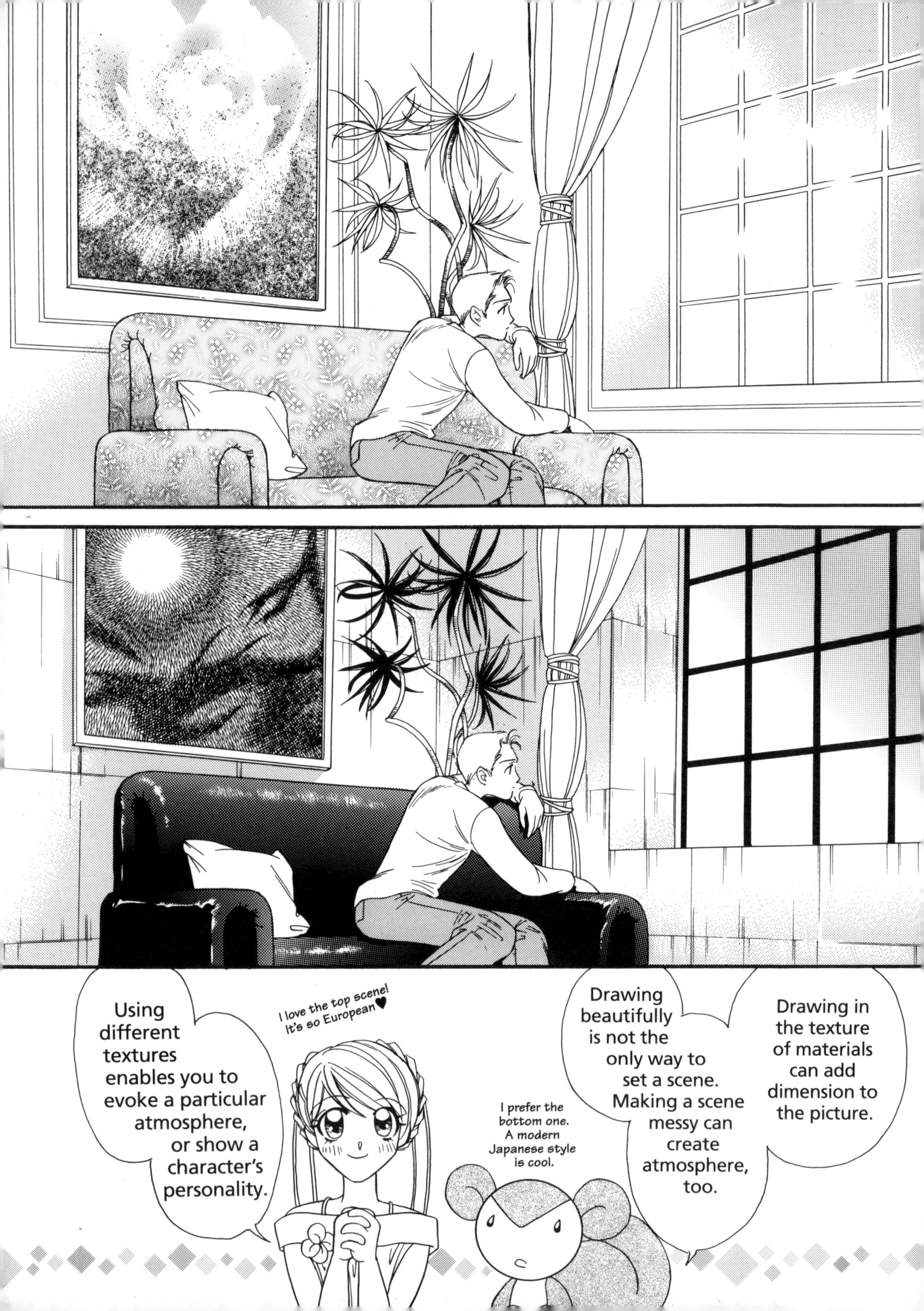
Drawing in the texture of materials can add dimension to the picture.
Drawing beautifully is not the only way to set a scene. Making a scene messy can create atmosphere, too.
I prefer the bottom one. A modern Japanese style is cool.
I love the top scene! It's so European♥
Using different textures enables you to evoke a particular atmosphere, or show a character's personality.

LESSON 2

EFFECTS

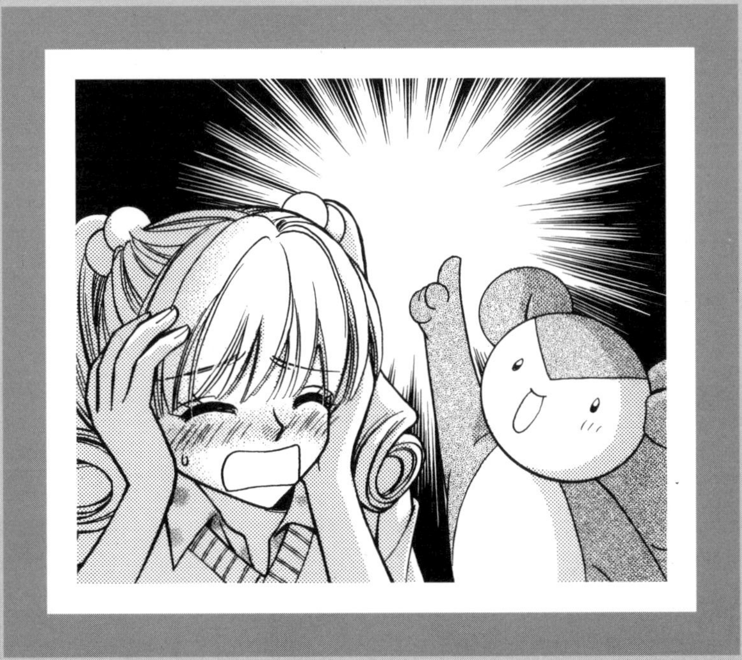

In this lesson we explain how to enhance your manga with special effects, including flashes and sound effects, as well as how to create different effects in ink or screen tone.

FLASHES

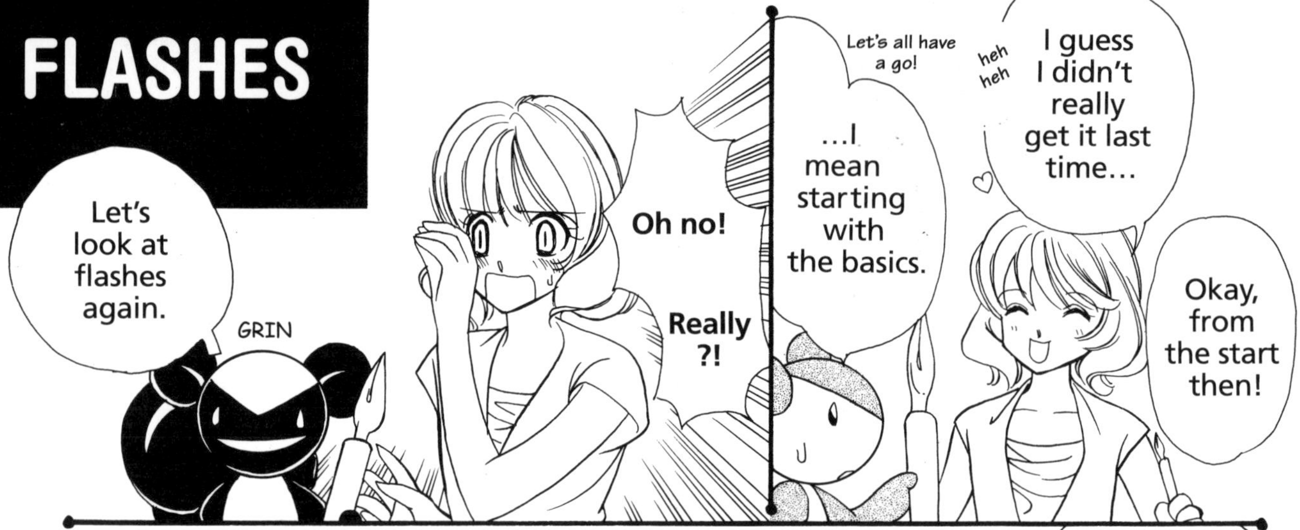
Let's look at flashes again.
GRIN
Oh no!
Really ?!
...I mean starting with the basics.
Let's all have a go!
heh heh
I guess I didn't really get it last time...
Okay, from the start then!

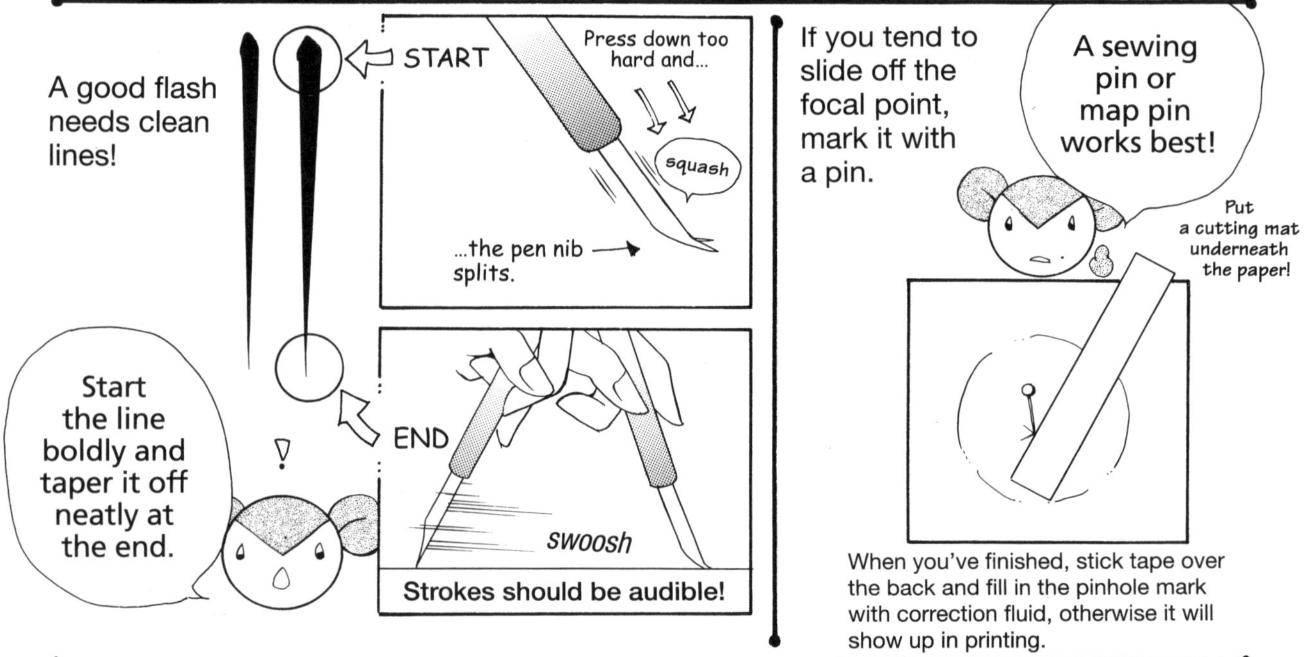
A good flash needs clean lines!
START
Press down too hard and...
squash
...the pen nib splits.
END
swoosh
Strokes should be audible!
Start the line boldly and taper it off neatly at the end.
If you tend to slide off the focal point, mark it with a pin.
A sewing pin or map pin works best!
Put a cutting mat underneath the paper!
When you've finished, stick tape over the back and fill in the pinhole mark with correction fluid, otherwise it will show up in printing.

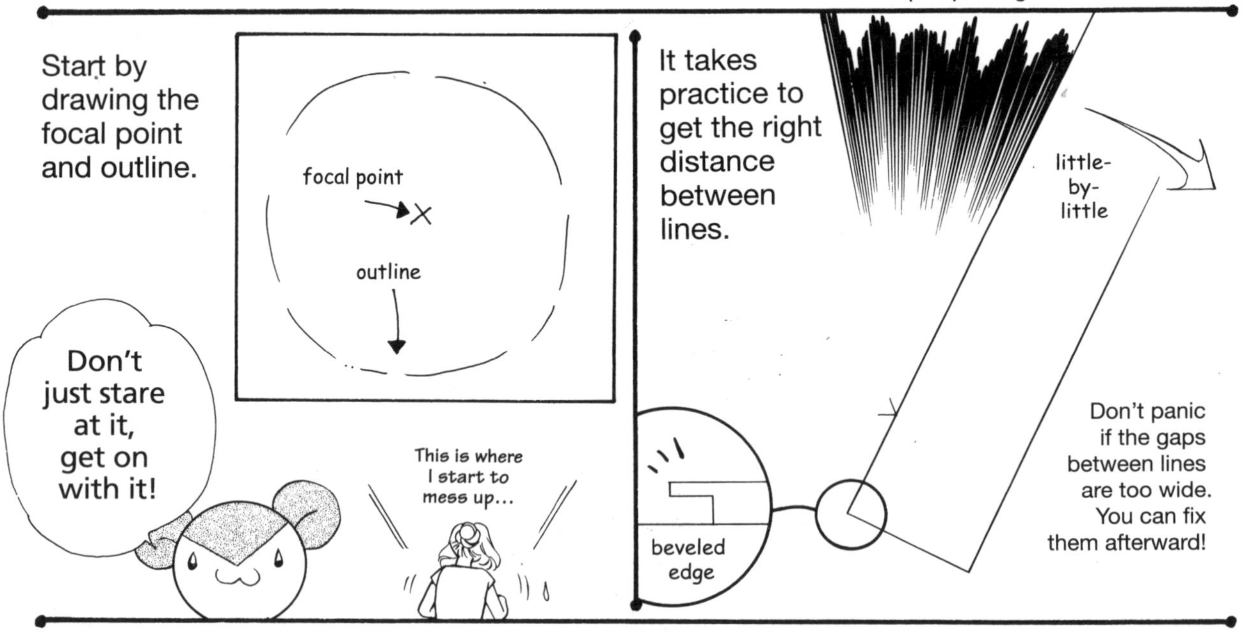
Start by drawing the focal point and outline.
focal point
outline
Don't just stare at it, get on with it!
This is where I start to mess up...
It takes practice to get the right distance between lines.
little-by-little
beveled edge
Don't panic if the gaps between lines are too wide. You can fix them afterward!

The finished result looks like this.
Now all you have to do is tidy it up.

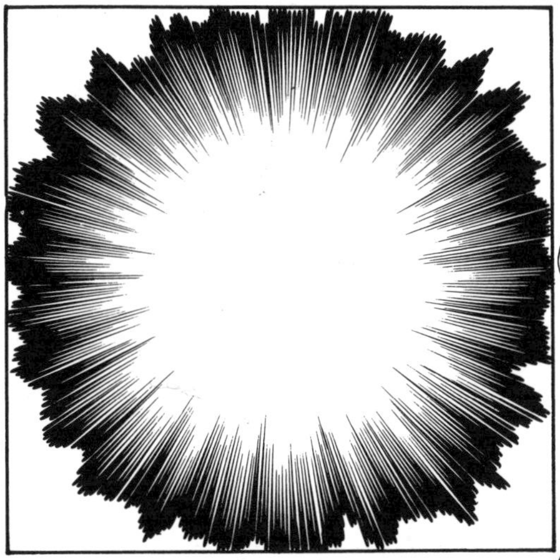

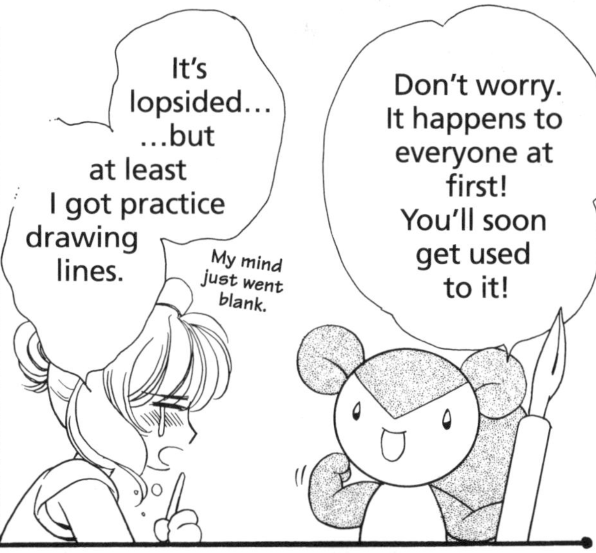
It's lopsided… …but at least I got practice drawing lines.
My mind just went blank.
Don't worry. It happens to everyone at first! You'll soon get used to it!

FLASH TYPES

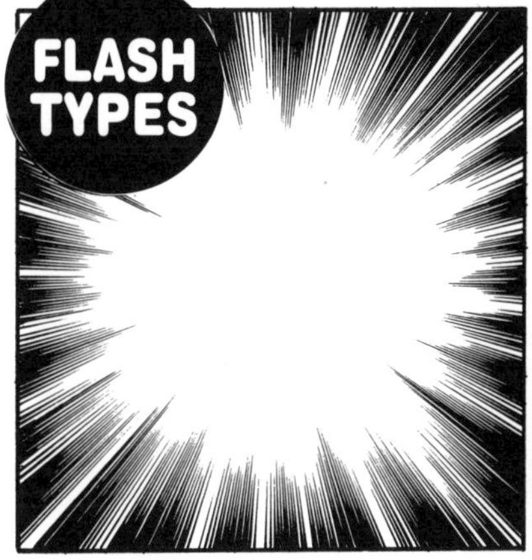
Big flash

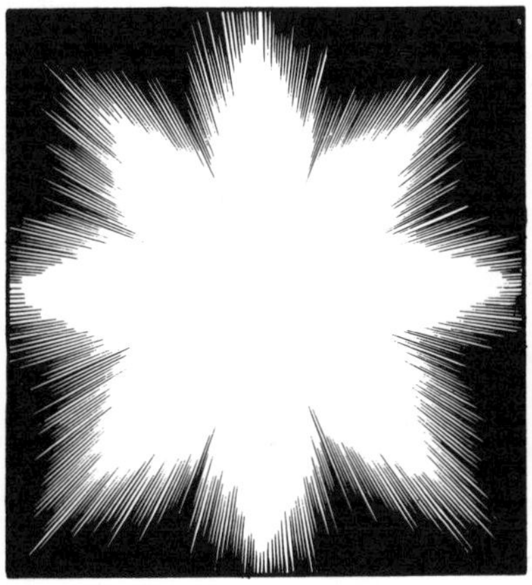
Star-shaped flash

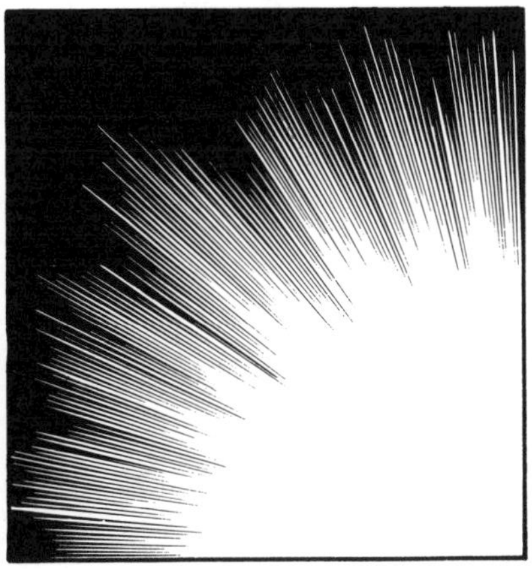
Partial flash

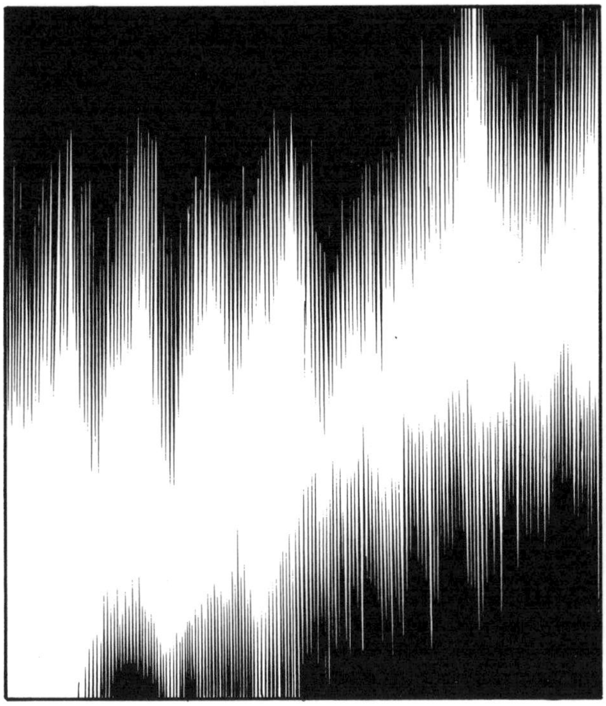
Straight line flash

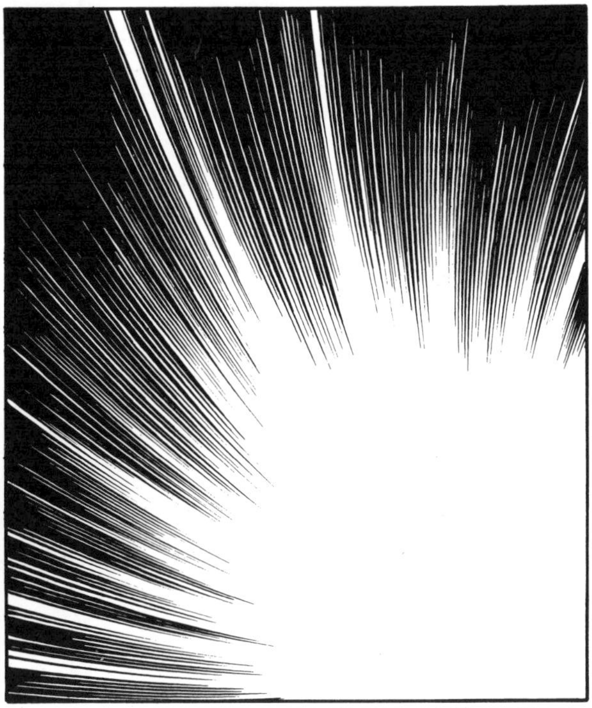
Curved line flash

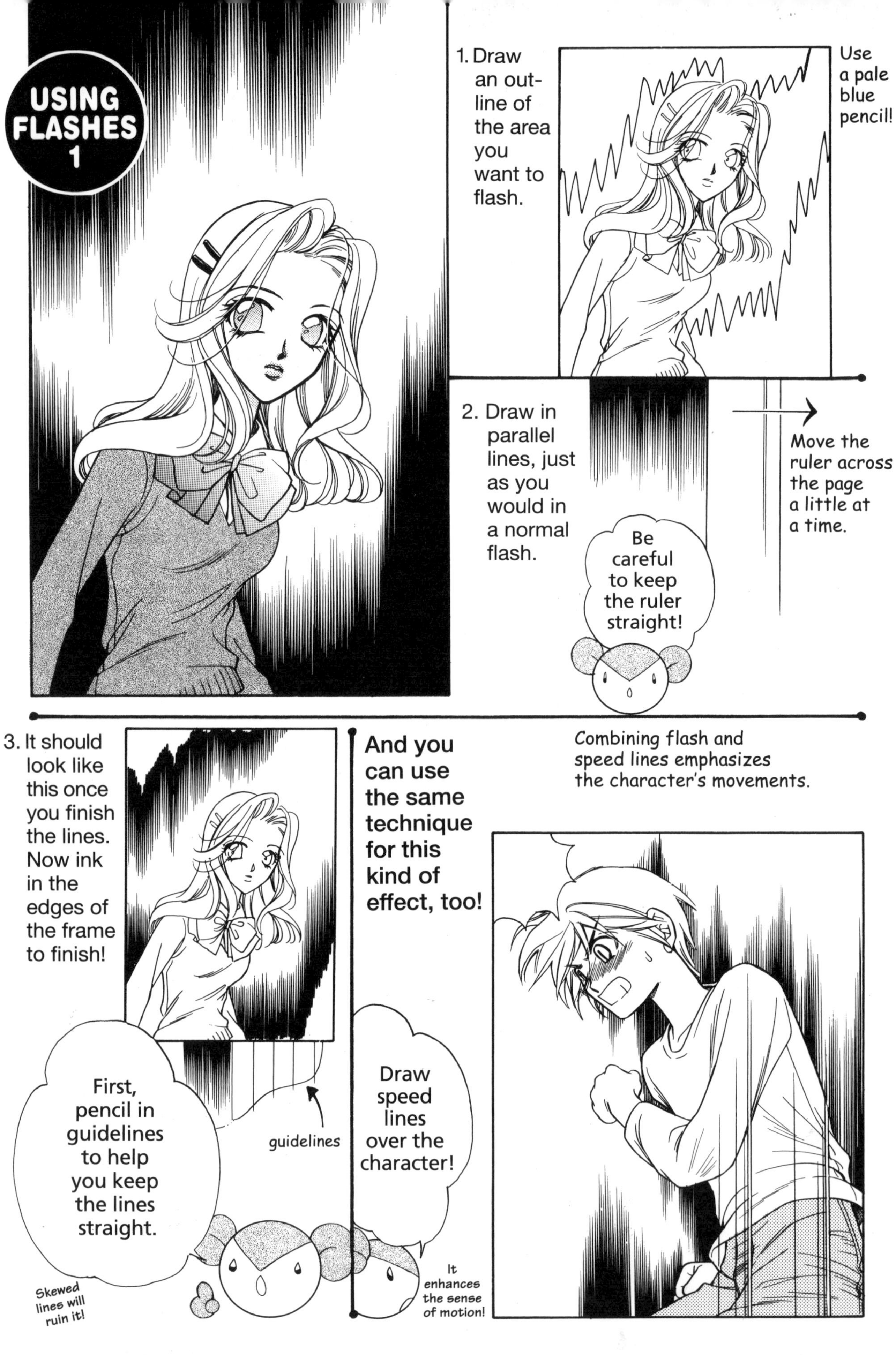
USING FLASHES 1
1. Draw an outline of the area you want to flash.
Use a pale blue pencil!
2. Draw in parallel lines, just as you would in a normal flash.
Move the ruler across the page a little at a time.
Be careful to keep the ruler straight!
3. It should look like this once you finish the lines. Now ink in the edges of the frame to finish!
First, pencil in guidelines to help you keep the lines straight.
guidelines
Skewed lines will ruin it!
And you can use the same technique for this kind of effect, too!
Draw speed lines over the character!
It enhances the sense of motion!
Combining flash and speed lines emphasizes the character's movements.

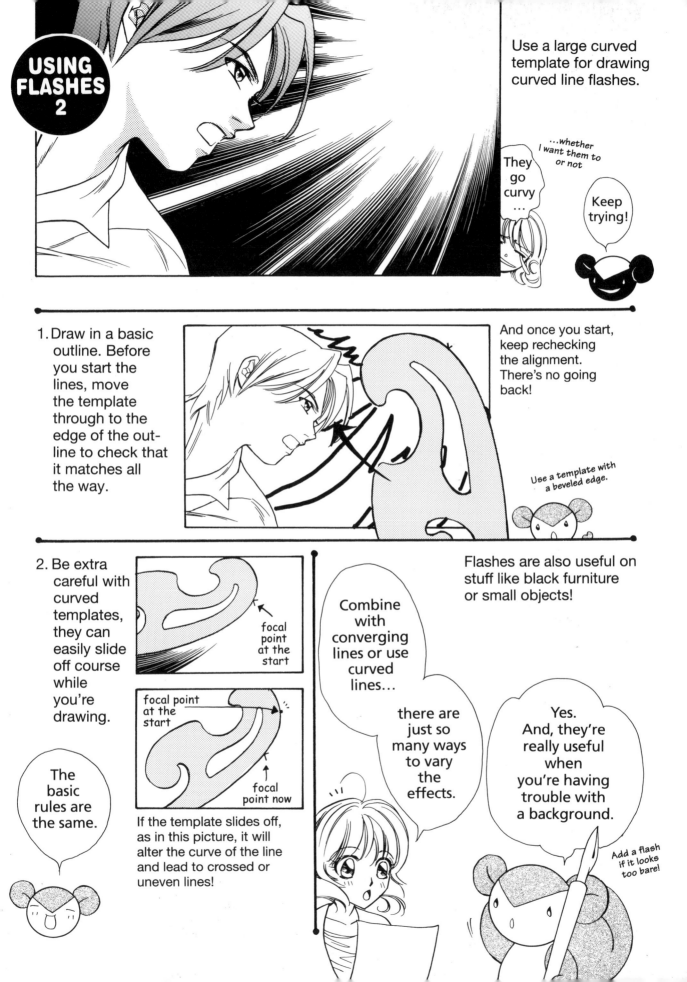

USING FLASHES 2

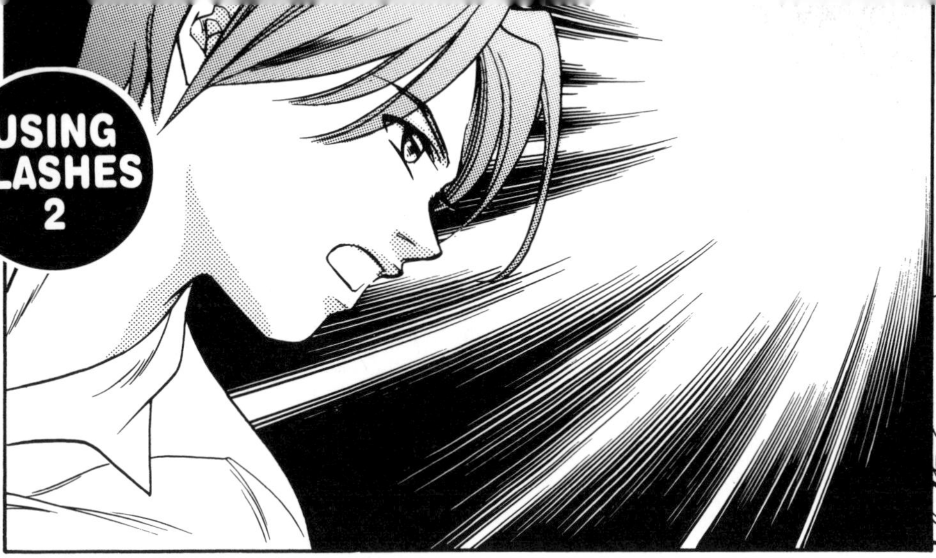

Use a large curved template for drawing curved line flashes.

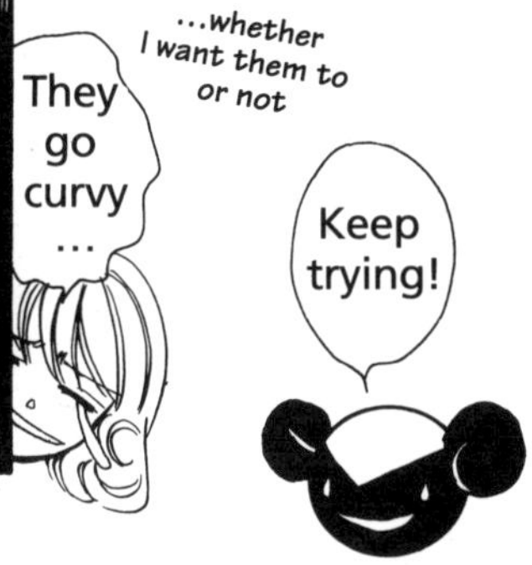

They go curvy …
…whether I want them to or not
Keep trying!

1. Draw in a basic outline. Before you start the lines, move the template through to the edge of the outline to check that it matches all the way.

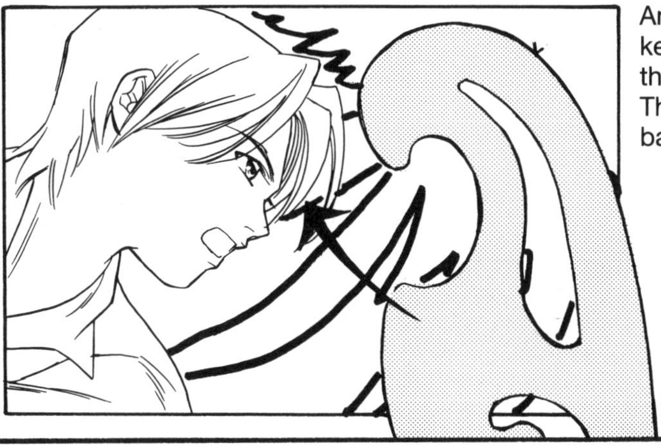

And once you start, keep rechecking the alignment. There's no going back!

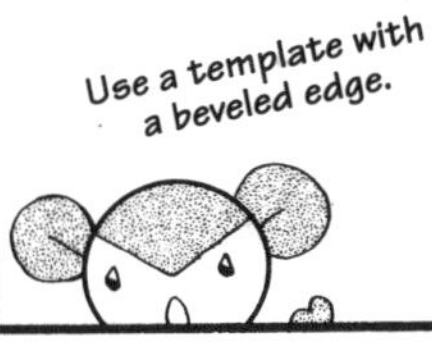

Use a template with a beveled edge.

2. Be extra careful with curved templates, they can easily slide off course while you're drawing.

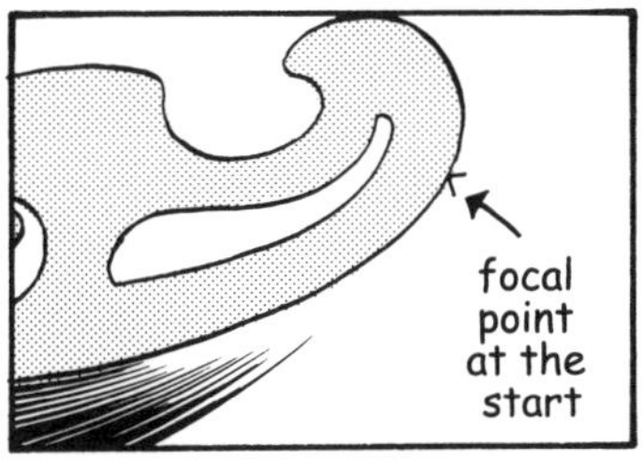

focal point at the start

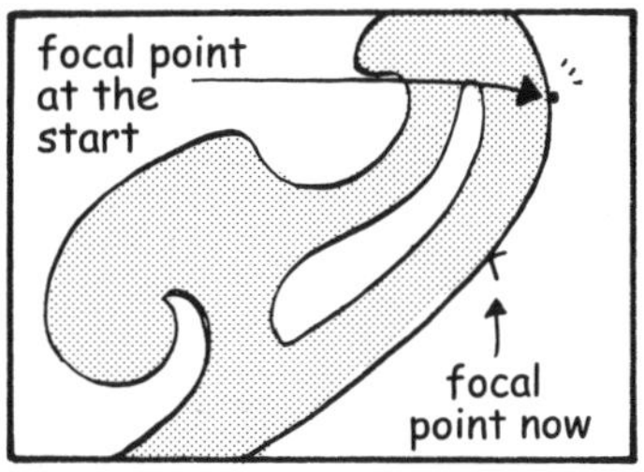

focal point at the start
focal point now

If the template slides off, as in this picture, it will alter the curve of the line and lead to crossed or uneven lines!

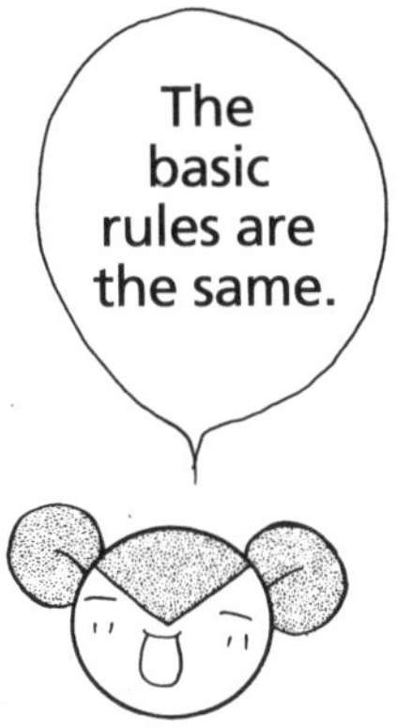

The basic rules are the same.

Flashes are also useful on stuff like black furniture or small objects!

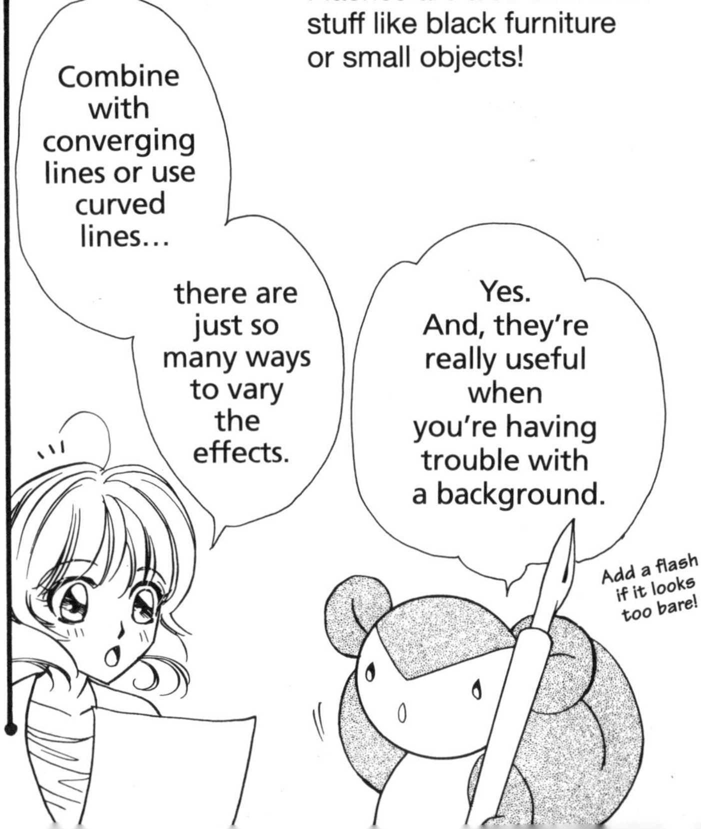

Combine with converging lines or use curved lines…
there are just so many ways to vary the effects.
Yes. And, they're really useful when you're having trouble with a background.
Add a flash if it looks too bare!

CONVERGING LINES

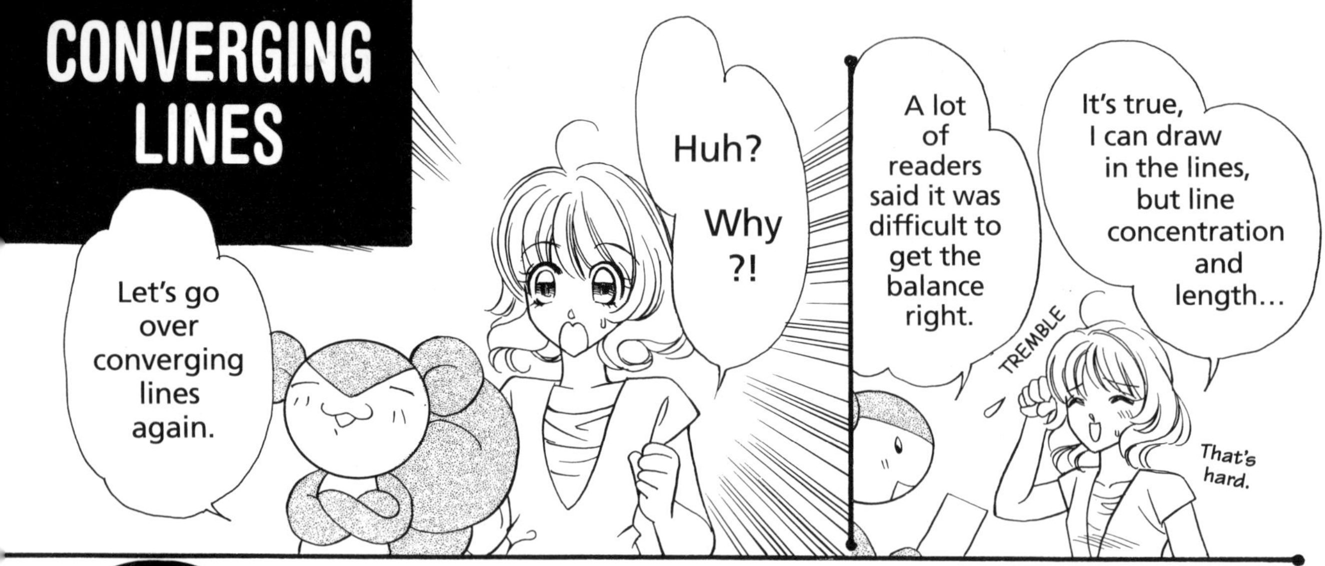
Let's go over converging lines again.
Huh?
Why ?!
A lot of readers said it was difficult to get the balance right.
It's true, I can draw in the lines, but line concentration and length...
TREMBLE
That's hard.

Basic Method

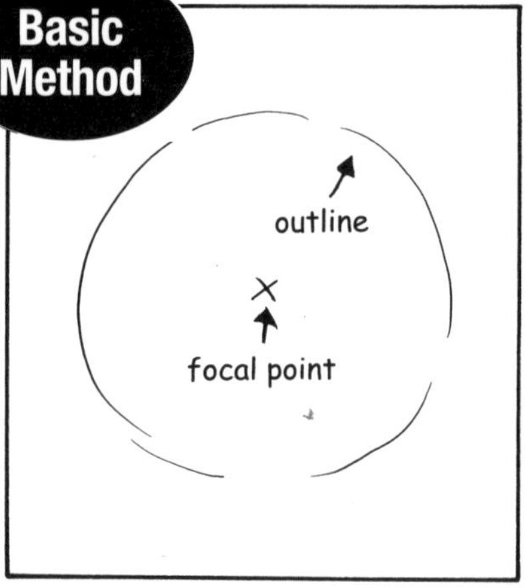
outline
focal point

1. Draw in the focal point and outline with a pale blue pencil!

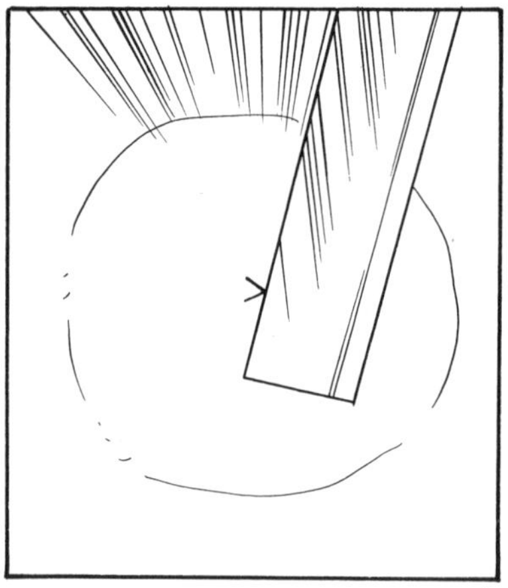

2. Use a ruler with a beveled edge, and taper the lines for a neat effect.

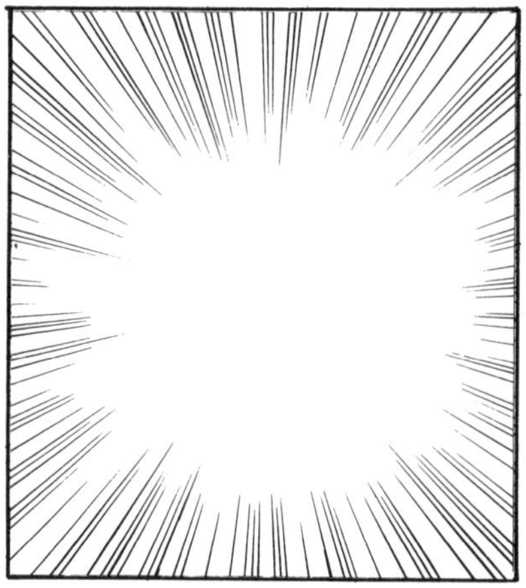

3. Erase the outline and focal point.

Getting the balance right

Lines drawn with identical gaps between them look lifeless. Draw groups of lines and vary the size of the gaps!

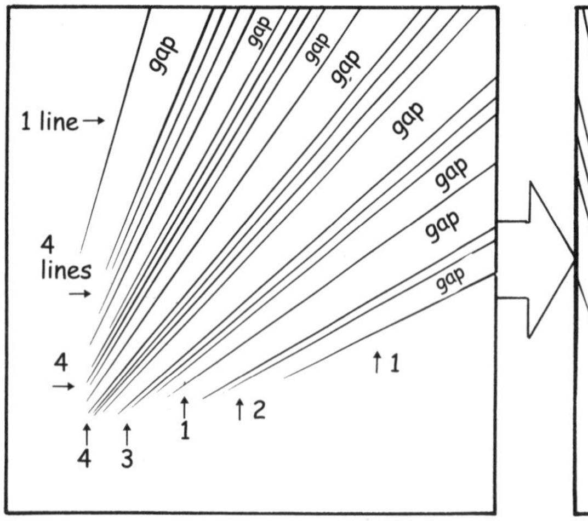
gap
gap
gap
gap
gap
gap
gap
gap
1 line→
4 lines →
4 →
↑ 4
↑ 3
↑ 1
↑ 2
↑ 1

It's easy to balance the grouping of lines this way.

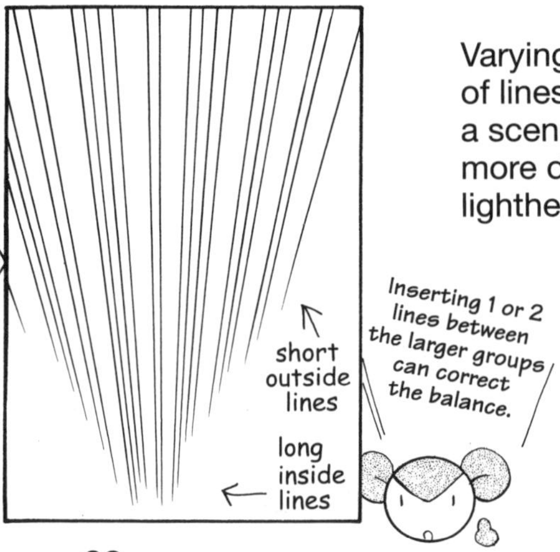
short outside lines
long inside lines
Inserting 1 or 2 lines between the larger groups can correct the balance.

Groups of 4 lines on the inside, with smaller groups of 1 or 2 on the outside look good.

Varying the groups of lines can enhance a scene to make it more dramatic or lighthearted.

Lighthearted effect

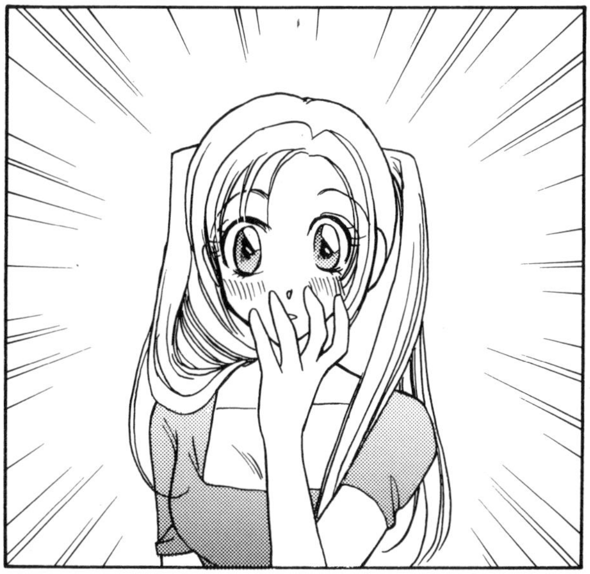

Dramatic effect

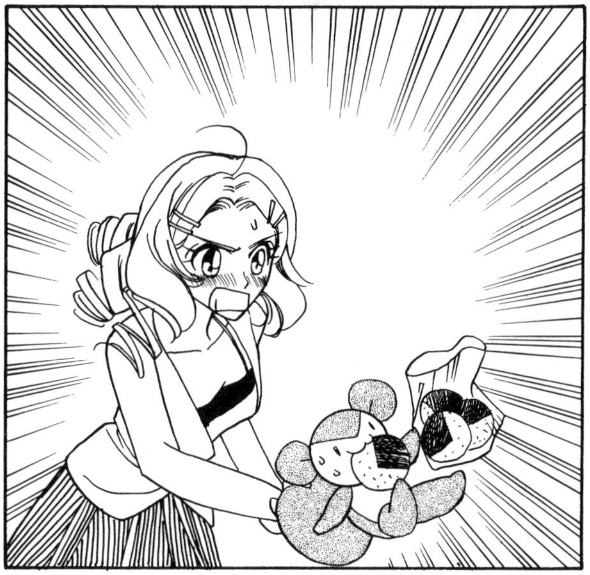

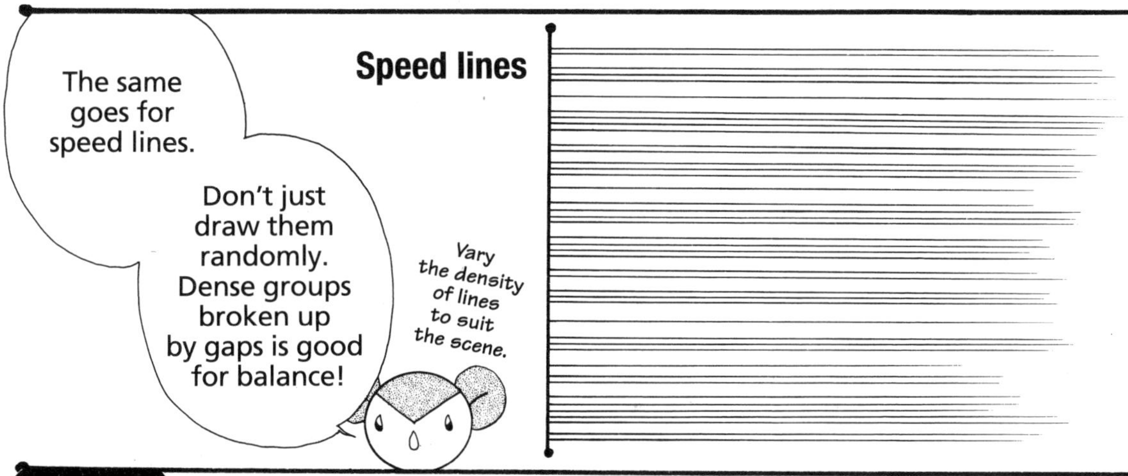
The same goes for speed lines.
Don't just draw them randomly. Dense groups broken up by gaps is good for balance!
Vary the density of lines to suit the scene.

Speed lines

SPEED LINES

Draw speed lines separately onto both the background and the character.

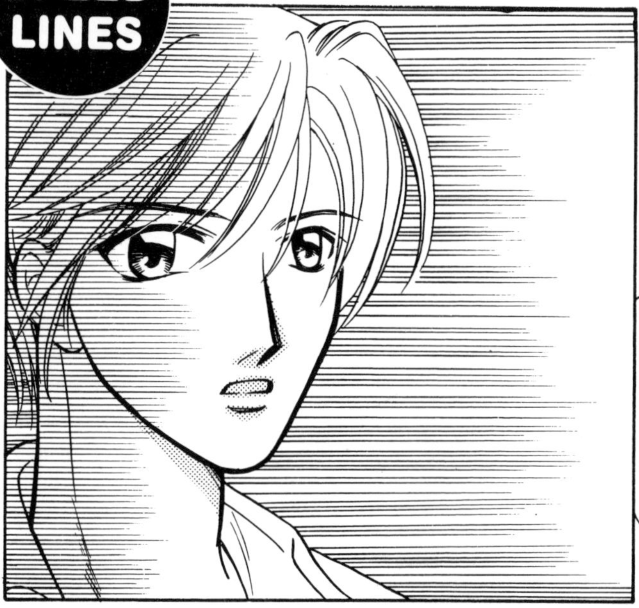

Draw speed lines on the background as usual, and then draw them onto the character. This is great for emotional rather than action scenes.

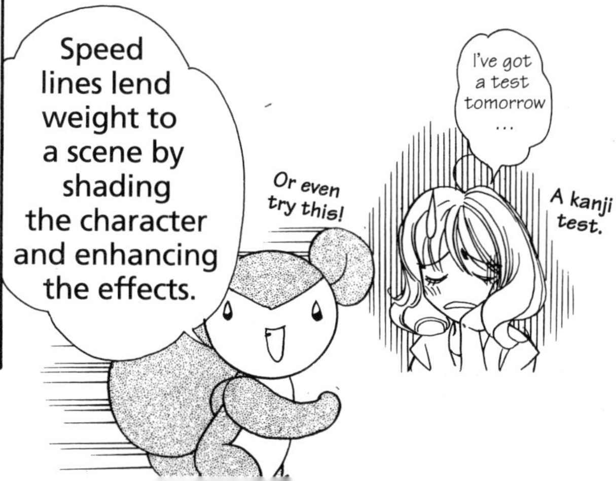
Speed lines lend weight to a scene by shading the character and enhancing the effects.
Or even try this!
I've got a test tomorrow ...
A kanji test.

EFFECTS WITH TONE

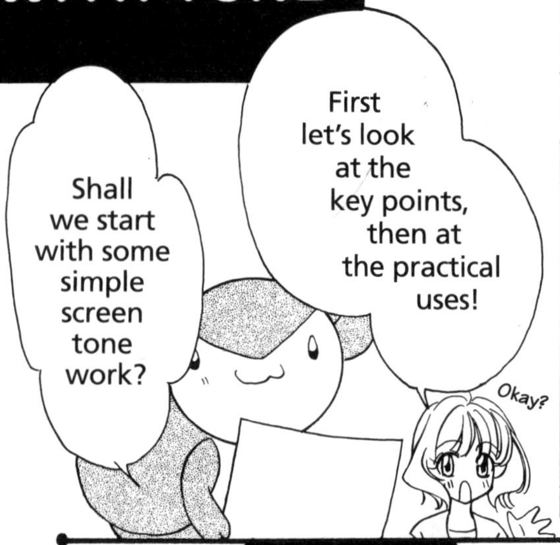
First let's look at the key points, then at the practical uses!
Shall we start with some simple screen tone work?
Okay?

Key Point 1

There are good and bad angles to scratch tone for a blurred effect.

Bad angles
Scratching tone off at these angles makes the lines of dots stand out.

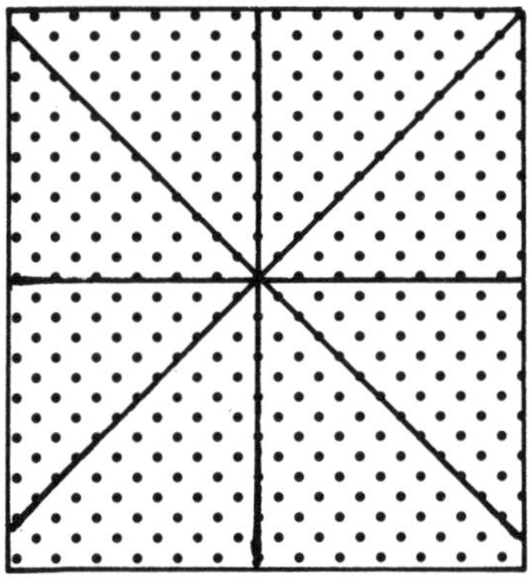

Good angles
Scratching tone off at these angles gives a great blurred effect.

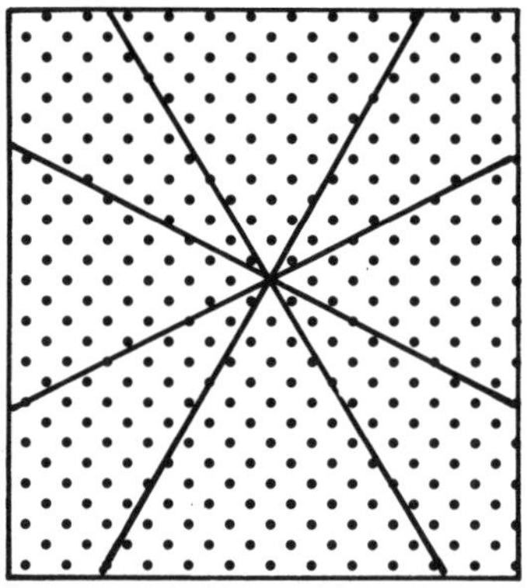

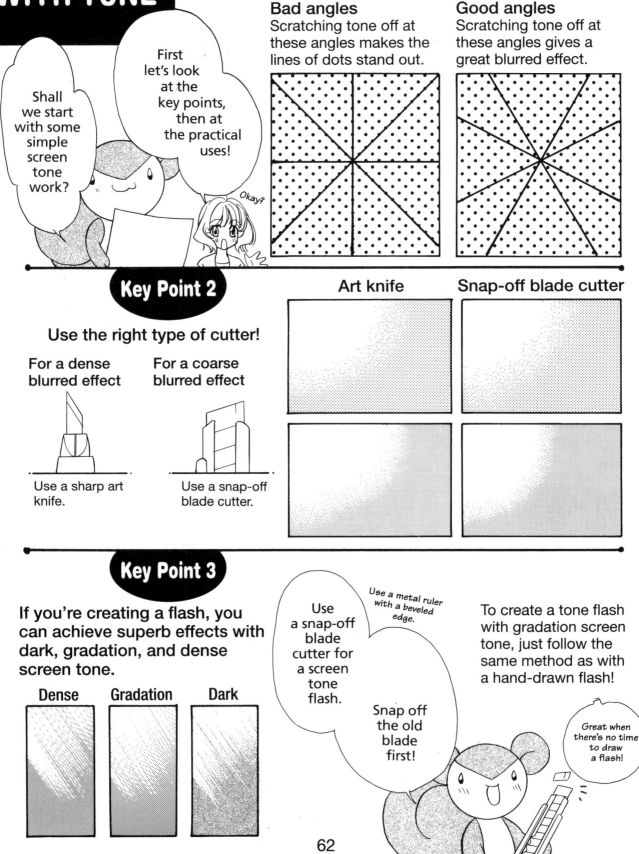

Key Point 2

Use the right type of cutter!

For a dense blurred effect

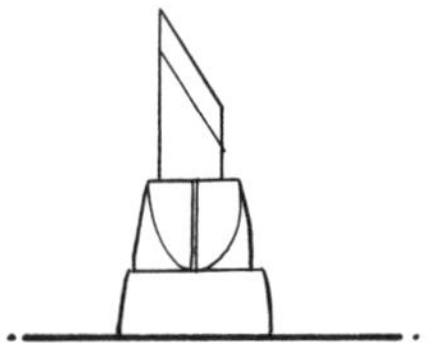

Use a sharp art knife.

For a coarse blurred effect

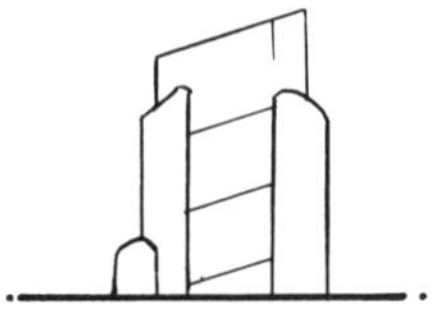

Use a snap-off blade cutter.

Art knife

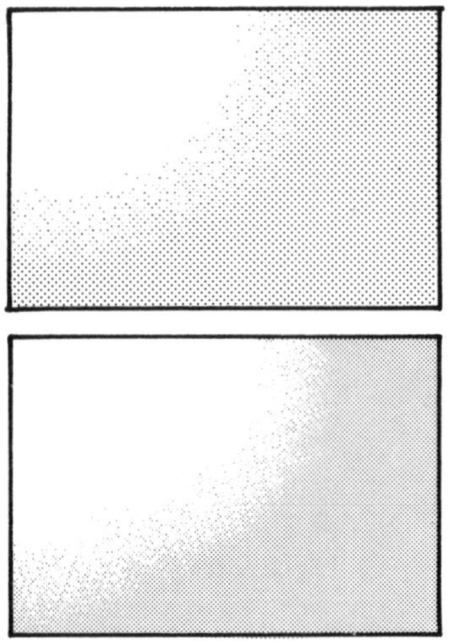

Snap-off blade cutter

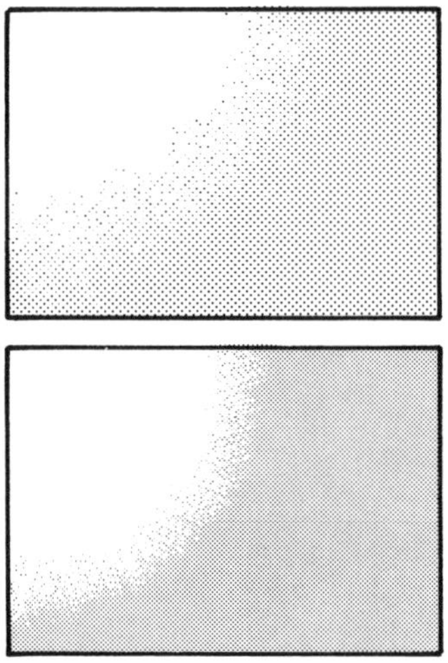

Key Point 3

If you're creating a flash, you can achieve superb effects with dark, gradation, and dense screen tone.

Dense **Gradation** **Dark**

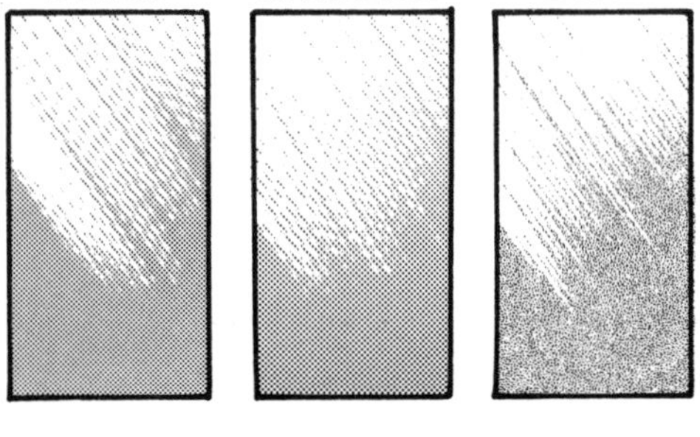

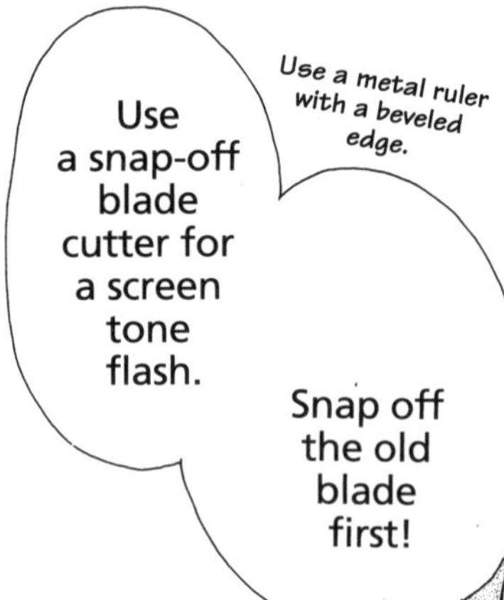
Use a snap-off blade cutter for a screen tone flash.
Use a metal ruler with a beveled edge.
Snap off the old blade first!

To create a tone flash with gradation screen tone, just follow the same method as with a hand-drawn flash!

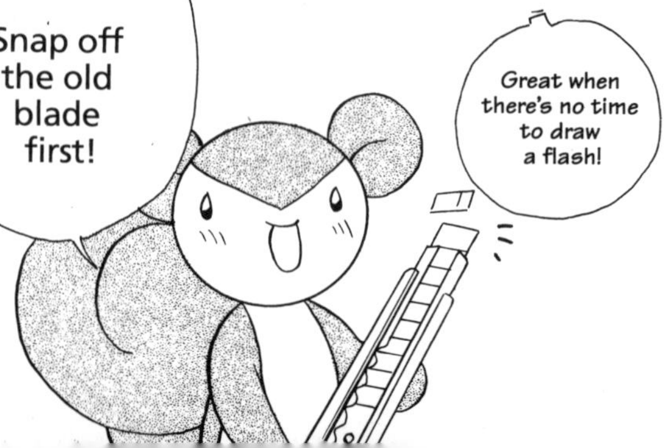
Great when there's no time to draw a flash!

BLURRED EFFECT

1. Apply the tone and draw in the outline.

Use a pale blue pencil!

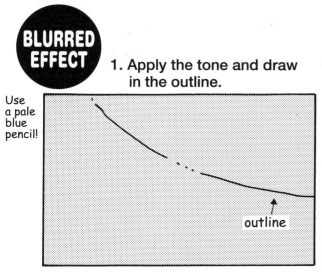

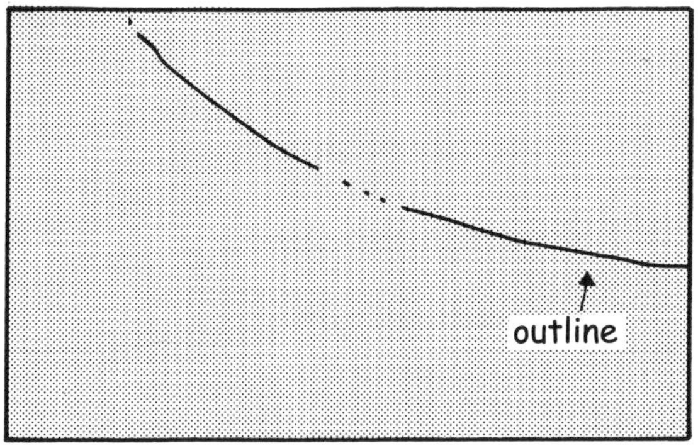
outline

2. If you're not confident, start by scratching the tone roughly inside the outline.

Watch out for the angles!

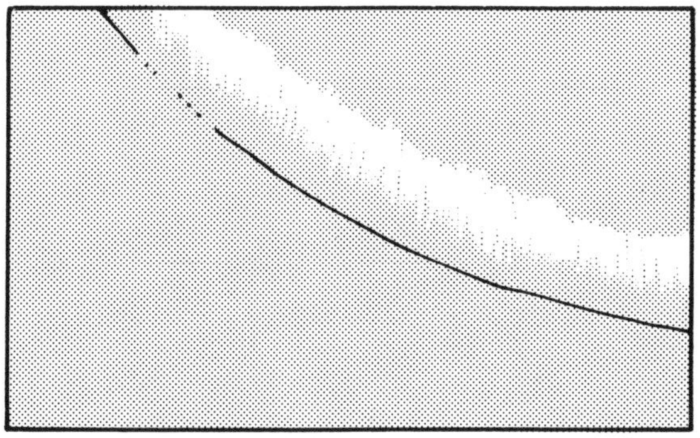

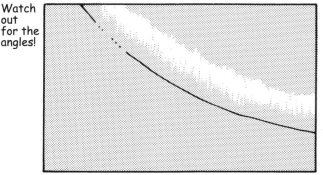

3. Make sure you scratch at good angles to create the blurred effect you want.

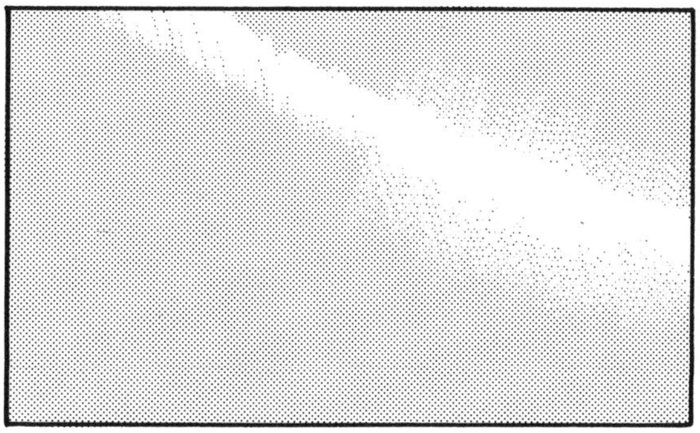

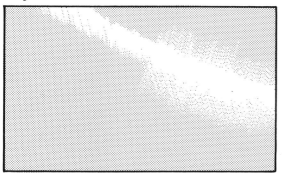

4. Lastly, remove any excess tone, then go over it lightly with an eraser.

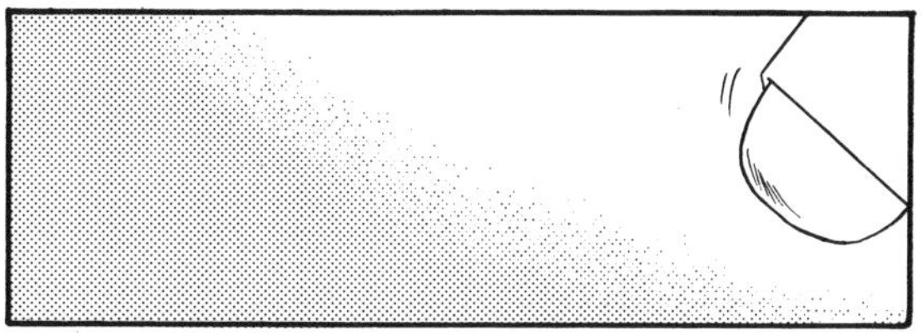

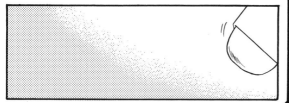

Make sure the outline is erased!

FLASH EFFECT

1. Apply the tone and draw in the focal point and outline.

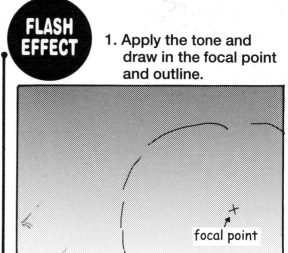

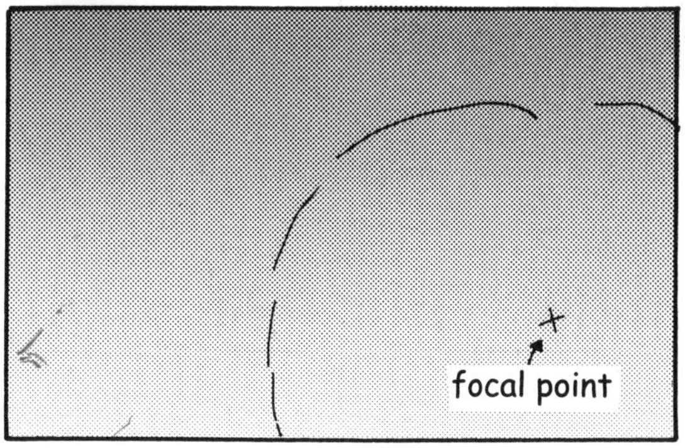
focal point

2. Use a metal ruler with a beveled edge.

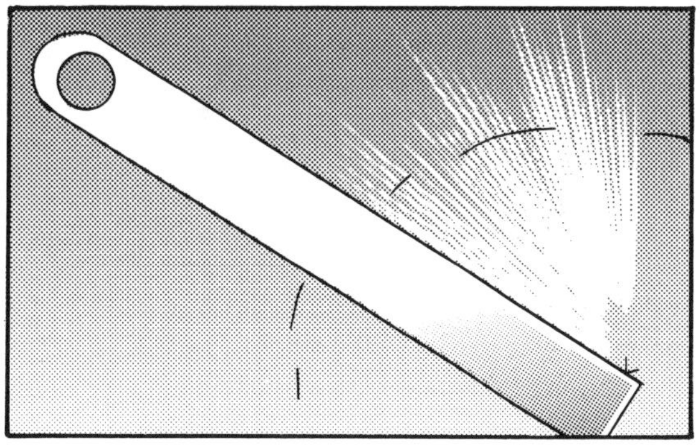

3. If a line of dots stands out, line up the ruler slightly off the focal point.

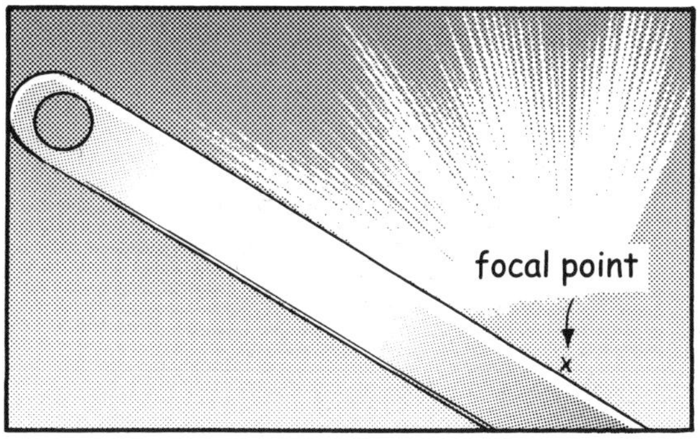
focal point

4. Finally, remove any excess and use an eraser to remove any residue.

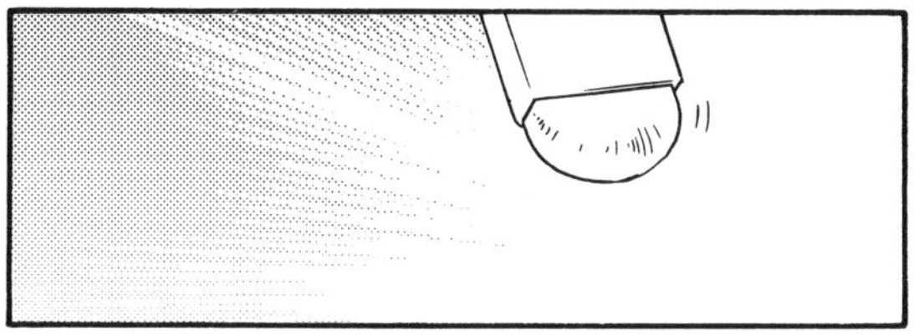

USING TONE EFFECTS 1

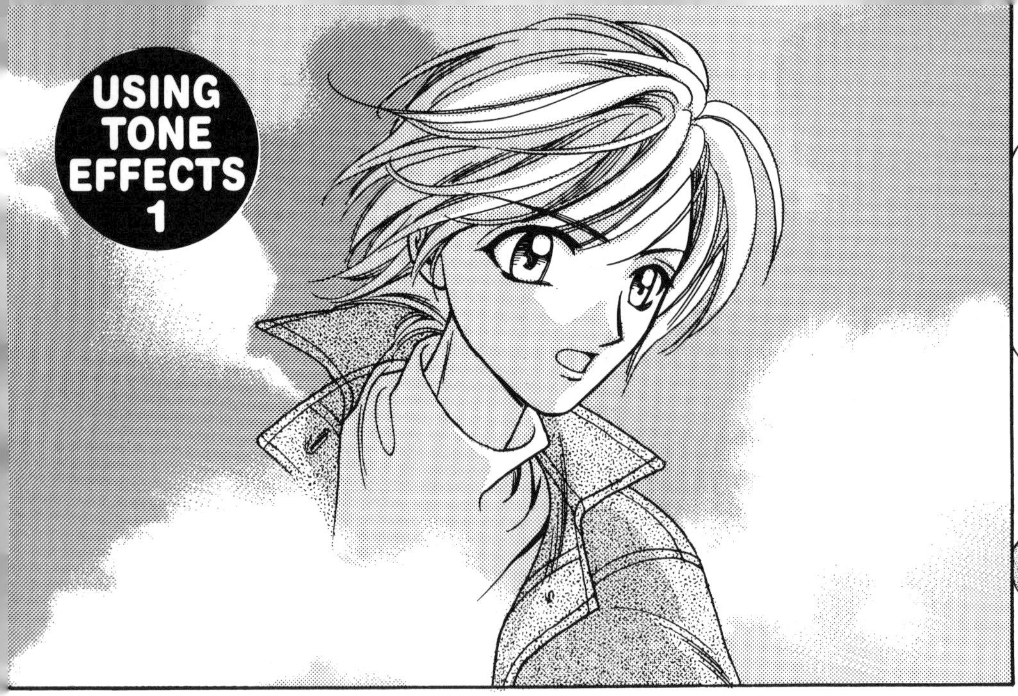

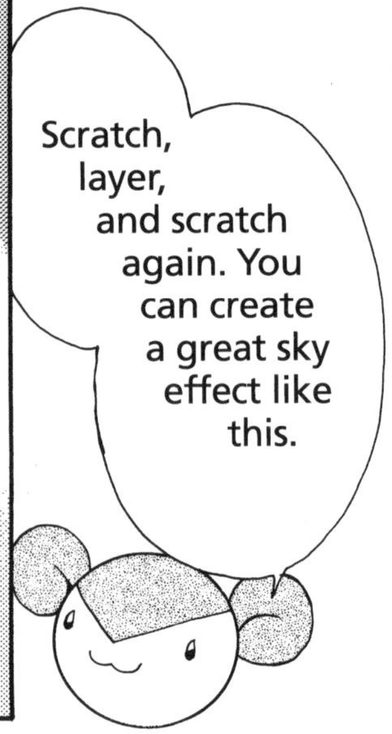
Scratch, layer, and scratch again. You can create a great sky effect like this.

1. Apply the screen tone and sketch in a rough outline. Think carefully about which parts you want to blur or leave blank.

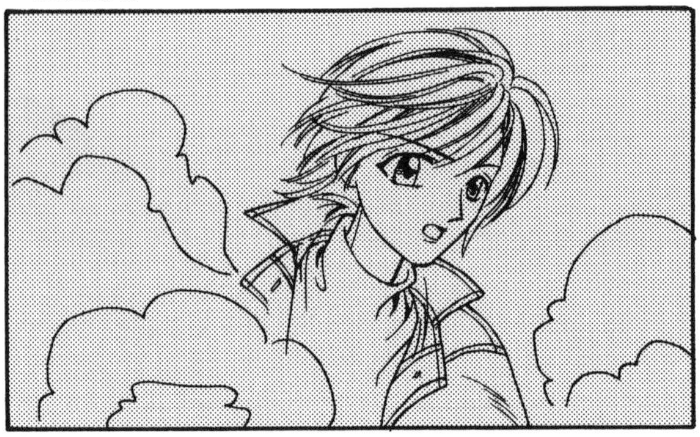

2. Scratch around the outline of the blank area with the edge of the cutter to create a soft blurred effect. This will make it look three-dimensional.

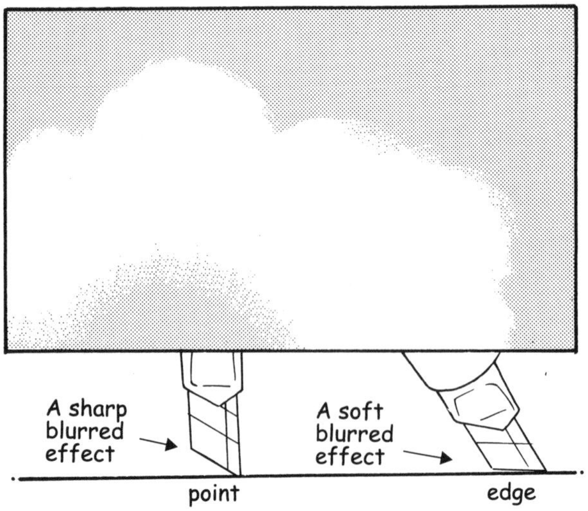
A sharp blurred effect
point
A soft blurred effect
edge

3. Remove any excess, and then apply a new layer. Look at the scratched area underneath as you draw in a new outline.

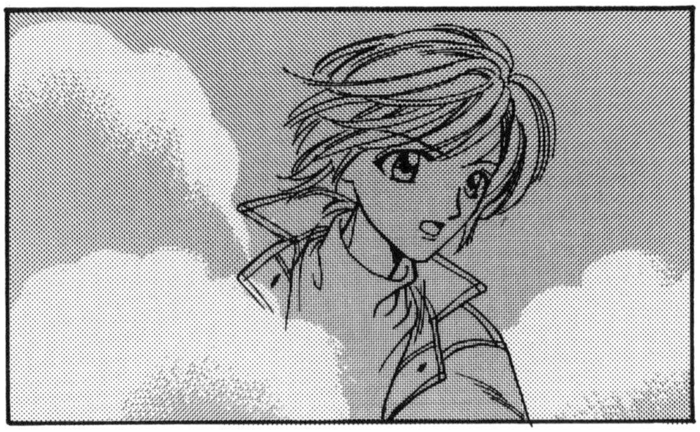

4. Scratch off tone as before. Overuse of layering will weaken the effect, so keep balance in mind at all times.

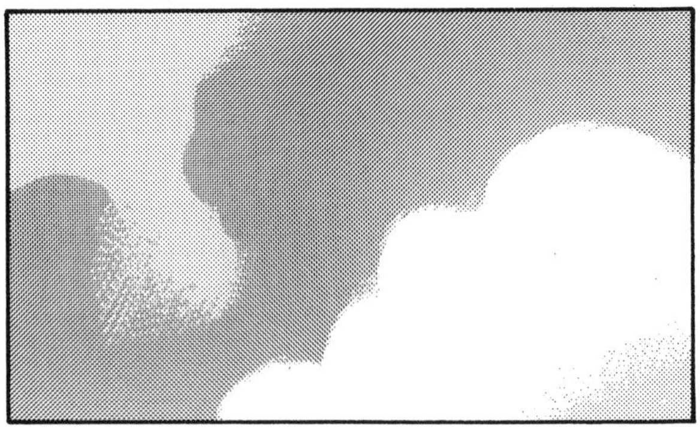

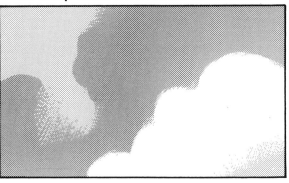

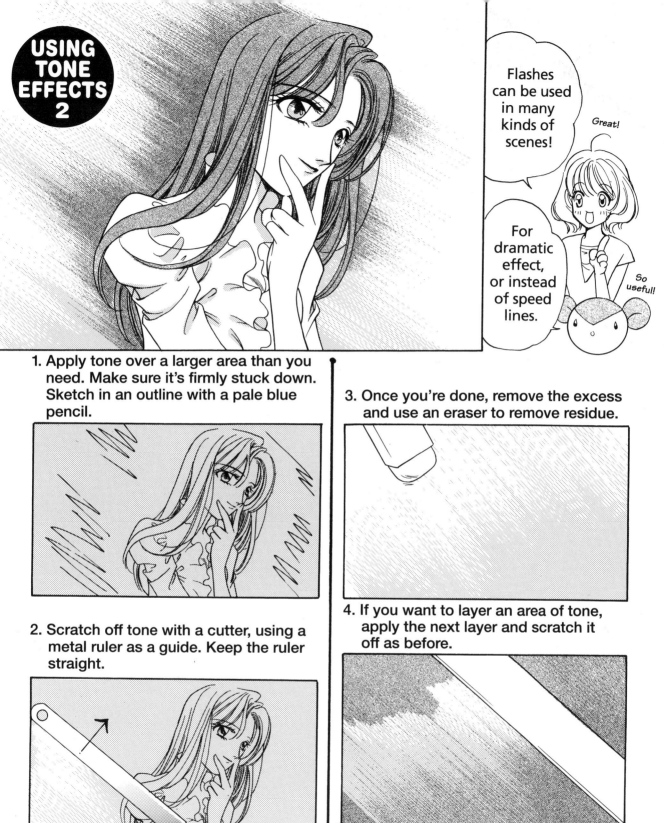

USING TONE EFFECTS 2

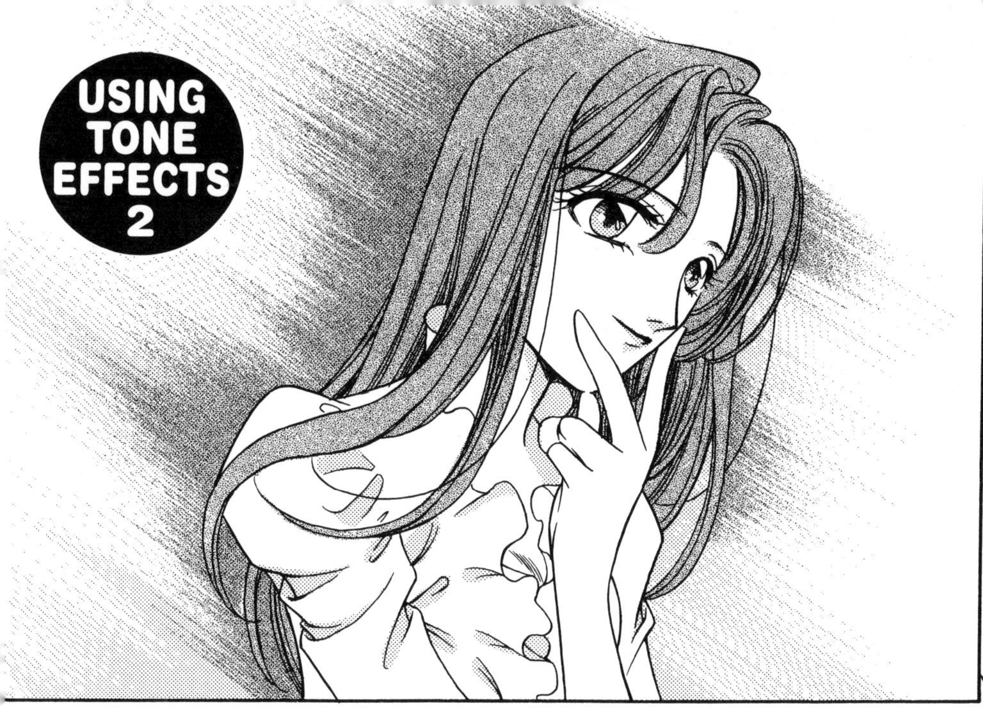

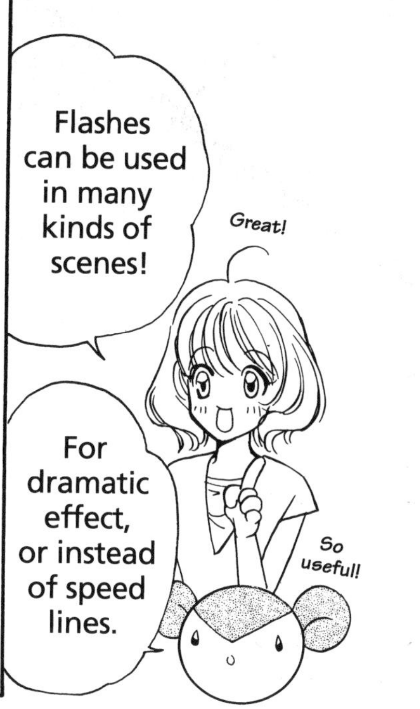
Flashes can be used in many kinds of scenes!
Great!
For dramatic effect, or instead of speed lines.
So useful!

1. Apply tone over a larger area than you need. Make sure it's firmly stuck down. Sketch in an outline with a pale blue pencil.

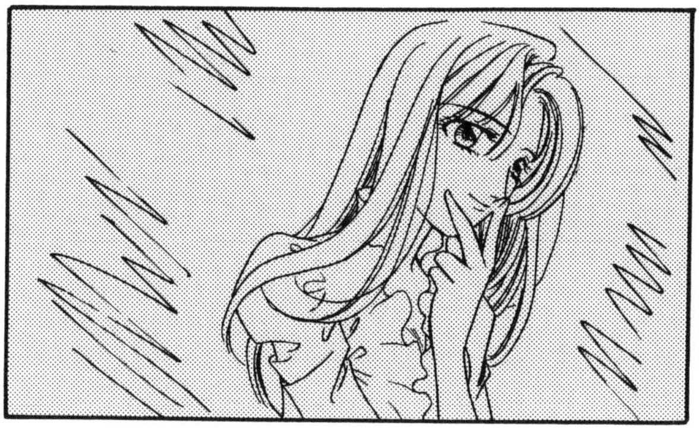

2. Scratch off tone with a cutter, using a metal ruler as a guide. Keep the ruler straight.

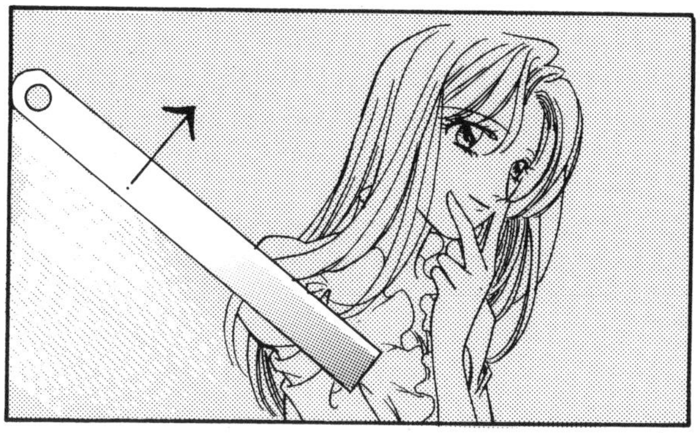

To scratch this side, turn the page upside ↑ down. Bear in mind that long lines look better than short ones.

3. Once you're done, remove the excess and use an eraser to remove residue.

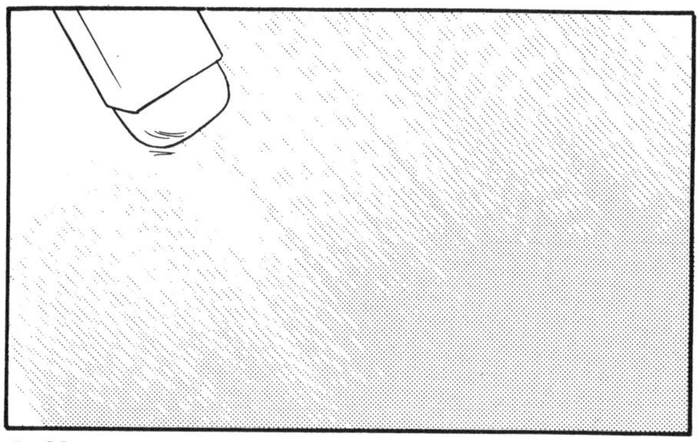

4. If you want to layer an area of tone, apply the next layer and scratch it off as before.

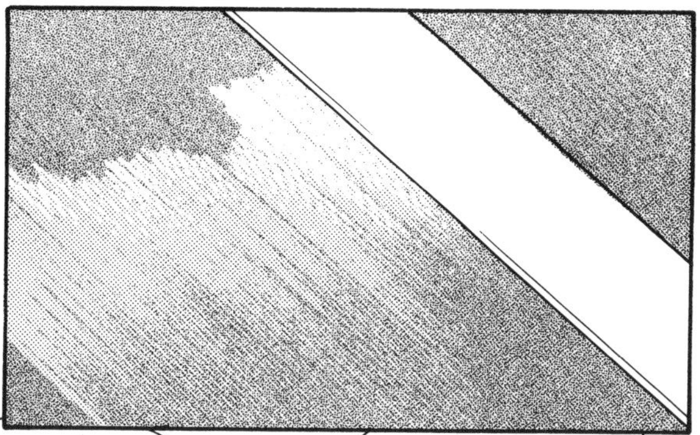

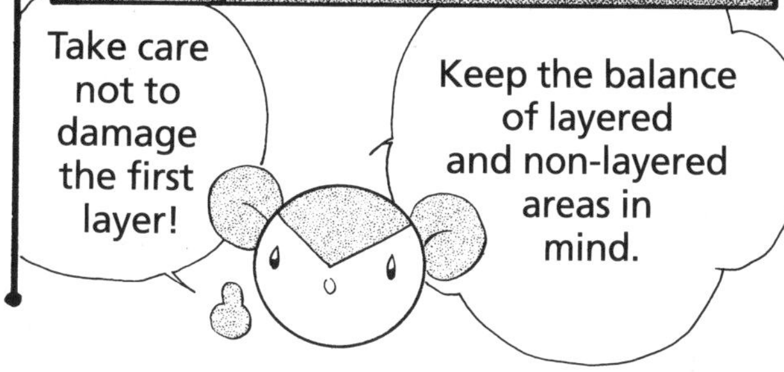
Take care not to damage the first layer!
Keep the balance of layered and non-layered areas in mind.

VARYING EFFECTS 1

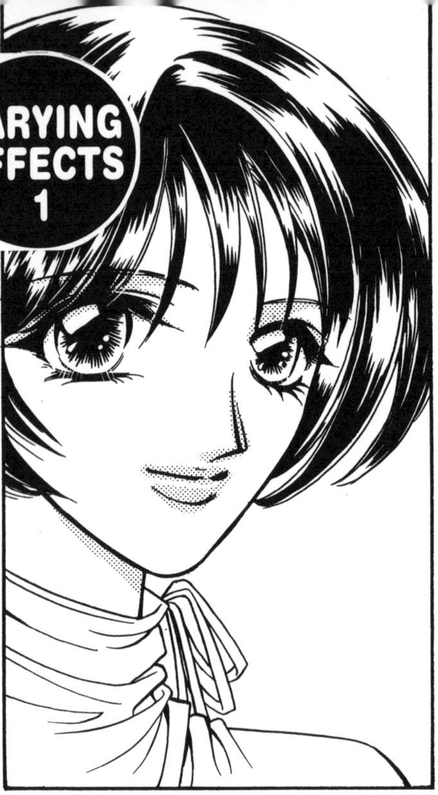

Ink effect

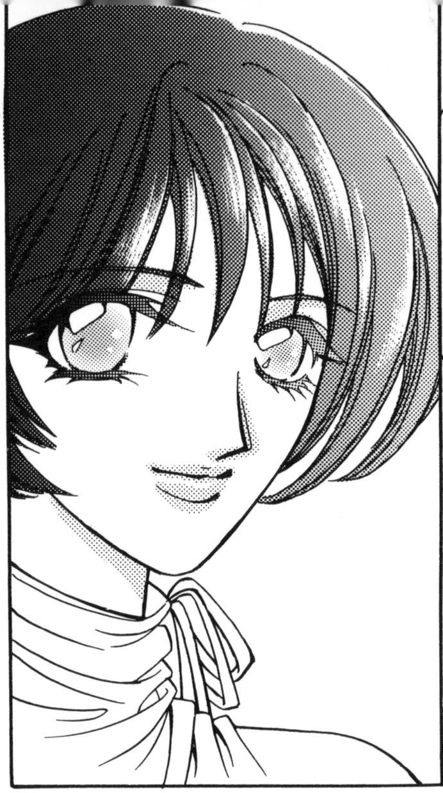

Tone effect

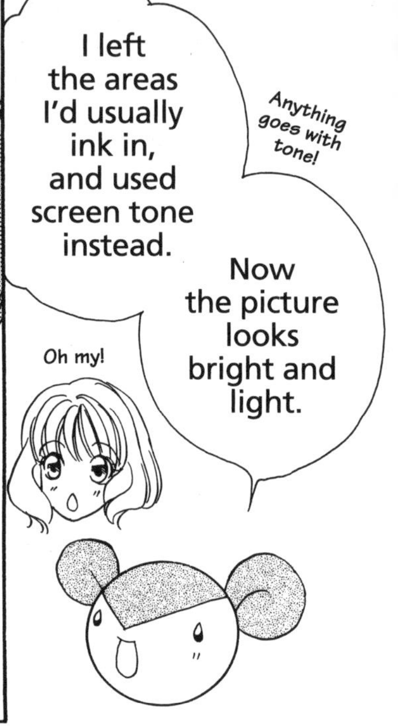
I left the areas I'd usually ink in, and used screen tone instead.
Anything goes with tone!
Now the picture looks bright and light.
Oh my!

VARYING EFFECTS 2

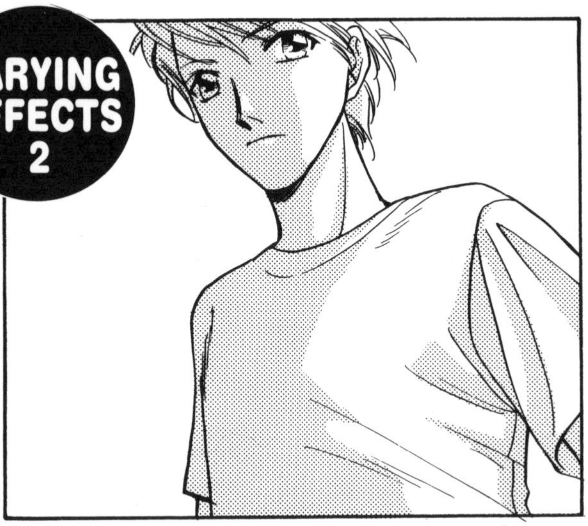

Standard screen tone for shading

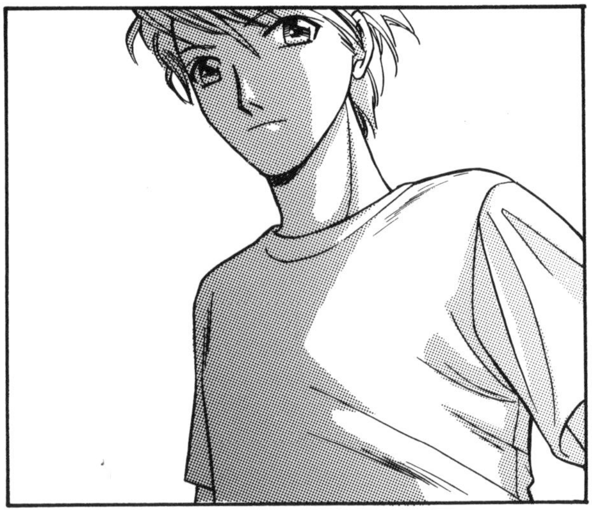

Gradation screen tone for shading

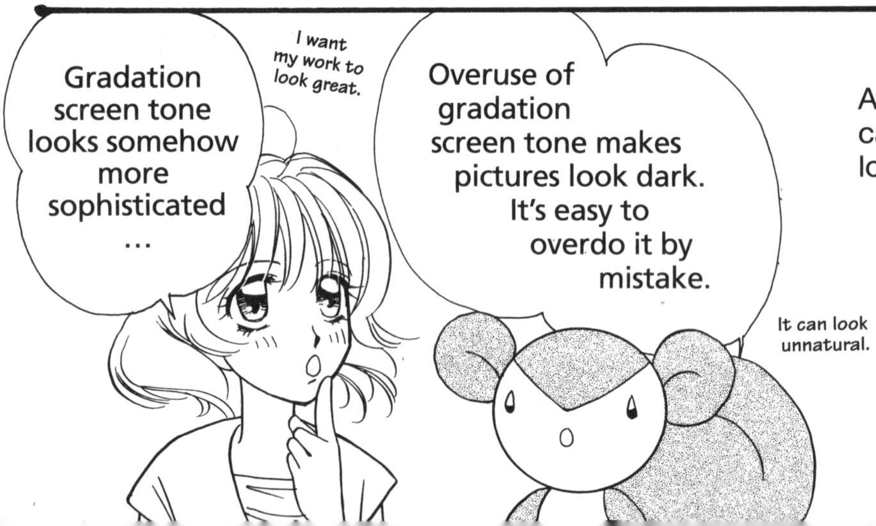
Gradation screen tone looks somehow more sophisticated …
I want my work to look great.
Overuse of gradation screen tone makes pictures look dark. It's easy to overdo it by mistake.
It can look unnatural.

And inking in backgrounds can sometimes make it look too dark.

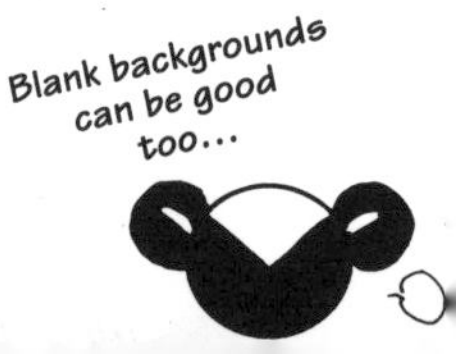
Blank backgrounds can be good too…

SOUND EFFECTS

In manga, we depict sounds with onomatopoeic words written on the background.

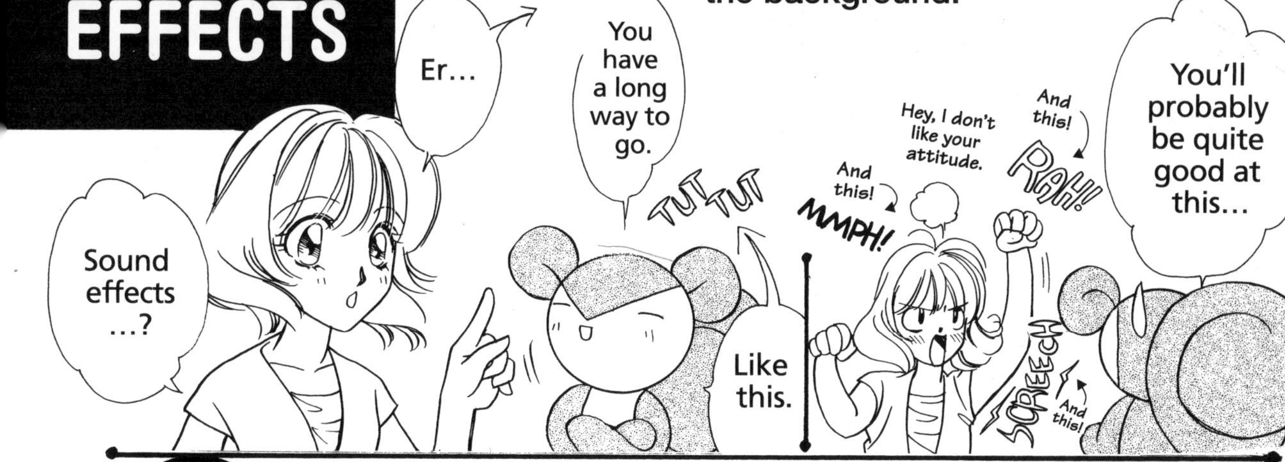
Sound effects …?
Er…
You have a long way to go.
TUT TUT
Like this.
And this!
MMPH!
Hey, I don't like your attitude.
And this!
RAH!
You'll probably be quite good at this…
SCREECH
And this!

VARIOUS

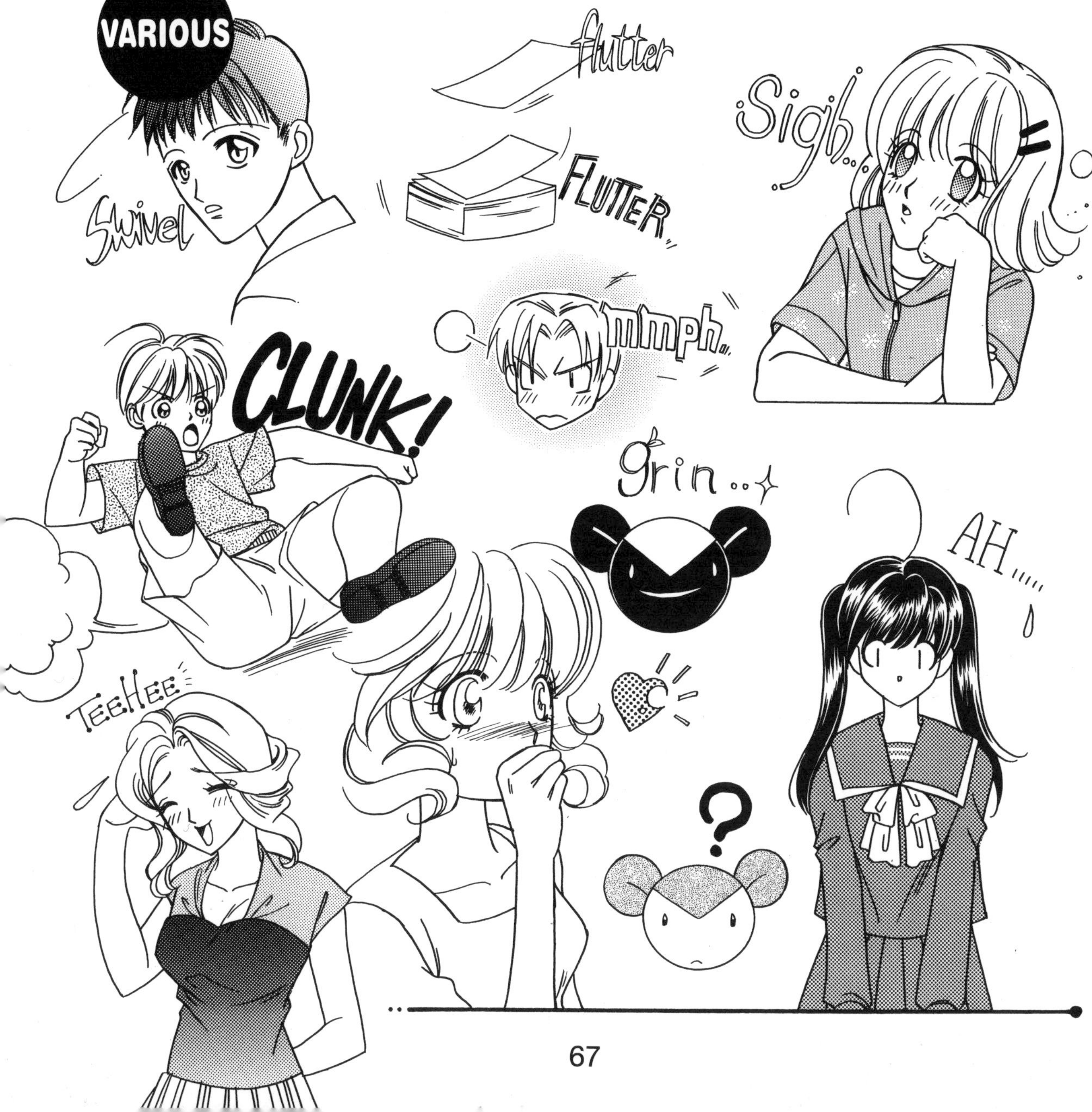
Swivel
flutter
FLUTTER
Sigh..
mmph..
CLUNK!
Grin..
AH.....
TEEHEE
?

What's important with sound effects is to use a style of letters that suits the mood or scene.

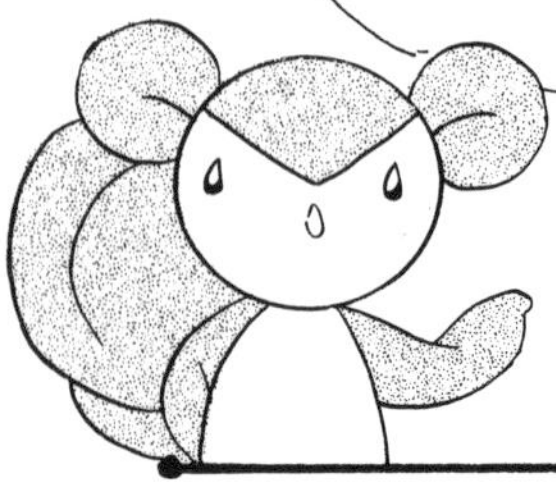

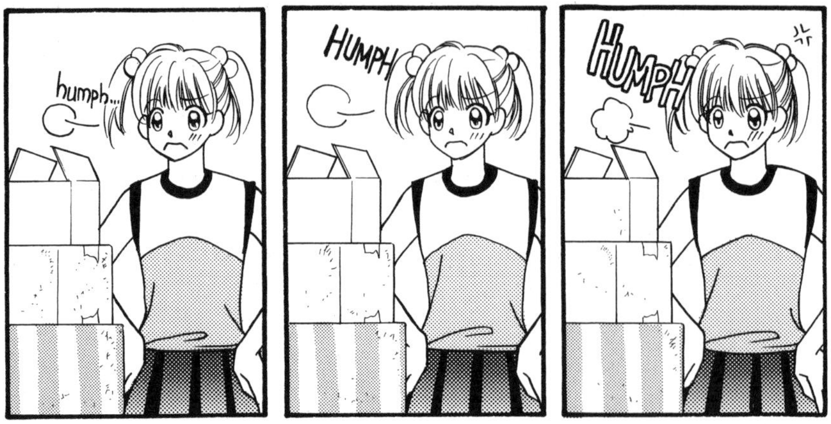
humph...
HUMPH
HUMPH

Here she's slightly annoyed.

Here she's more annoyed.

Here she's really annoyed!

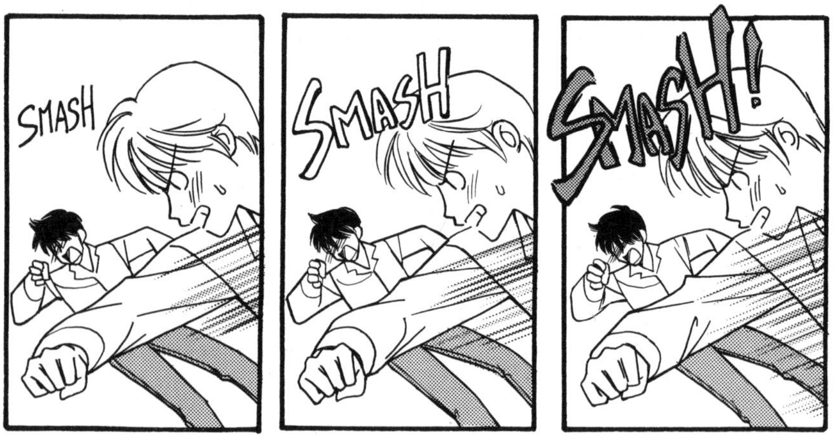
SMASH
SMASH
SMASH!

This punch won't knock anyone out!

A normal punch.

A knockout punch.

The mood and importance of a panel changes depending on the style of lettering used.

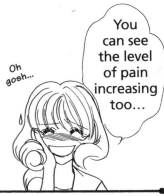

You can see the level of pain increasing too...

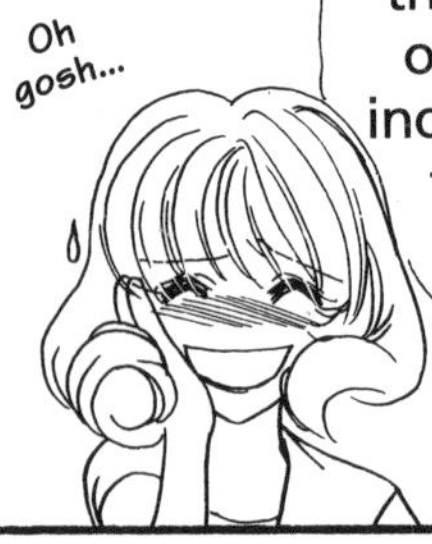
Oh gosh...

And you can change the appearance of weight with the style of lettering.

And make use of colors, too—white looks light and black looks heavy.

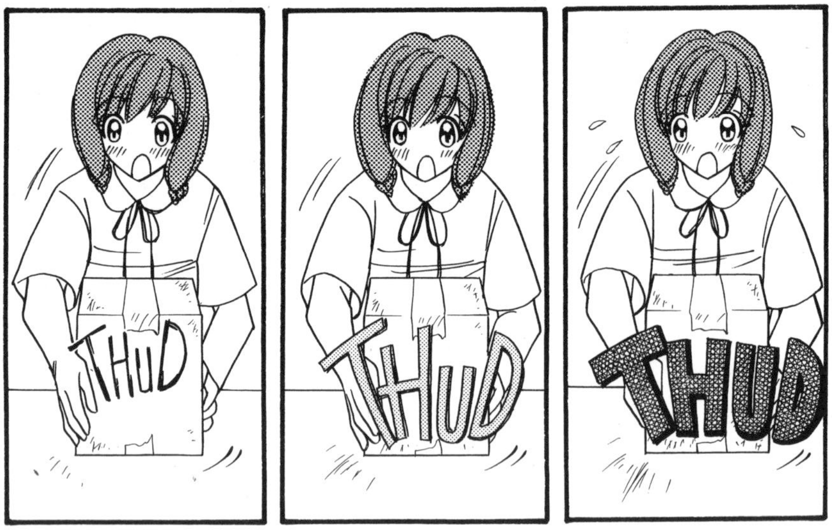
THUD
THUD
THUD

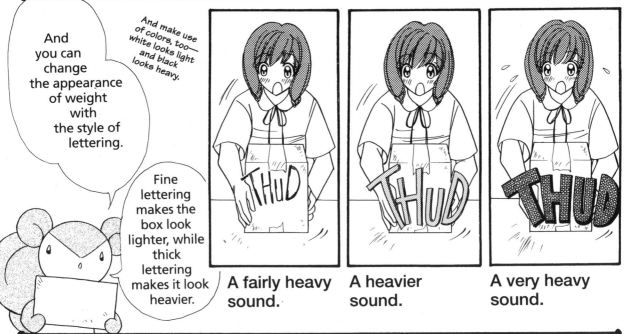

A fairly heavy sound.

A heavier sound.

A very heavy sound.

Fine lettering makes the box look lighter, while thick lettering makes it look heavier.

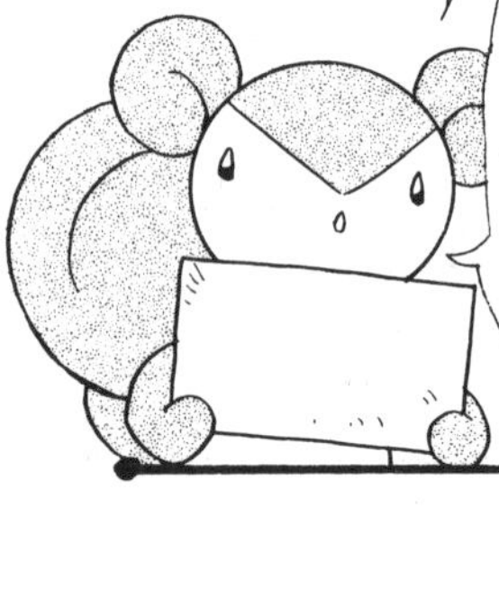

Not all sound effects are 'true' sounds.

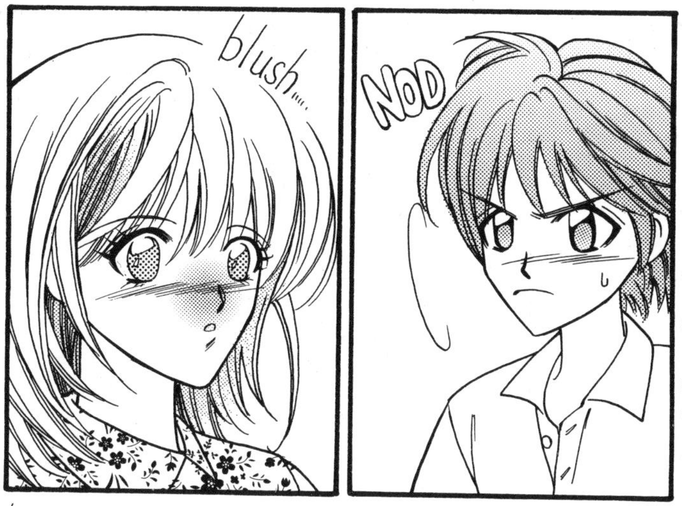
blush...
NOD

Her face turns red.

He answers with a nod.

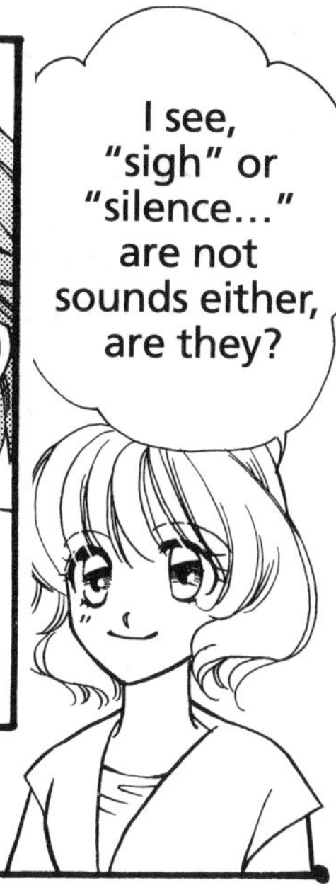
I see, "sigh" or "silence..." are not sounds either, are they?

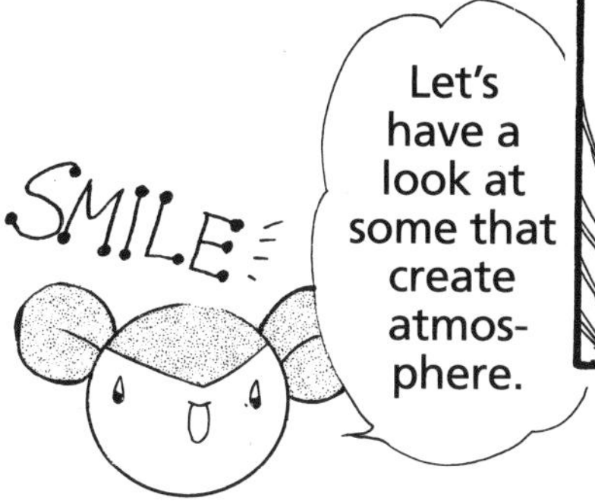
SMILE
Let's have a look at some that create atmos-phere.

Use different pens or tone according to the scene or style of letters you want!

Magic marker or brush pen.

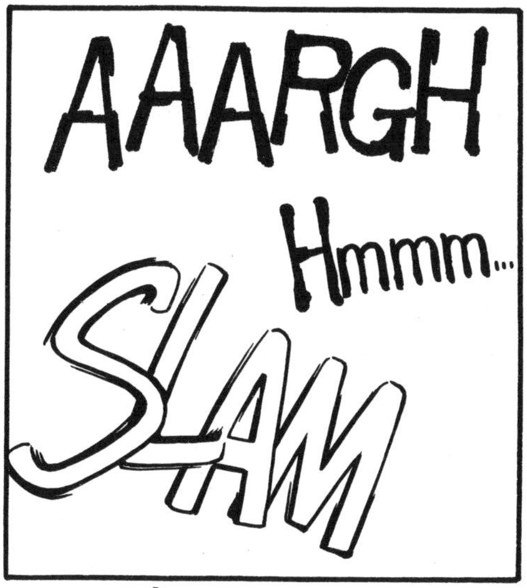
AAARGH
Hmmm...
SLAM

Fine line marker or round nib.

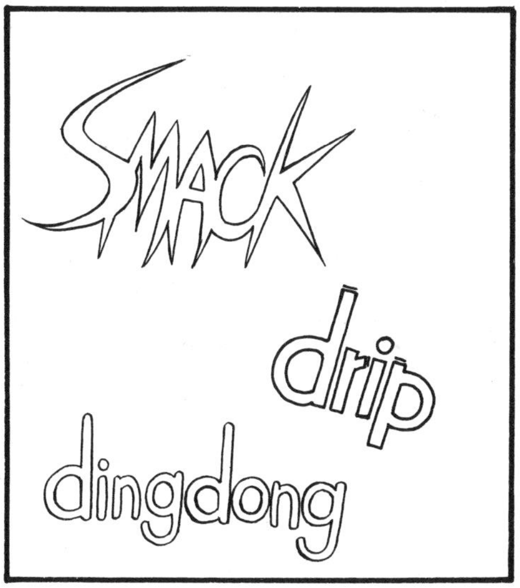
SMACK
drip
dingdong

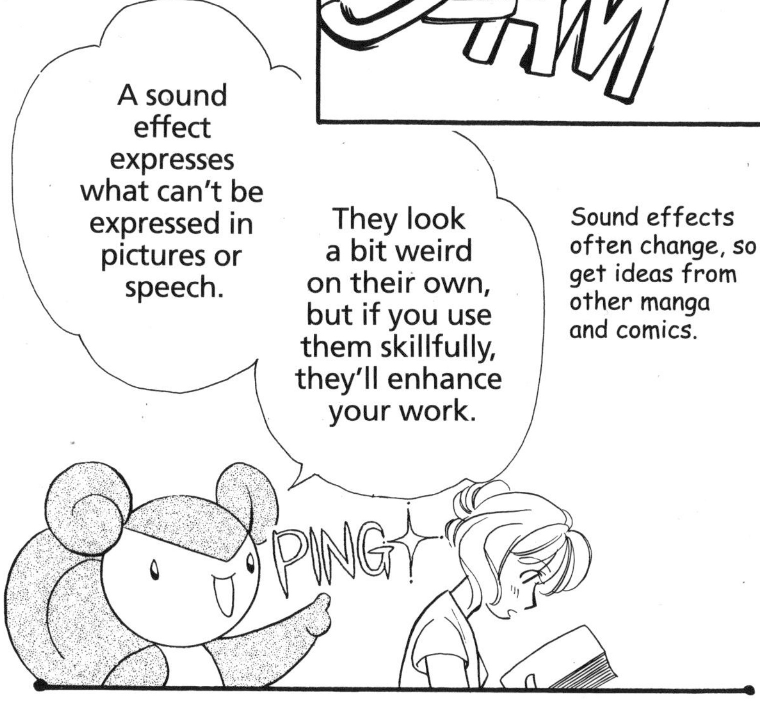
A sound effect expresses what can't be expressed in pictures or speech.
They look a bit weird on their own, but if you use them skillfully, they'll enhance your work.
PING

Sound effects often change, so get ideas from other manga and comics.

Screen tone.

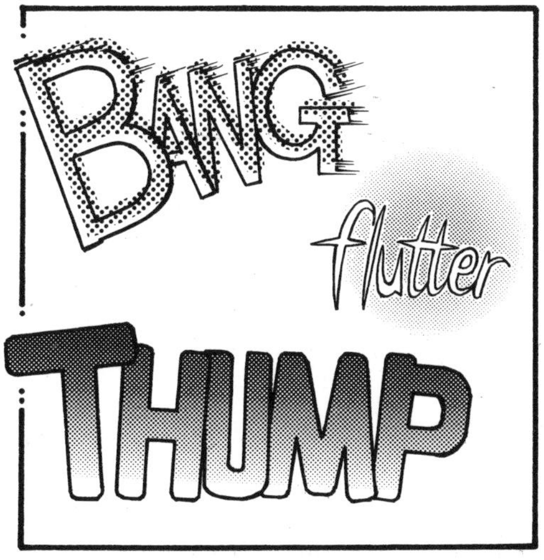
BANG
flutter
THUMP

Heavy sounds

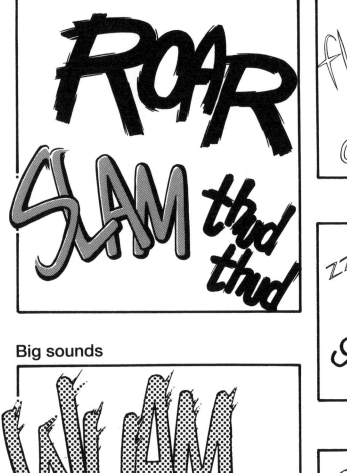

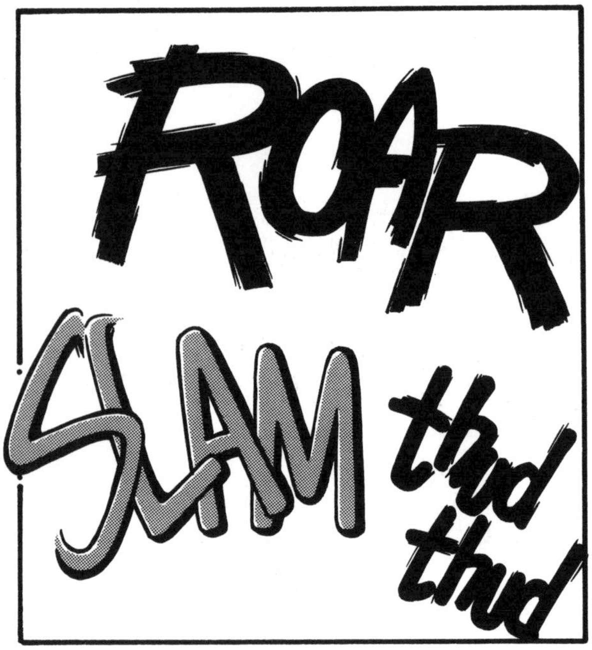
ROAR
SLAM
thud
thud

Big sounds

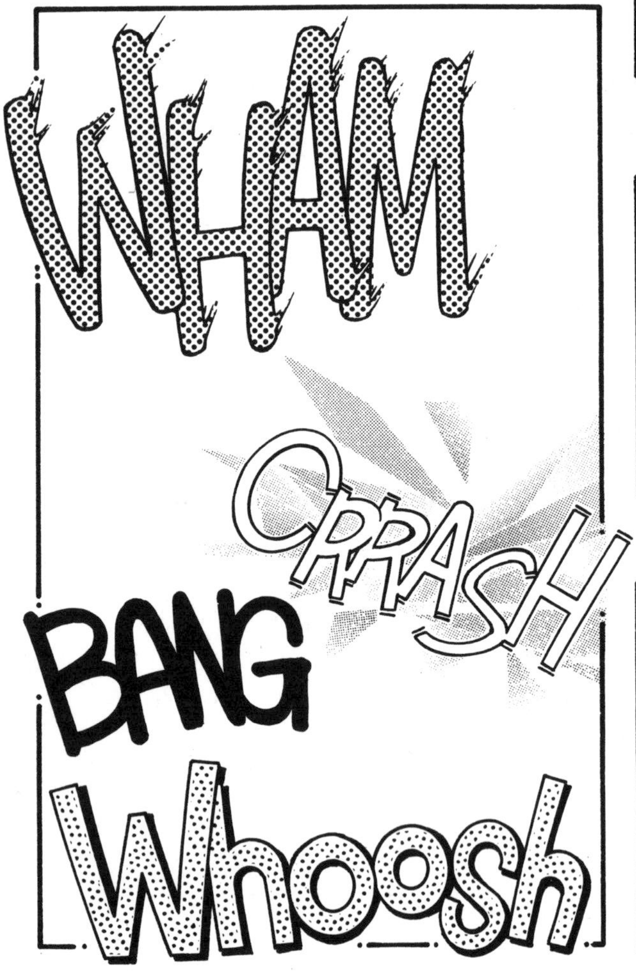
WHAM
CRRASH
BANG
Whoosh

Light sounds

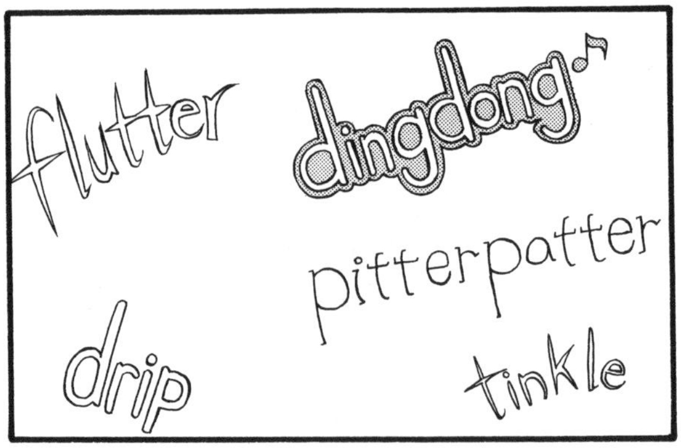
flutter
dingdong
pitterpatter
drip
tinkle

Small sounds

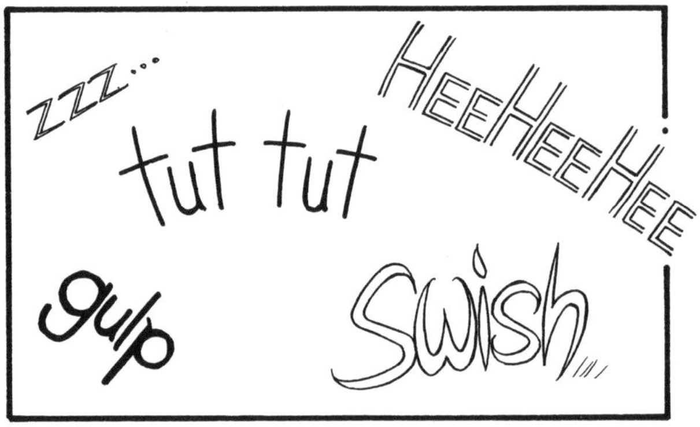
zzz...
HeeHeeHee
tut tut
gulp
Swish

Sounds that can be quiet or loud

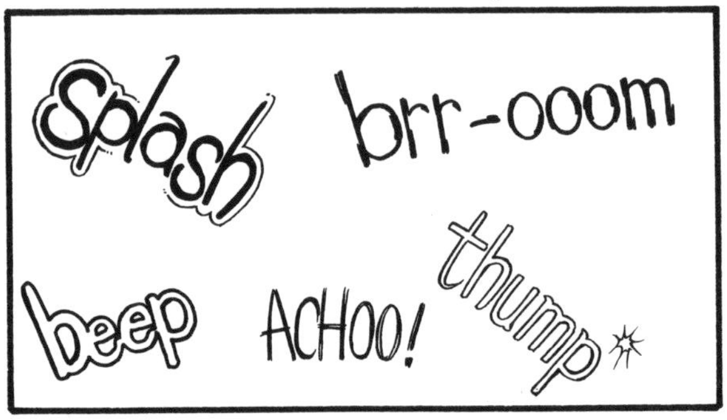
Splash
brr-ooom
beep
ACHOO!
thump

Not "true" sounds

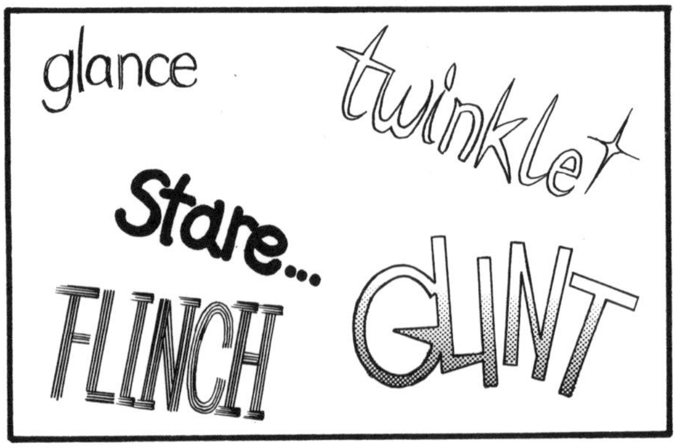
glance
twinkle
Stare...
FLINCH
GLINT

LESSON 3
BACKGROUNDS

Now that you've mastered the more advanced techniques
for drawing characters and special effects,
you're ready to take on the background.
This will really make a difference in your manga!
Let's have a look at indoor
and outdoor backgrounds, and using tone and ink to
depict daytime and night scenes!

BACKGROUNDS

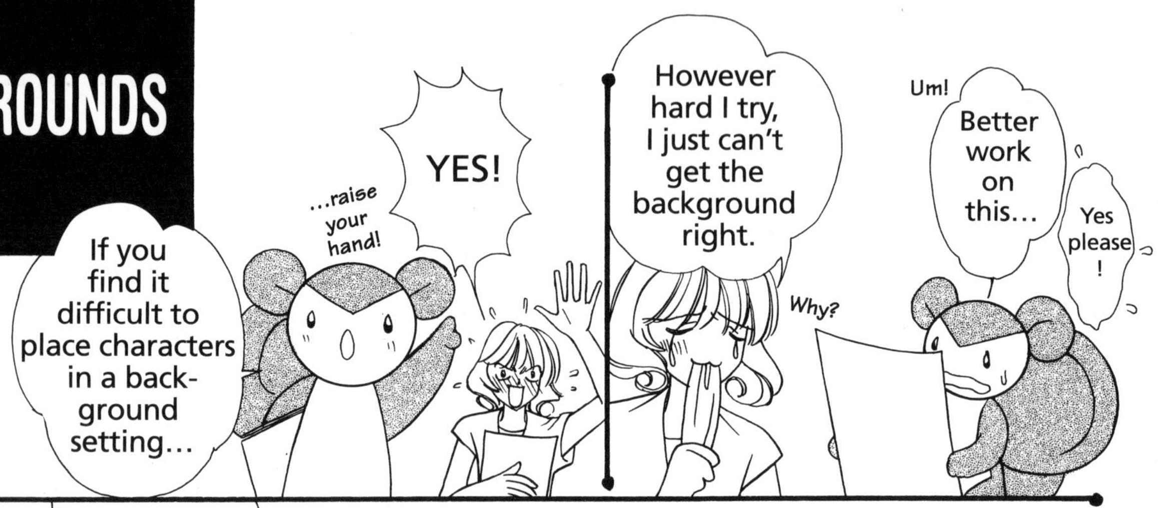
If you find it difficult to place characters in a back-ground setting…
…raise your hand!
YES!
However hard I try, I just can't get the background right.
Why?
Um!
Better work on this…
Yes please!

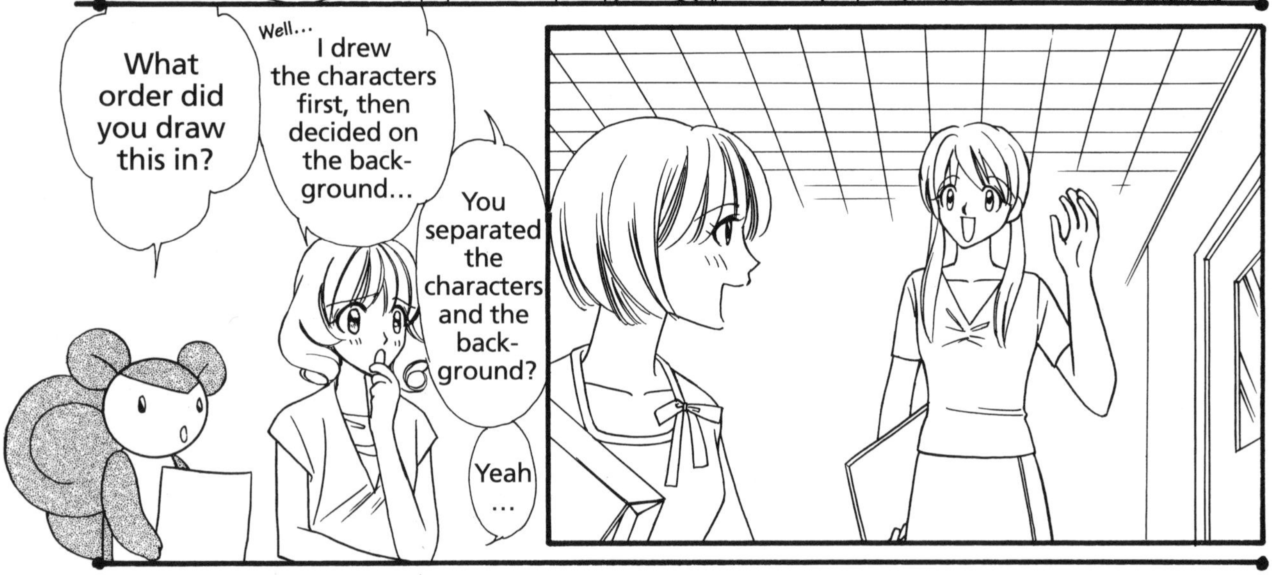
What order did you draw this in?
Well…
I drew the characters first, then decided on the back-ground…
You separated the characters and the back-ground?
Yeah…

Drawing a scene.
The main character meets a friend in the school corridor. Use one-point perspective.

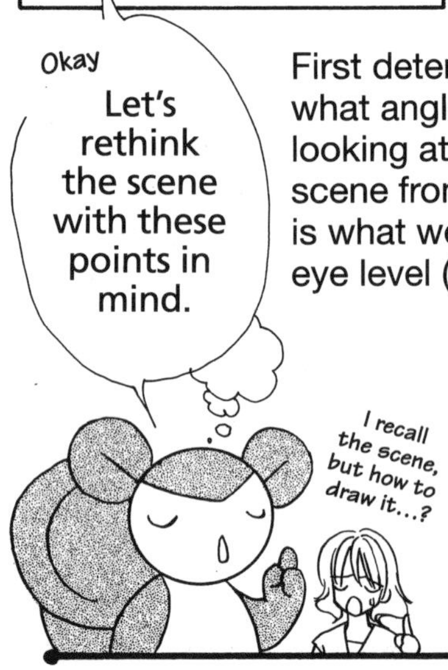
Okay
Let's rethink the scene with these points in mind.
I recall the scene, but how to draw it…?

First determine what angle you're looking at the scene from. This is what we call the eye level (EL).

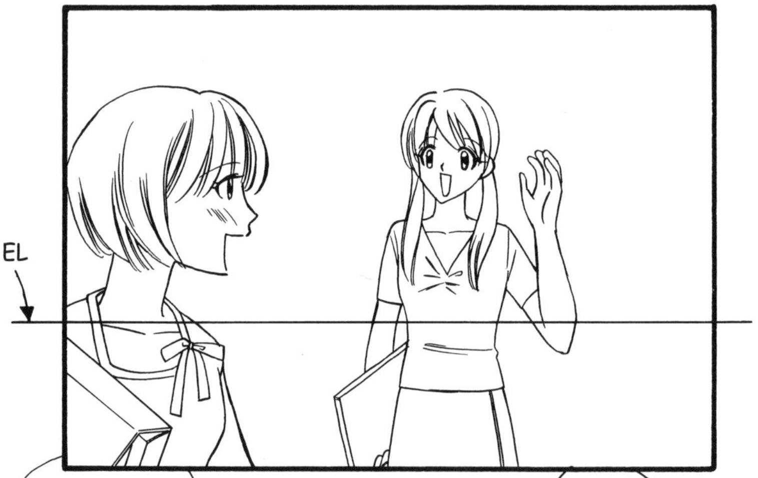
EL

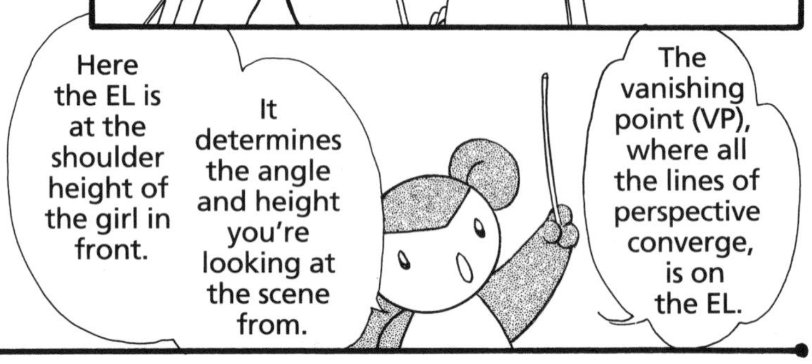
Here the EL is at the shoulder height of the girl in front.
It determines the angle and height you're looking at the scene from.
The vanishing point (VP), where all the lines of perspective converge, is on the EL.

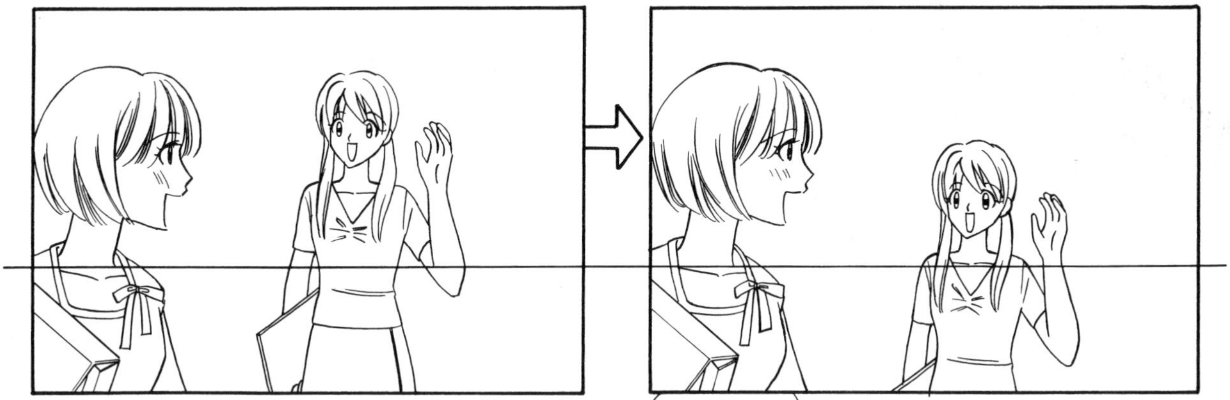

One-point perspective

The girl in front is the main figure. Both girls are about the same height, so draw their shoulders at the same level. Then you can adjust the perspective to make the girl behind appear closer or further away. This works as long as they're standing on a flat surface.

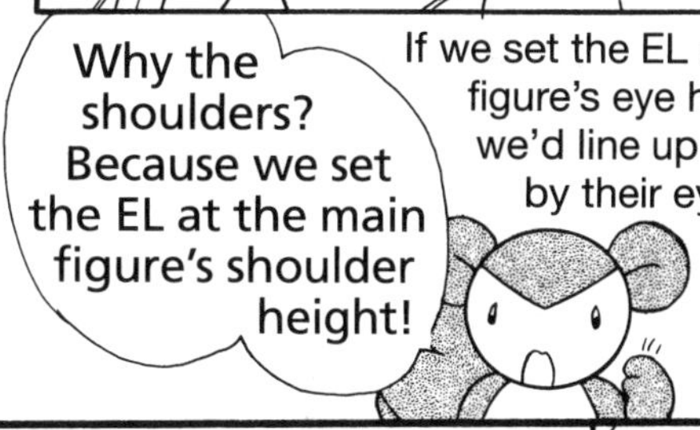
Why the shoulders? Because we set the EL at the main figure's shoulder height!

If we set the EL at the main figure's eye height, then we'd line up characters by their eyes instead.

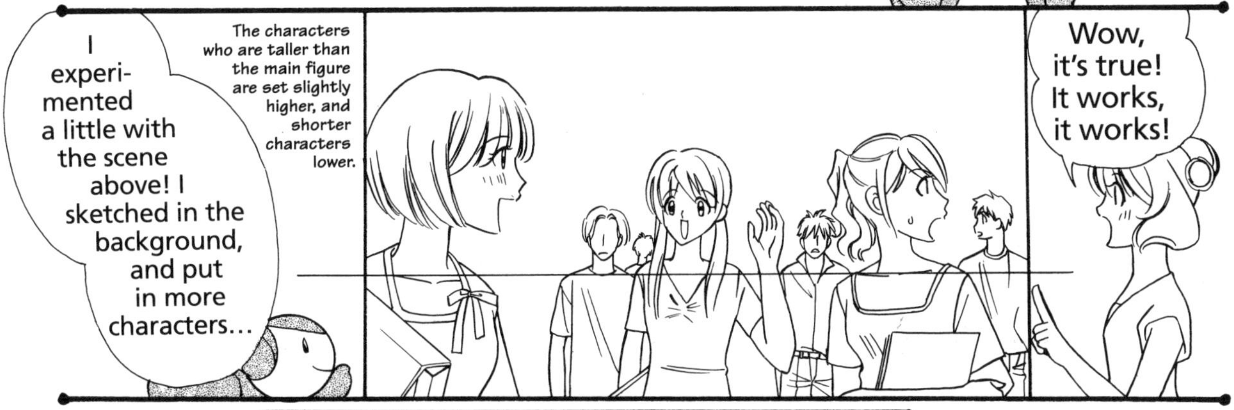
I experi-mented a little with the scene above! I sketched in the background, and put in more characters...
The characters who are taller than the main figure are set slightly higher, and shorter characters lower.
Wow, it's true! It works, it works!

Now we've fixed the characters, let's take a look at the background.

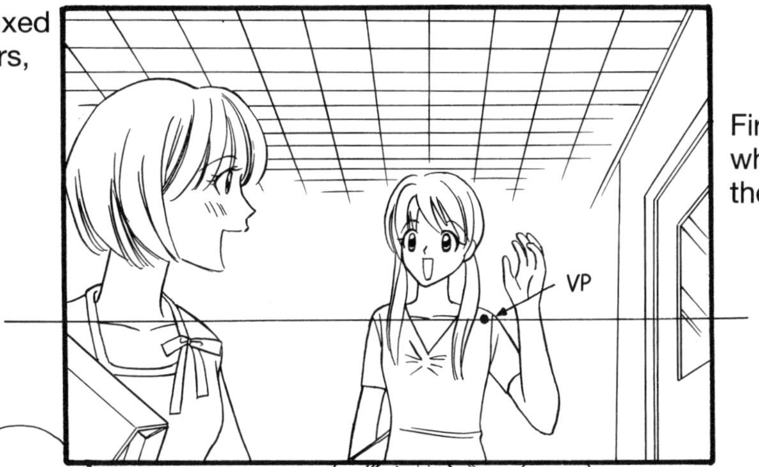
VP

First decide where to position the VP on the EL.

Use your imagination to visualize how the perspective expands from the VP.

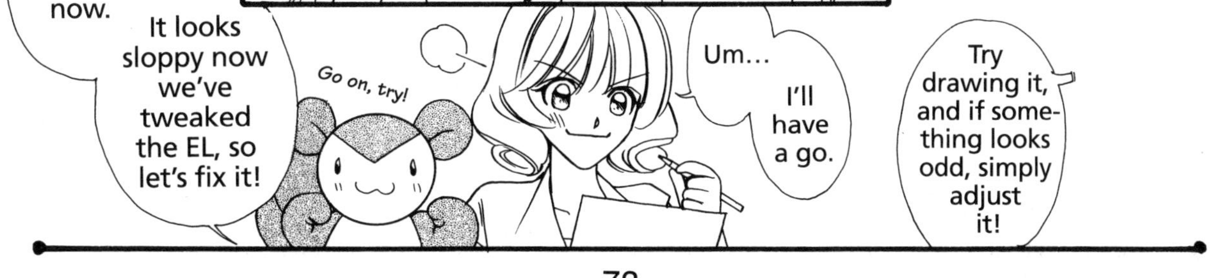
This is how it looks now.
It looks sloppy now we've tweaked the EL, so let's fix it!
Go on, try!
Um...
I'll have a go.
Try drawing it, and if some-thing looks odd, simply adjust it!

To calculate the height of windows and doors, first determine the distance between the girls and the walls on each side, then imagine each girl against the wall and scale the windows and doors to her size.

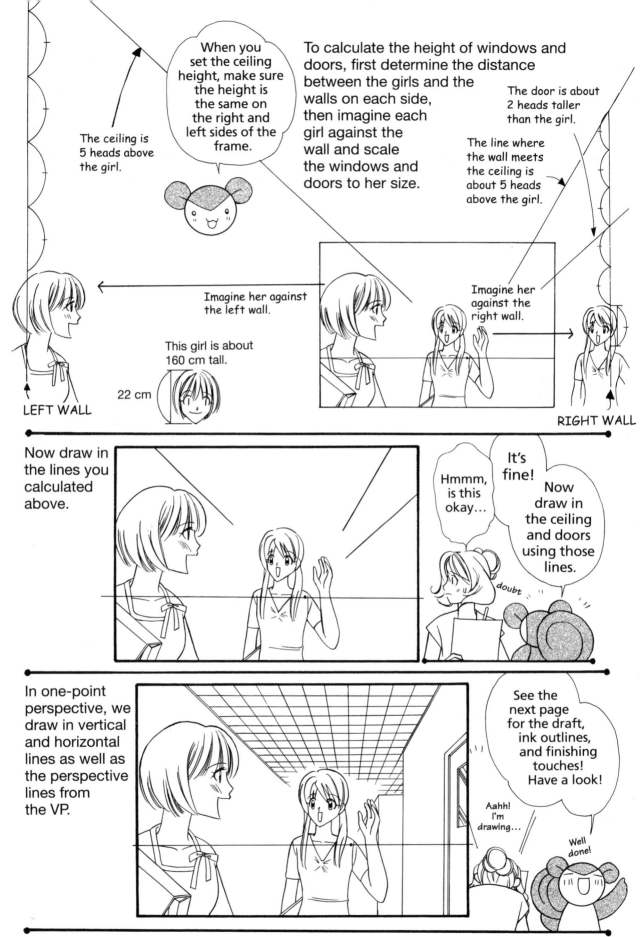

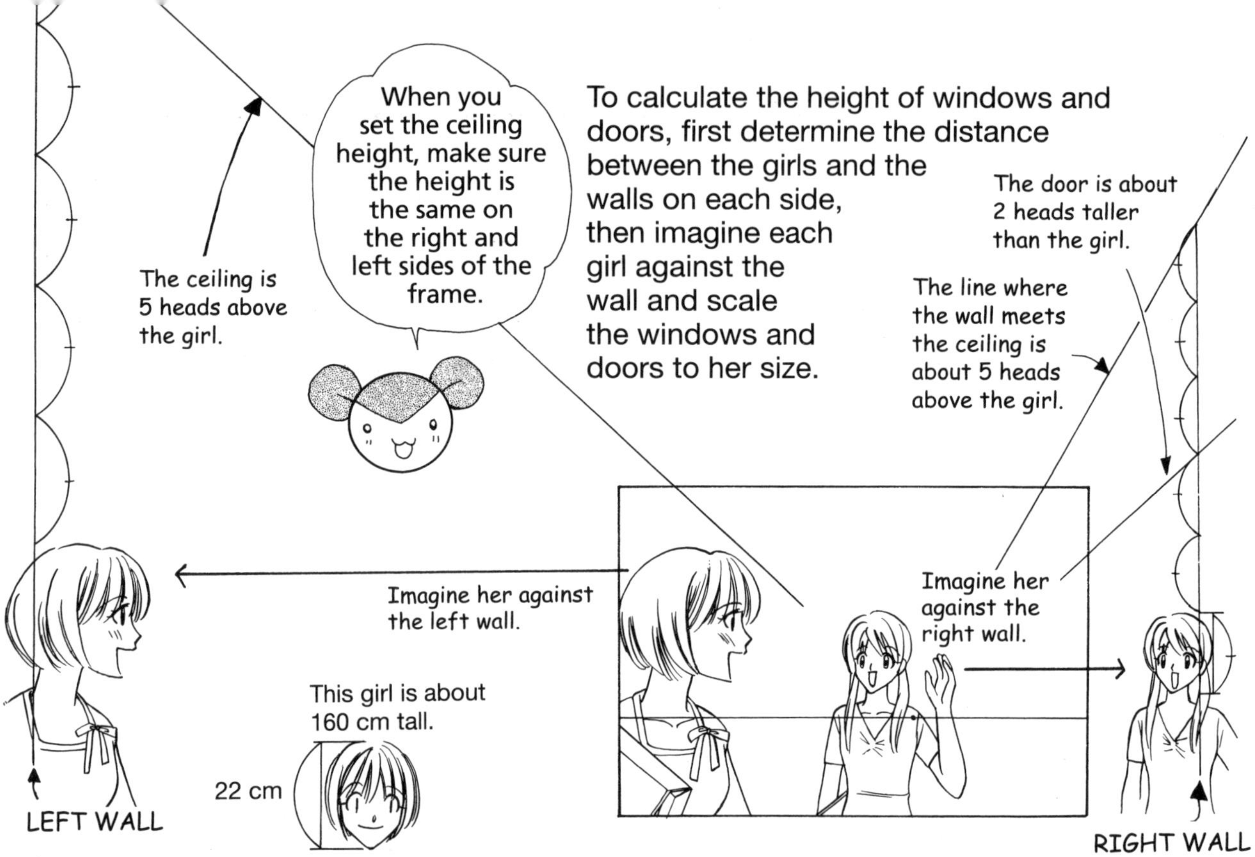
The ceiling is 5 heads above the girl.
When you set the ceiling height, make sure the height is the same on the right and left sides of the frame.
The door is about 2 heads taller than the girl.
The line where the wall meets the ceiling is about 5 heads above the girl.
Imagine her against the left wall.
Imagine her against the right wall.
This girl is about 160 cm tall.
22 cm
LEFT WALL
RIGHT WALL

Now draw in the lines you calculated above.

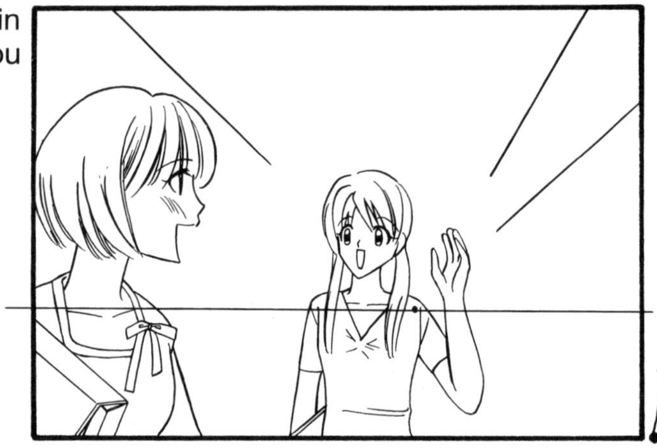

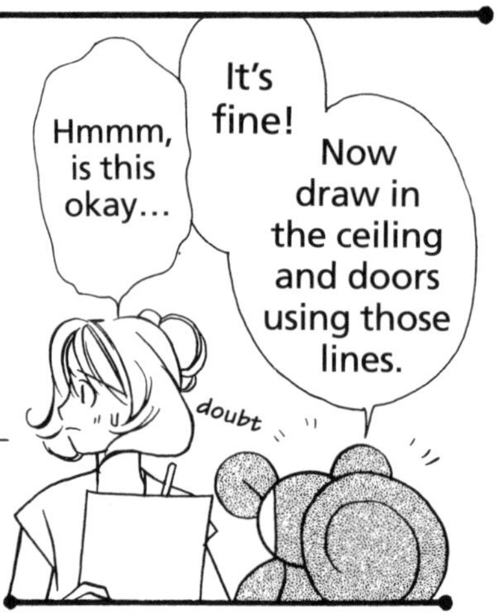
Hmmm, is this okay...
It's fine! Now draw in the ceiling and doors using those lines.
doubt

In one-point perspective, we draw in vertical and horizontal lines as well as the perspective lines from the VP.

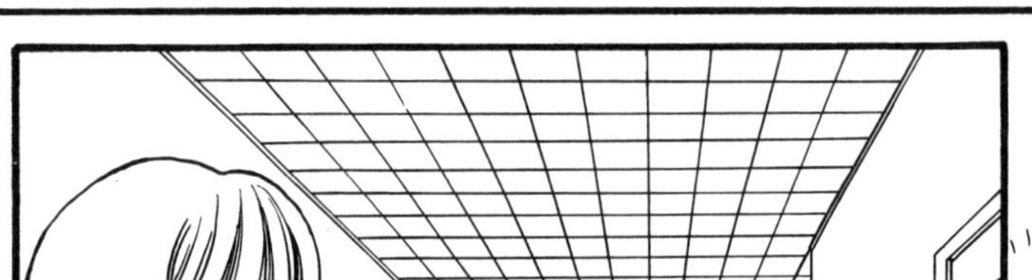

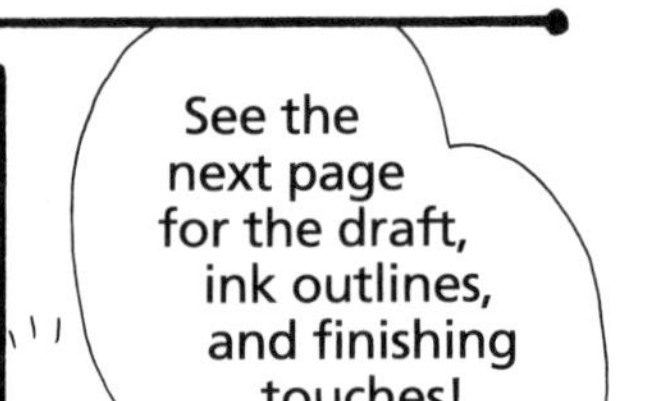
See the next page for the draft, ink outlines, and finishing touches! Have a look!
Aahh! I'm drawing...
Well done!

DRAFT When you're drafting, you must correct all mistakes until it's perfect. It's really hard to correct your work after inking in outlines, so make sure you get it right first.

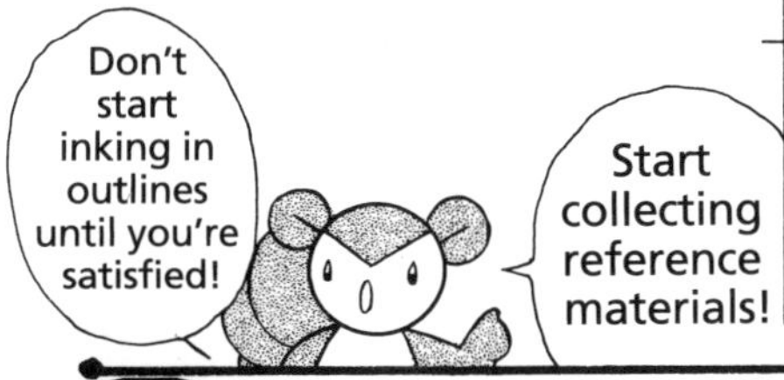
Don't start inking in outlines until you're satisfied!
Start collecting reference materials!

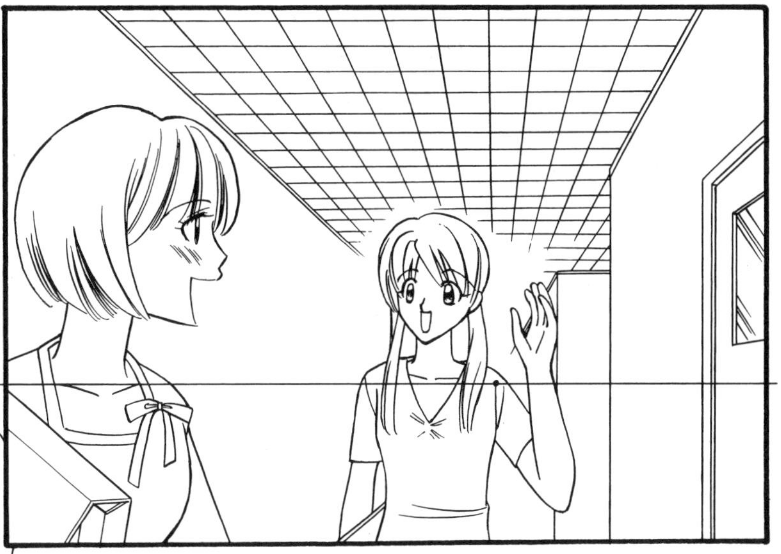

OUTLINES Ink in the characters first! But if there are objects in front of them, start with these instead. Always start with the closest object or character and work back.

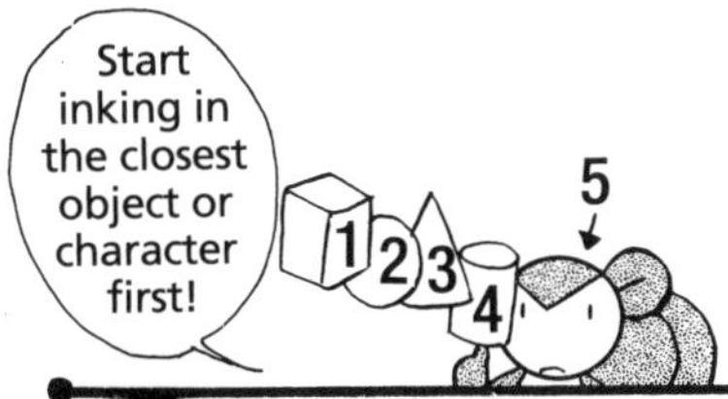
Start inking in the closest object or character first!
1
2
3
4
5

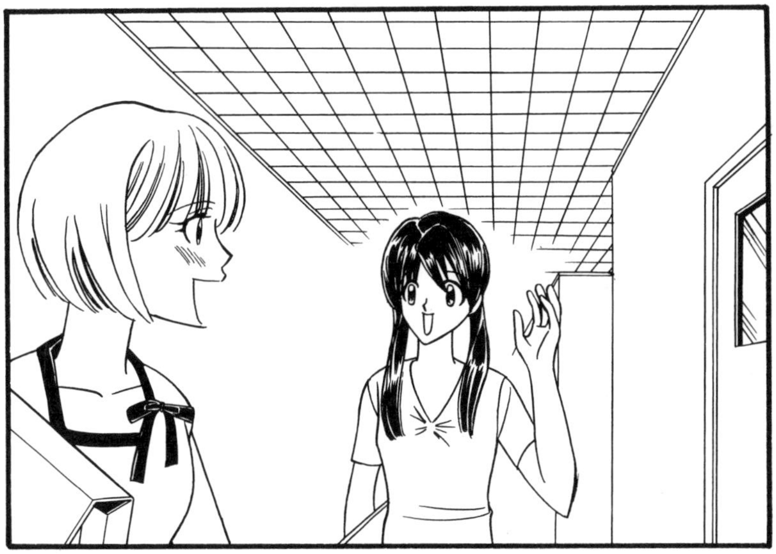

FINISHING TOUCHES Apply screen tone only after inking in outlines and effects! If you apply tone first, the ink will bleed between the paper and tone. Too much background screen tone can weaken a character's presence. Either use screen tone modestly, or use a light color.

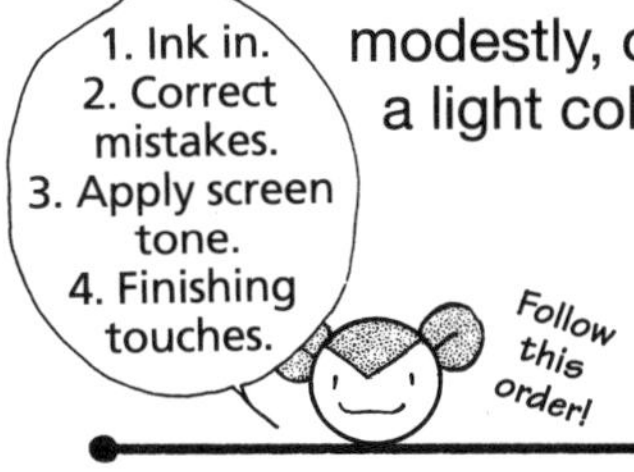
1. Ink in.
2. Correct mistakes.
3. Apply screen tone.
4. Finishing touches.
Follow this order!

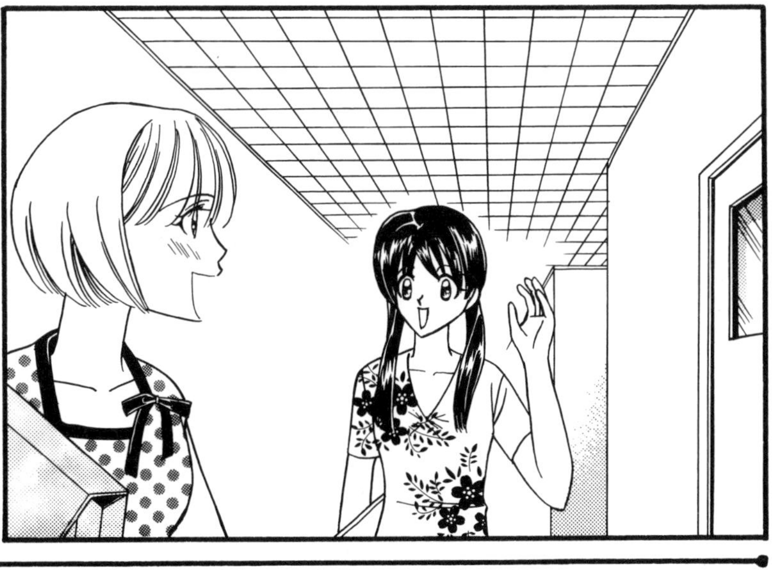

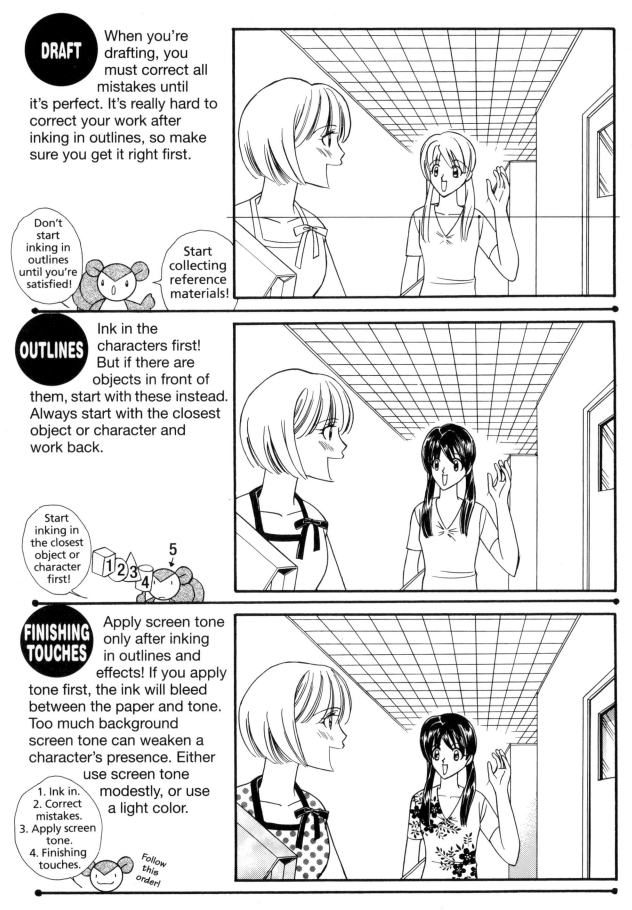

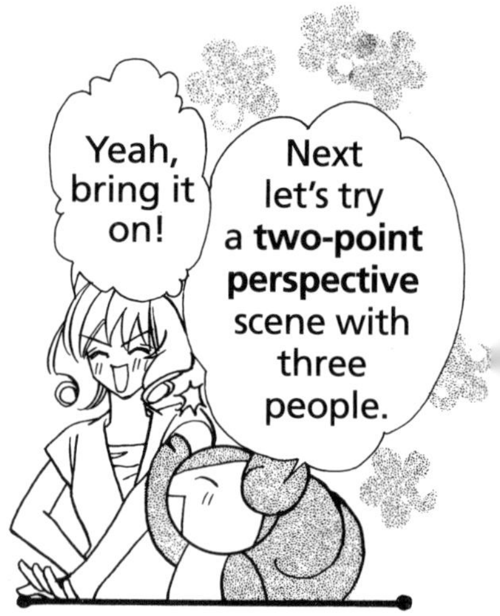
Next let's try a **two-point perspective** scene with three people.
Yeah, bring it on!

A girl is window shopping with her boyfriend. I set the EL at the height of the girl's eyes.

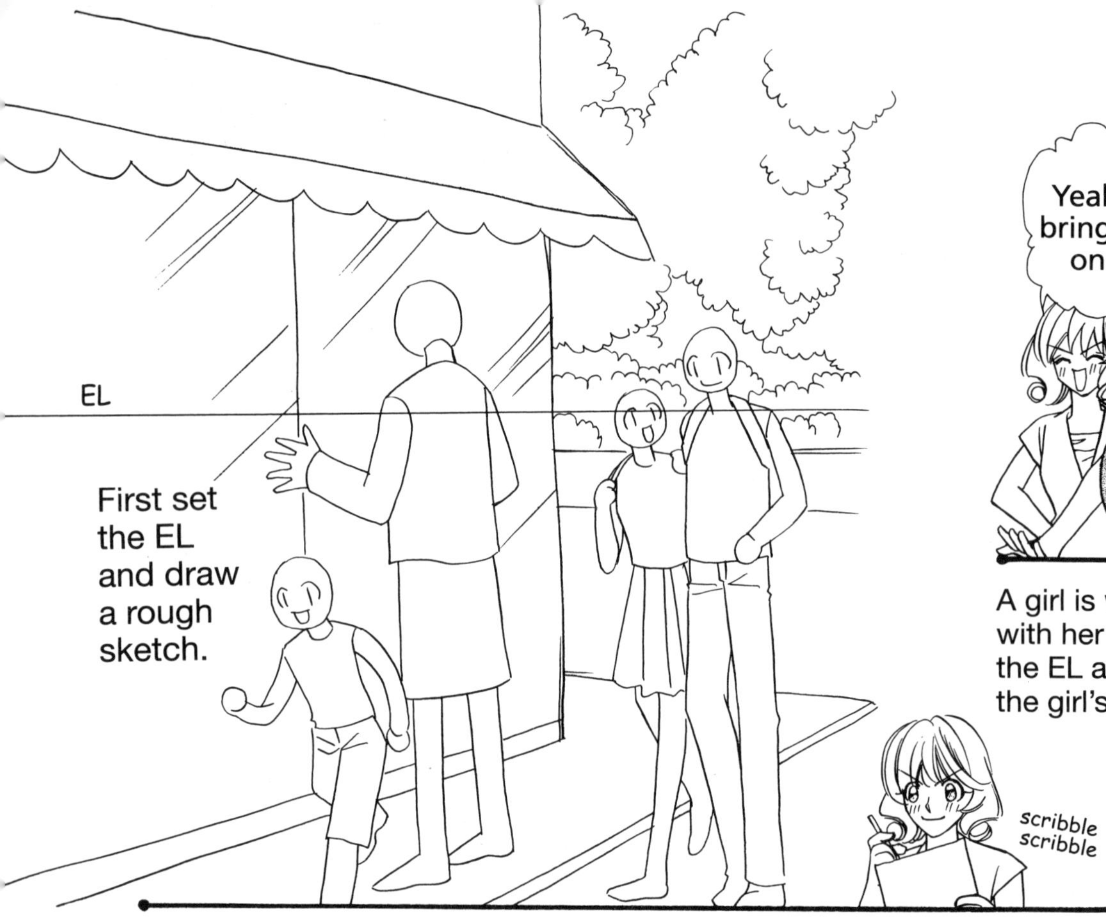
EL
First set the EL and draw a rough sketch.
scribble scribble

The right VP is on the line of the shop window canopy, and the left VP is on the line of the garden behind. Use the girl and her boyfriend as the main figures and scale the other characters and objects to their heights.

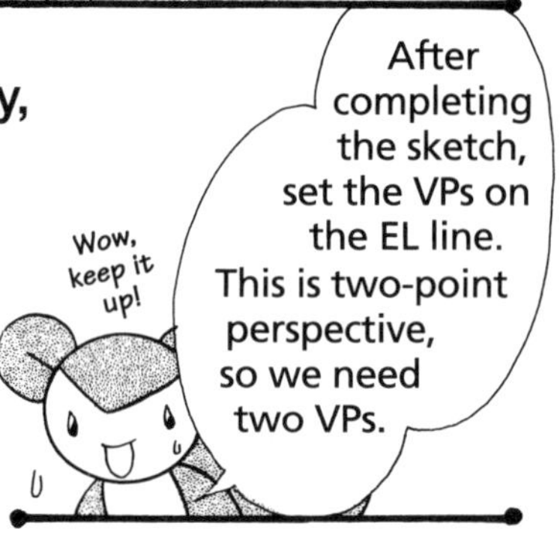
After completing the sketch, set the VPs on the EL line. This is two-point perspective, so we need two VPs.
Wow, keep it up!

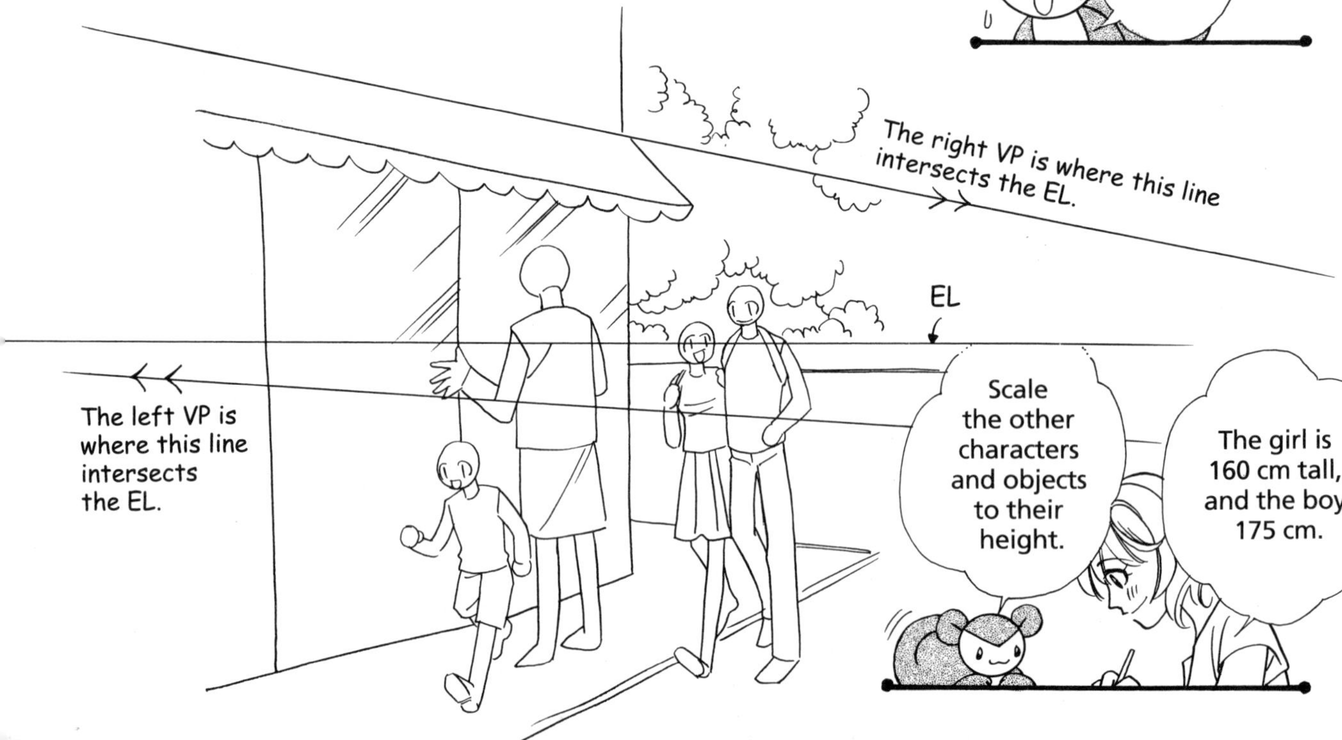
The right VP is where this line intersects the EL.
EL
The left VP is where this line intersects the EL.
The girl is 160 cm tall, and the boy 175 cm.
Scale the other characters and objects to their height.

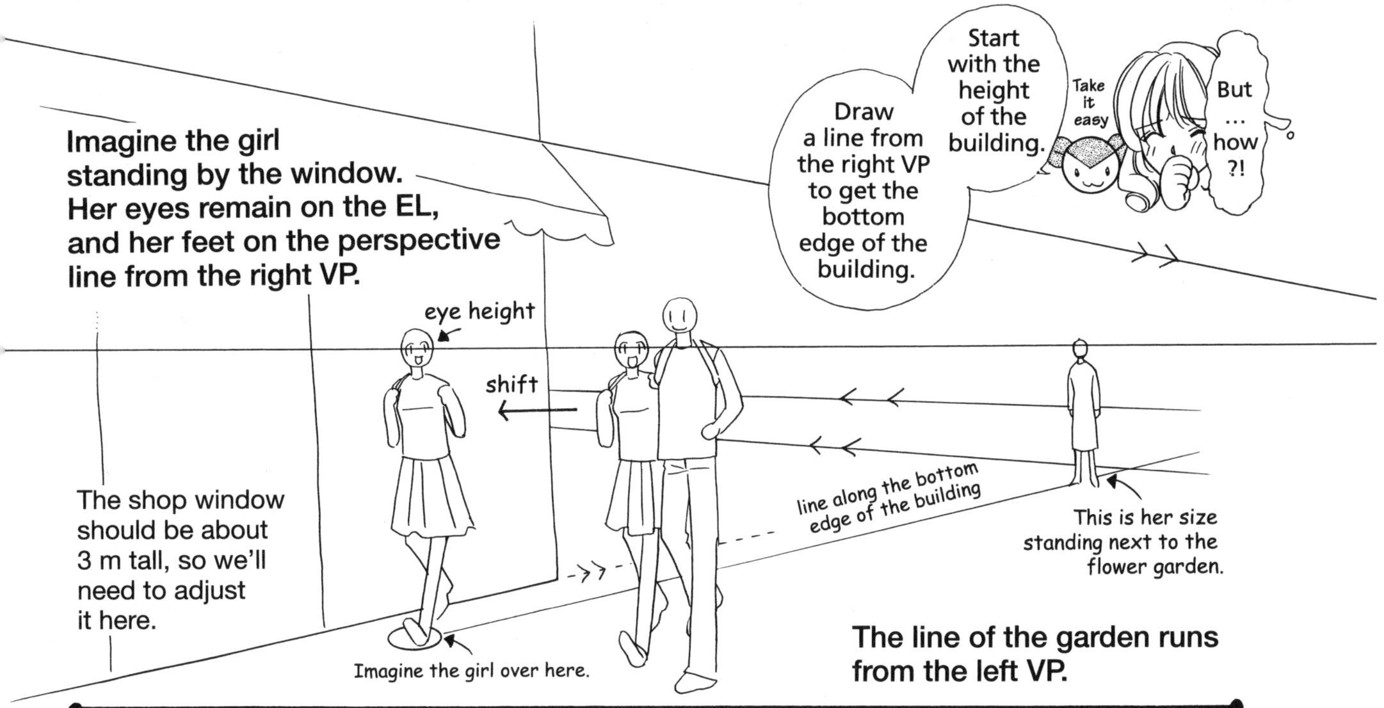
But ... how ?!
Take it easy
Start with the height of the building.
Draw a line from the right VP to get the bottom edge of the building.
Imagine the girl standing by the window. Her eyes remain on the EL, and her feet on the perspective line from the right VP.
eye height
shift
line along the bottom edge of the building
This is her size standing next to the flower garden.
The shop window should be about 3 m tall, so we'll need to adjust it here.
Imagine the girl over here.
The line of the garden runs from the left VP.

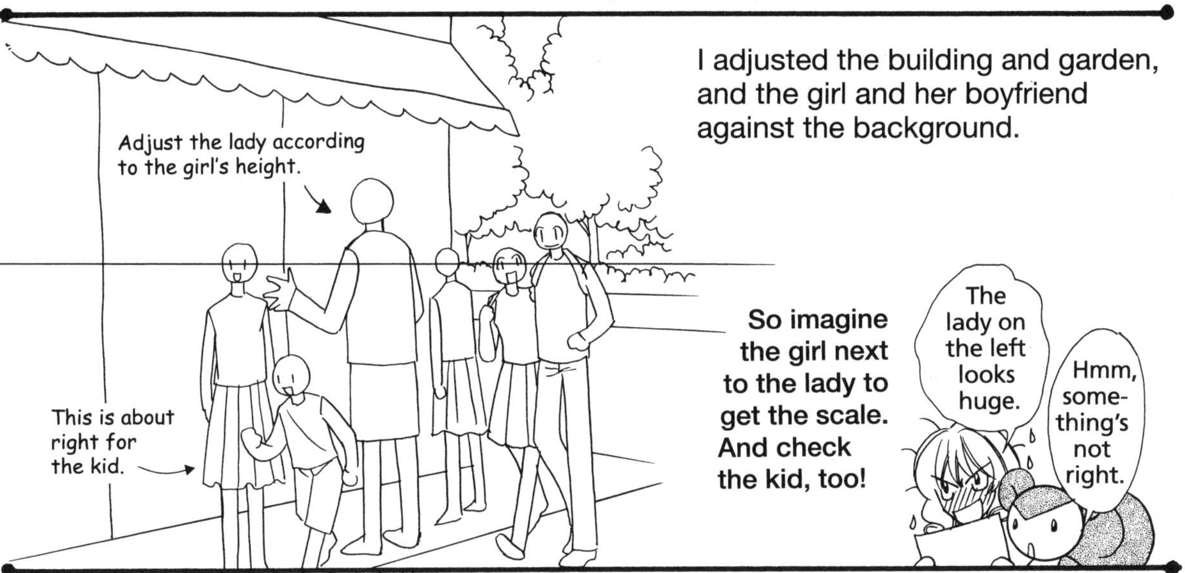
I adjusted the building and garden, and the girl and her boyfriend against the background.
Adjust the lady according to the girl's height.
This is about right for the kid.
Hmm, some-thing's not right.
The lady on the left looks huge.
So imagine the girl next to the lady to get the scale. And check the kid, too!

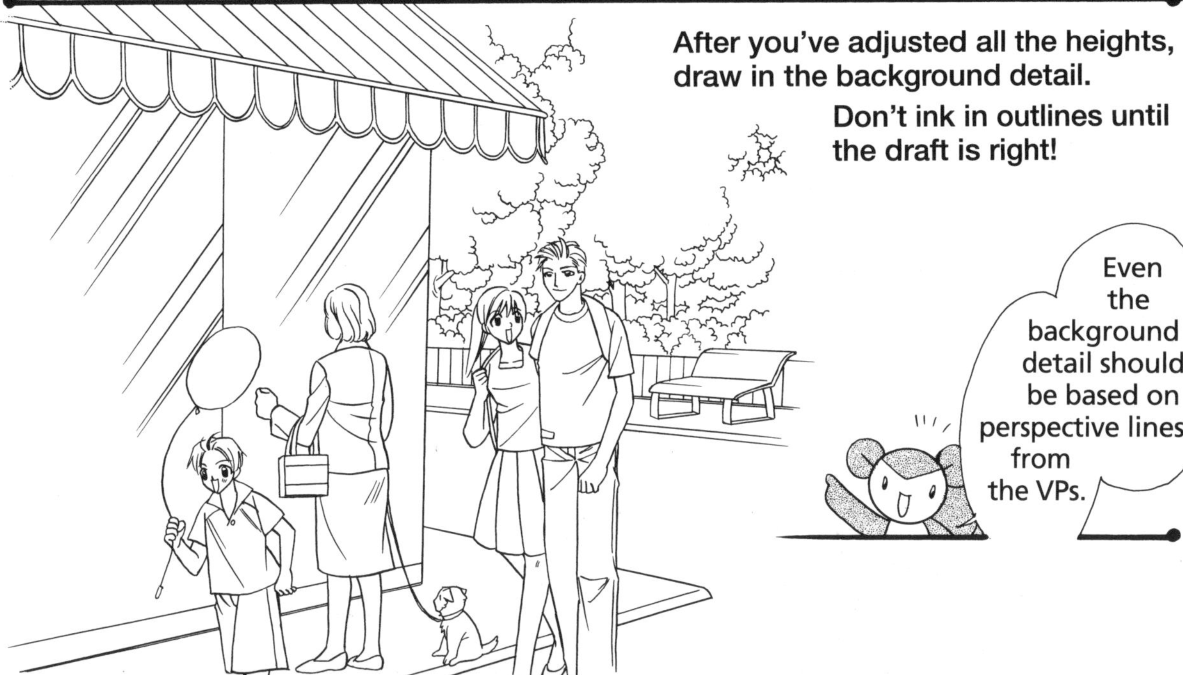
After you've adjusted all the heights, draw in the background detail.
Don't ink in outlines until the draft is right!
Even the background detail should be based on perspective lines from the VPs.

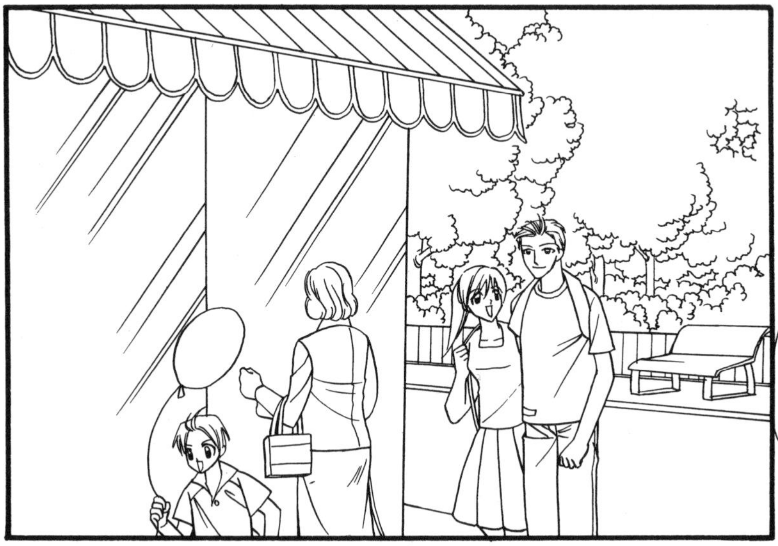

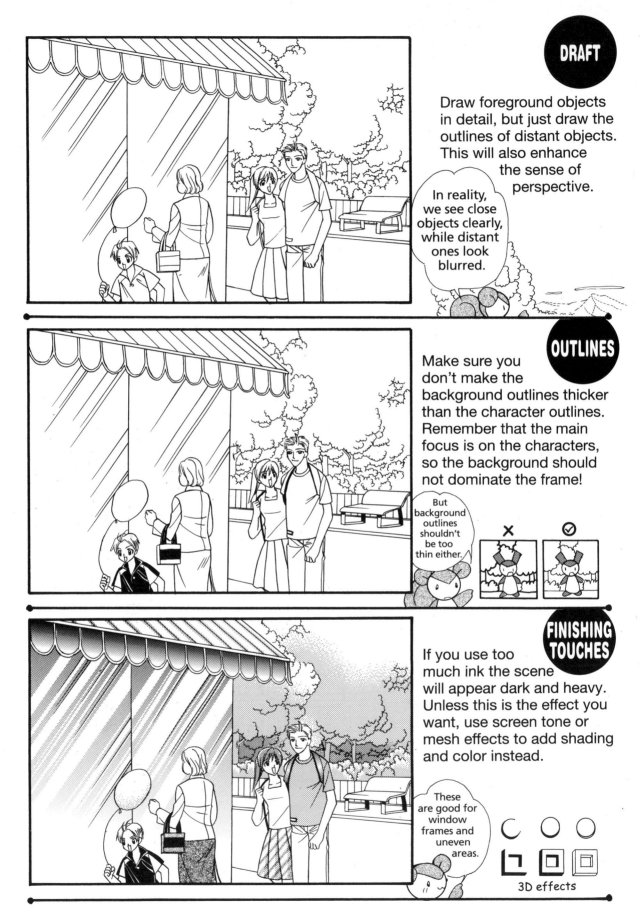

DRAFT

Draw foreground objects in detail, but just draw the outlines of distant objects. This will also enhance the sense of perspective.

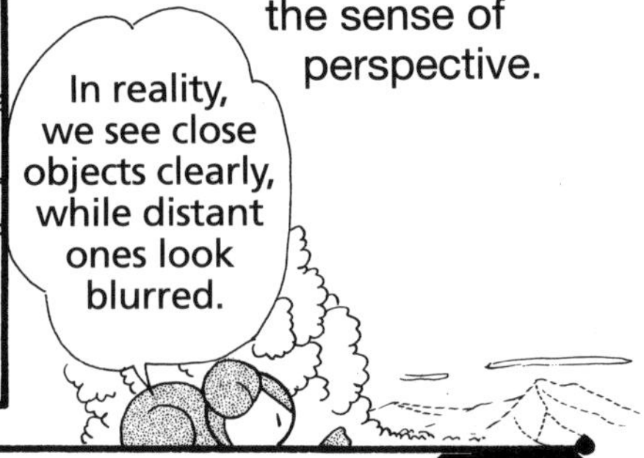
In reality, we see close objects clearly, while distant ones look blurred.

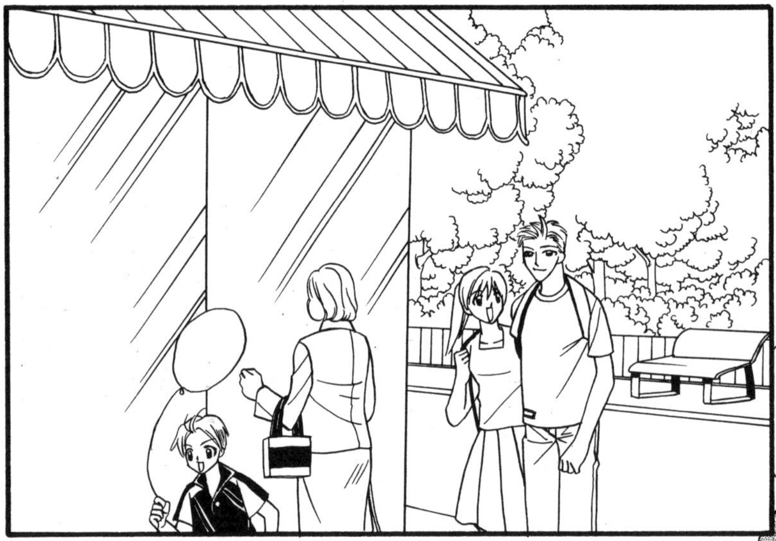

OUTLINES

Make sure you don't make the background outlines thicker than the character outlines. Remember that the main focus is on the characters, so the background should not dominate the frame!

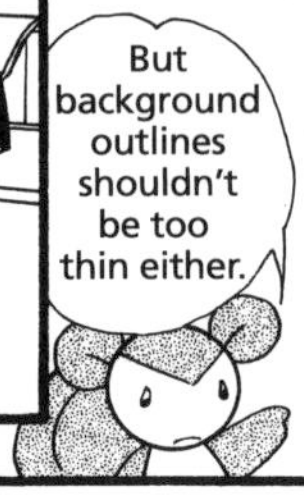
But background outlines shouldn't be too thin either.

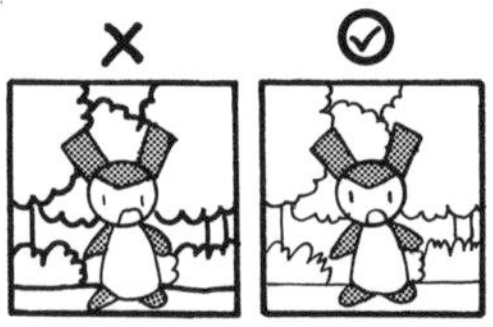

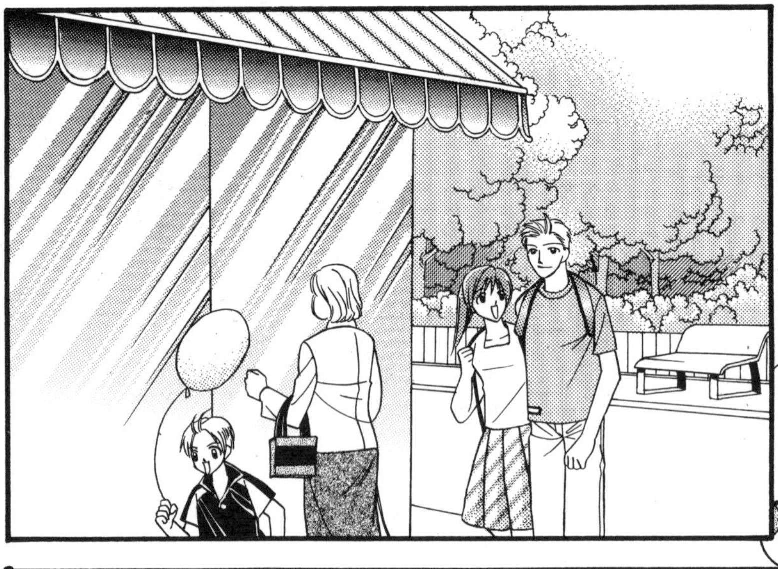

FINISHING TOUCHES

If you use too much ink the scene will appear dark and heavy. Unless this is the effect you want, use screen tone or mesh effects to add shading and color instead.

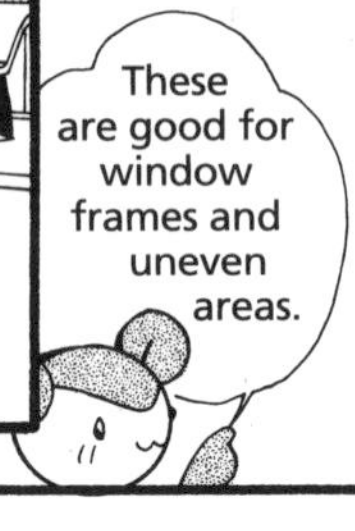
These are good for window frames and uneven areas.

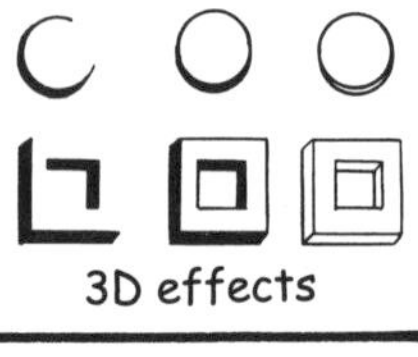
3D effects

TIME EFFECTS

A building looks different in the daytime and at night. The subtleties you read in the scene also change.

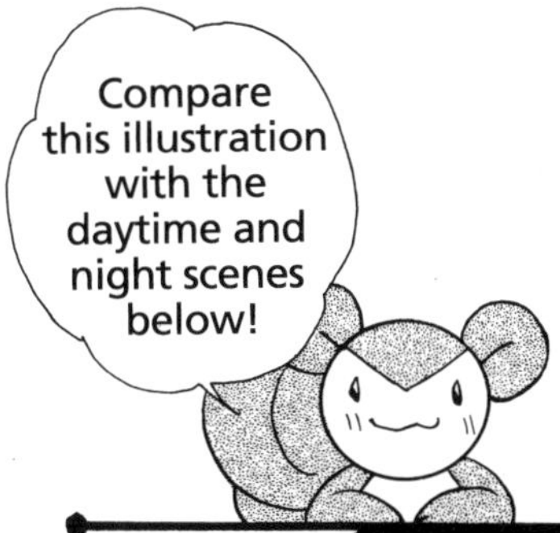
Compare this illustration with the daytime and night scenes below!

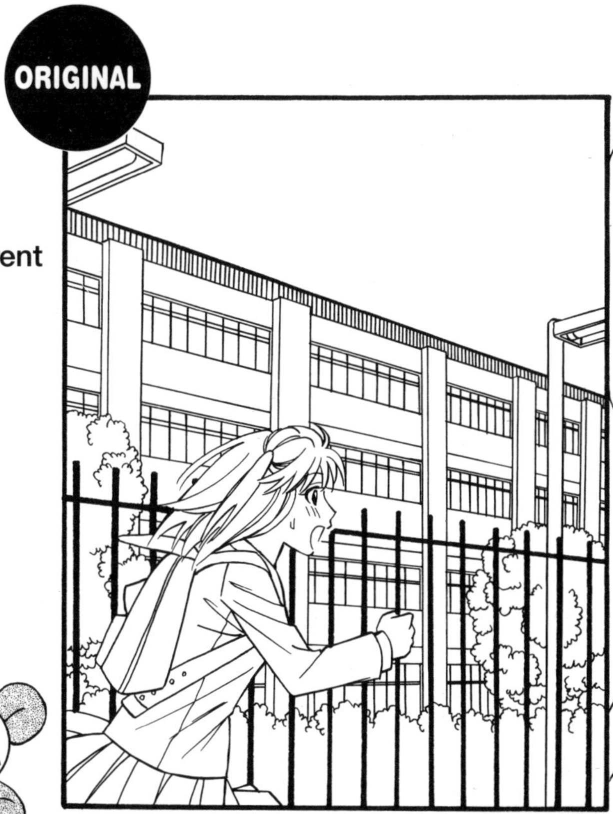
ORIGINAL

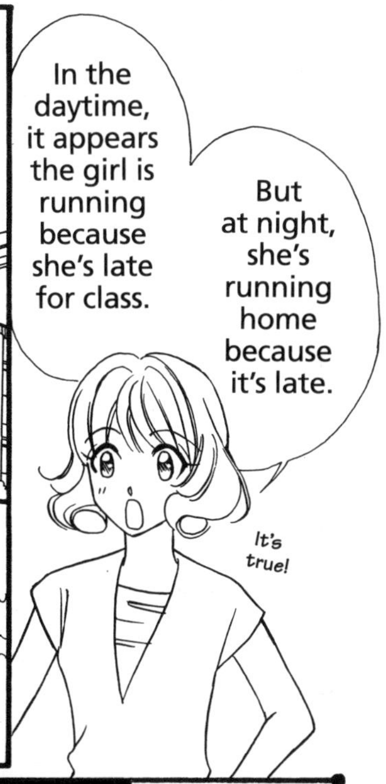
In the daytime, it appears the girl is running because she's late for class.
But at night, she's running home because it's late.
It's true!

The windows are dark as the lights inside are off.

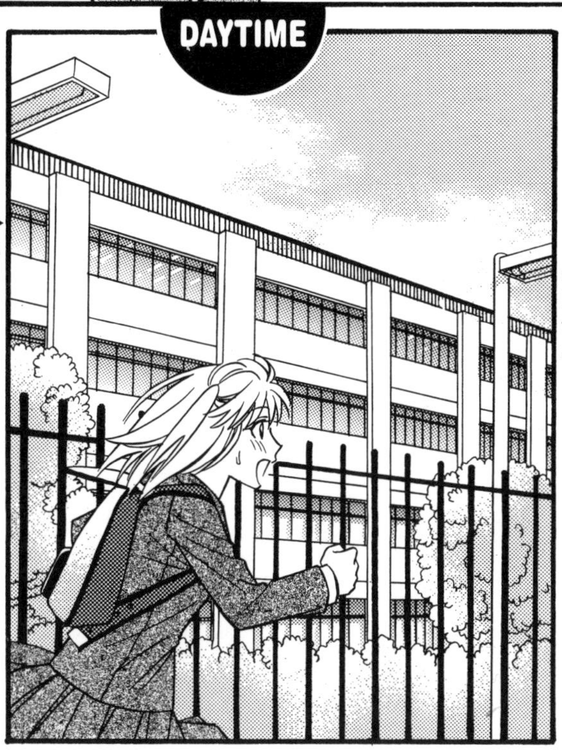
DAYTIME

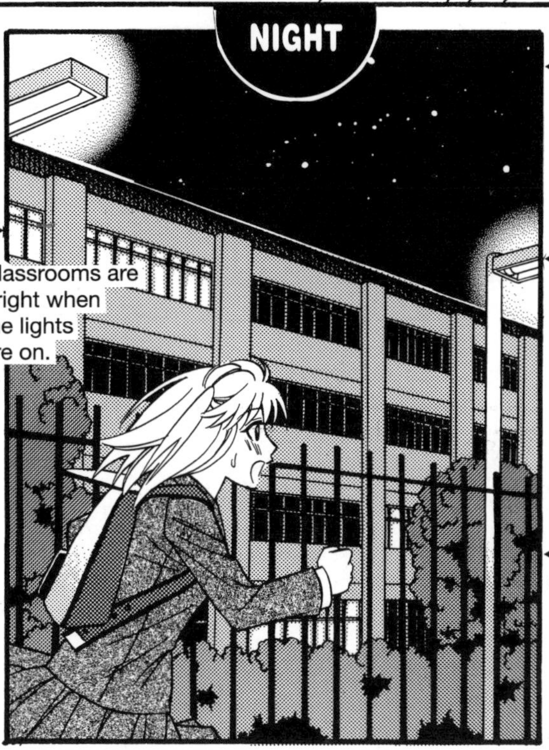
NIGHT
Classrooms are bright when the lights are on.

White ink for stars.

Halo of light around street-lights.

Ink in shadows.

In the daytime scene, the light shines from above so shadows appear mainly under objects or in any recesses. The scene is bright, so don't ink in large areas. Scratch screen tone off trees and leaves for highlights where the sunlight falls.

The background in a night scene is dark, so use gradation or dark screen tone. Areas around streetlights should be slightly lighter, and shadows inked in. Use dark gradation screen tone on the sky, and if it's a clear night depict stars with white ink.

OVERHEAD PERSPECTIVE

This is when the EL is set above the characters.

Draw your sketch with this in mind. It's only a sketch, it doesn't have to be exact!

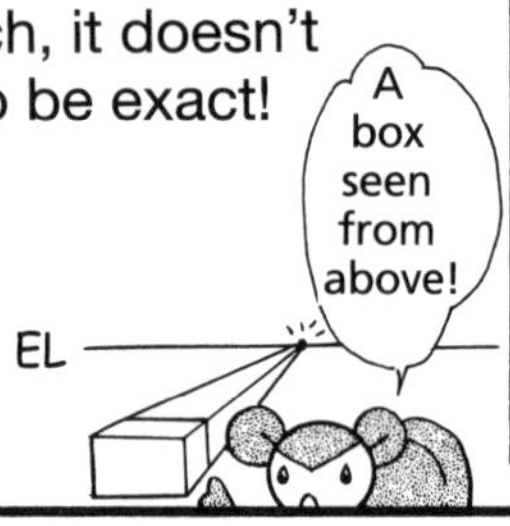
A box seen from above!
EL

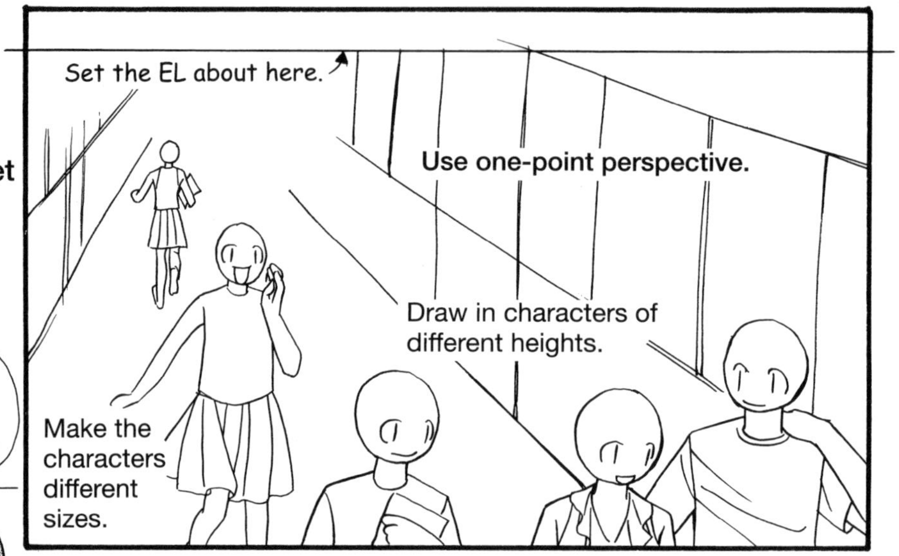
Set the EL about here.
Use one-point perspective.
Draw in characters of different heights.
Make the characters different sizes.

Set the EL, then determine where to position the VP.

Start by drawing the floor line on the right.

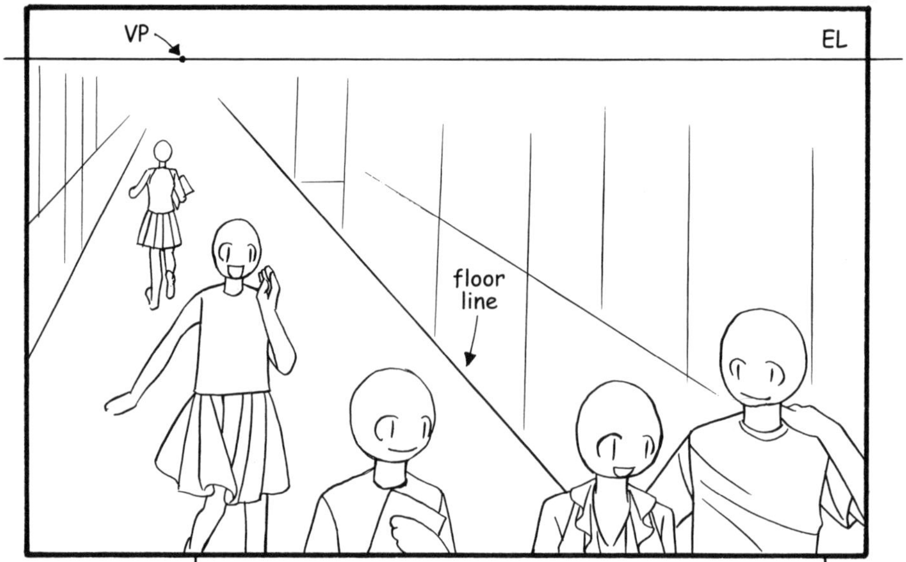
VP
EL
floor line

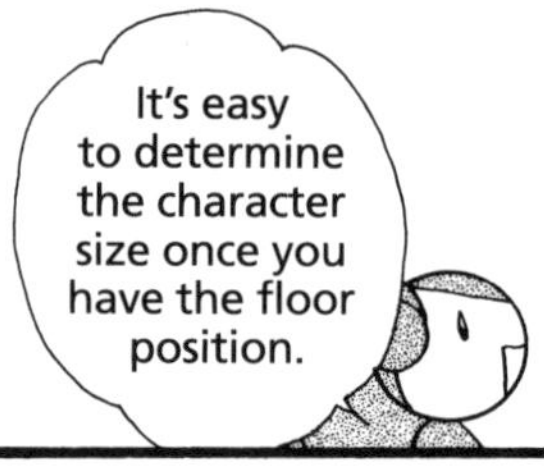
It's easy to determine the character size once you have the floor position.

Draw in the main figure's body, including her feet. Draw in two more characters using the feet position and height of the main figure as a scale.

Now adjust any awkward looking parts of the sketch.

Make the girl behind the same height as the girl in front on the left.

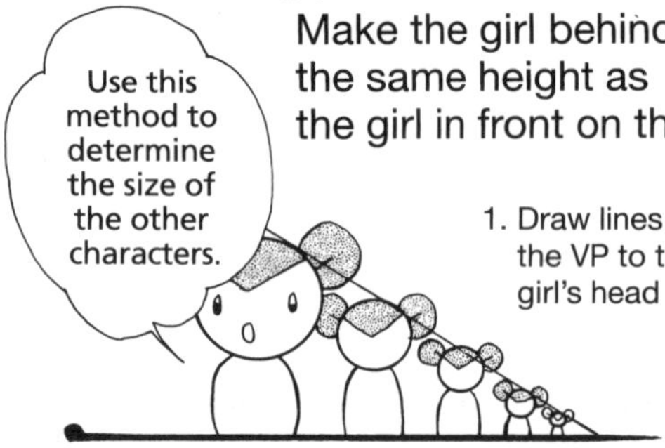
Use this method to determine the size of the other characters.

1. Draw lines from the VP to the front girl's head and feet.

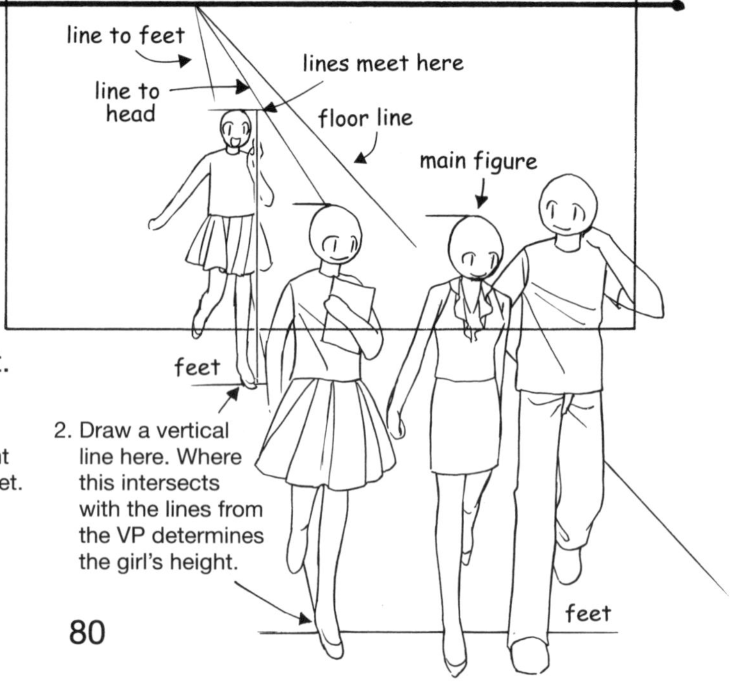
line to feet
line to head
lines meet here
floor line
main figure
feet
feet

2. Draw a vertical line here. Where this intersects with the lines from the VP determines the girl's height.

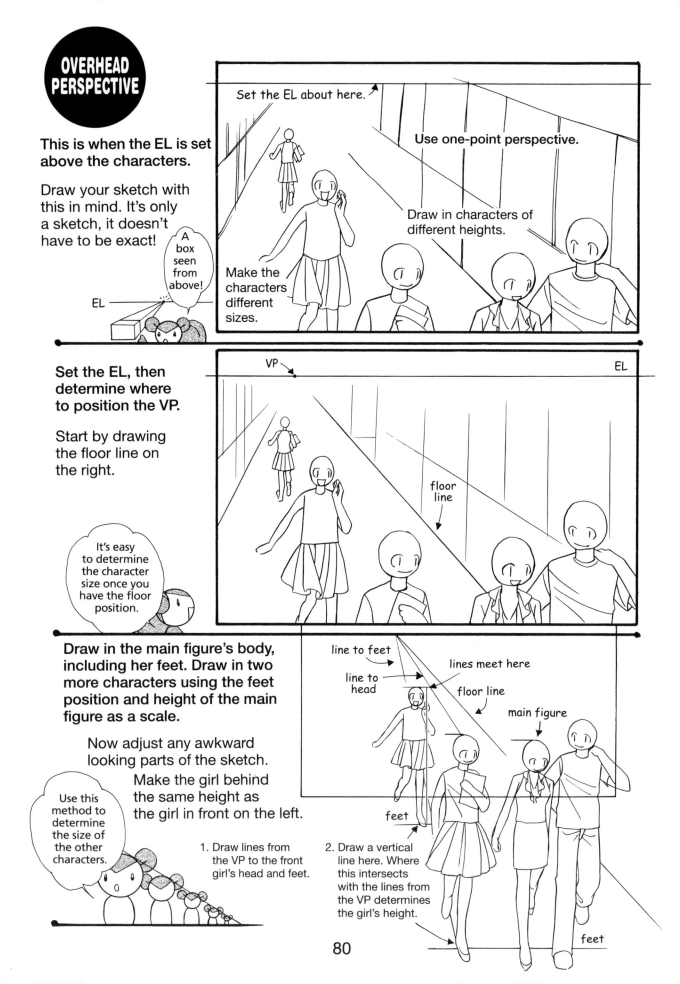

An overhead view should feel like you're seeing the characters from above! That sense increases the closer to the foreground.

Use the characters' heights as a scale when you're drawing in the background details.

The area around the VP should be blurred, so don't draw fine detail here. This will enhance the perspective.

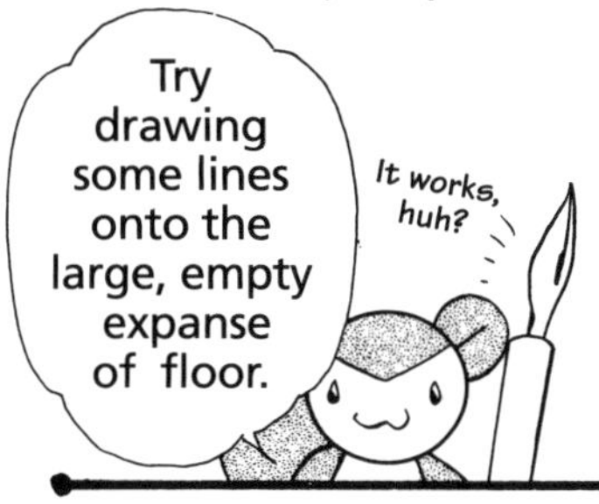
Try drawing some lines onto the large, empty expanse of floor.
It works, huh?

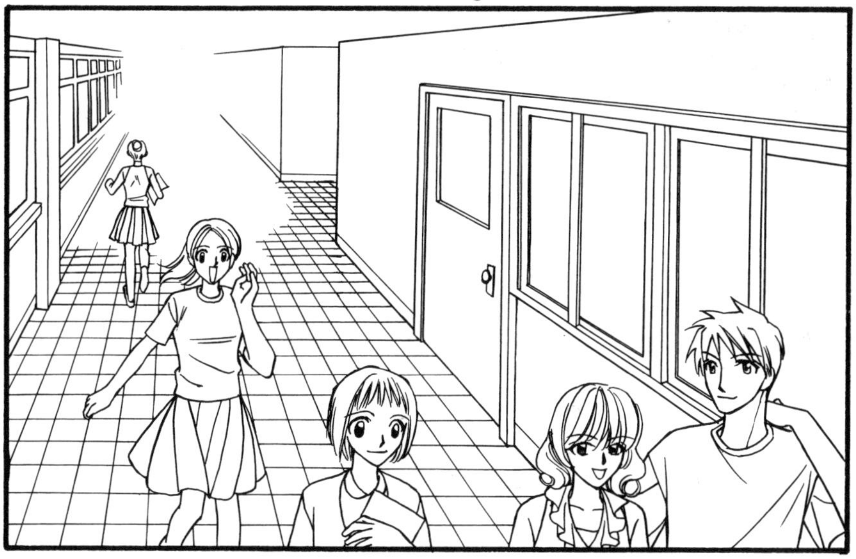

Start inking in the character outlines first. Pay attention to hard and soft textures.

Don't let background outlines dominate the character outlines. Floor details should be light.

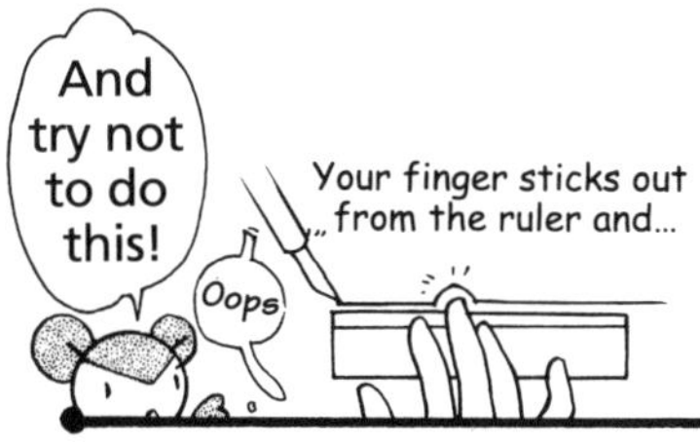
And try not to do this!
Your finger sticks out from the ruler and...
Oops

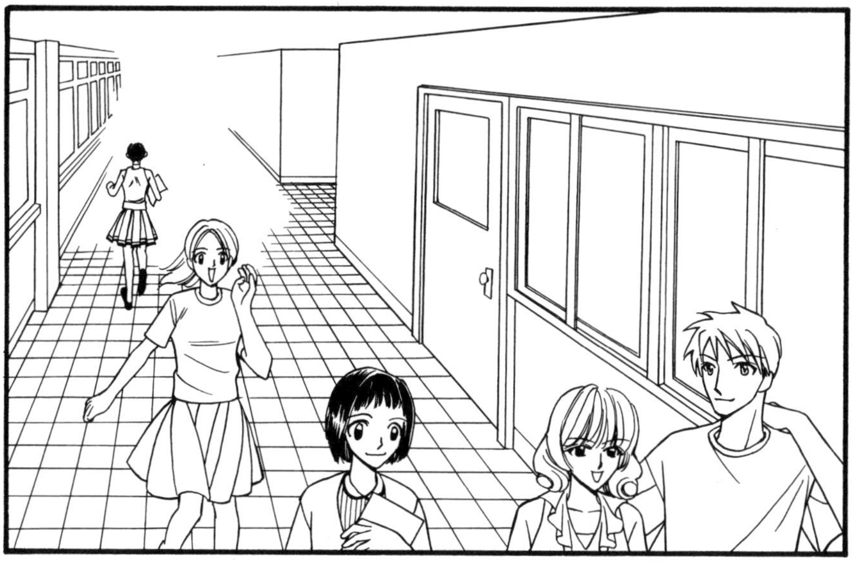

For daytime scenes, ink in the windows lightly and use light screen tone for the finishing touches!

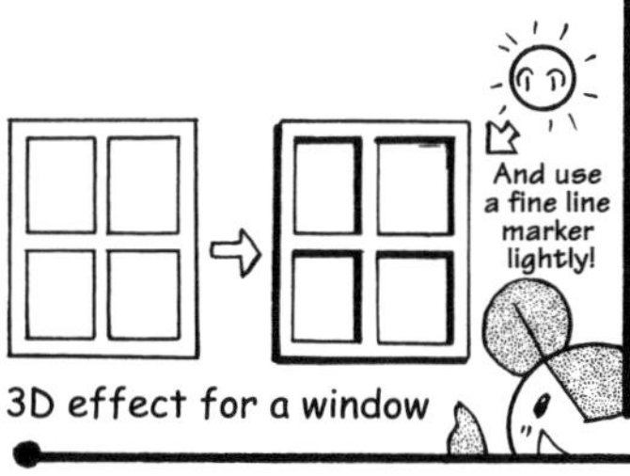
And use a fine line marker lightly!
3D effect for a window

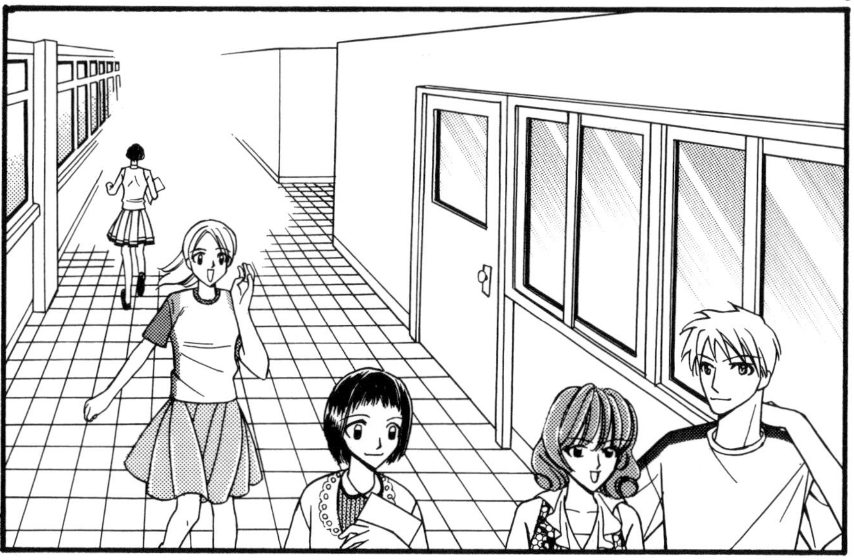

LOW PERSPECTIVE

The viewing angle is from below, so the EL is set lower.

Try not to make the angle too sharp (unless you want that effect).

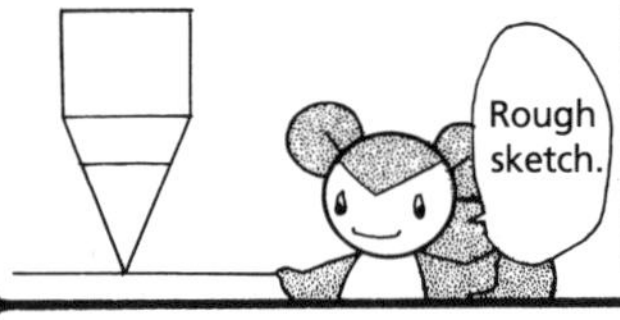
Rough sketch.

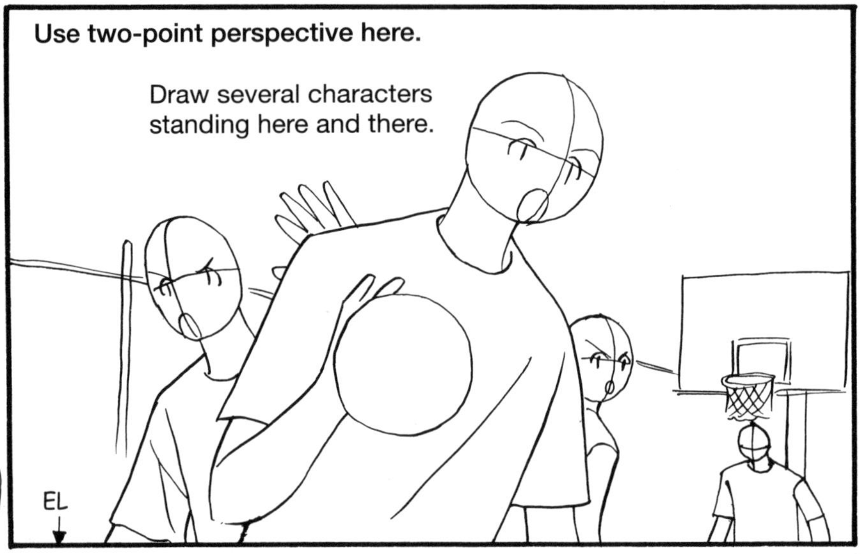
Use two-point perspective here.
Draw several characters standing here and there.
EL

Set the EL, then decide the character sizes.

The foreground character is the main figure. The EL is at his waist height, so adjust the other characters' waists to this height, too. That's the main part done.

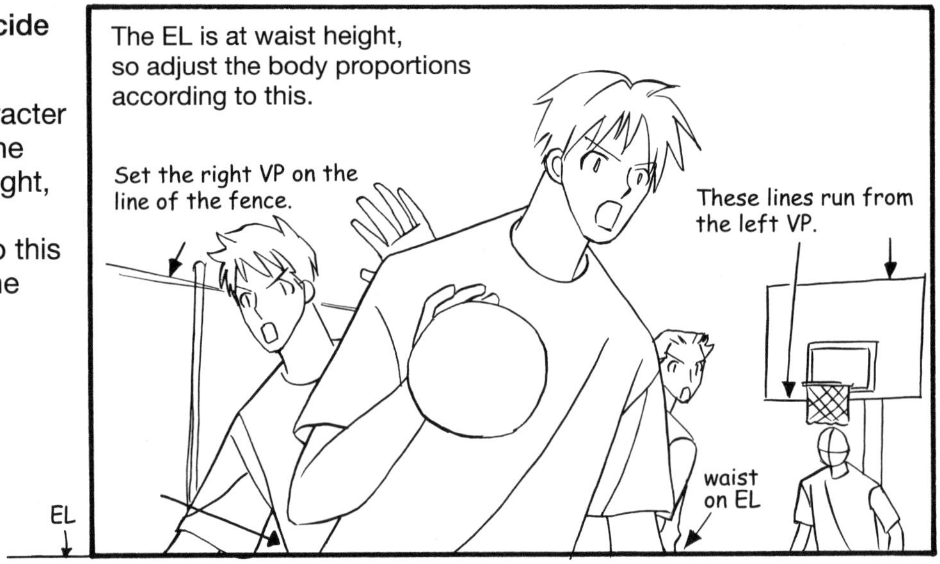
The EL is at waist height, so adjust the body proportions according to this.
Set the right VP on the line of the fence.
These lines run from the left VP.
waist on EL
EL

Adjust the height of the fence and the size of the backboard.

Scale objects to the height of the characters.

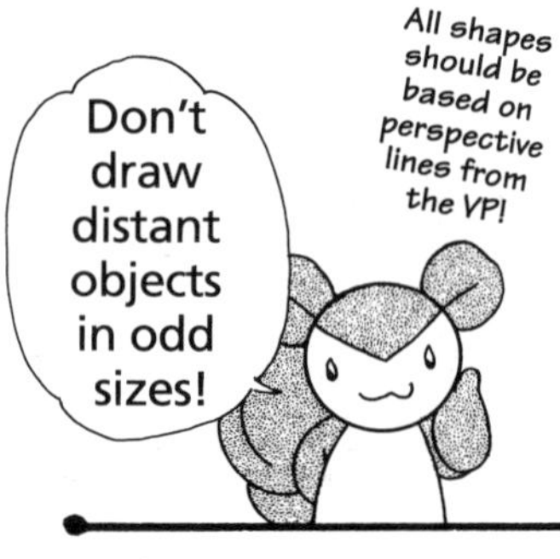
Don't draw distant objects in odd sizes!
All shapes should be based on perspective lines from the VP!

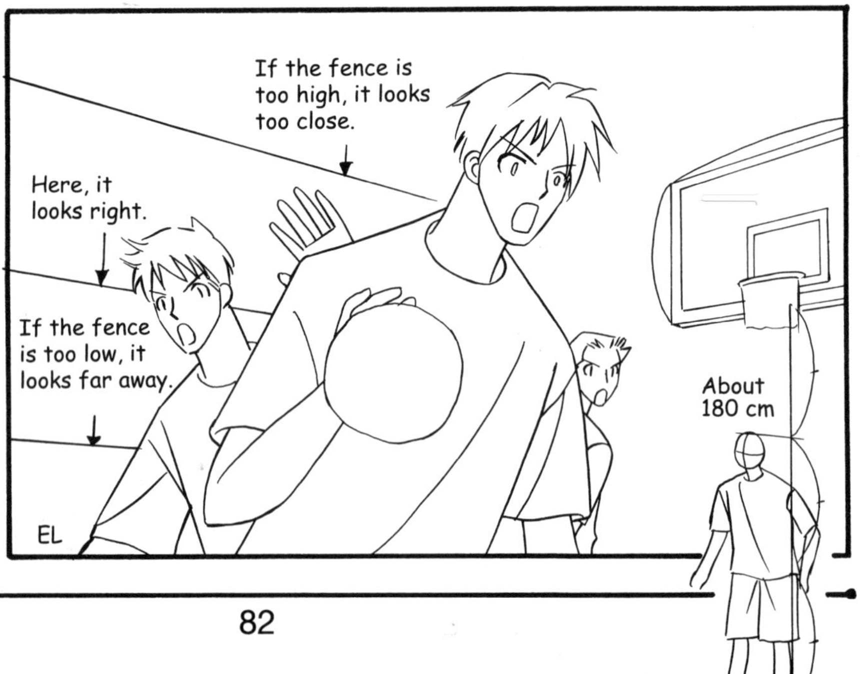
If the fence is too high, it looks too close.
Here, it looks right.
If the fence is too low, it looks far away.
About 180 cm
EL

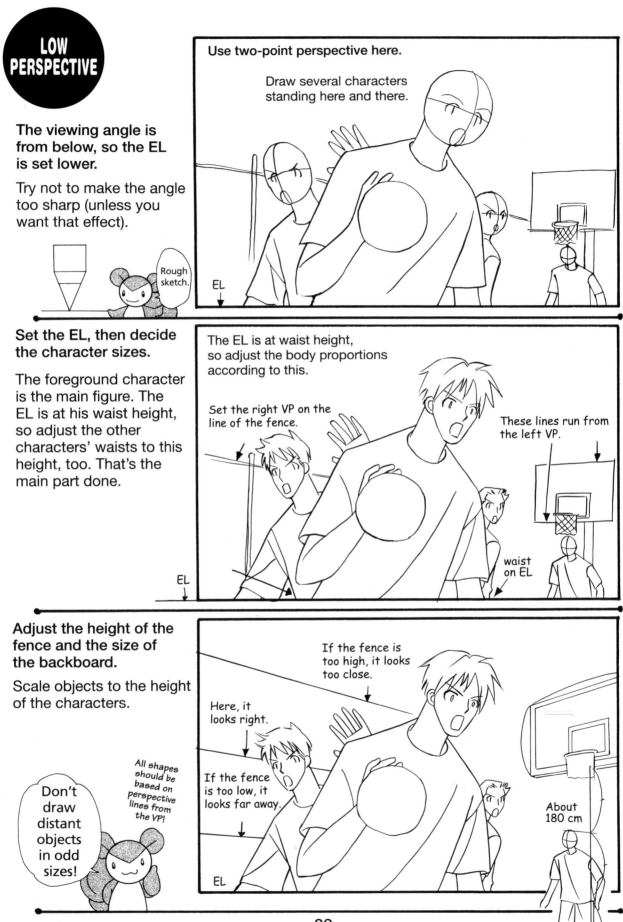

After determining the sizes of background objects, draw in details.

Remember that you're looking upwards from below when you draw the angle of the faces and clothing folds!

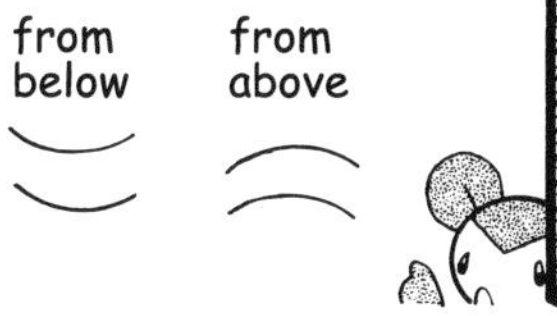
from below
from above

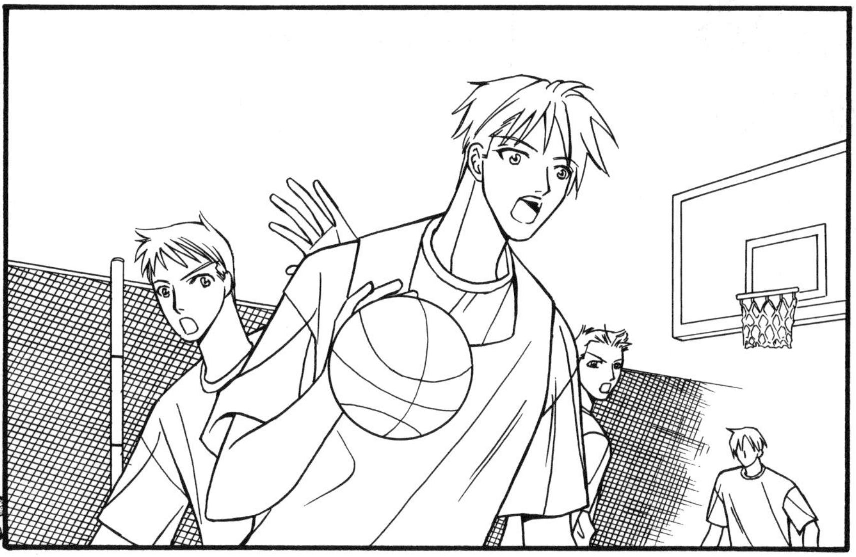

Ink in the outlines.

Always start with the foreground character or objects in the foreground. The fence is quite far away so you don't need much detail. Blur in places to make the characters stand out better.

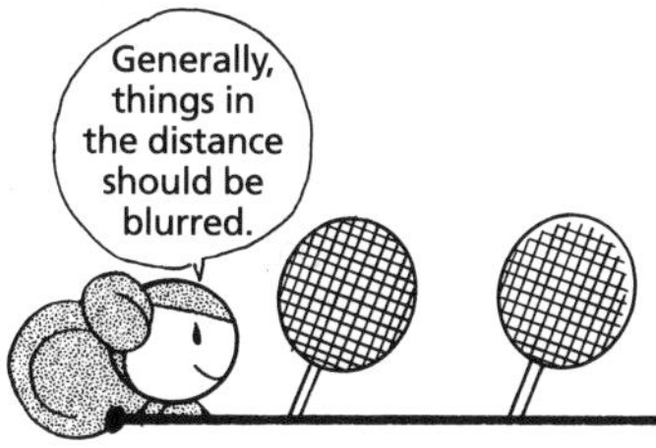
Generally, things in the distance should be blurred.

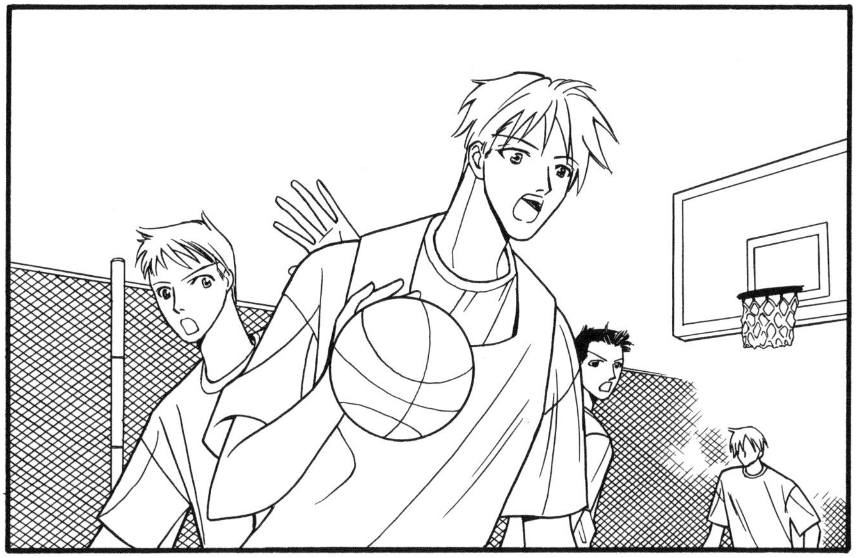

Go easy on the finishing touches, there aren't many shadows. Scratch off screen tone for highlights on the dark-colored jerseys. Apply a light screen tone for the sky, and scratch off patches for clouds.

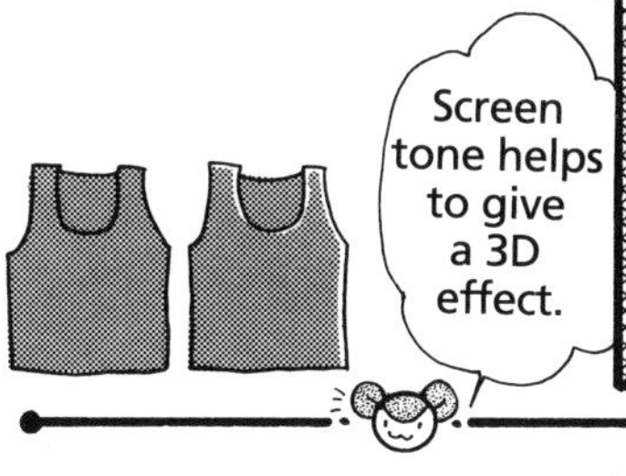
Screen tone helps to give a 3D effect.

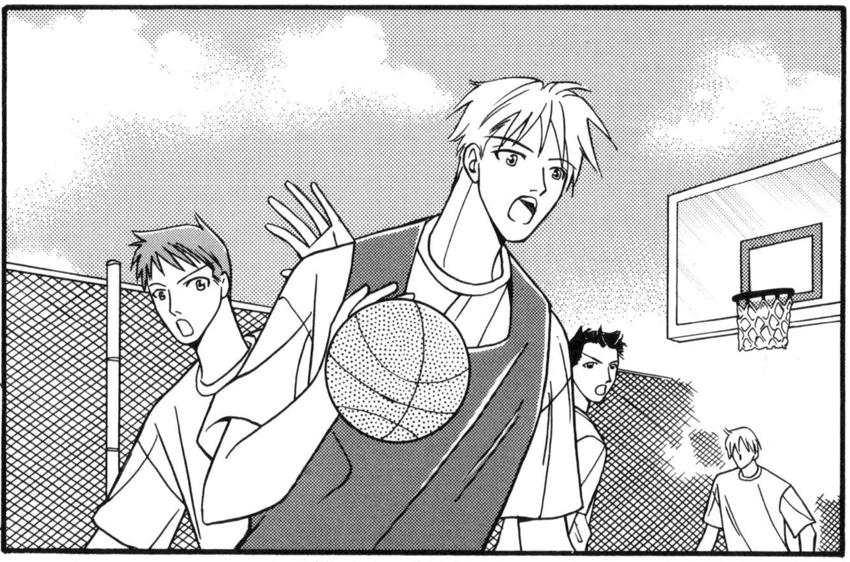

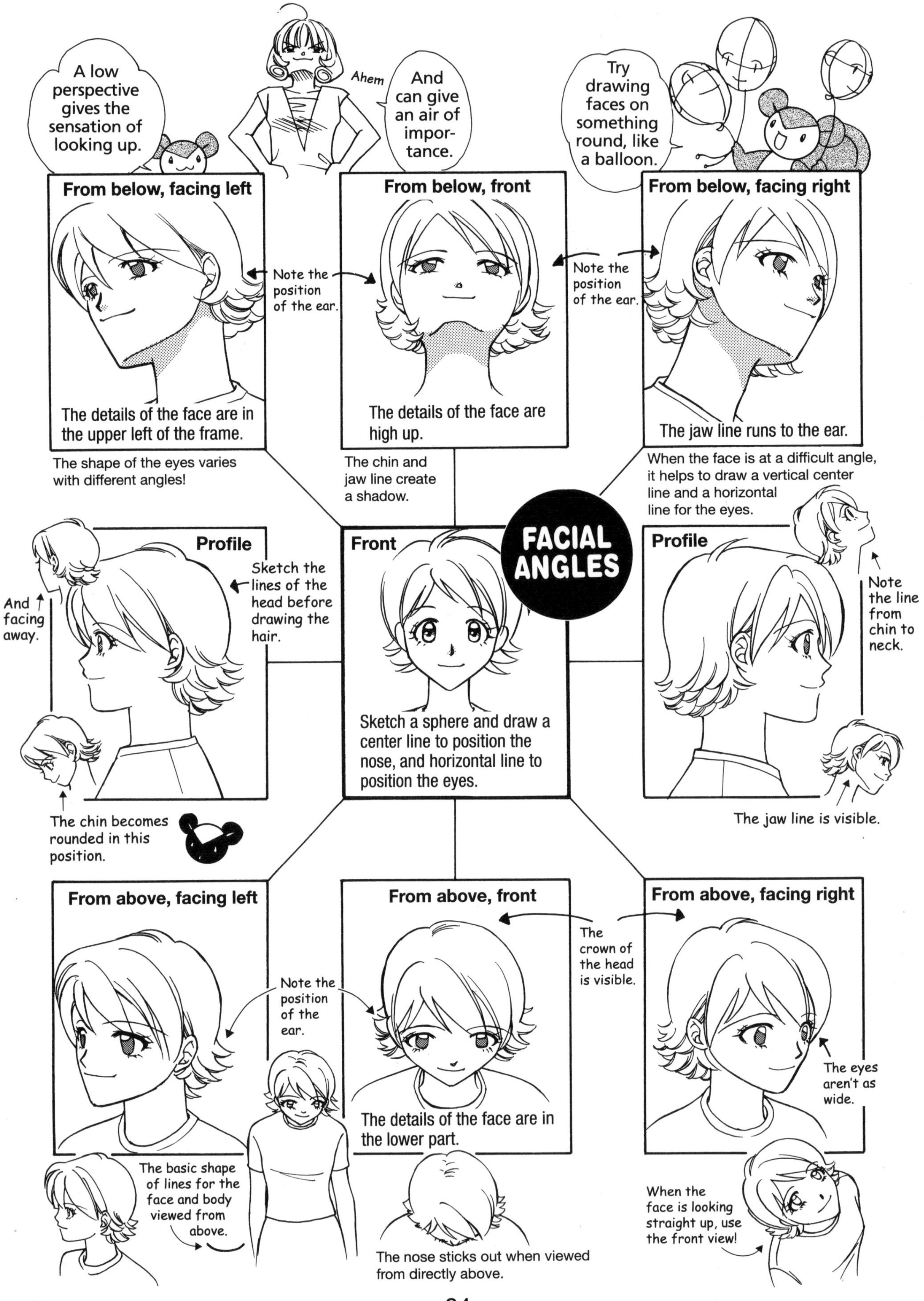
A low perspective gives the sensation of looking up.
Ahem
And can give an air of impor-tance.
Try drawing faces on something round, like a balloon.
From below, facing left
Note the position of the ear.
The details of the face are in the upper left of the frame.
The shape of the eyes varies with different angles!
From below, front
The details of the face are high up.
The chin and jaw line create a shadow.
From below, facing right
Note the position of the ear.
The jaw line runs to the ear.
When the face is at a difficult angle, it helps to draw a vertical center line and a horizontal line for the eyes.
FACIAL ANGLES
Profile
And facing away.
Sketch the lines of the head before drawing the hair.
The chin becomes rounded in this position.
Front
Sketch a sphere and draw a center line to position the nose, and horizontal line to position the eyes.
Profile
Note the line from chin to neck.
The jaw line is visible.
From above, facing left
Note the position of the ear.
The basic shape of lines for the face and body viewed from above.
From above, front
The crown of the head is visible.
The details of the face are in the lower part.
The nose sticks out when viewed from directly above.
From above, facing right
The eyes aren't as wide.
When the face is looking straight up, use the front view!

LESSON 4
COLOR MANGA

Now that you've honed your technique
in black-and-white,
why not try your hand at color?
Let's look at how to use color inks,
color markers, and airbrushes!

There are many types of ink, pens, and other materials to experiment with, but here's what you need to get started.

Color ink

There are many colors and types of ink. Transparent ink lets colors underneath show through, while opaque ink covers other colors. There are water-soluble and water-resistant types of ink. You can also use a dye or a pigment to produce different finishes.

Color markers

Color markers range from water-soluble to oil-based and alcohol-based types. There are many different nibs, but the brush pen is particularly handy. Markers dry very quickly, though, so if you don't work fast the color will look patchy.

↓ **Brushes**

Water cup
(for washing brushes)
Some water cups have lids that double ↓ as palettes.

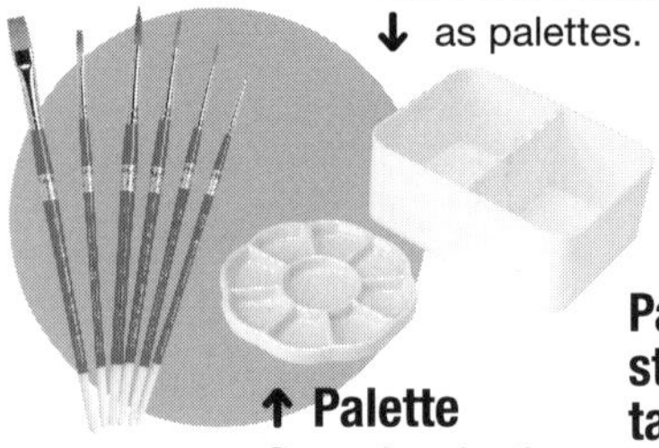

Paper stretching ↓ board

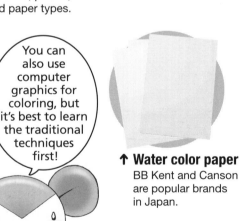

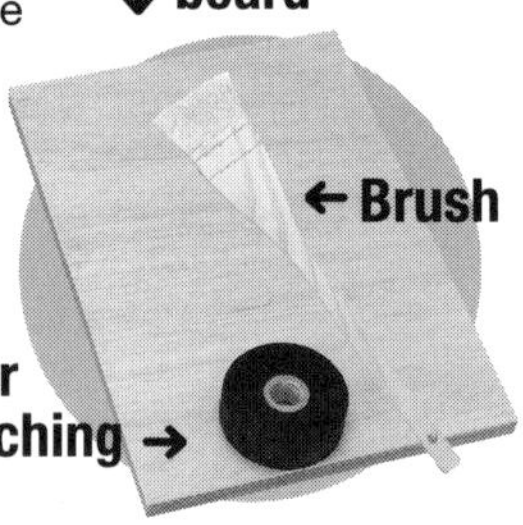

← **Brush**

Paper stretching → tape

↑ **Palette**
Ceramic, plastic, and paper types.

Brushes, water cups, palettes, and other essentials

When you're painting with color ink, things like brushes, palettes, water cups, and paper stretching boards are essential. Brushes with natural hair bristles are easy to use, but nylon will do to begin with. Palettes come in porcelain, plastic, and handy disposable paper types. Any clean container can be used as a water cup. See page 93 for more on paper stretching.

You can also use computer graphics for coloring, but it's best to learn the traditional techniques first!

↑ **Water color paper**
BB Kent and Canson are popular brands in Japan.

Color manuscript paper

Choosing the right paper is important when drawing in color! Go for one that matches your colors or design: white paper will display bright colors well, while an off-white paper will produce a softer effect. Also, pick a size larger than you actually need!

 ←**Fine BB Kent paper (natural)**
This takes the ink well, and is suitable for airbrushes too.

Marker paper

Alcohol-based markers do not dissolve copy toner, so you can use them to color a photocopy of the original. If you think copy paper is too thin, or if you want bright marker colors to stand out clearly, try using special marker paper like the one shown here. Also, beware that ink bleeds through thin paper!

↑ **Marker paper**

COLOR INK

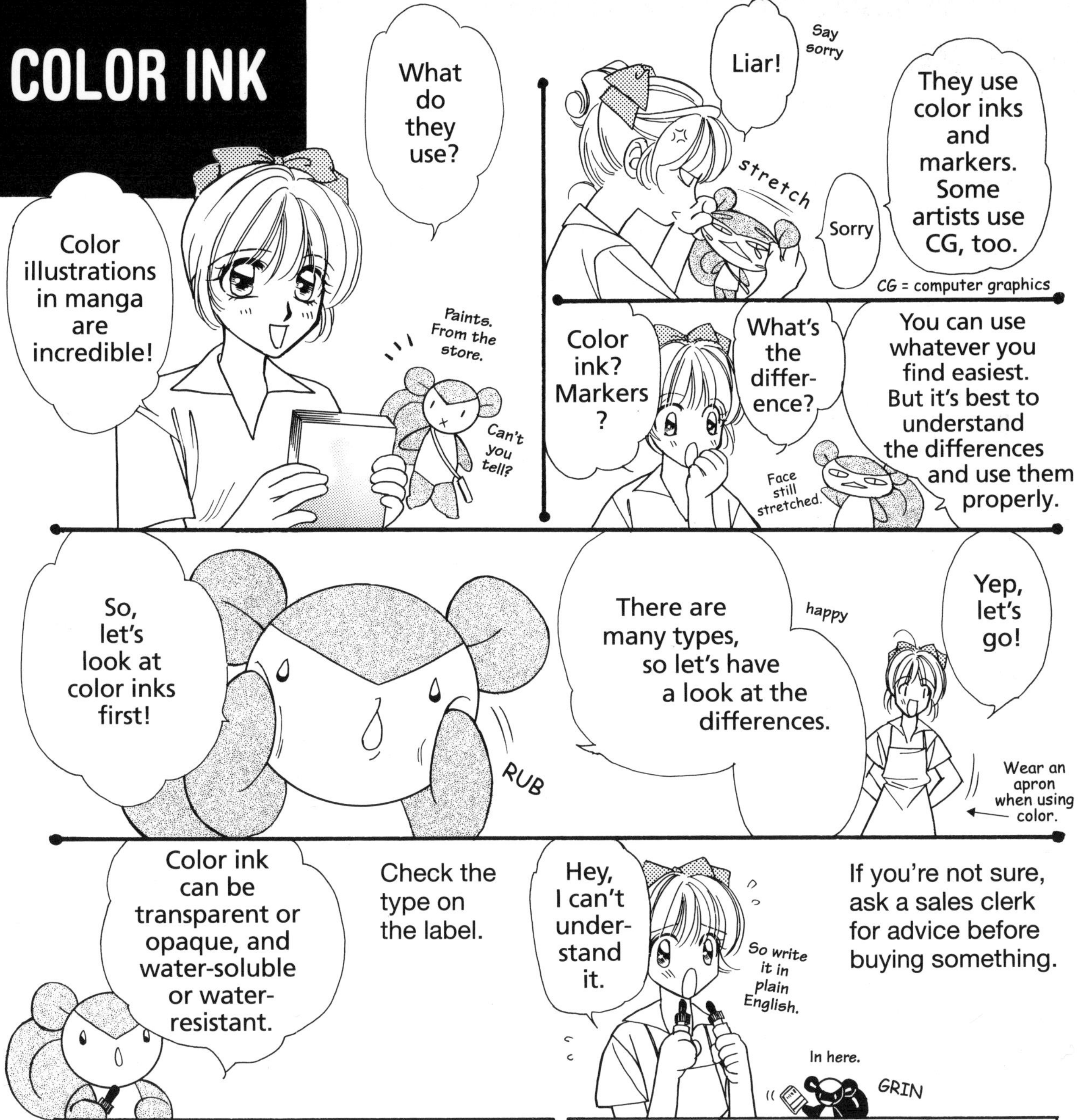
Color illustrations in manga are incredible!
What do they use?
Paints. From the store.
Can't you tell?
Liar!
Say sorry
stretch
Sorry
They use color inks and markers. Some artists use CG, too.
CG = computer graphics
Color ink? Markers?
What's the differ-ence?
You can use whatever you find easiest. But it's best to understand the differences and use them properly.
Face still stretched.
So, let's look at color inks first!
RUB
There are many types, so let's have a look at the differences.
happy
Yep, let's go!
Wear an apron when using color.
Color ink can be transparent or opaque, and water-soluble or water-resistant.
Check the type on the label.
Hey, I can't under-stand it.
So write it in plain English.
If you're not sure, ask a sales clerk for advice before buying something.
In here.
GRIN

Transparent water colors
Bright, strong colors that allow colors and lines underneath to show through. You can adjust the color by diluting with water. These inks are often used for color manuscripts.

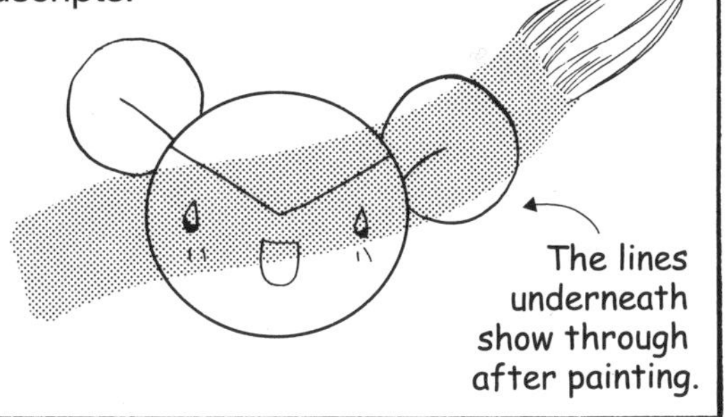
The lines underneath show through after painting.

Opaque water-based colors
Compared to transparent water colors, these inks have a matte effect, and do not allow the lines and colors underneath to show through.They can be mixed to create new colors.

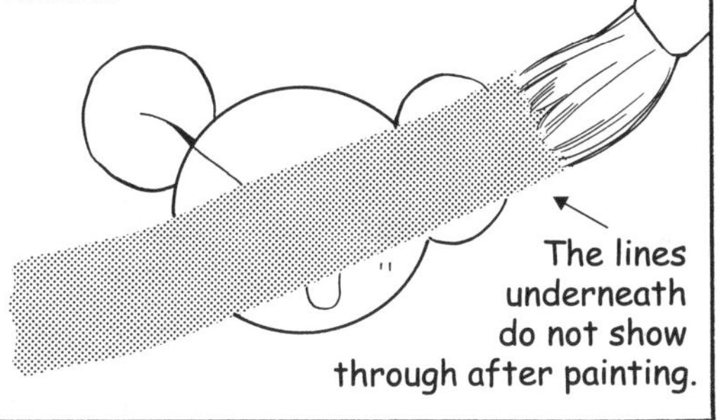
The lines underneath do not show through after painting.

Water-soluble (water-based) colors will still dissolve in water even after the ink has dried, so you can also create blurred effects. There's a wide range of colors, too.

Inks are further divided into dyes and pigments.

Shake pigments well before use.
That's helpful but...
There's so much...

Water-resistant colors do not dissolve in water after drying, so they are useful for painting layers of color. There are many opaque water-resistant colors.

Dyes
These are transparent bright, strong colors. There is a wide range of colors. However, dyes fade quickly when exposed to light. Bear this in mind when you store your work.

Pigments
There is a limited range of colors, but they don't fade quickly so are ideal for work you want to keep for a long time! The pigment base tends to settle in the bottle, so give it a good shake before use.

Waterproof means water-resistant.

Choose the ink that suits you.
Bring this along to help you when buying ink!
Look at the table below!
Confused ?

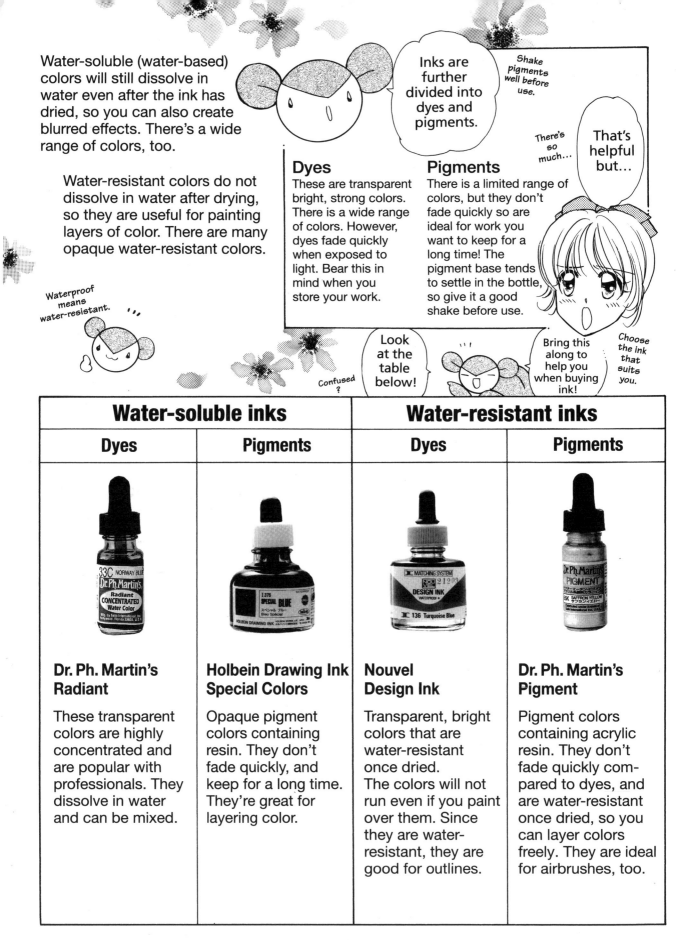

Water-soluble inks		Water-resistant inks	
Dyes	**Pigments**	**Dyes**	**Pigments**
Dr. Ph. Martin's Radiant These transparent colors are highly concentrated and are popular with professionals. They dissolve in water and can be mixed.	**Holbein Drawing Ink Special Colors** Opaque pigment colors containing resin. They don't fade quickly, and keep for a long time. They're great for layering color.	**Nouvel Design Ink** Transparent, bright colors that are water-resistant once dried. The colors will not run even if you paint over them. Since they are water-resistant, they are good for outlines.	**Dr. Ph. Martin's Pigment** Pigment colors containing acrylic resin. They don't fade quickly compared to dyes, and are water-resistant once dried, so you can layer colors freely. They are ideal for airbrushes, too.

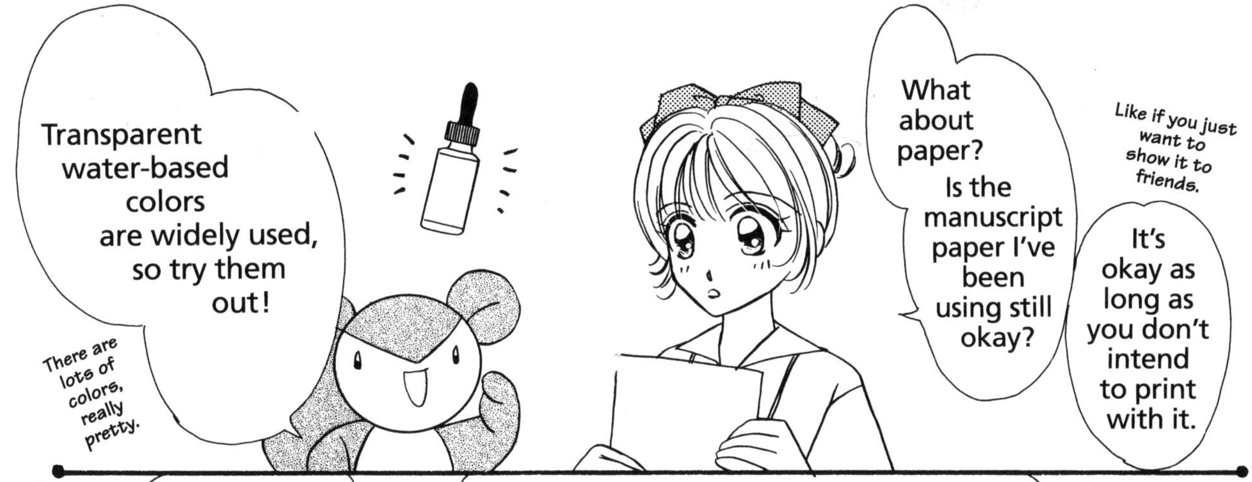
Transparent water-based colors are widely used, so try them out!
There are lots of colors, really pretty.
What about paper? Is the manuscript paper I've been using still okay?
Like if you just want to show it to friends.
It's okay as long as you don't intend to print with it.

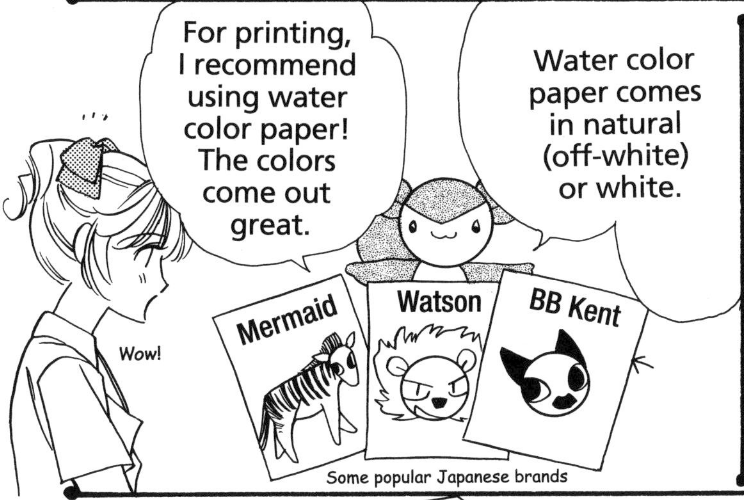
For printing, I recommend using water color paper! The colors come out great.
Water color paper comes in natural (off-white) or white.
Wow!
Mermaid
Watson
BB Kent
Some popular Japanese brands

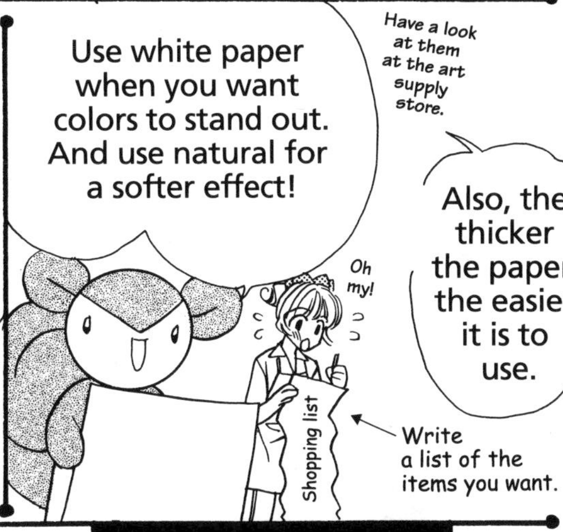
Use white paper when you want colors to stand out. And use natural for a softer effect!
Have a look at them at the art supply store.
Also, the thicker the paper, the easier it is to use.
Oh my!
Shopping list
Write a list of the items you want.

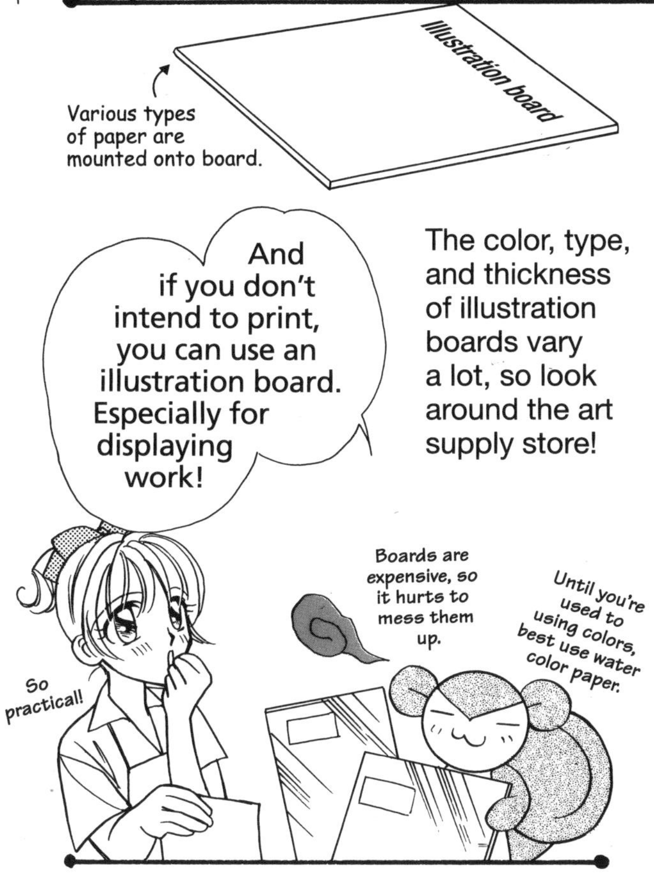
Illustration board
Various types of paper are mounted onto board.
And if you don't intend to print, you can use an illustration board. Especially for displaying work!
The color, type, and thickness of illustration boards vary a lot, so look around the art supply store!
Boards are expensive, so it hurts to mess them up.
Until you're used to using colors, best use water color paper.
So practical!

ESSENTIAL COLORING KIT

- Color inks
- Paper, e.g. water color paper, illustration board
- Brush for water colors
- Palette
- Water cup (for cleaning brushes)
- Towel or tissue (for wiping brushes)
- Test paper (of similar quality to your working paper)
- Tools for inking in outlines

Other useful items

- Light box tracer
- Paper stretching board
- Paper stretching tape
- Stapler
- Tracing paper
- Old clothes or apron to wear when painting

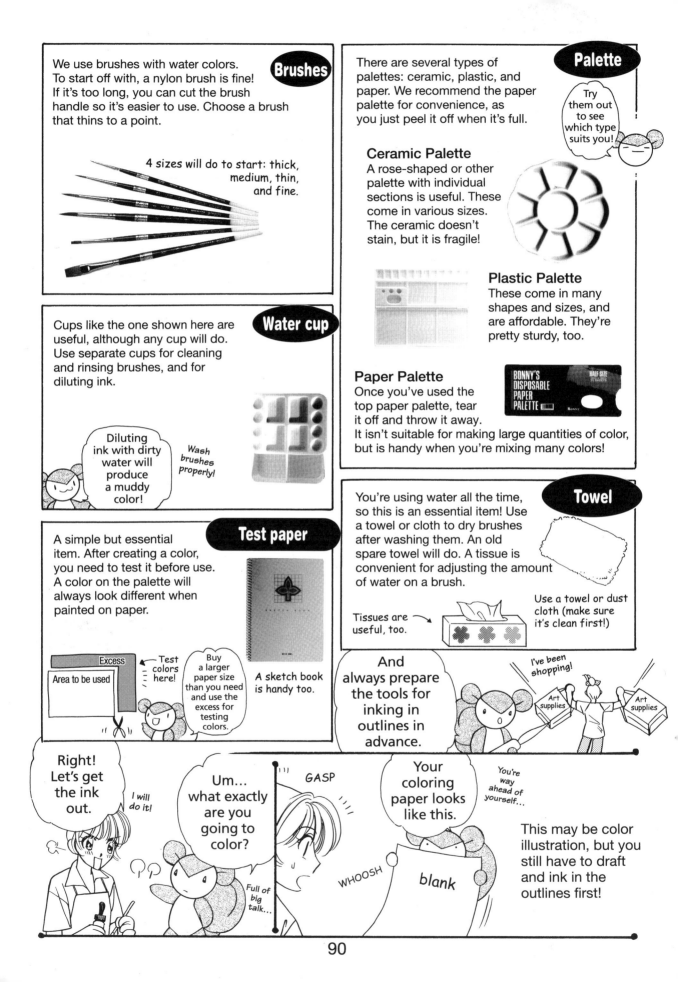

Brushes

We use brushes with water colors. To start off with, a nylon brush is fine! If it's too long, you can cut the brush handle so it's easier to use. Choose a brush that thins to a point.

4 sizes will do to start: thick, medium, thin, and fine.

Palette

There are several types of palettes: ceramic, plastic, and paper. We recommend the paper palette for convenience, as you just peel it off when it's full.

Try them out to see which type suits you!

Ceramic Palette
A rose-shaped or other palette with individual sections is useful. These come in various sizes. The ceramic doesn't stain, but it is fragile!

Plastic Palette
These come in many shapes and sizes, and are affordable. They're pretty sturdy, too.

Paper Palette
Once you've used the top paper palette, tear it off and throw it away.

BONNY'S
DISPOSABLE
PAPER
PALETTE
HALF SIZE

It isn't suitable for making large quantities of color, but is handy when you're mixing many colors!

Water cup

Cups like the one shown here are useful, although any cup will do. Use separate cups for cleaning and rinsing brushes, and for diluting ink.

Diluting ink with dirty water will produce a muddy color!
Wash brushes properly!

Towel

You're using water all the time, so this is an essential item! Use a towel or cloth to dry brushes after washing them. An old spare towel will do. A tissue is convenient for adjusting the amount of water on a brush.

Tissues are useful, too.

Use a towel or dust cloth (make sure it's clean first!)

Test paper

A simple but essential item. After creating a color, you need to test it before use. A color on the palette will always look different when painted on paper.

A sketch book is handy too.

Excess
Area to be used
Test colors here!
Buy a larger paper size than you need and use the excess for testing colors.

And always prepare the tools for inking in outlines in advance.
I've been shopping!
Art supplies
Art supplies

Right! Let's get the ink out.
I will do it!
Um... what exactly are you going to color?
Full of big talk...

GASP
Your coloring paper looks like this.
You're way ahead of yourself...
WHOOSH
blank
This may be color illustration, but you still have to draft and ink in the outlines first!

STEPS IN COLOR ILLUSTRATION

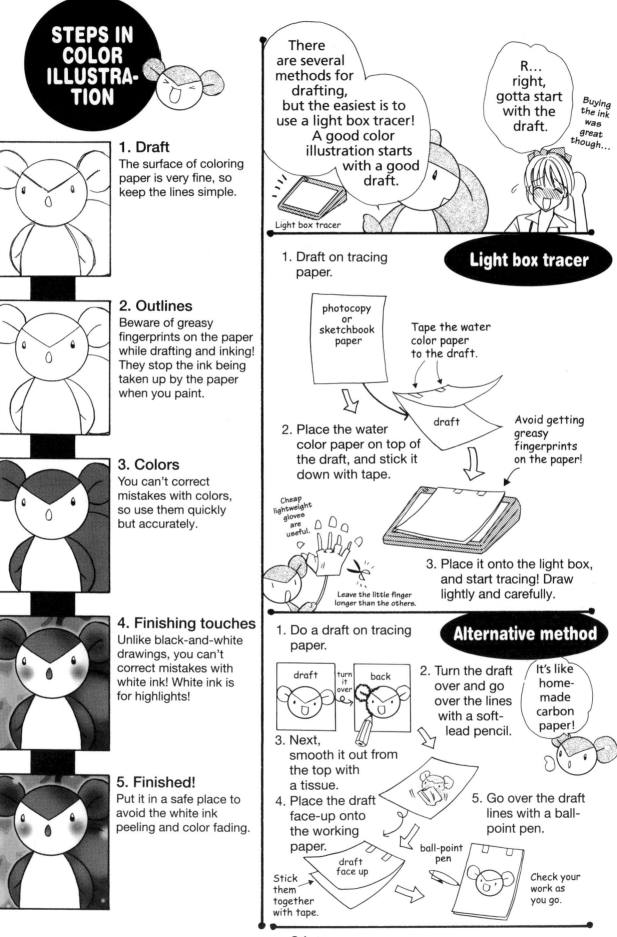

1. Draft
The surface of coloring paper is very fine, so keep the lines simple.

2. Outlines
Beware of greasy fingerprints on the paper while drafting and inking! They stop the ink being taken up by the paper when you paint.

3. Colors
You can't correct mistakes with colors, so use them quickly but accurately.

4. Finishing touches
Unlike black-and-white drawings, you can't correct mistakes with white ink! White ink is for highlights!

5. Finished!
Put it in a safe place to avoid the white ink peeling and color fading.

There are several methods for drafting, but the easiest is to use a light box tracer! A good color illustration starts with a good draft.

R... right, gotta start with the draft.

Buying the ink was great though...

Light box tracer

Light box tracer

1. Draft on tracing paper.

photocopy or sketchbook paper

Tape the water color paper to the draft.

draft

2. Place the water color paper on top of the draft, and stick it down with tape.

Avoid getting greasy fingerprints on the paper!

Cheap lightweight gloves are useful.

Leave the little finger longer than the others.

3. Place it onto the light box, and start tracing! Draw lightly and carefully.

Alternative method

1. Do a draft on tracing paper.

draft — turn it over → back

2. Turn the draft over and go over the lines with a soft-lead pencil.

It's like home-made carbon paper!

3. Next, smooth it out from the top with a tissue.

4. Place the draft face-up onto the working paper.

Stick them together with tape.

draft face up

5. Go over the draft lines with a ball-point pen.

ball-point pen

Check your work as you go.

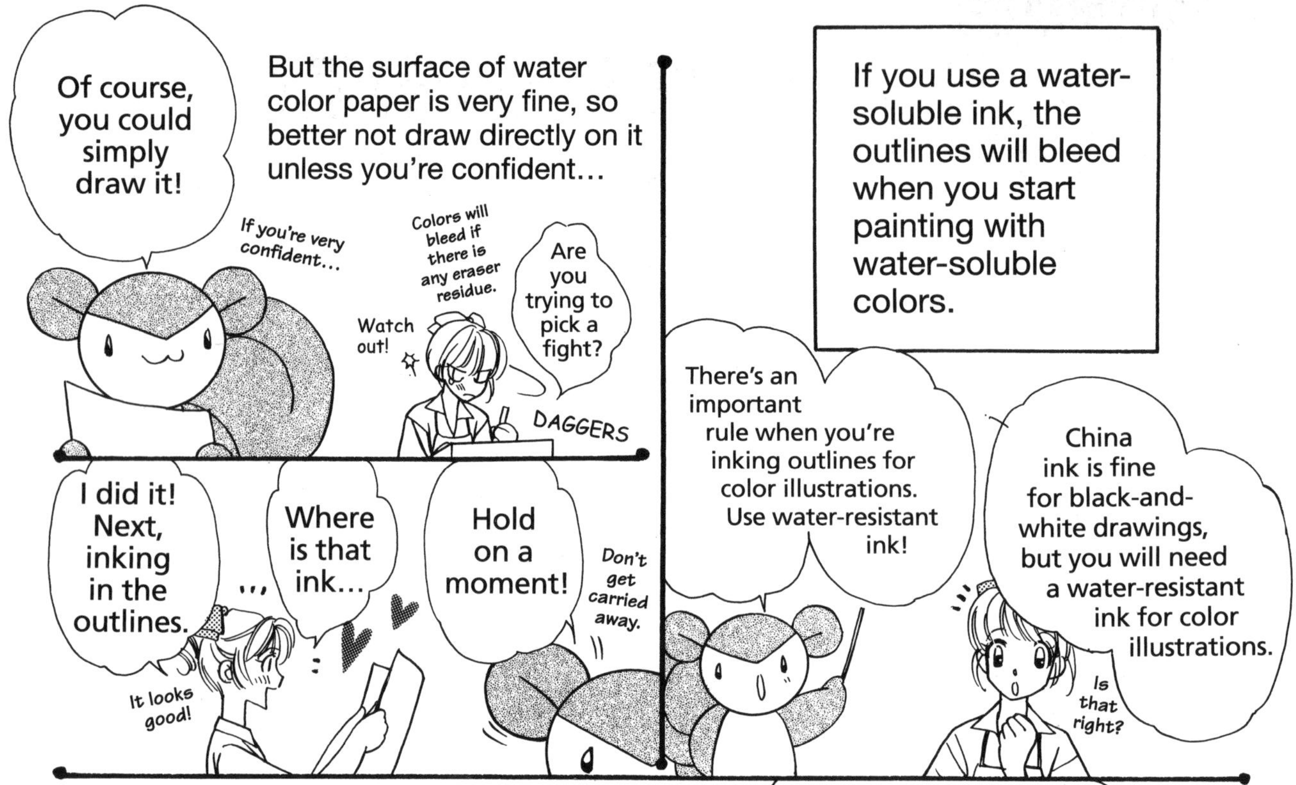
Of course, you could simply draw it!
But the surface of water color paper is very fine, so better not draw directly on it unless you're confident…
If you're very confident…
Colors will bleed if there is any eraser residue.
Watch out!
Are you trying to pick a fight?
DAGGERS
I did it! Next, inking in the outlines.
It looks good!
…
Where is that ink…
Hold on a moment!
Don't get carried away.
If you use a water-soluble ink, the outlines will bleed when you start painting with water-soluble colors.
There's an important rule when you're inking outlines for color illustrations. Use water-resistant ink!
China ink is fine for black-and-white drawings, but you will need a water-resistant ink for color illustrations.
Is that right?

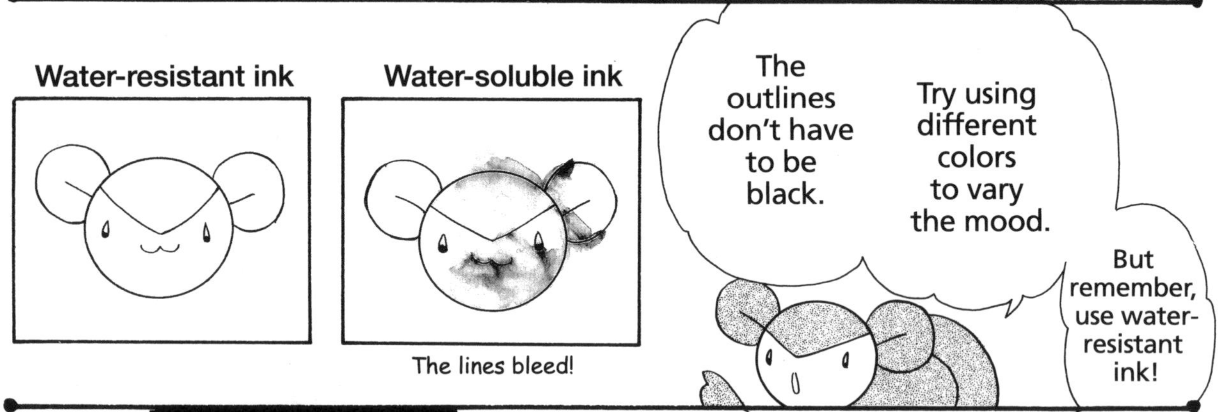
Water-resistant ink
Water-soluble ink
The lines bleed!
The outlines don't have to be black.
Try using different colors to vary the mood.
But remember, use water-resistant ink!

FOR OUTLINES

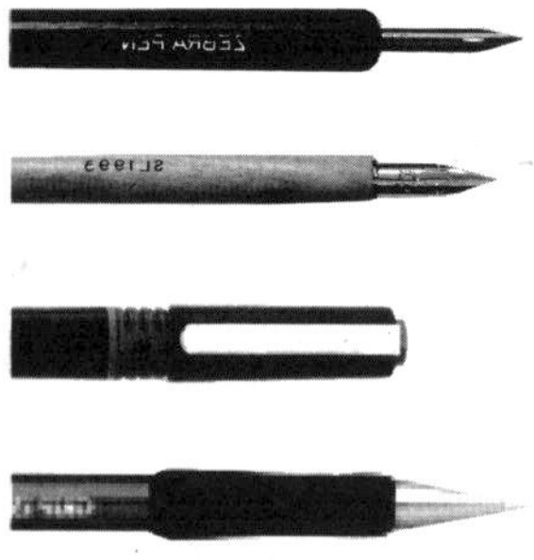

Normal pen nibs or water-resistant ink drawing pens are fine.

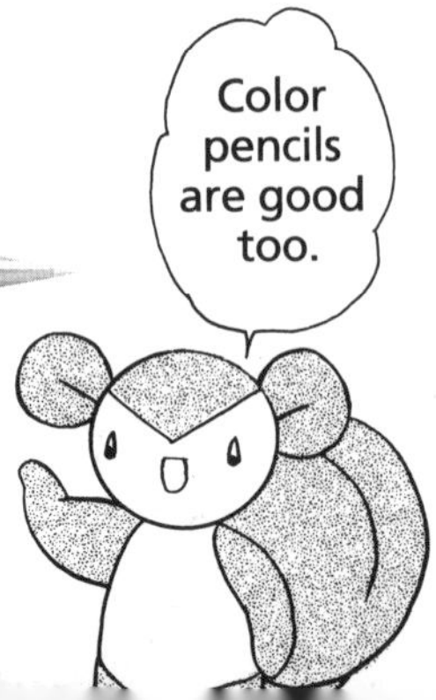
Color pencils are good too.

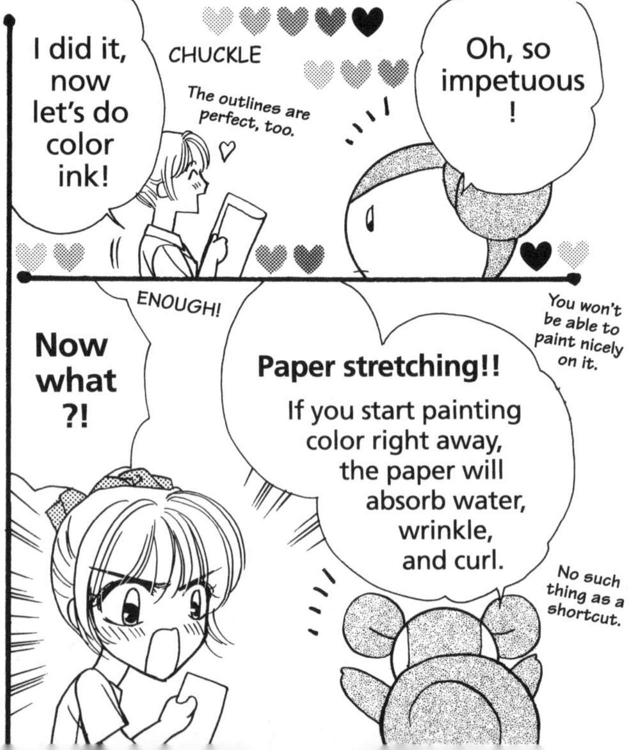
I did it, now let's do color ink!
CHUCKLE
The outlines are perfect, too.
Oh, so impetuous!
ENOUGH!
Now what?!
Paper stretching!!
If you start painting color right away, the paper will absorb water, wrinkle, and curl.
You won't be able to paint nicely on it.
No such thing as a shortcut.

PAPER STRETCHING KIT

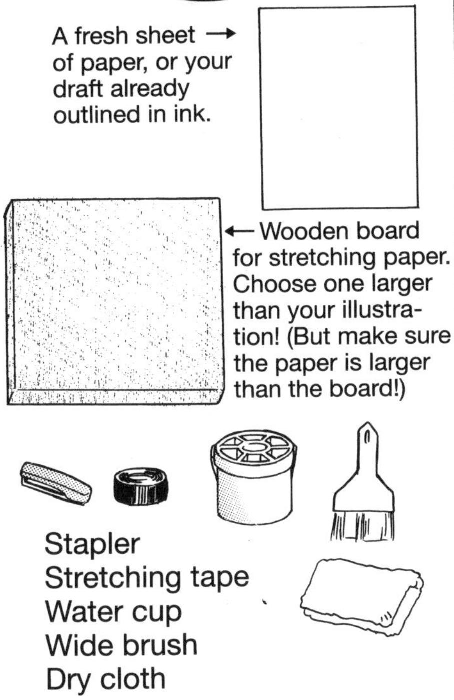
A fresh sheet of paper, or your draft already outlined in ink.
Wooden board for stretching paper. Choose one larger than your illustration! (But make sure the paper is larger than the board!)
Stapler
Stretching tape
Water cup
Wide brush
Dry cloth

Method

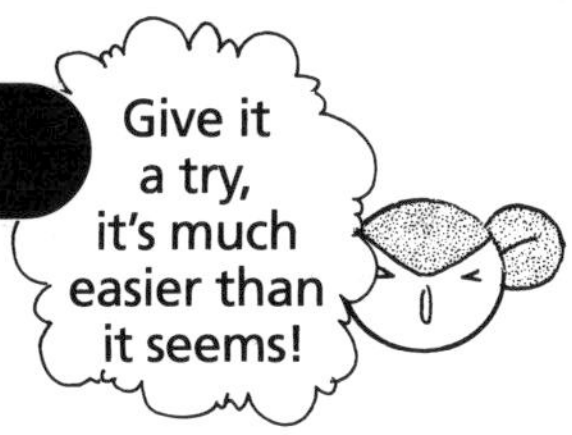
Give it a try, it's much easier than it seems!

1. Brush water onto the back of the paper. Spread a good amount of water evenly until the paper stops absorbing it.

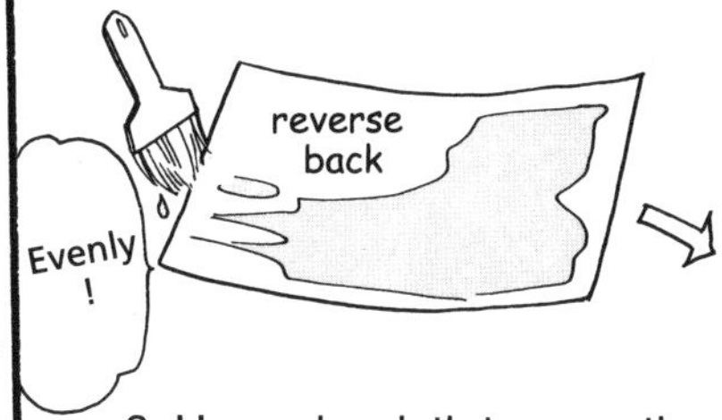
Evenly !
reverse back

2. Turn the paper over and put the wet side face down onto the panel.

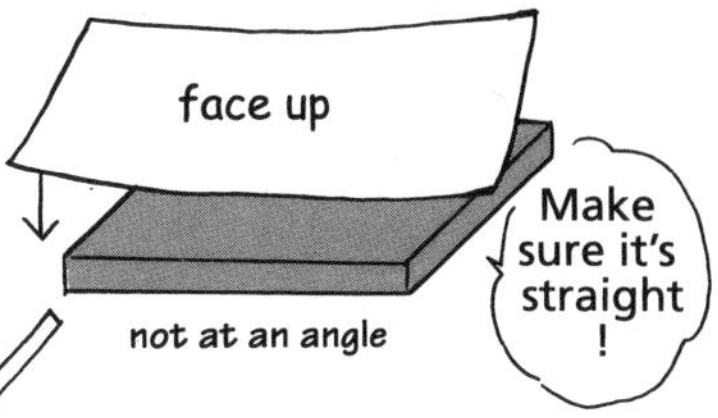
face up
Make sure it's straight !
not at an angle

3. Use a dry cloth to smooth out the paper from the center toward the edges to get rid of any air bubbles.

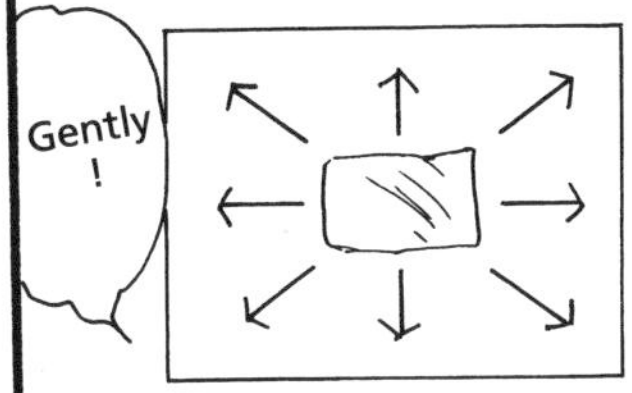
Gently !

4. Fold over the edges and staple.

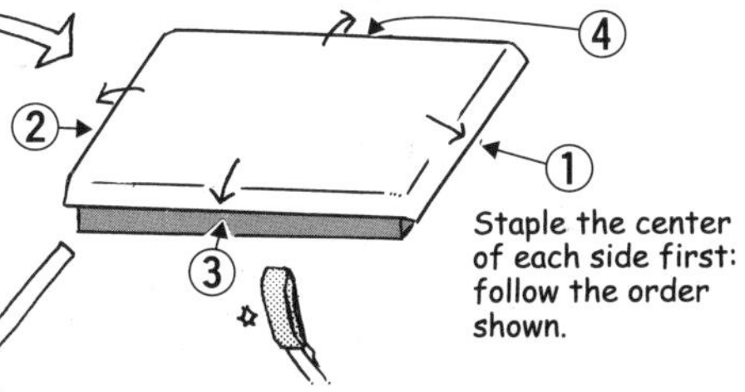
4
2
1
3
Staple the center of each side first: follow the order shown.

5. Next fold the corners down, and staple.

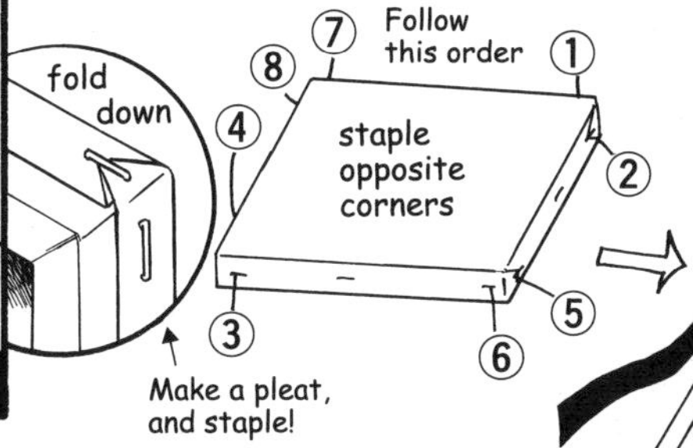
fold down
Follow this order
7
8
1
4
2
staple opposite corners
3
6
5
Make a pleat, and staple!

6. Cut some paper-stretching tape to the right length, and wet it with water while sticking it around the edge.

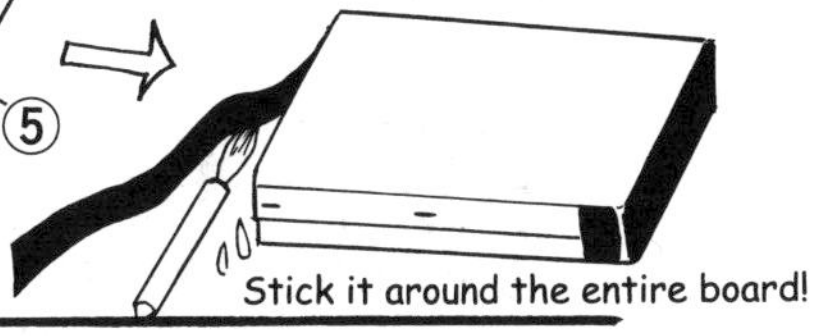
Stick it around the entire board!

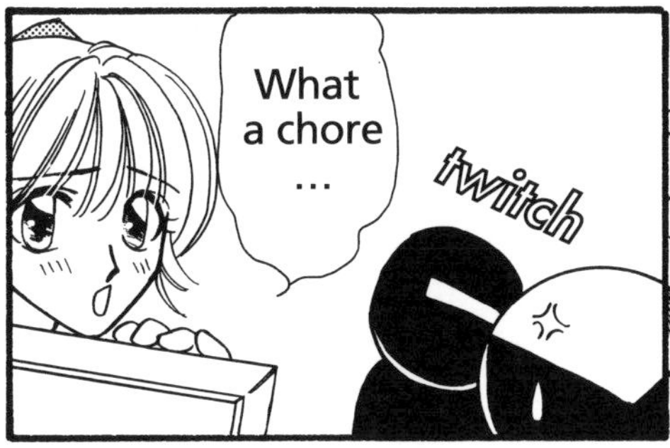
What a chore ...
twitch

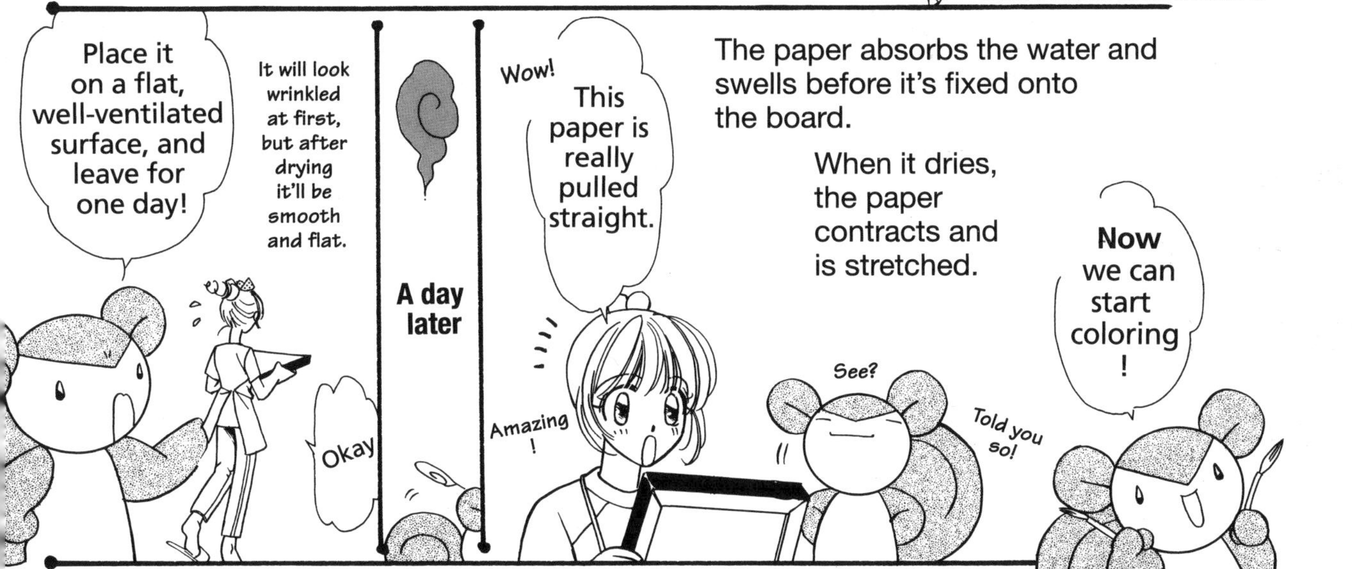
Place it on a flat, well-ventilated surface, and leave for one day!
It will look wrinkled at first, but after drying it'll be smooth and flat.
Okay
A day later
Wow!
This paper is really pulled straight.
Amazing !
The paper absorbs the water and swells before it's fixed onto the board.
When it dries, the paper contracts and is stretched.
See?
Told you so!
Now we can start coloring !

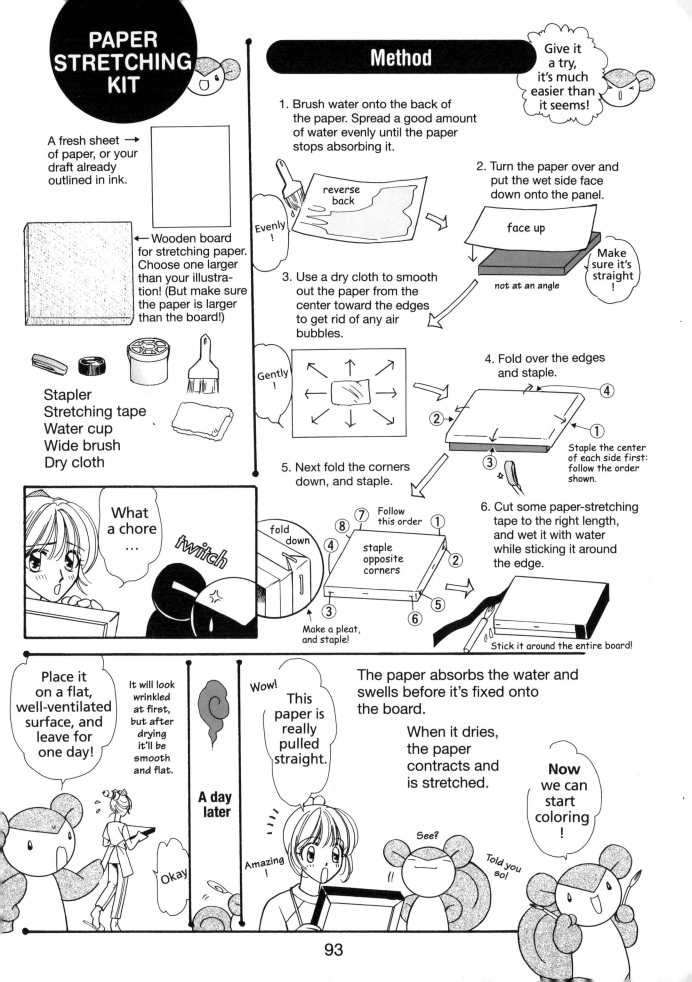

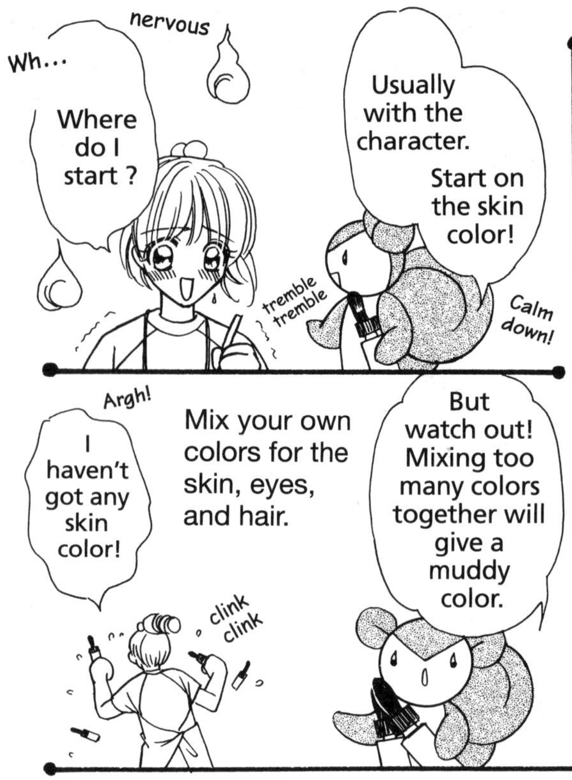
nervous
Wh... Where do I start ?
Usually with the character.
Start on the skin color!
tremble tremble
Calm down!
Argh! I haven't got any skin color!
Mix your own colors for the skin, eyes, and hair.
But watch out! Mixing too many colors together will give a muddy color.
clink clink

Try mixing colors until you create one you like. Make a note of the recipe so you won't forget it!

Write down the number of parts used for each ink color! And note who or what it's for.

Skin color (for Mei)
- Orange 1 part
- Brown 1/2 part
- Yellow 2 parts
- Pink 1/4 part

Hair color (for Mei)
- Brown 2 parts
- Orange 1 part
- Blue— a dab

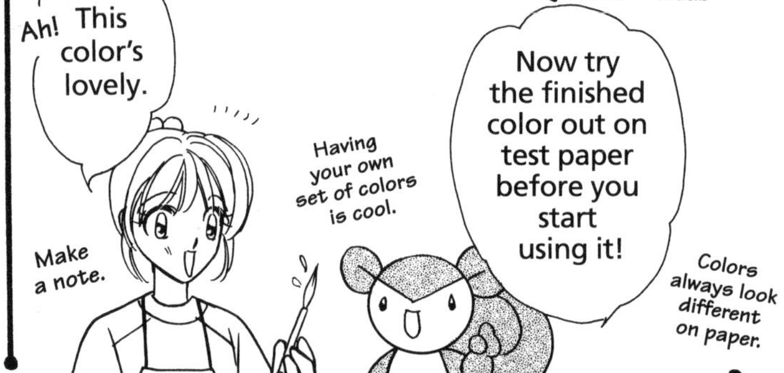
Ah! This color's lovely.
Make a note.
Having your own set of colors is cool.
Now try the finished color out on test paper before you start using it!
Colors always look different on paper.

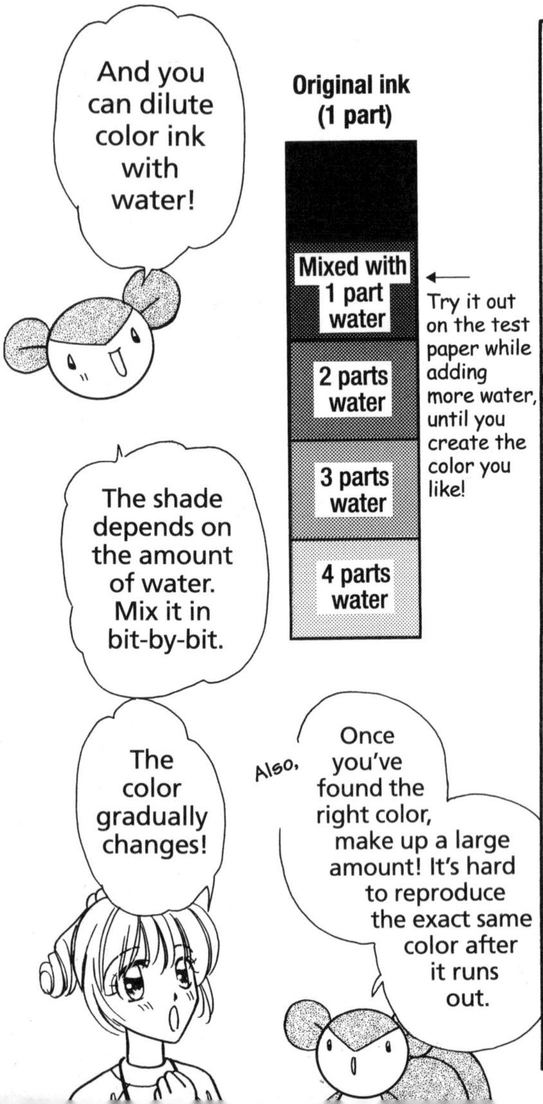
And you can dilute color ink with water!
Original ink (1 part)
Mixed with 1 part water
2 parts water
3 parts water
4 parts water
Try it out on the test paper while adding more water, until you create the color you like!
The shade depends on the amount of water. Mix it in bit-by-bit.
The color gradually changes!
Also, Once you've found the right color, make up a large amount! It's hard to reproduce the exact same color after it runs out.

Painting with color!

1. Brush water over the area you wish to color. Be accurate: don't dampen areas not for coloring. And don't soak the paper with too much water.

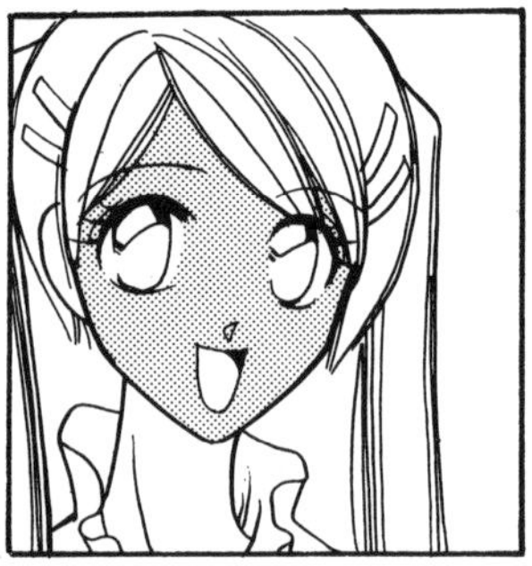

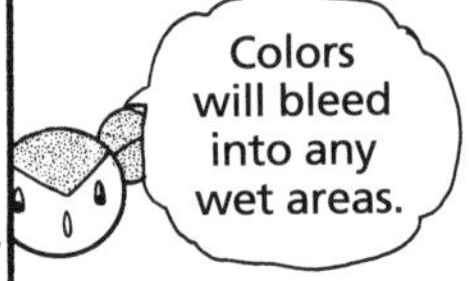
Colors will bleed into any wet areas.

2. Paint the prepared color on lightly before the surface dries. Moisten the brush with a small amount of water. Start with a light shade! Keep checking the result as you paint.

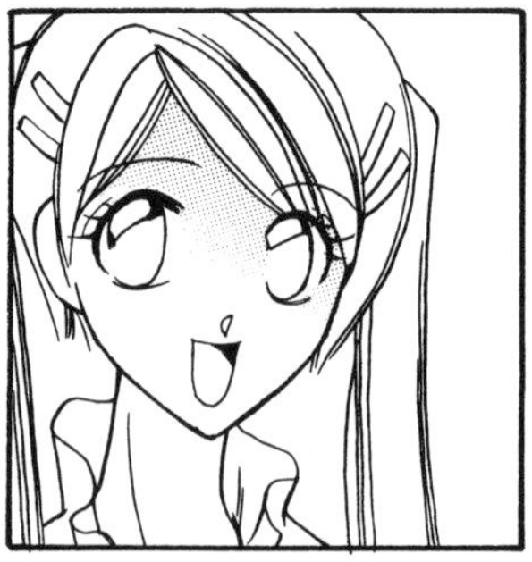

3. Before it dries, start layering color onto the areas where you want rich color, or dark areas of shading. Add layers of the same color and it will darken naturally!

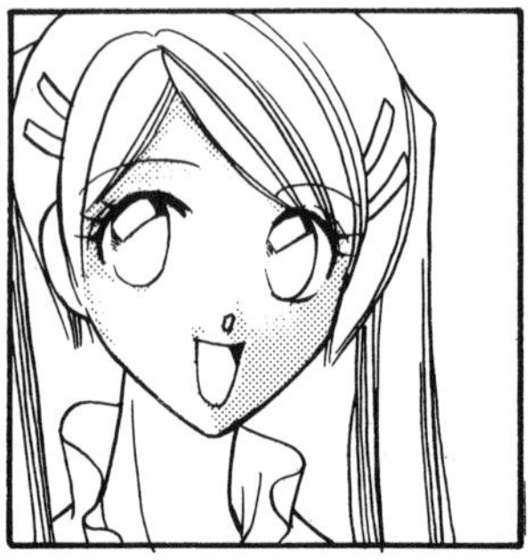

If the color turns too dark, gently press down onto it with a tissue neatly folded into four. But don't try to rub it!

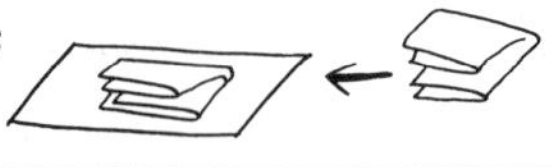
Gently press down and peel it off!

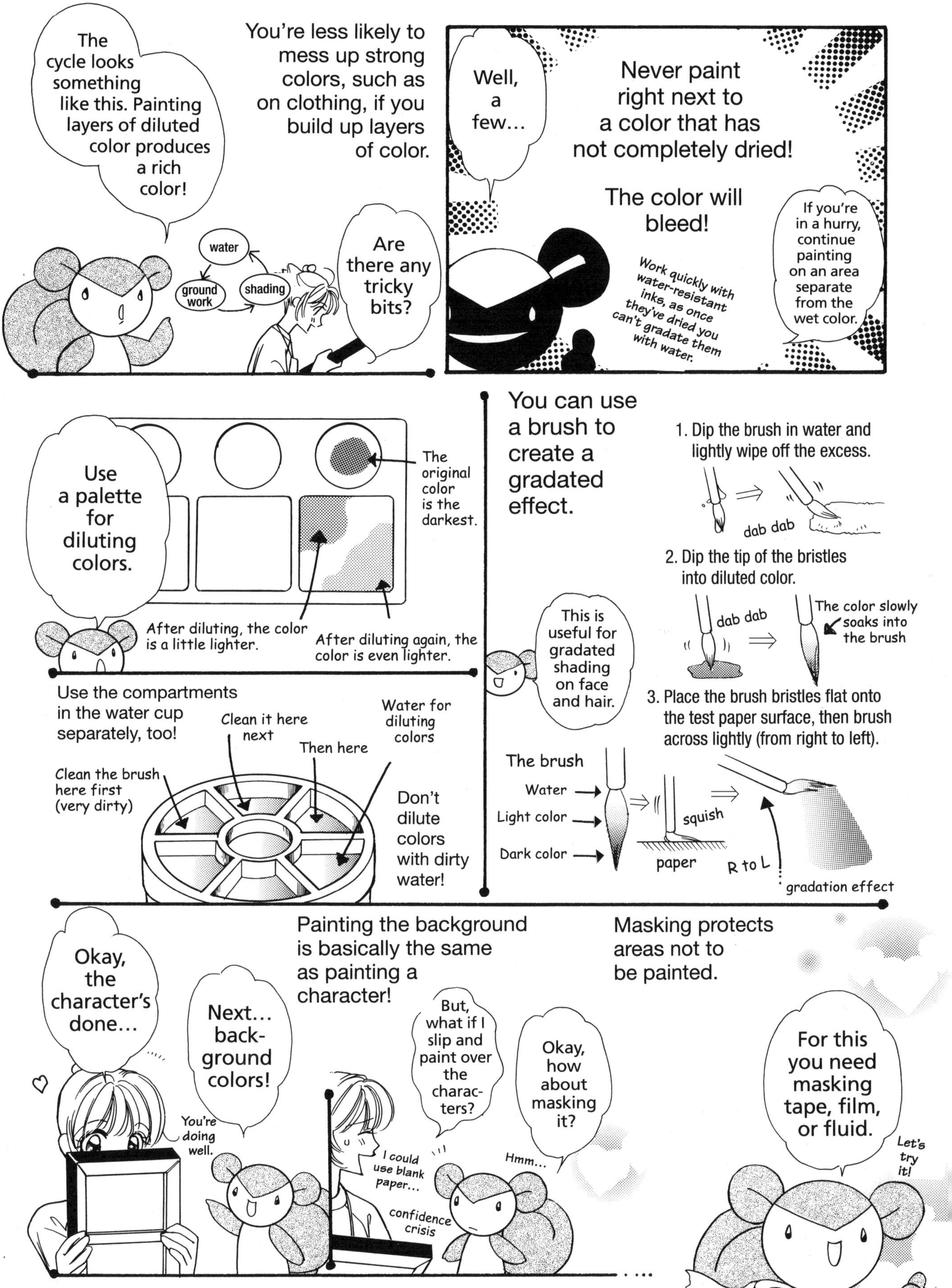

The cycle looks something like this. Painting layers of diluted color produces a rich color!
water
shading
ground work
You're less likely to mess up strong colors, such as on clothing, if you build up layers of color.
Are there any tricky bits?
Well, a few…
Never paint right next to a color that has not completely dried!
The color will bleed!
Work quickly with water-resistant inks, as once they've dried you can't gradate them with water.
If you're in a hurry, continue painting on an area separate from the wet color.
Use a palette for diluting colors.
The original color is the darkest.
After diluting, the color is a little lighter.
After diluting again, the color is even lighter.
Use the compartments in the water cup separately, too!
Clean the brush here first (very dirty)
Clean it here next
Then here
Water for diluting colors
Don't dilute colors with dirty water!
You can use a brush to create a gradated effect.
1. Dip the brush in water and lightly wipe off the excess.
dab dab
2. Dip the tip of the bristles into diluted color.
dab dab
The color slowly soaks into the brush
This is useful for gradated shading on face and hair.
3. Place the brush bristles flat onto the test paper surface, then brush across lightly (from right to left).
The brush
Water
Light color
Dark color
squish
paper
R to L
gradation effect
Okay, the character's done…
Next… back-ground colors!
You're doing well.
Painting the background is basically the same as painting a character!
But, what if I slip and paint over the charac-ters?
I could use blank paper…
confidence crisis
Okay, how about masking it?
Hmm…
Masking protects areas not to be painted.
For this you need masking tape, film, or fluid.
Let's try it!

Masking tape and film

1. Apply tape or film to the area you want to protect. Cover a larger area than you need to.

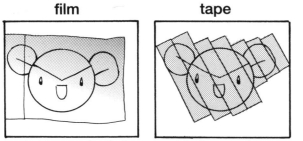

film
tape

Don't press too hard when you stick the tape down, or it will rip the paper when you peel it off! Press down only around the edges to avoid air bubbles.

2. Cut lightly around the shape you want to protect using a snap-off blade cutter. Be careful not to cut the paper underneath!

Air bubble
Masking tape
Paper
cross section

Ink will bleed into the masked area through air bubbles like this. Don't leave creases when sticking the tape down.

3. Now start painting around the masking. Wait until the colors are dry before peeling off the tape.

Peel the tape off slowly and gently.
Peel too quickly and you'll rip the paper!
Film and tape are not suitable for masking fine detail.

Masking fluid

1. Dip your brush or pen into the masking fluid and paint over the area you want to protect.

Masking fluid can't be used with some color inks or papers, so always check the label first.

2. Wait until the masking fluid is dry before starting to paint. Once the illustration is dry, masking fluid can be removed with a special cleaner, or peeled off, depending on the type.

Don't rub too hard with the cleaner.

Masking fluid is not suitable for large areas.
So tape and film are for big areas, and masking fluid is for small areas.
I see...

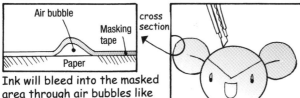

And if you prefer not to use an adhesive mask on your work…
Make the template smaller than the area it's masking.

1. If you don't like sticking film and tape onto your work, you can mask it with a paper template.

2. Place the template over the area and stick tape or film over it.

Template
Masking tape
Paper

cross-section

3. Remove the excess tape, and paint the background!

Illustration
Template

The template is smaller than the picture.

Stick masking tape or film over it.

Press the edges of the tape down firmly.

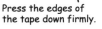

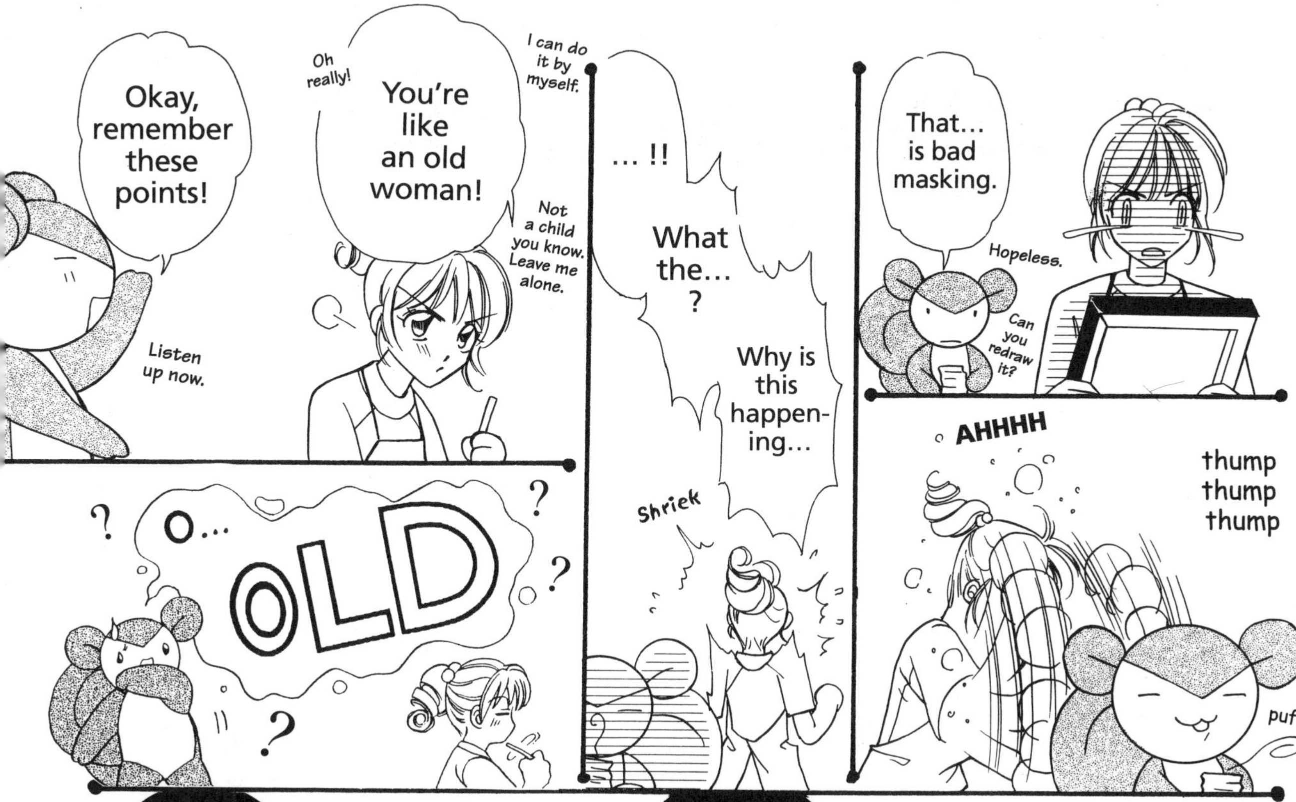
Okay, remember these points!
Listen up now.
Oh really!
You're like an old woman!
I can do it by myself.
Not a child you know. Leave me alone.
O...
OLD
... !!
What the...?
Why is this happening...
Shriek
That... is bad masking.
Hopeless.
Can you redraw it?
AHHHH
thump thump thump
puff

KEY POINT 1

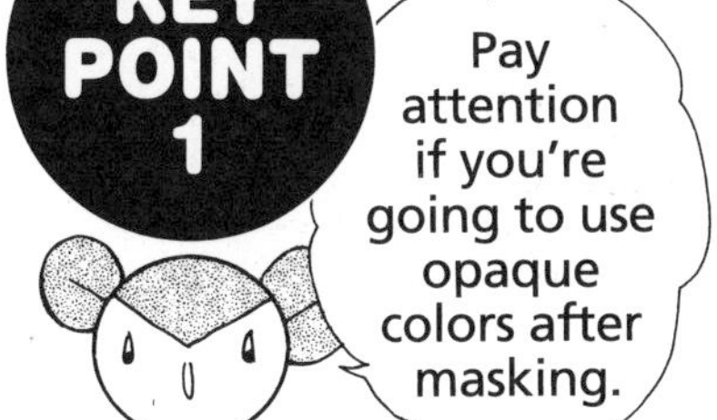
Pay attention if you're going to use opaque colors after masking.

1. If you paint opaque colors onto this masking...

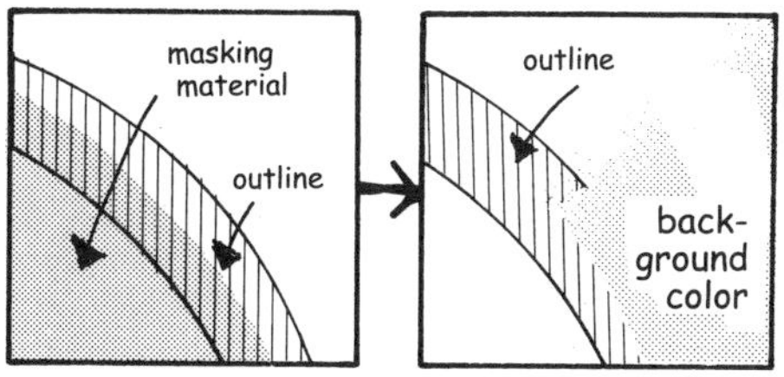
masking material
outline
outline
back-ground color

...they will erase part of the outline.

2. You can prevent this by making sure you cut around the outside edge of the outline so that it is completely covered by the masking material.

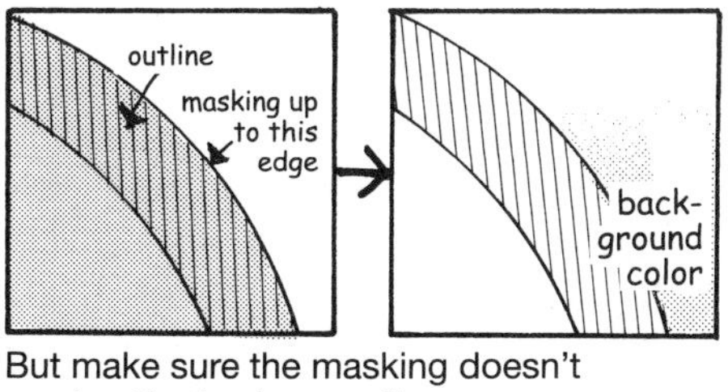
outline
masking up to this edge
back-ground color

But make sure the masking doesn't overlap the background!

KEY POINT 2

1. Take care when peeling off masking. Paper covered with masking looks like this...

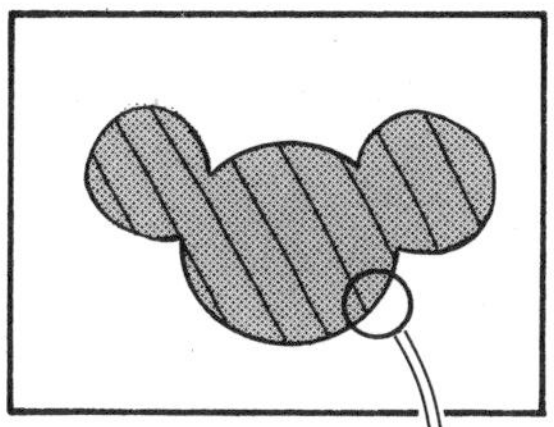

cross-section

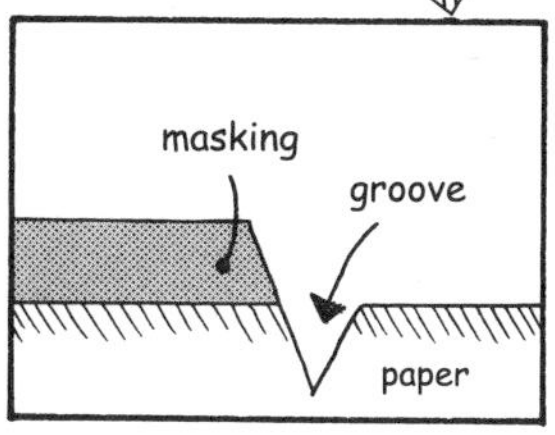
masking
groove
paper

When you cut the masking, the cutter makes a slight groove around the outline.

2. Peel from the edge like this and...

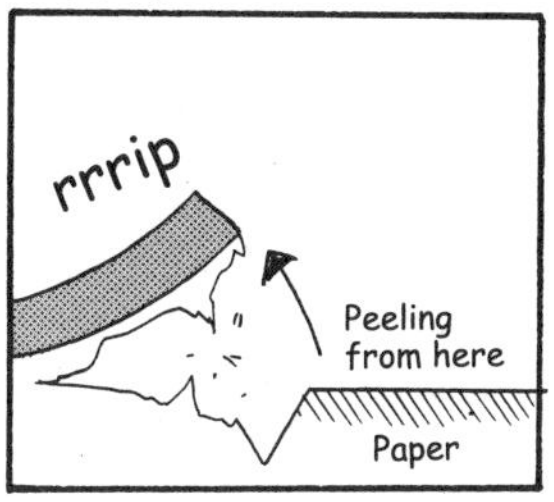
rrrip
Peeling from here
Paper

It will probably rip the paper off, too. Therefore...

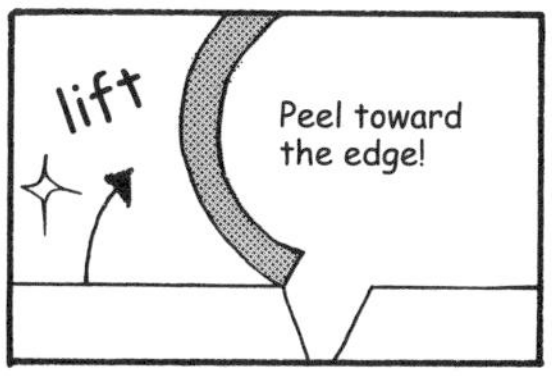
lift
Peel toward the edge!

...gently peel the masking off toward the groove instead.

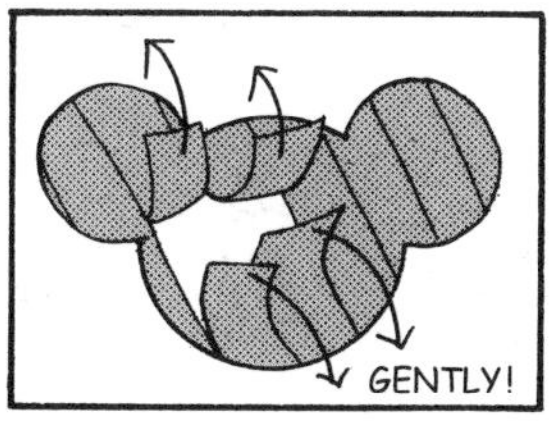
GENTLY!

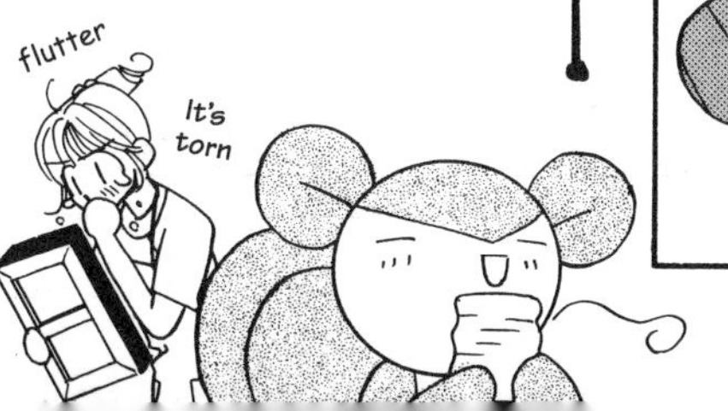
flutter
It's torn

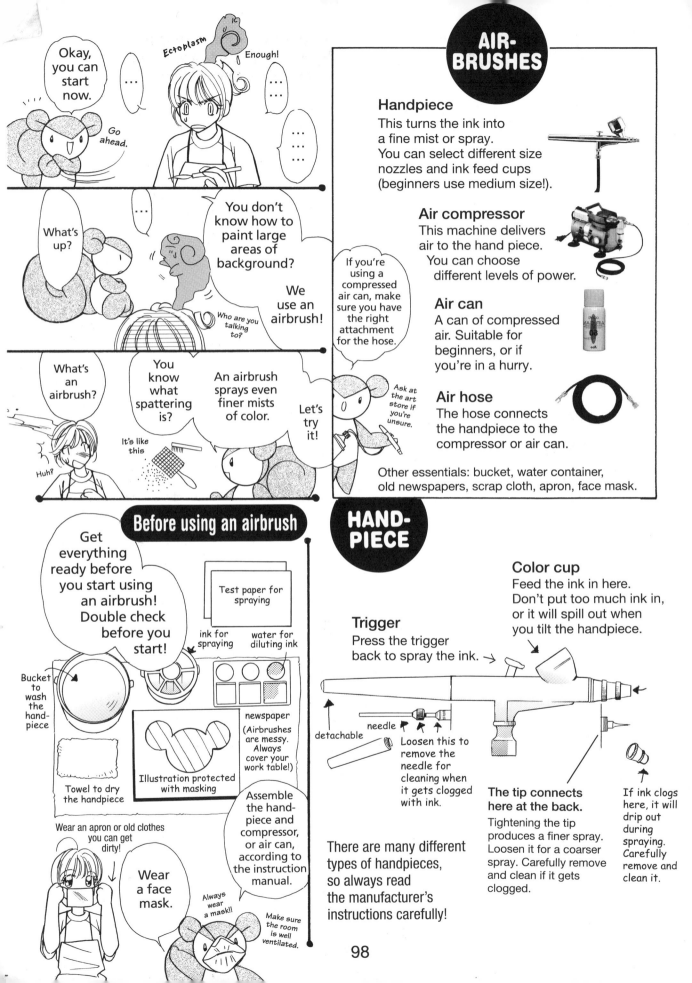

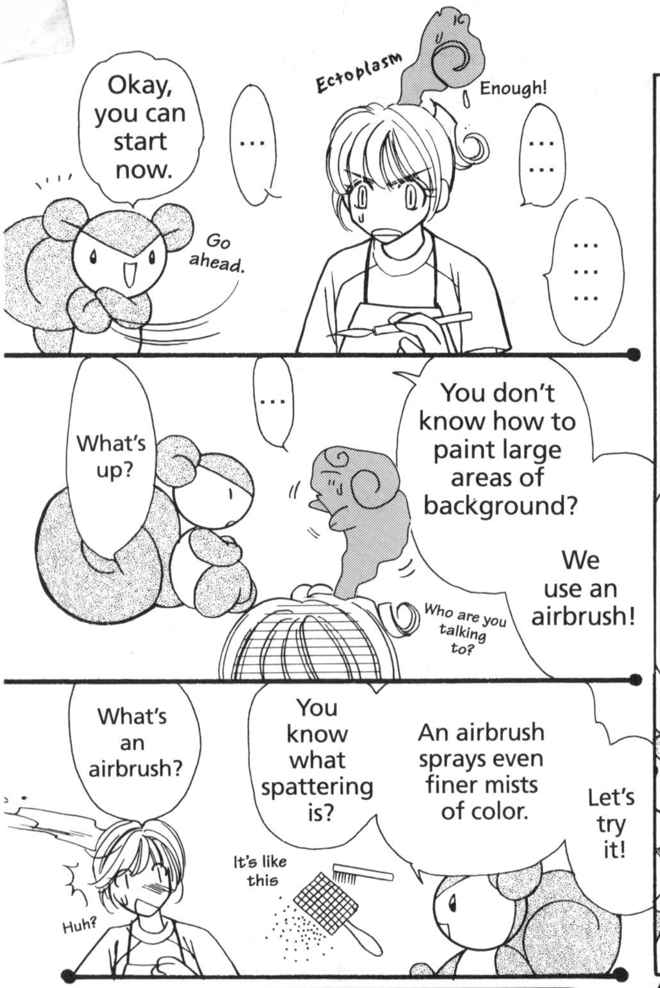
Okay, you can start now.
Go ahead.
...
Ectoplasm
Enough!
......
....
What's up?
...
You don't know how to paint large areas of background?
We use an airbrush!
Who are you talking to?
What's an airbrush?
Huh?
You know what spattering is?
It's like this
An airbrush sprays even finer mists of color.
Let's try it!

AIR-BRUSHES

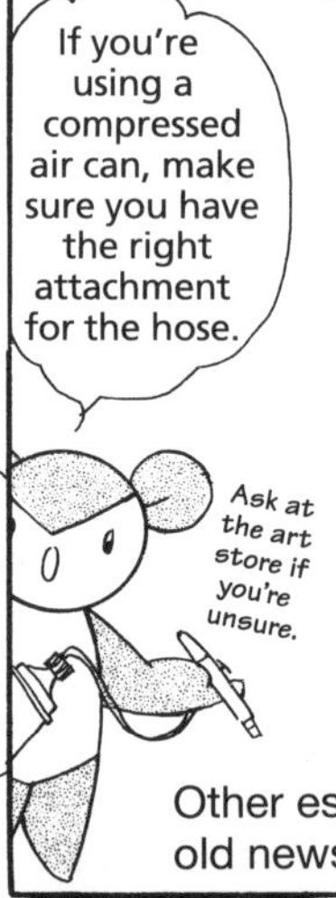
If you're using a compressed air can, make sure you have the right attachment for the hose.
Ask at the art store if you're unsure.

Handpiece

This turns the ink into a fine mist or spray. You can select different size nozzles and ink feed cups (beginners use medium size!).

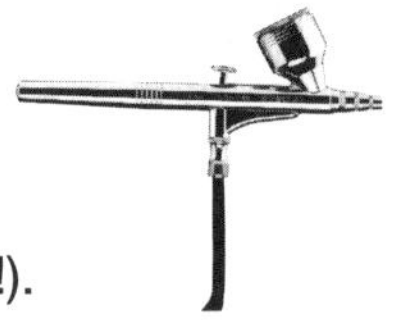

Air compressor

This machine delivers air to the hand piece. You can choose different levels of power.

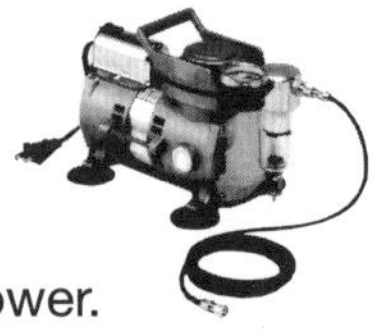

Air can

A can of compressed air. Suitable for beginners, or if you're in a hurry.

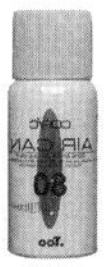

Air hose

The hose connects the handpiece to the compressor or air can.

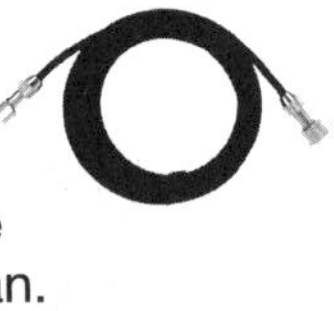

Other essentials: bucket, water container, old newspapers, scrap cloth, apron, face mask.

Before using an airbrush

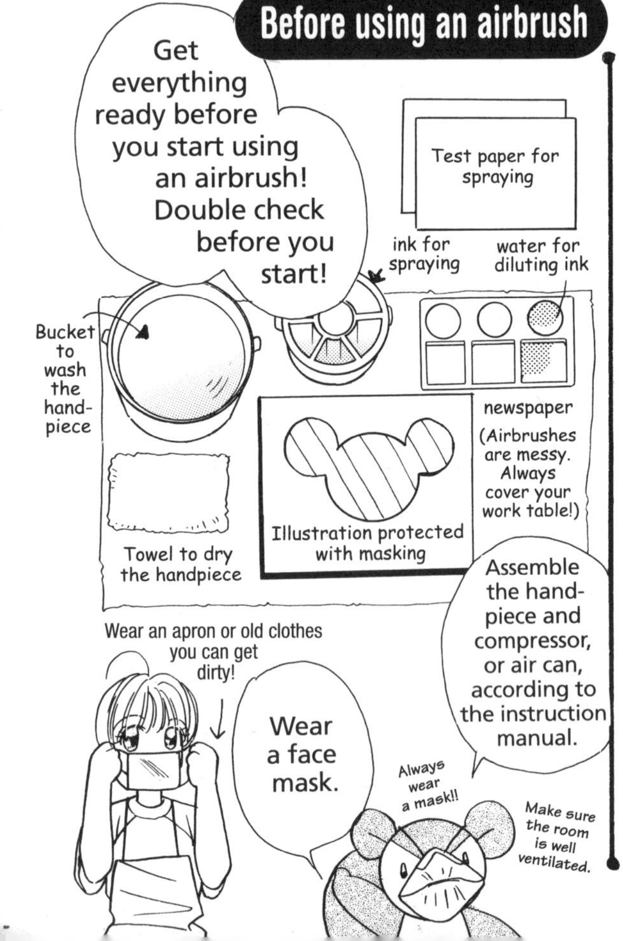
Get everything ready before you start using an airbrush! Double check before you start!
Test paper for spraying
ink for spraying
water for diluting ink
Bucket to wash the hand-piece
newspaper (Airbrushes are messy. Always cover your work table!)
Towel to dry the handpiece
Illustration protected with masking
Assemble the hand-piece and compressor, or air can, according to the instruction manual.
Wear an apron or old clothes you can get dirty!
Wear a face mask.
Always wear a mask!!
Make sure the room is well ventilated.

HAND-PIECE

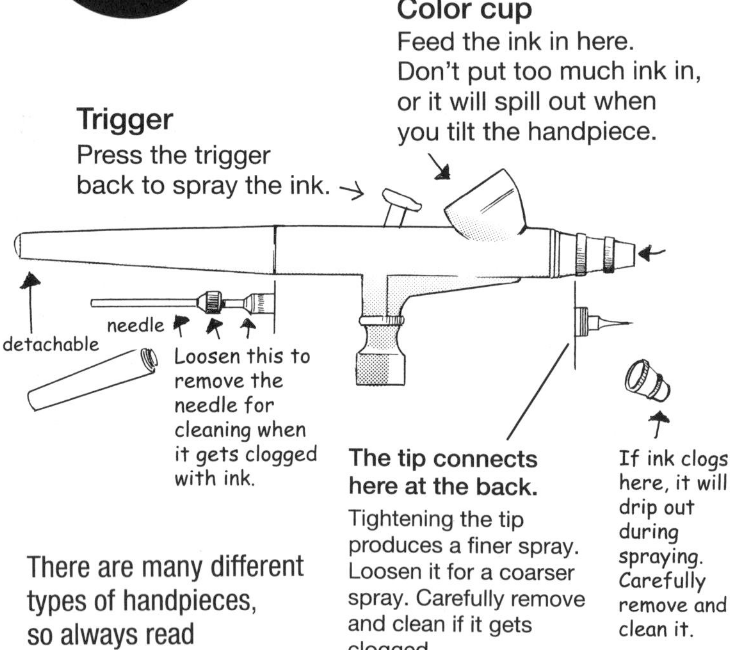
Color cup
Feed the ink in here. Don't put too much ink in, or it will spill out when you tilt the handpiece.
Trigger
Press the trigger back to spray the ink.
detachable
needle
Loosen this to remove the needle for cleaning when it gets clogged with ink.
The tip connects here at the back.
Tightening the tip produces a finer spray. Loosen it for a coarser spray. Carefully remove and clean if it gets clogged.
If ink clogs here, it will drip out during spraying. Carefully remove and clean it.

There are many different types of handpieces, so always read the manufacturer's instructions carefully!

Ink

When using an airbrush, prepare a larger amount of color than normal as it tends to run out quickly.
Keep it in several small containers.

Film cases are great for keeping ink in.

Dilute tube and acrylic paints into a smooth consistency, as handpieces clog up easily with thick paints!
Old paints clog up easily too.

Changing ink and cleaning the handpiece

Just splashing the handpiece about in a bucket or sink is not enough! Any ink left inside the handpiece will harden afterward, so it must be thoroughly flushed out!

1. Feed water into the color cup.

water

2. Press your finger over the nozzle while depressing the trigger.

depress
cover

3. This will force the air back through the color cup. Repeat 2–3 times, spray as normal, and repeat.

bubble bubble
As the ink is washed out, the water gets dirty.

4. Change the dirty water and repeat until the water stays clean.

Argh!
squirt
That's what happens when you don't press firmly on the nozzle.
And do it well away from your illustration!

How to use an airbrush

1. First, pour water into the color cup and do a test spray to make sure it's working properly!

Fill the color cup about half full with water.

Take care not to spray water onto your illustration!

2. Next, pour some ink into the color cup and test spray it on scrap paper.

pull back to release ink
2
1 depress
Make sure the water or ink doesn't clog up here!

Depressing the trigger releases air, and simultaneously pulling it back releases the ink.

3. If you like the color, start spraying it onto your illustration. To begin with, don't spray too close to the illustration.

If you tilt the handpiece too much, you'll spill the ink!

Spraying is easier if you tilt the illustration.

4. Use transparent inks when you want the different layers of color to show through, and opaque inks when you want bold, bright colors that stand out.

Use opaque white ink for high-lights.
Either standard white ink or special airbrush white ink is fine.

5. When you want to use a different color, first flush out the old ink using the above method, then add the new ink to the color cup. The new color will mix with the old if you do not flush the handpiece out properly!

squirt
bucket

6. Finally, peel off the masking and add highlights to hair or clothes with white ink.

Don't mess up when spraying highlights! Do a test spray first!

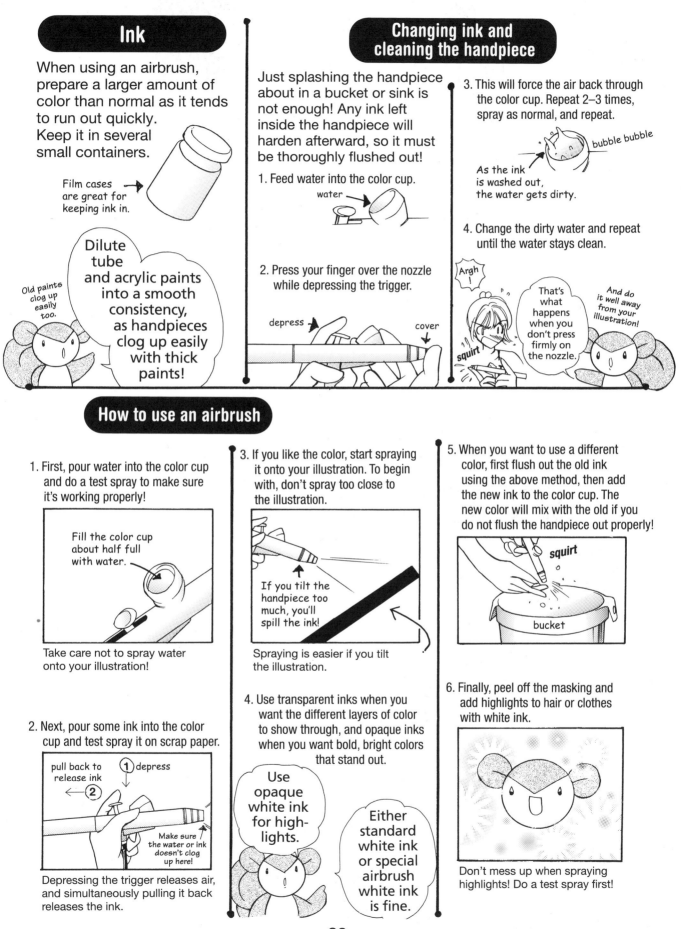

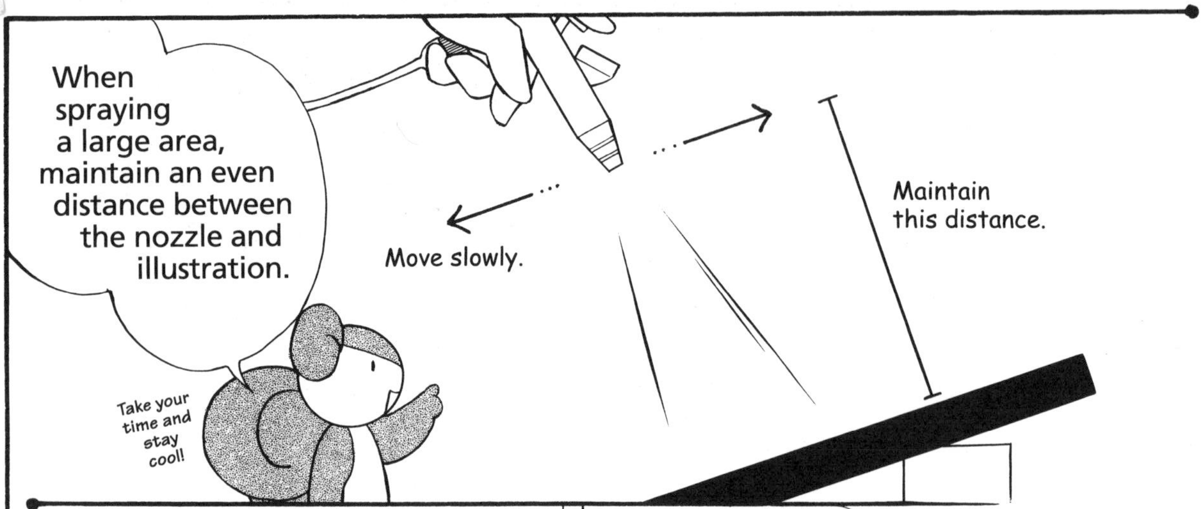
When spraying a large area, maintain an even distance between the nozzle and illustration.
Move slowly.
Maintain this distance.
Take your time and stay cool!

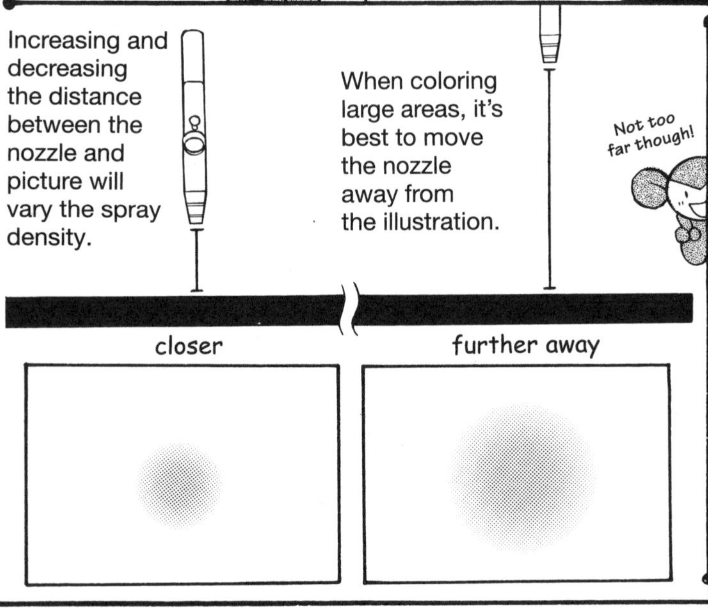
Increasing and decreasing the distance between the nozzle and picture will vary the spray density.
When coloring large areas, it's best to move the nozzle away from the illustration.
closer
further away

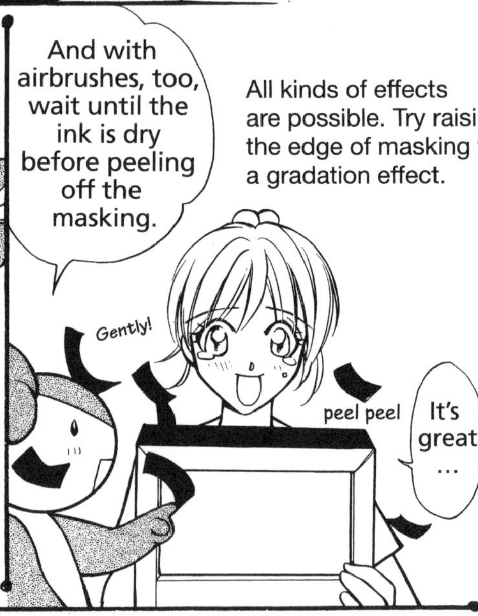
Not too far though!
And with airbrushes, too, wait until the ink is dry before peeling off the masking.
All kinds of effects are possible. Try raising the edge of masking for a gradation effect.
Gently!
peel peel
It's great ...

Finishing touches

When finishing with white ink, use a brush or pen as usual on eyebrows or hair.

When you have completed the illustration, give your tools a good clean. And store them in a special container or box. That way they'll be ready to use next time you need them.

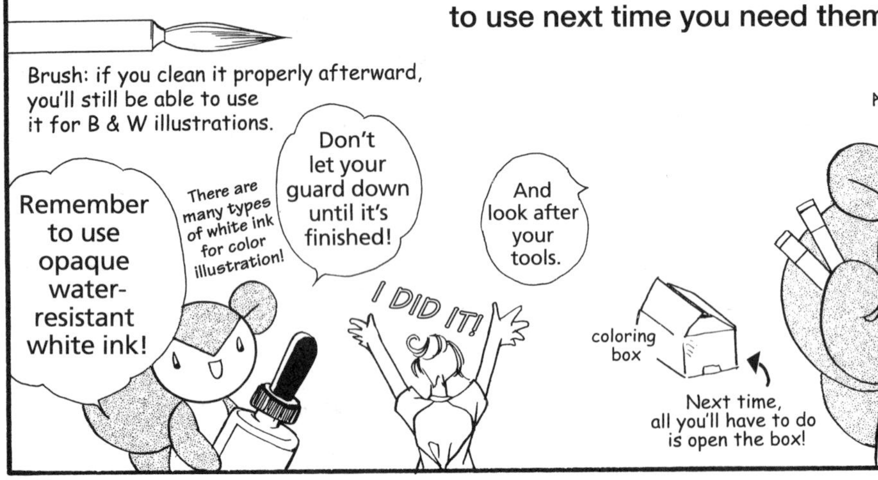
Brush: if you clean it properly afterward, you'll still be able to use it for B & W illustrations.
Remember to use opaque water-resistant white ink!
There are many types of white ink for color illustration!
Don't let your guard down until it's finished!
I DID IT!
And look after your tools.
coloring box
Next time, all you'll have to do is open the box!

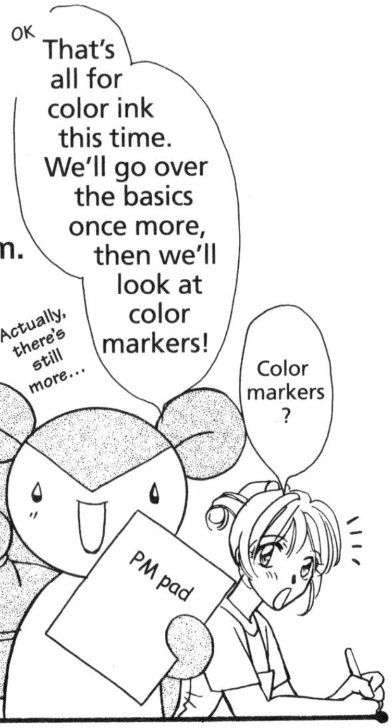
OK
That's all for color ink this time. We'll go over the basics once more, then we'll look at color markers!
Actually, there's still more...
Color markers ?
PM pad

COLORING STEPS

Working quickly is important with color. Have everything you need ready before starting.

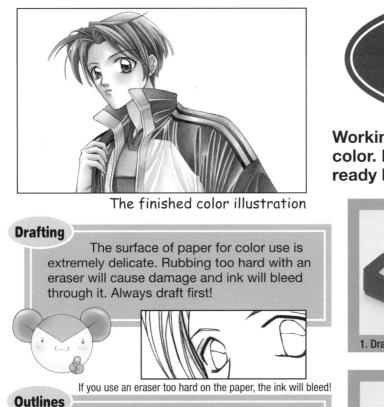

The finished color illustration

Drafting

The surface of paper for color use is extremely delicate. Rubbing too hard with an eraser will cause damage and ink will bleed through it. Always draft first!

If you use an eraser too hard on the paper, the ink will bleed!

Outlines

Using colors other than black for the outlines will make an illustration look interesting. But you must use a water-resistant ink.

If you don't use water-resistant ink, the outlines will bleed!

Coloring

When diluting color ink, remember that the amount of water you add will change the shade!

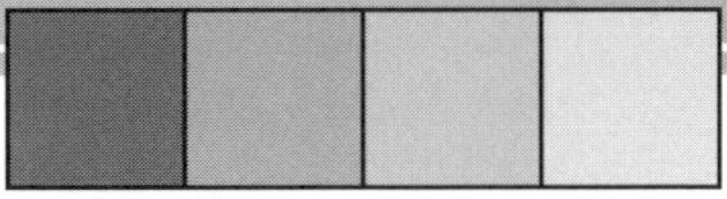

Ink 1	Ink 1: water 2	Ink 1: water 4	Ink 1: water 7

Finishing

Use opaque water-resistant white ink to add highlights to the eyebrows and eyes. This should prevent the colors underneath from bleeding.

1. Drafting A light box is useful for drafting.

2. Inking in outlines Don't get greasy fingerprints onto your work.

3. Applying colors Start painting lighter colors first.

Prepare 2 or 3 colors in advance!

4. Finishing touches Add highlights with white ink.

Turn over for an essential guide to painting colors

PAINTING WITH COLOR INK

Start with the light shades, and then add darker colors. It's best to paint areas of skin first.

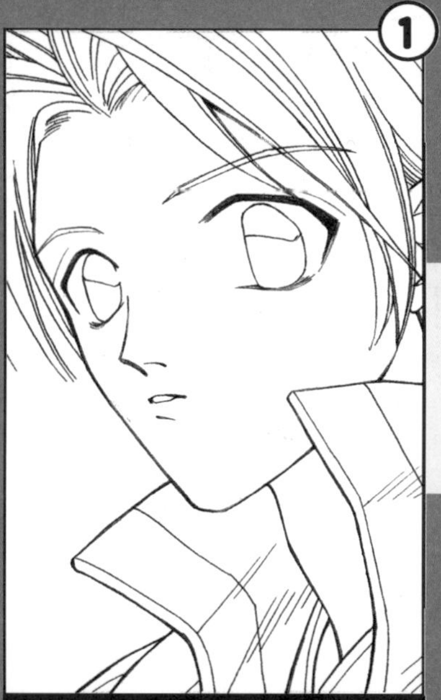
1

Paint water on the areas you want to color using a brush. Make sure that it doesn't bleed to other parts of the illustration. Don't use too much water, just enough to moisten the paper.

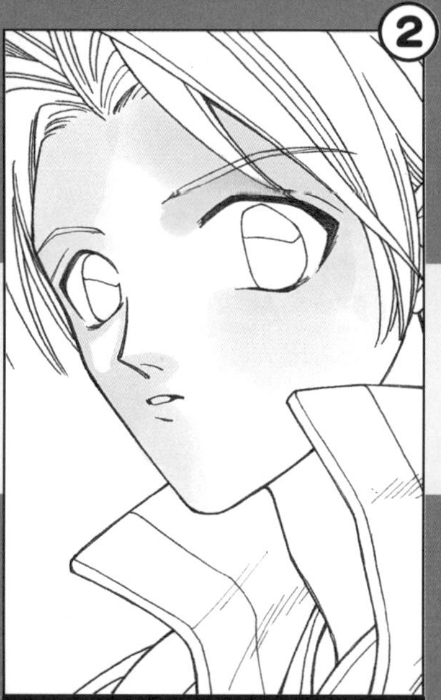
2

Next, carefully paint on the lightest shade while the paper is still moist. Slightly moisten the brush with water before painting with color ink.

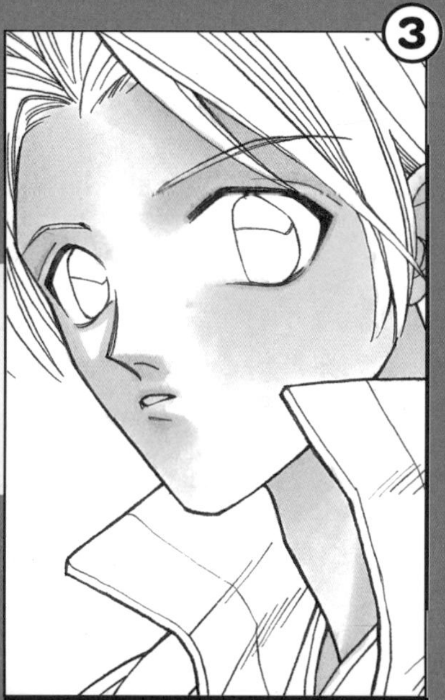
3

Before the ink dries, add further layers to create shading and darker colors. Layers of the same color or a slightly darker one will give a natural richness to the color.

Dilute the finished color with water

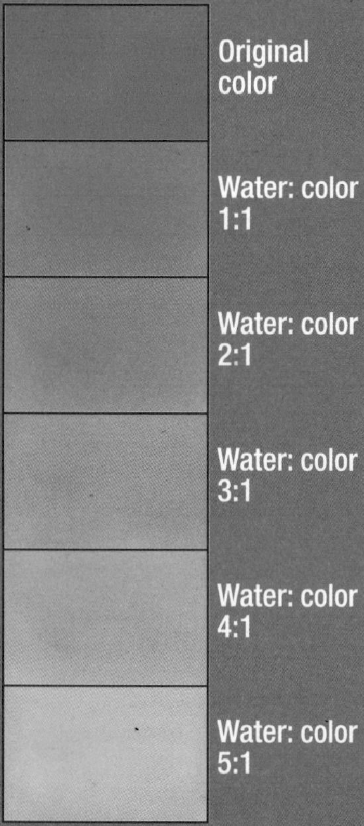
Original color
Water: color 1:1
Water: color 2:1
Water: color 3:1
Water: color 4:1
Water: color 5:1

How to mix colors

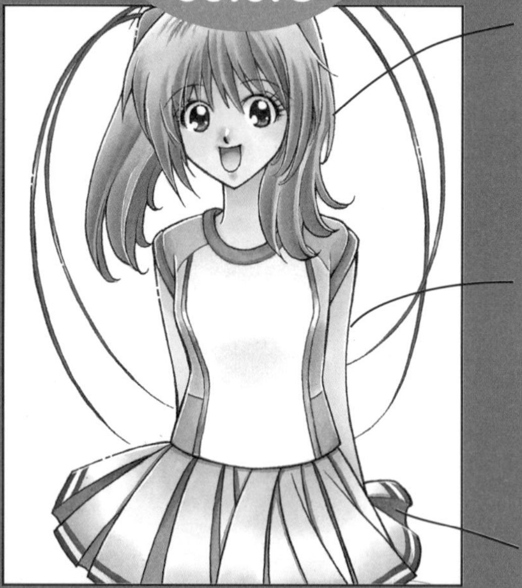

It's fine to use ready-mixed colors, or create new ones. Don't mix too many together, or you will get a muddy color.

• hair color

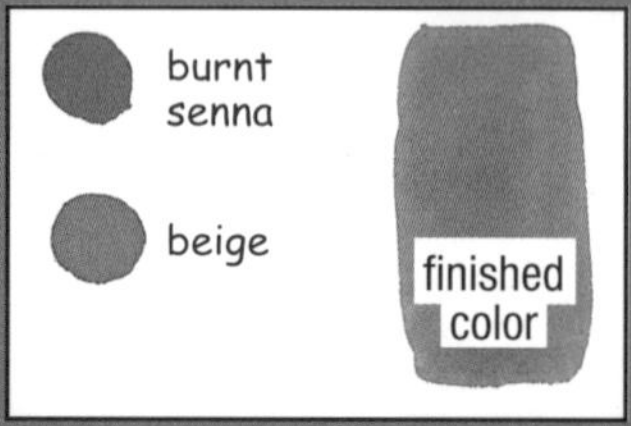
burnt senna
beige
finished color

• skin color

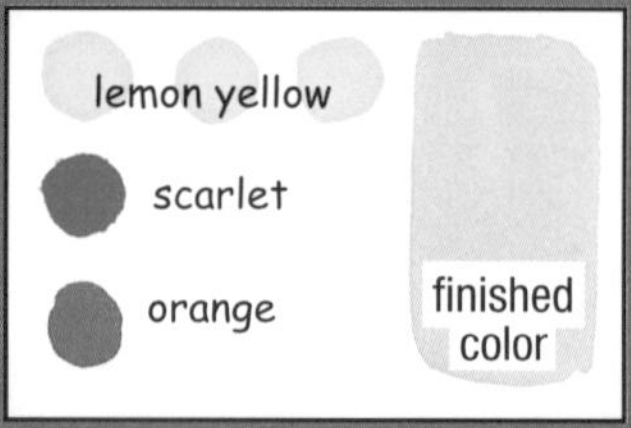
lemon yellow
scarlet
orange
finished color

• clothing color

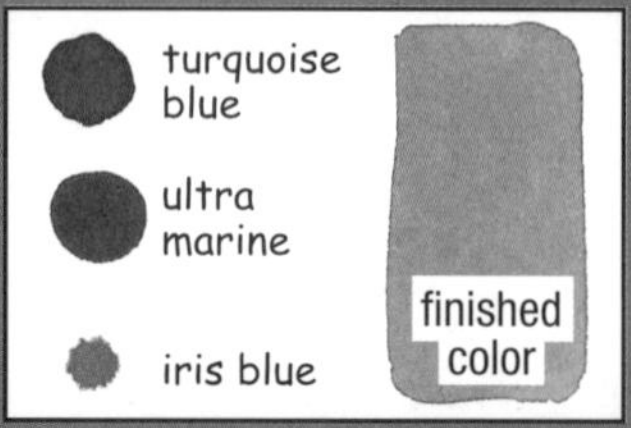
turquoise blue
ultra marine
iris blue
finished color

COLORING WITH COLOR MARKERS

Alcohol-based color markers dry very quickly, so you must work fast!

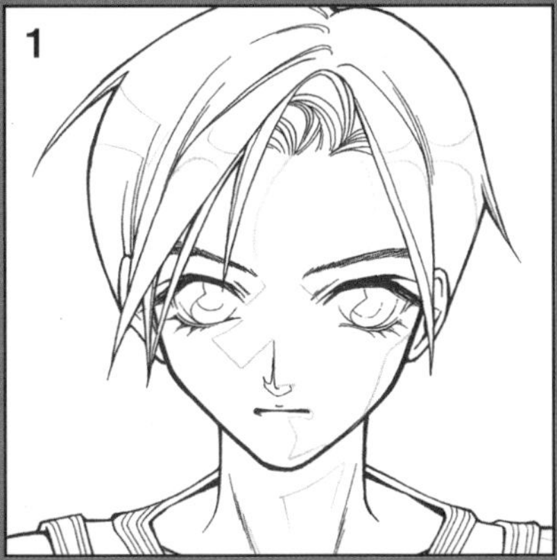
1

This is a photocopy of the original. If you're worried about coloring quickly, sketch an outline with a pale blue pencil.

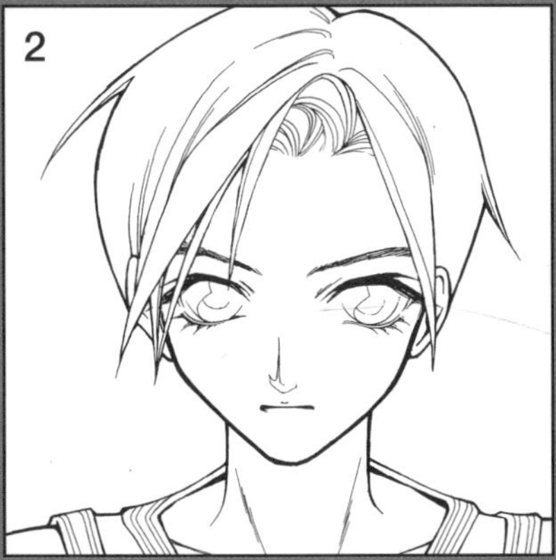
2

Apply colorless blender to the area you want to color. At this point, you can also apply it to the areas to be left white.

But don't apply colorless blender to the pupils, whites of the eyes, or mouth.

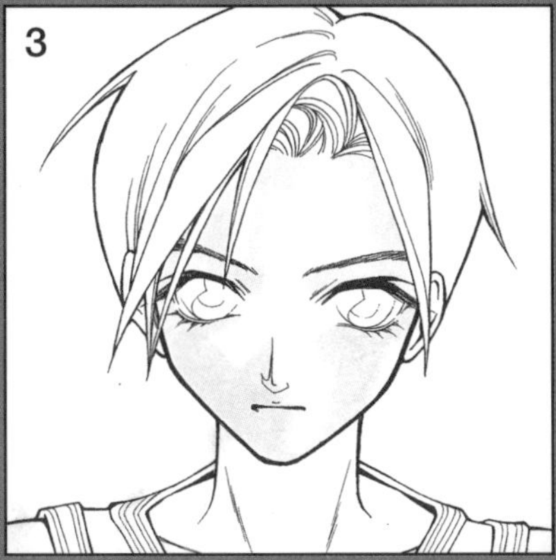
3

Apply the lightest color before the colorless blender dries.

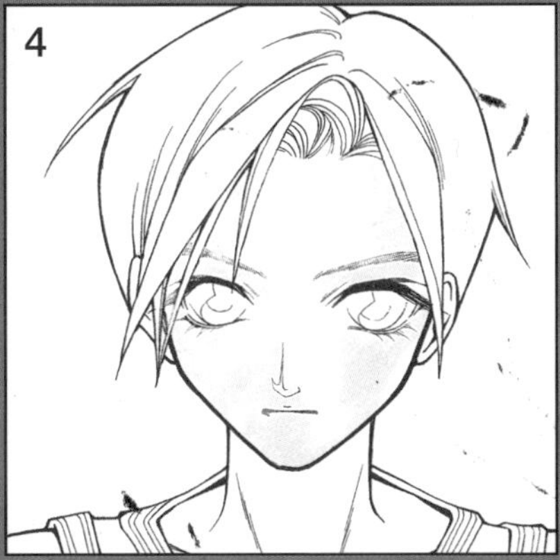
4

Quickly apply colorless blender where you want gradation.

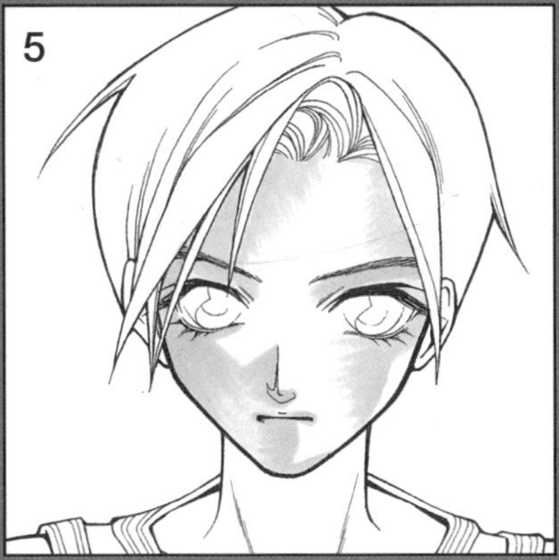
5

Layer more of the same or a slightly darker color where you want shading.

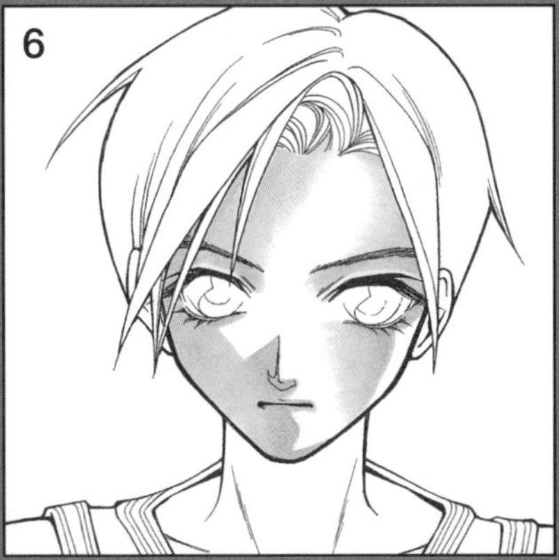
6

Gradate the edges of layered darker color using the lightest color.

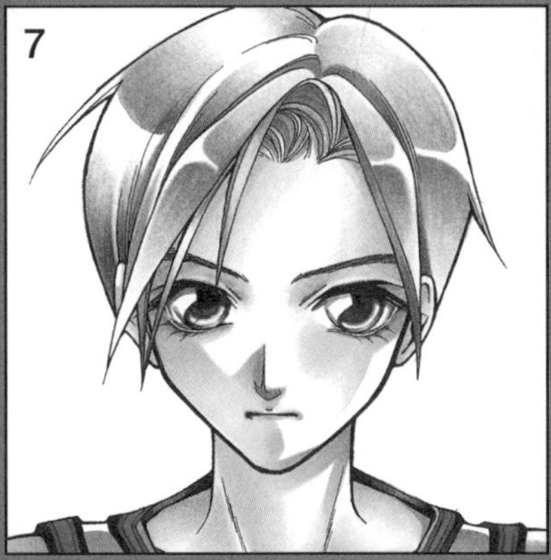
7

For the finishing touches, use a color pencil to add fine shading and detail to the eyebrows and hair.

After deciding where to paint and what colors to use, work quickly. The result will be patchy if you hesitate!

The finished color illustration

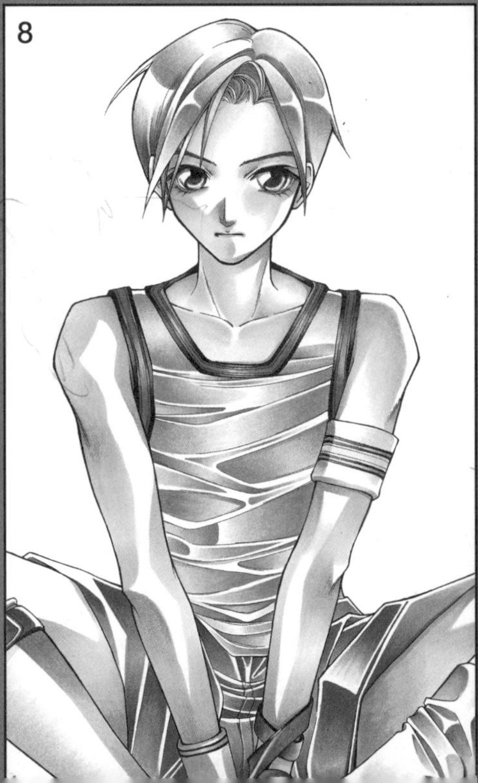
8

COLOR MARKERS

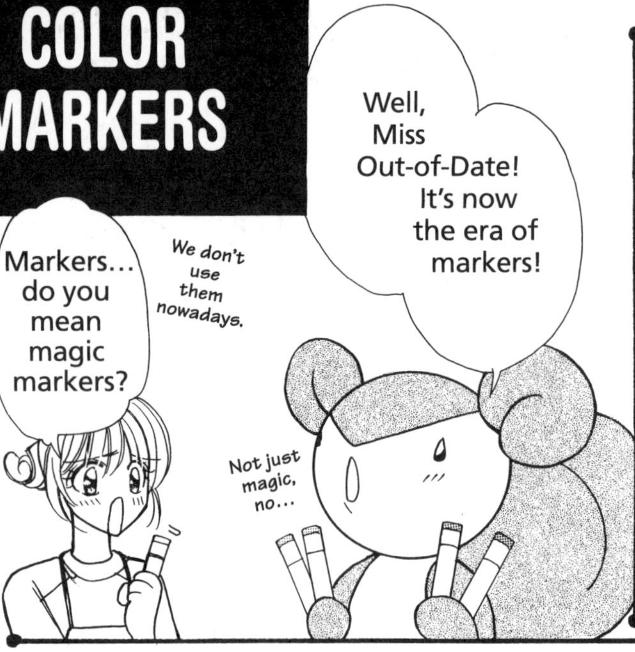
Markers... do you mean magic markers?
We don't use them nowadays.
Well, Miss Out-of-Date! It's now the era of markers!
Not just magic, no...

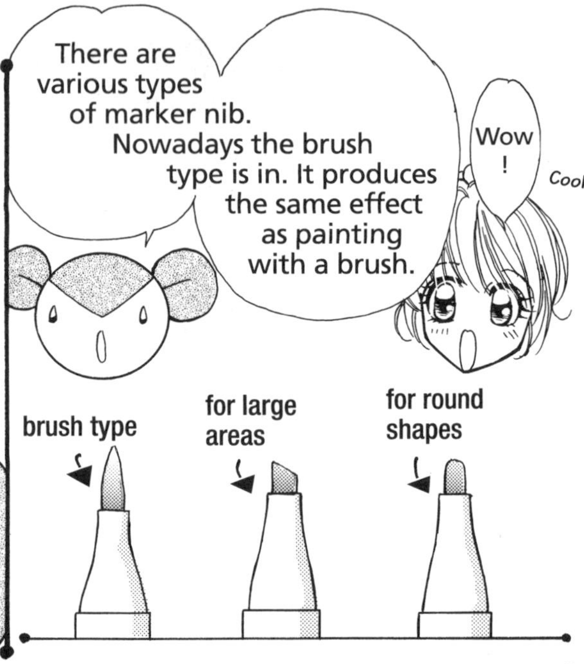
There are various types of marker nib. Nowadays the brush type is in. It produces the same effect as painting with a brush.
Wow!
Cool!
brush type
for large areas
for round shapes

There are also various types, including water-soluble and alcohol-based markers. Use them as much as you like— if you can afford to!

Water-soluble markers

Soluble in water, so blurring or gradation can be achieved easily by running a wet brush over it. The colors are translucent, but become muddy if you paint over them.

Alcohol-based markers

Do not become muddy if you paint over them, and dry very quickly. There are many colors and nib types—brush pens are popular. Alcohol markers do not dissolve copy toner or wrinkle paper, even thin photocopy paper.

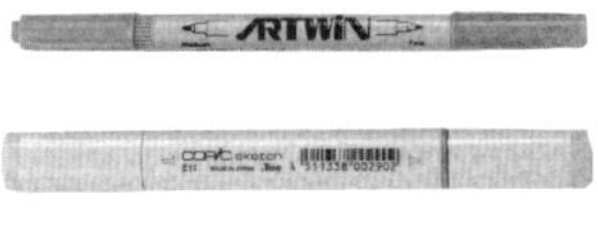
ARTWIN

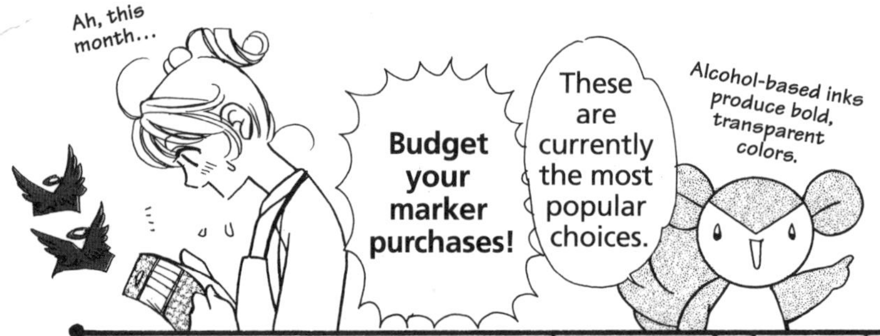
Ah, this month...
Budget your marker purchases!
These are currently the most popular choices.
Alcohol-based inks produce bold, transparent colors.

The great thing about markers is that, unlike color inks, they don't need any preparation!

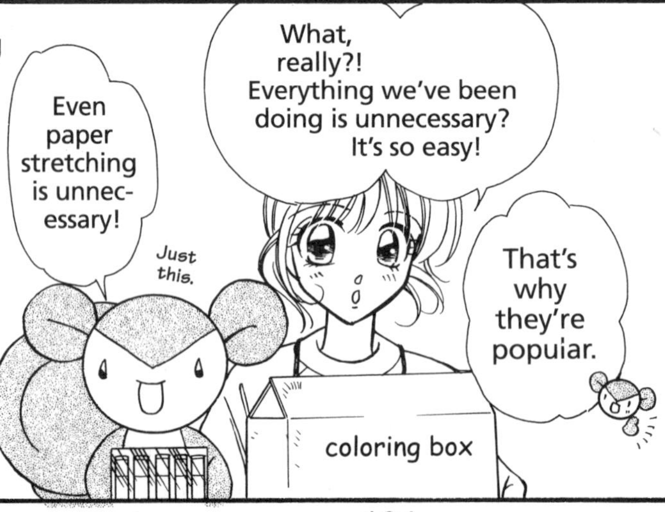
Even paper stretching is unnecessary!
What, really?! Everything we've been doing is unnecessary? It's so easy!
Just this.
That's why they're popular.
coloring box

Let's have a look at the popular alcohol-based ink markers Copic Sketch and Copic Ciao!

Copic Sketch

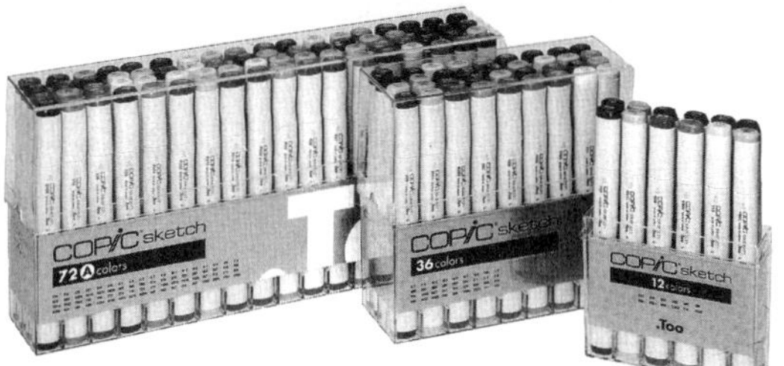

298 colors

Copic Sketch is the word in markers at the moment. The super brush nib is essential for hand-drawn details, and the broad nib is great for filling in large areas. They're compatible with the Copic ABS airbrush.

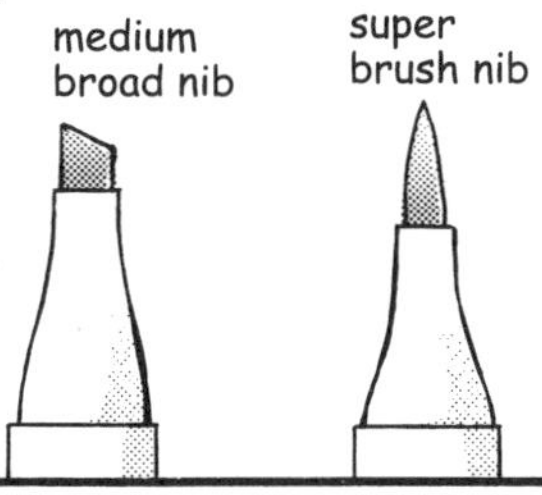

medium broad nib

super brush nib

Copic Ciao

The Copic Ciao range is similar to Copic Sketch, but includes only the most popular colors, and is cheaper. Ciao cannot be used with the ABS.

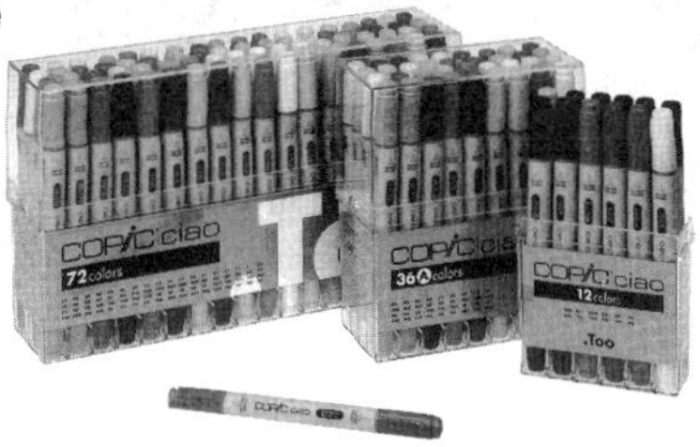

144 colors

Sketch and Ciao markers all have a brush-type nib, so using them feels like painting with color inks!

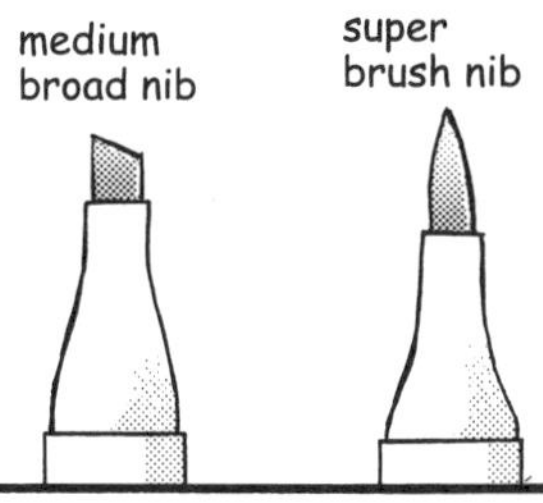

medium broad nib

super brush nib

Copic Sketch and Ciao

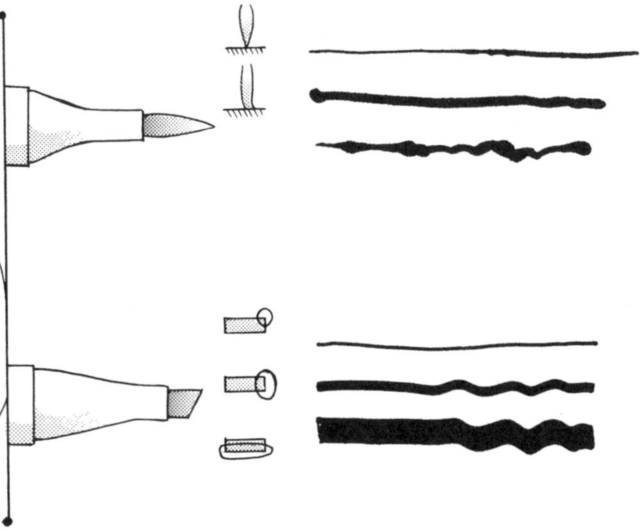

You can draw lines of varying thickness according to the nib type and angle. Try it out!

I've gotta try the super brush nib!

COLOR MARKER KIT

Ink for outlines
Some markers and types of ink for outlines do not work well together!

White Ink
Correction fluid or white ink for highlights are normally okay with markers.

Color pencils
Usually okay with markers.

Paper
Choose paper with a smooth, flat surface for even coloring. Remember that ink bleeds through thin paper!

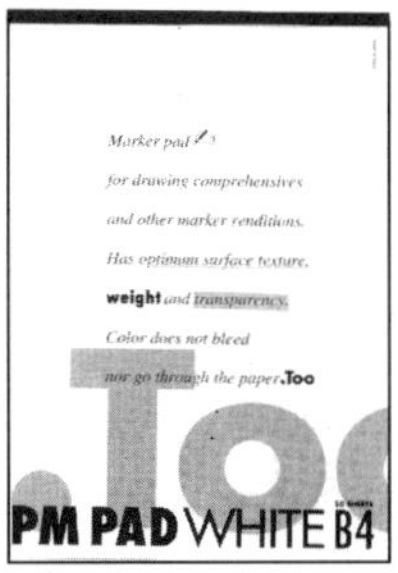

Marker pad
for drawing comprehensives and other marker renditions. Has optimum surface texture.
weight and transparency.
Color does not bleed.
ink go through the paper. Too

PM PAD WHITE B4

Multiliners or fine line markers work well with alcohol-based markers.

Even so, best test them first to make sure.

Use water-resistant ink with water-soluble markers!

hee hee hee

It's so simple!

hee hee hee

105

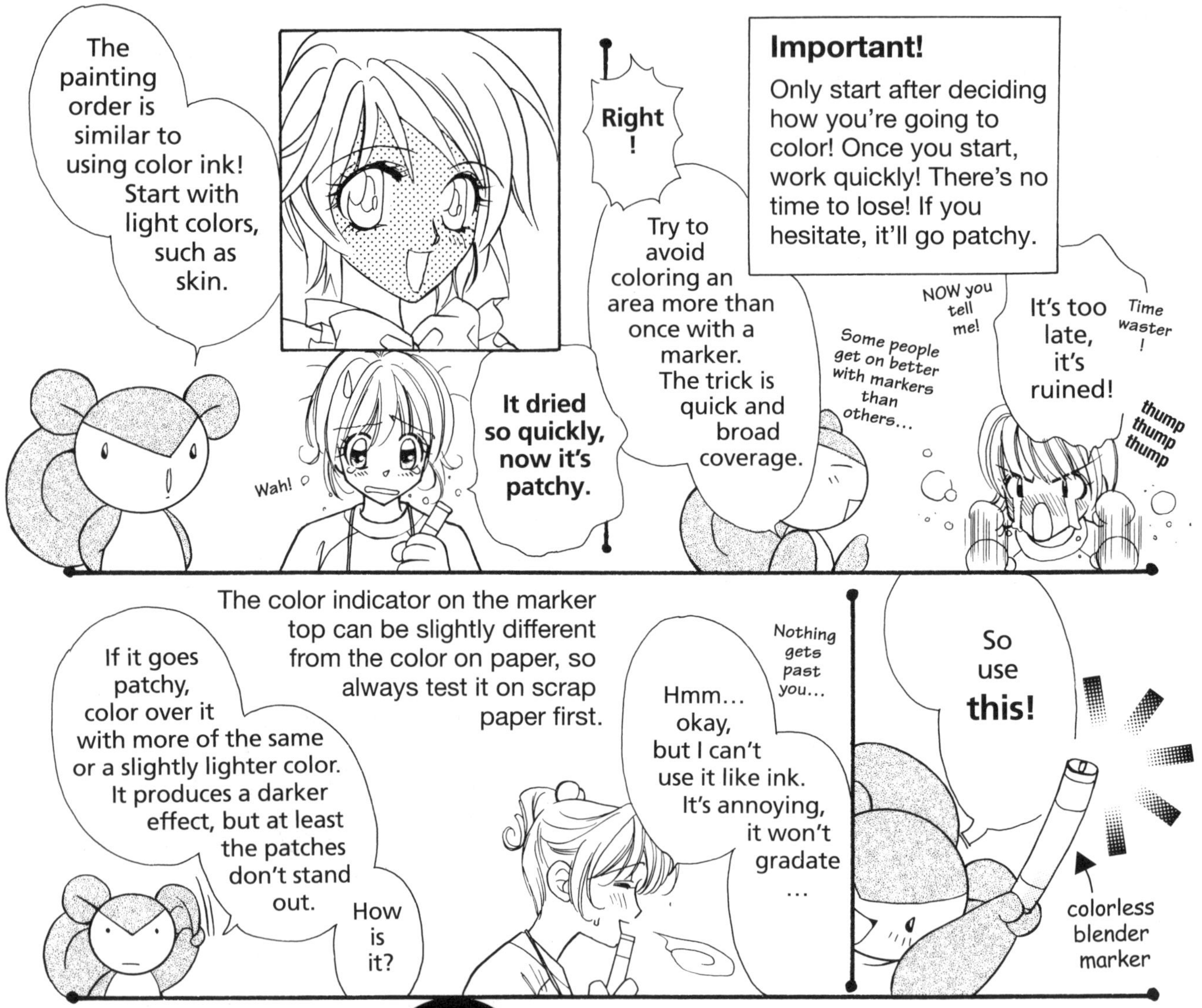
The painting order is similar to using color ink! Start with light colors, such as skin.
Wah!
It dried so quickly, now it's patchy.
Right!
Try to avoid coloring an area more than once with a marker. The trick is quick and broad coverage.
Important!
Only start after deciding how you're going to color! Once you start, work quickly! There's no time to lose! If you hesitate, it'll go patchy.
Some people get on better with markers than others…
NOW you tell me!
It's too late, it's ruined!
Time waster!
thump thump thump
The color indicator on the marker top can be slightly different from the color on paper, so always test it on scrap paper first.
If it goes patchy, color over it with more of the same or a slightly lighter color. It produces a darker effect, but at least the patches don't stand out.
How is it?
Hmm… okay, but I can't use it like ink. It's annoying, it won't gradate …
Nothing gets past you…
So use this!
colorless blender marker

Copic Sketch and Ciao #0 marker is a colorless blender marker. It contains solvent thinner to dissolve marker ink.

GRADATION 1

1. First apply the color.

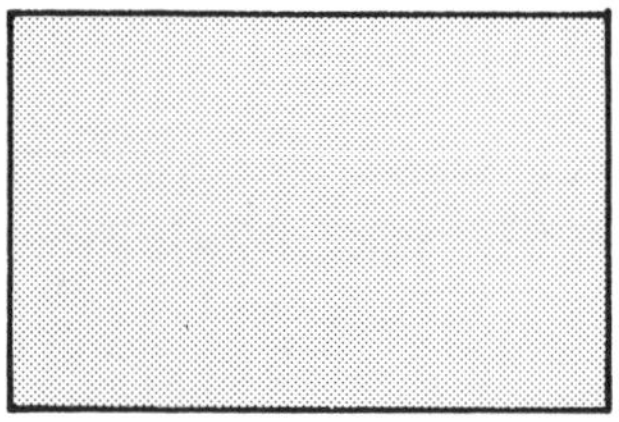

2. Apply the colorless blender over it before the ink dries.

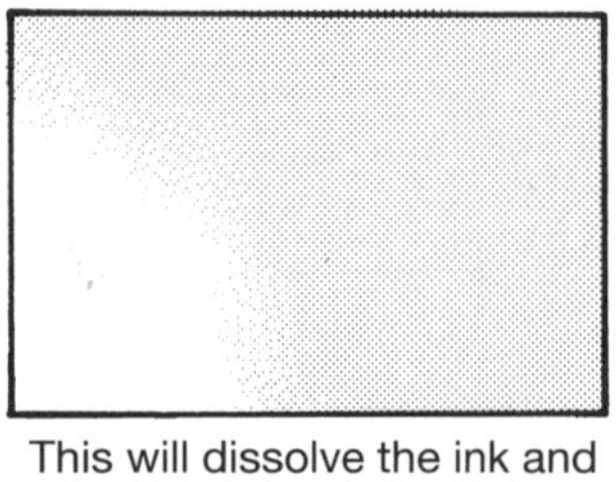

This will dissolve the ink and cause natural gradation.

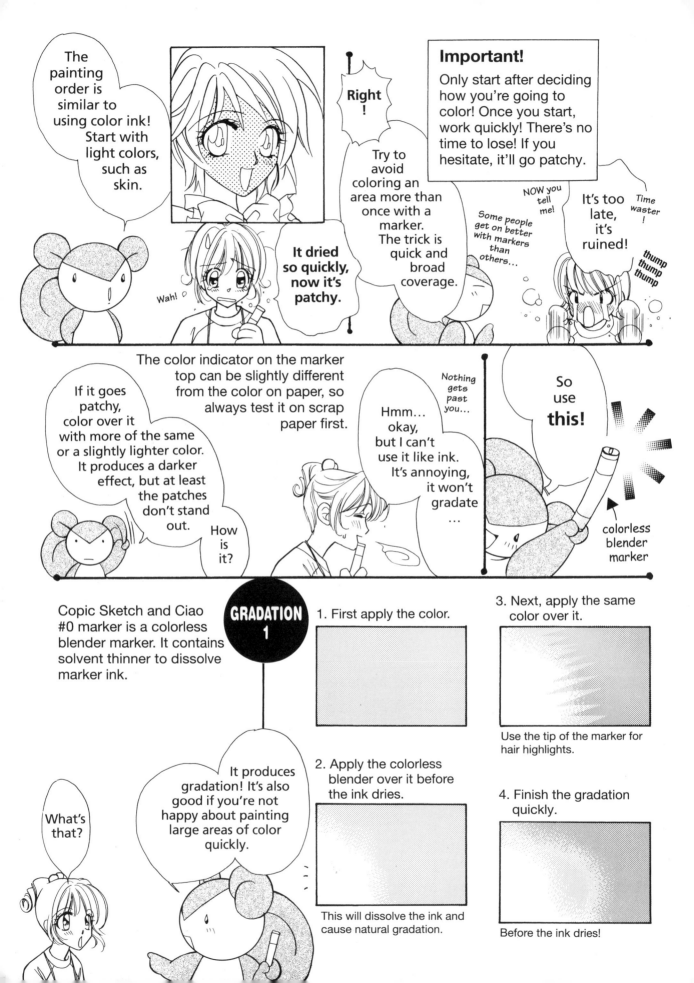

3. Next, apply the same color over it.

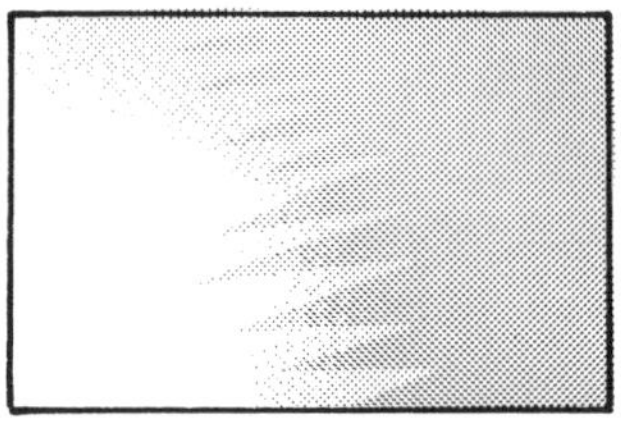

Use the tip of the marker for hair highlights.

4. Finish the gradation quickly.

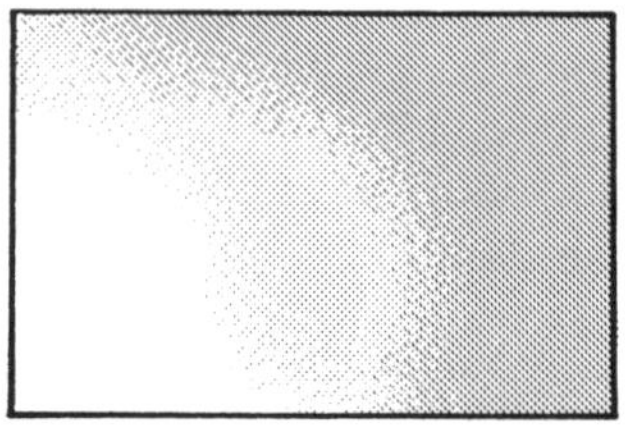

Before the ink dries!

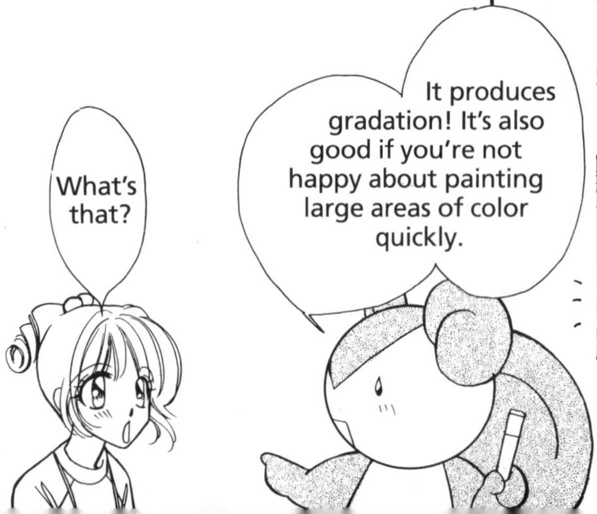
What's that?
It produces gradation! It's also good if you're not happy about painting large areas of color quickly.

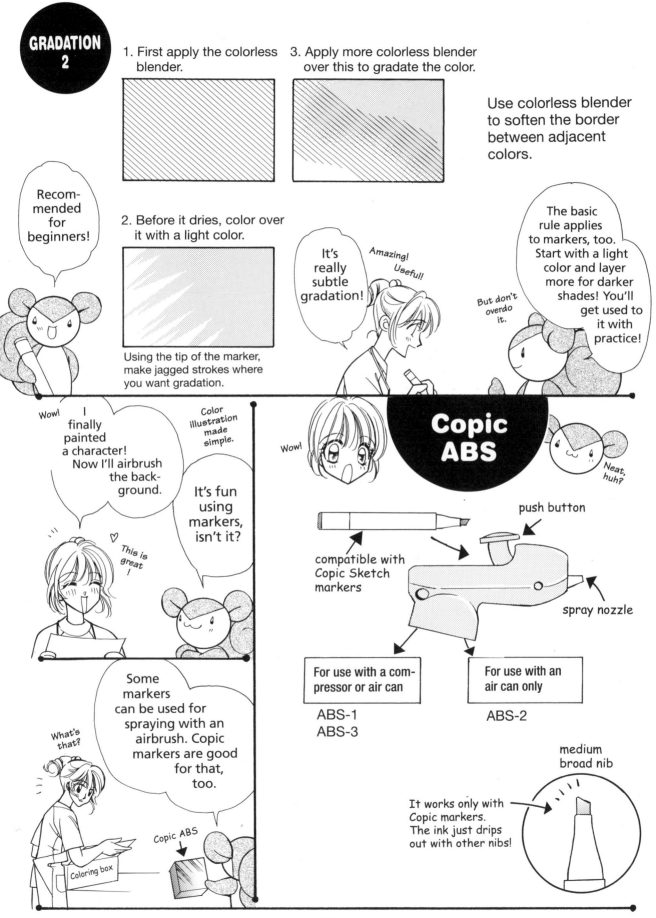

GRADATION 2

1. First apply the colorless blender.

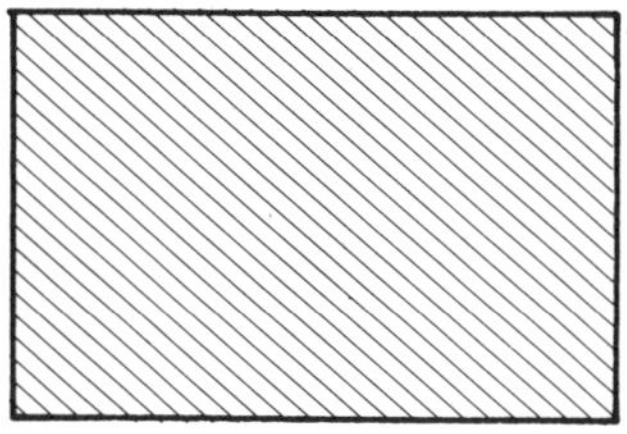

2. Before it dries, color over it with a light color.

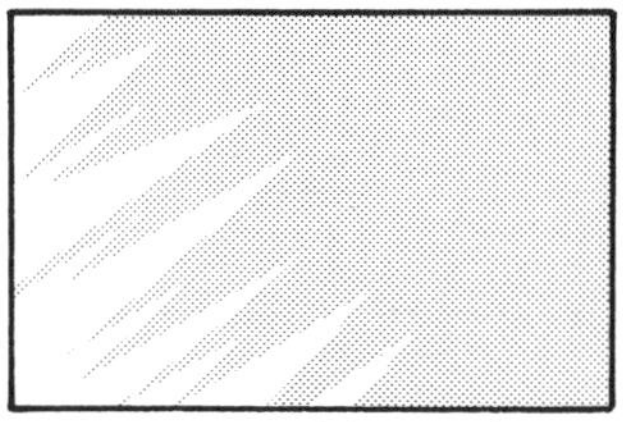

Using the tip of the marker, make jagged strokes where you want gradation.

3. Apply more colorless blender over this to gradate the color.

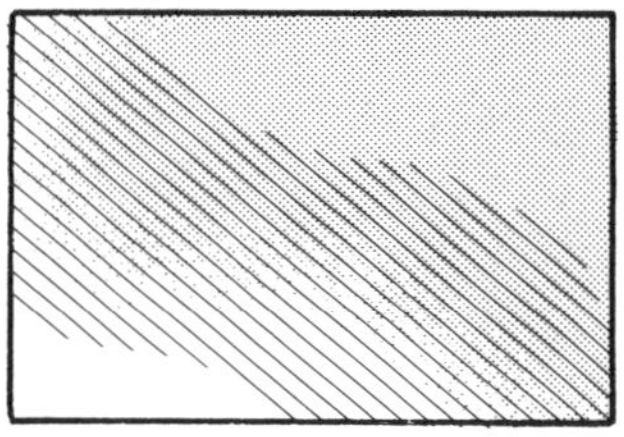

Use colorless blender to soften the border between adjacent colors.

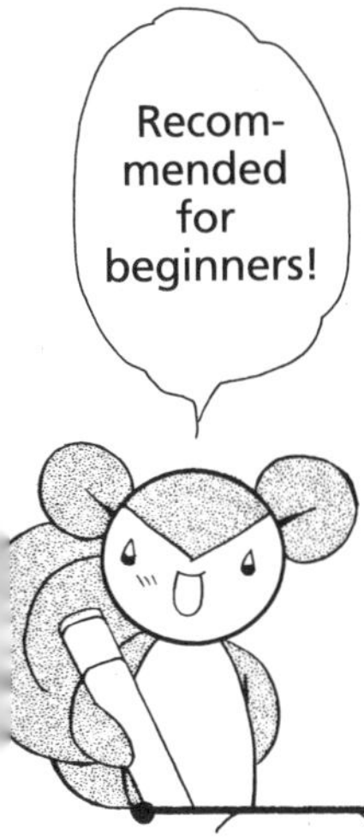
Recom-mended for beginners!

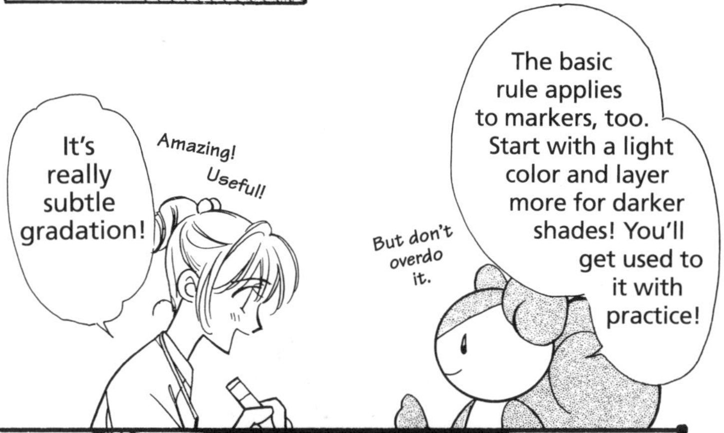
It's really subtle gradation!
Amazing!
Useful!
But don't overdo it.
The basic rule applies to markers, too. Start with a light color and layer more for darker shades! You'll get used to it with practice!

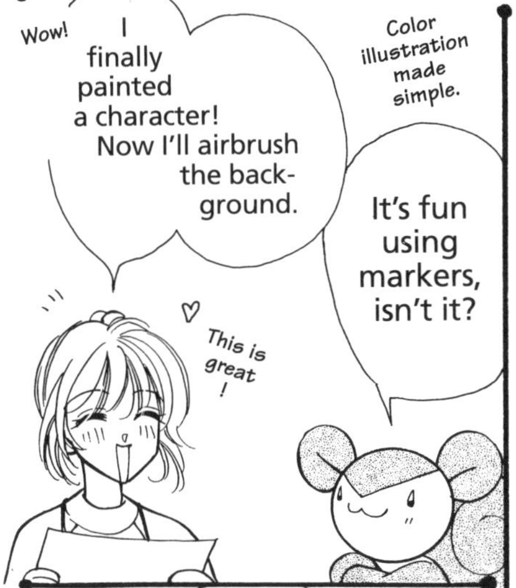
Wow!
I finally painted a character! Now I'll airbrush the back-ground.
Color illustration made simple.
It's fun using markers, isn't it?
This is great!

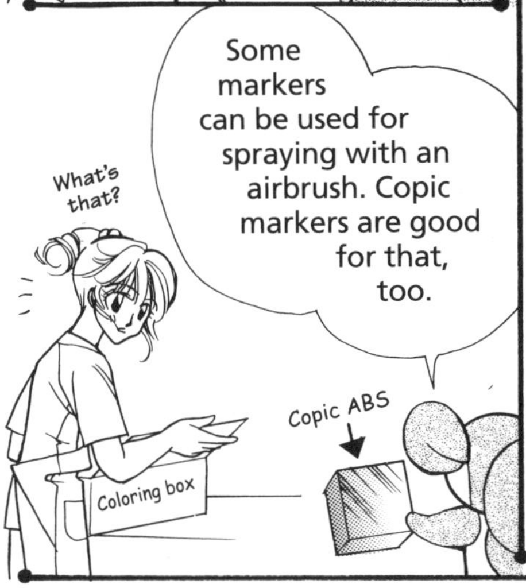
What's that?
Some markers can be used for spraying with an airbrush. Copic markers are good for that, too.
Copic ABS
Coloring box

Copic ABS

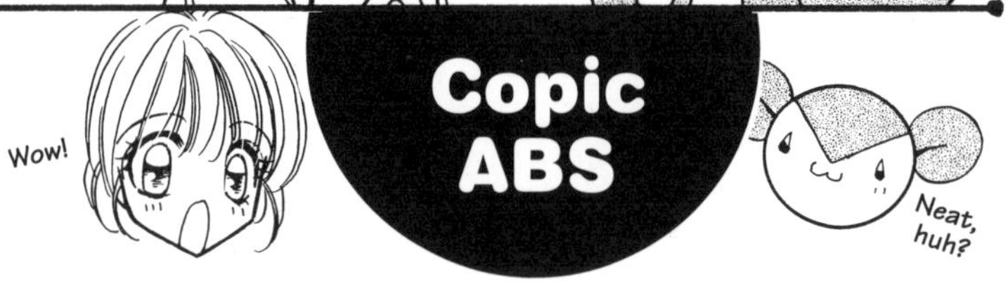
Wow!
Neat, huh?

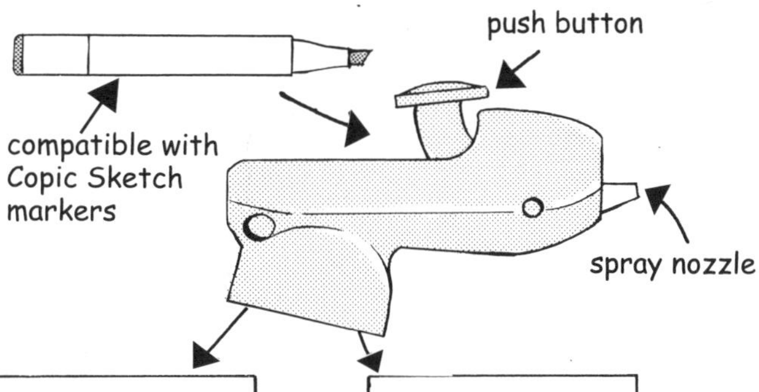
push button
compatible with Copic Sketch markers
spray nozzle

For use with a compressor or air can	For use with an air can only
ABS-1 ABS-3	ABS-2

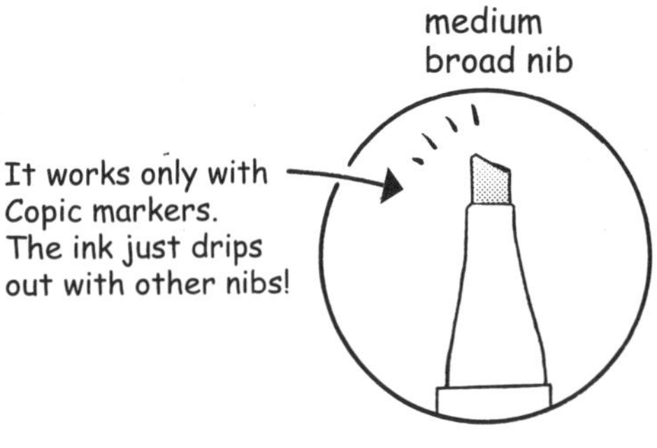
medium broad nib
It works only with Copic markers. The ink just drips out with other nibs!

USING THE ABS

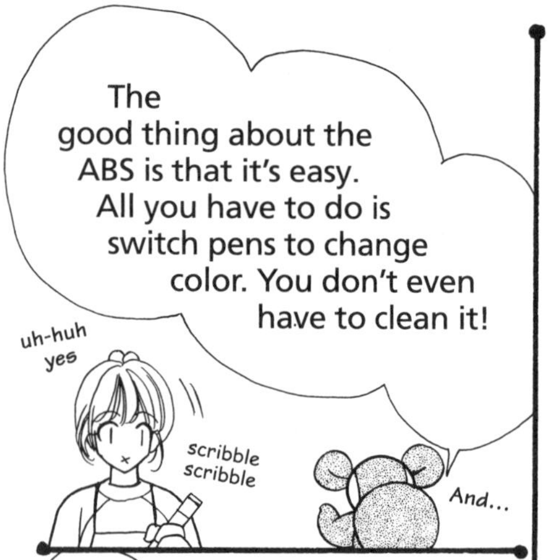
The good thing about the ABS is that it's easy. All you have to do is switch pens to change color. You don't even have to clean it!
uh-huh yes
scribble scribble
And...

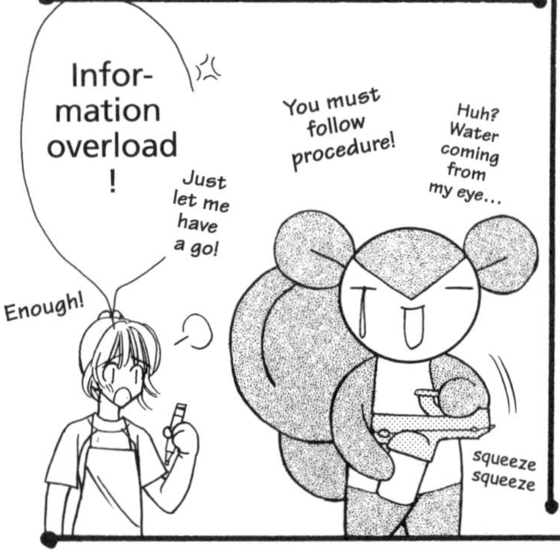
Information overload!
Just let me have a go!
You must follow procedure!
Huh? Water coming from my eye...
Enough!
squeeze squeeze

1. Mask the areas you want to protect.

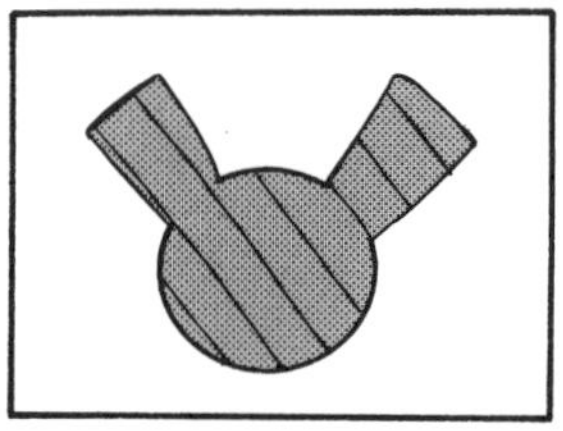

2. Choose a marker color and insert it into the ABS.

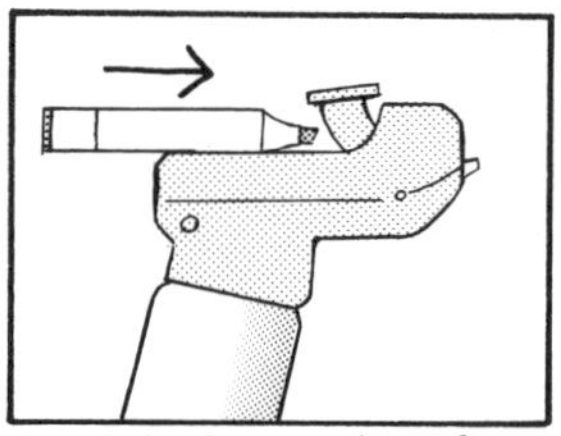

Read the instructions for attaching an air can, and assemble it properly!

3. Do a test spray on scrap paper before you start on your picture.

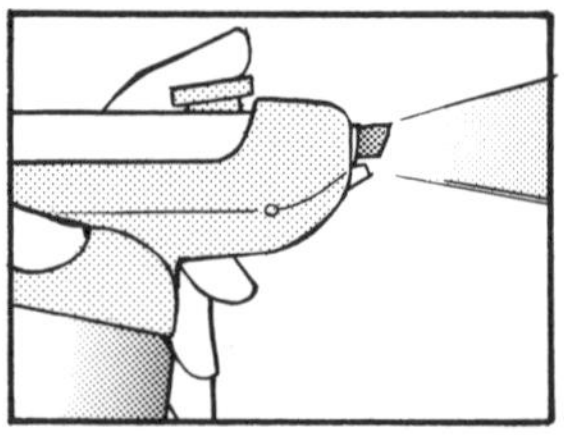

If you spray from too far away, the color will not adhere well to the surface.

4. To change colors, simply remove the marker and insert a new one!

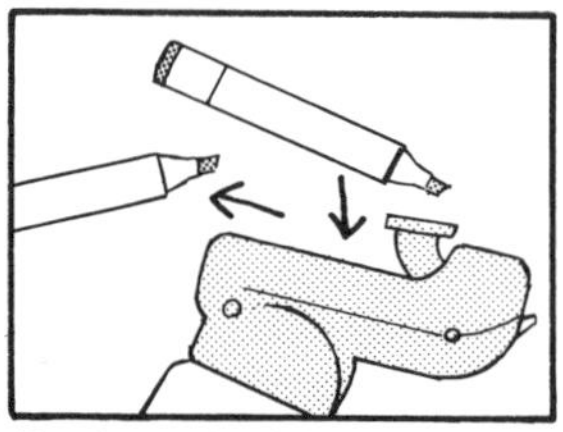

Replace the lid firmly on used markers! And keep an eye on the amount of air in the air can.

The air can gets cold while you're using the ABS and may sometimes get blocked. When this happens, give it a break for a while to let it warm up before starting to spray again.

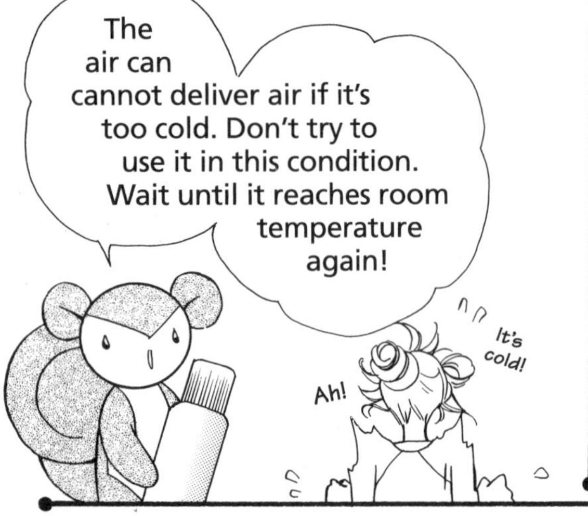
The air can cannot deliver air if it's too cold. Don't try to use it in this condition. Wait until it reaches room temperature again!
It's cold!
Ah!

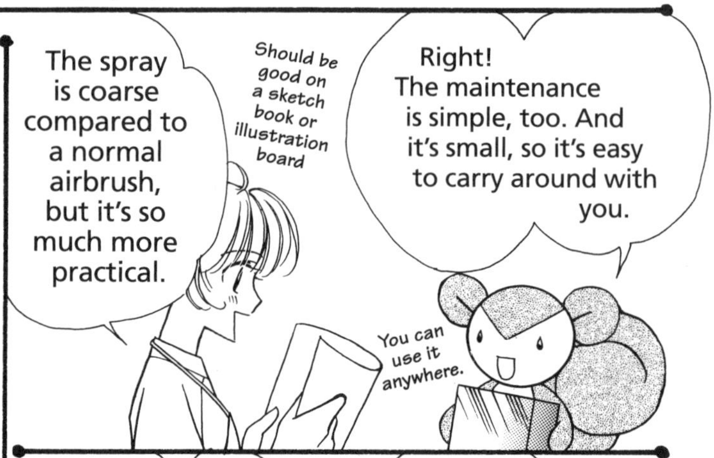
The spray is coarse compared to a normal airbrush, but it's so much more practical.
Should be good on a sketch book or illustration board
Right! The maintenance is simple, too. And it's small, so it's easy to carry around with you.
You can use it anywhere.

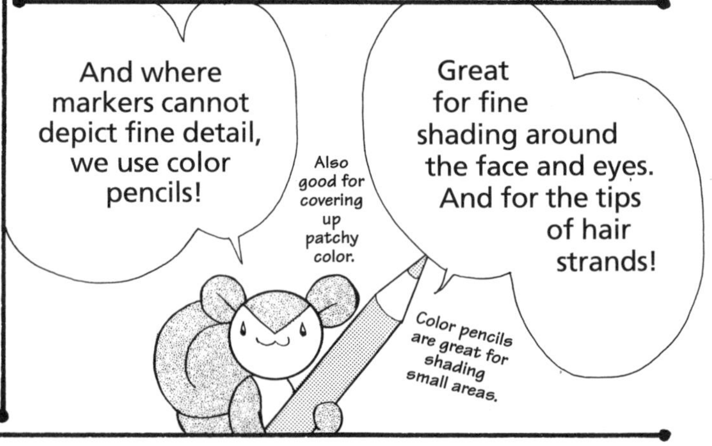
And where markers cannot depict fine detail, we use color pencils!
Also good for covering up patchy color.
Great for fine shading around the face and eyes. And for the tips of hair strands!
Color pencils are great for shading small areas.

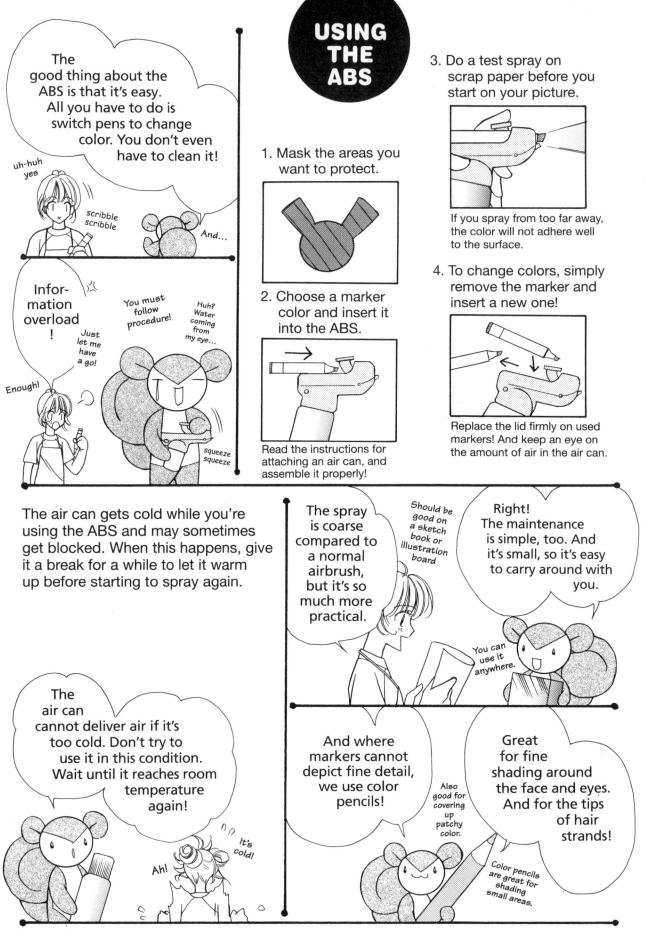

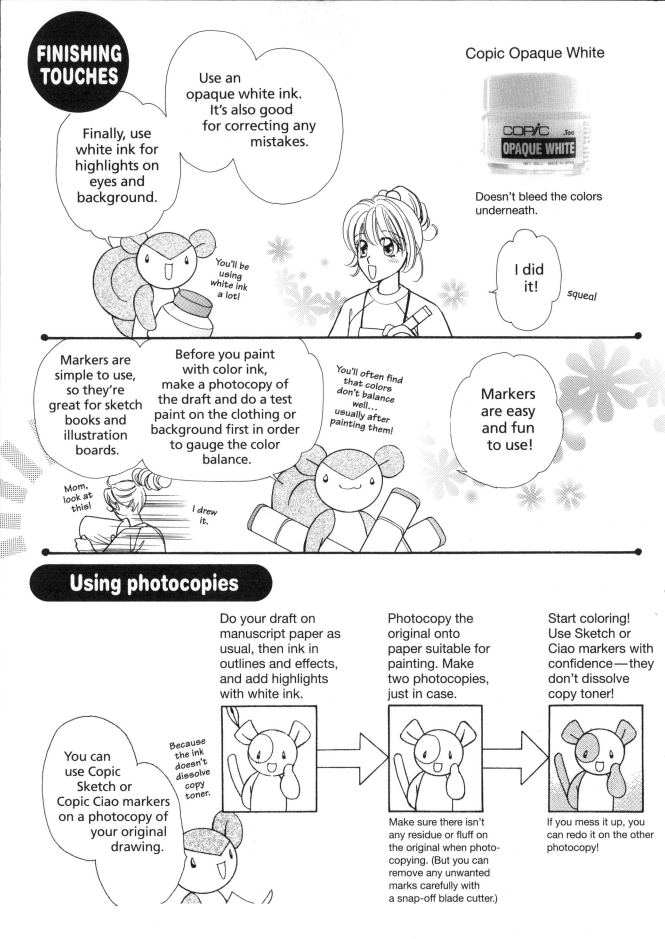

FINISHING TOUCHES

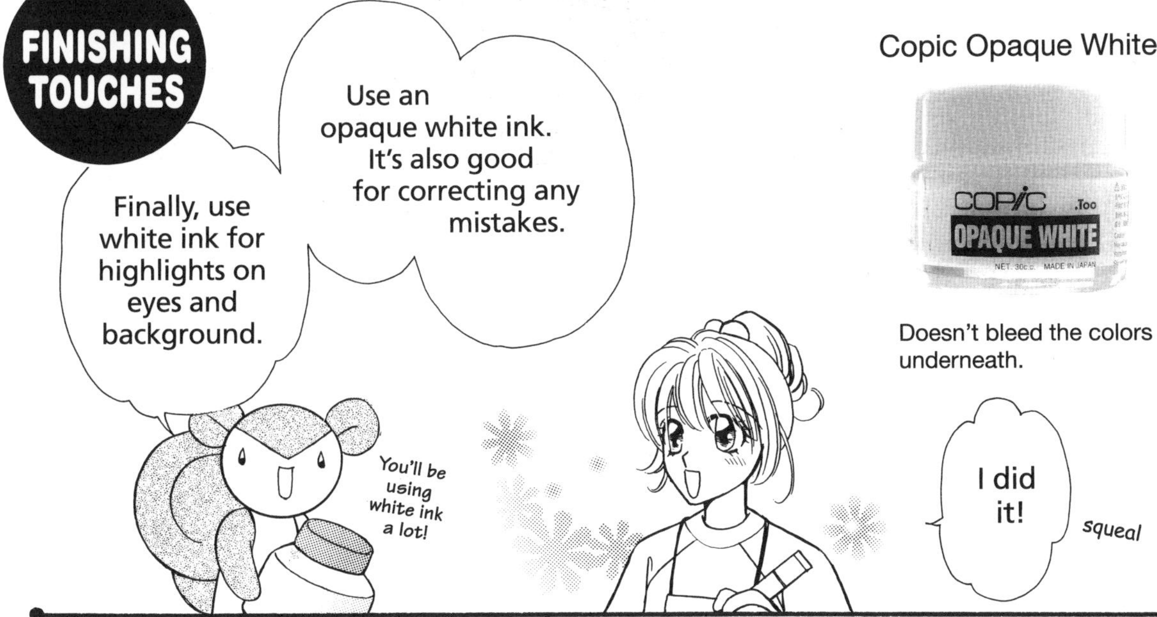

Finally, use white ink for highlights on eyes and background.
Use an opaque white ink. It's also good for correcting any mistakes.
You'll be using white ink a lot!
I did it!
squeal
COPIC .Too
OPAQUE WHITE

Copic Opaque White

Doesn't bleed the colors underneath.

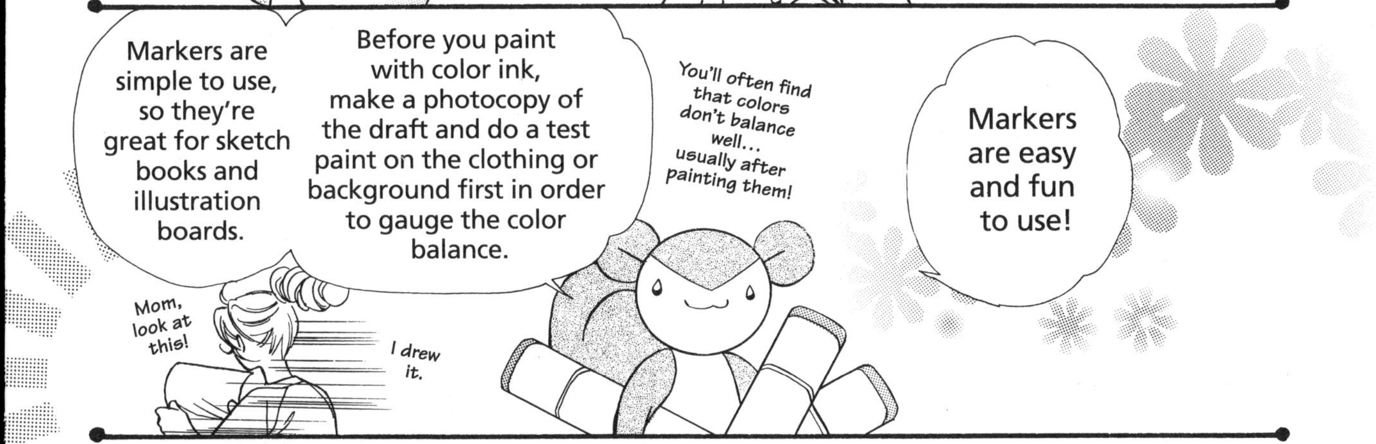

Markers are simple to use, so they're great for sketch books and illustration boards.
Before you paint with color ink, make a photocopy of the draft and do a test paint on the clothing or background first in order to gauge the color balance.
Mom, look at this!
I drew it.
You'll often find that colors don't balance well... usually after painting them!
Markers are easy and fun to use!

Using photocopies

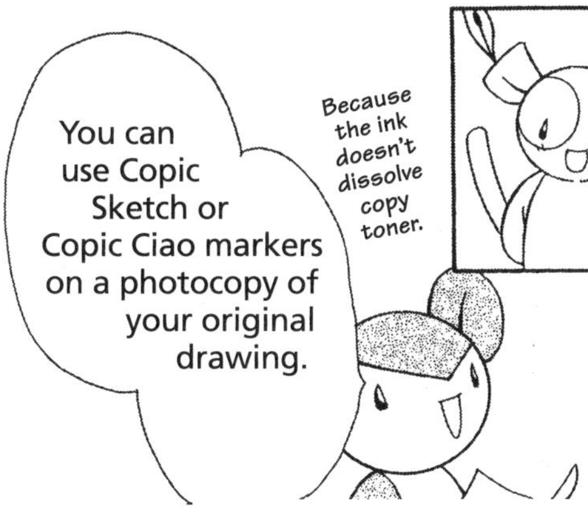

You can use Copic Sketch or Copic Ciao markers on a photocopy of your original drawing.
Because the ink doesn't dissolve copy toner.

Do your draft on manuscript paper as usual, then ink in outlines and effects, and add highlights with white ink.

Photocopy the original onto paper suitable for painting. Make two photocopies, just in case.

Start coloring! Use Sketch or Ciao markers with confidence—they don't dissolve copy toner!

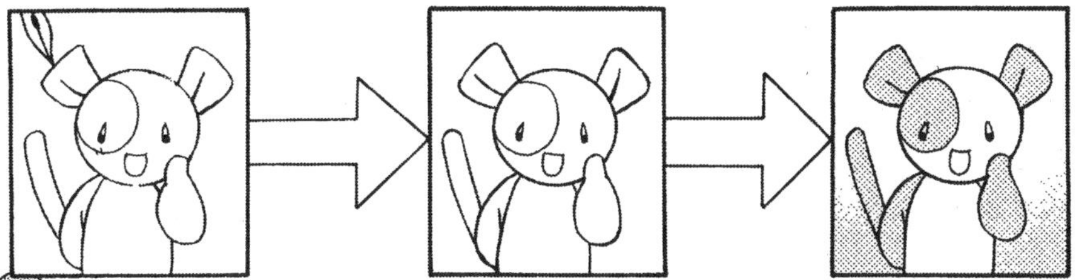

Make sure there isn't any residue or fluff on the original when photo-copying. (But you can remove any unwanted marks carefully with a snap-off blade cutter.)

If you mess it up, you can redo it on the other photocopy!

LET'S COLOR AN ILLUSTRATION WITH BACKGROUND

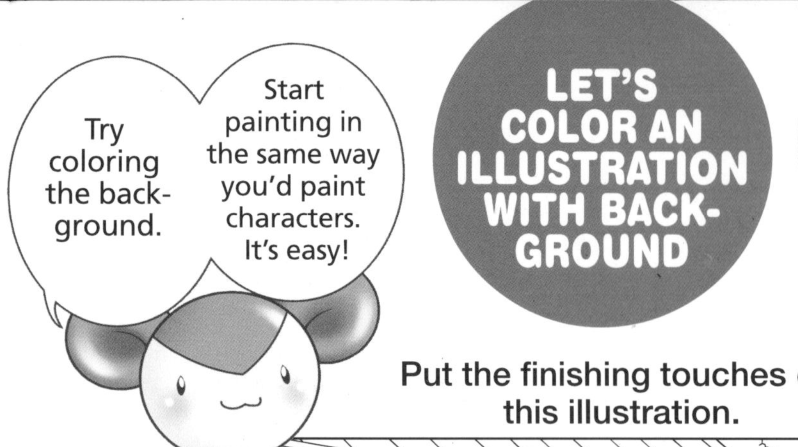
Try coloring the back-ground.
Start painting in the same way you'd paint characters. It's easy!

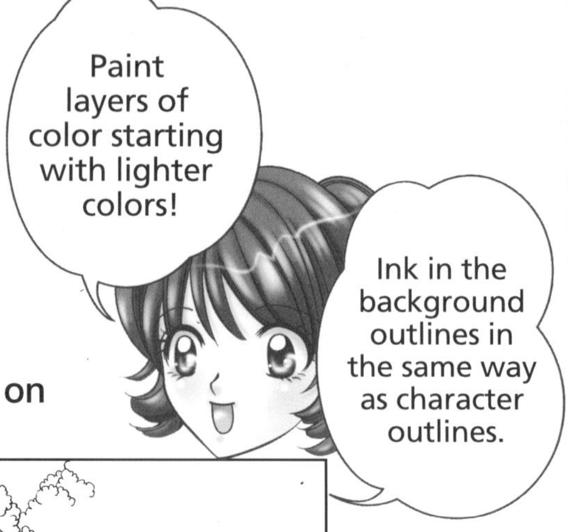
Paint layers of color starting with lighter colors!
Ink in the background outlines in the same way as character outlines.

Put the finishing touches on this illustration.

Here we've used Dr. Ph. Martin's Color Inks on Fine BB Kent paper. The outlines are in a water-resistant brown ink.

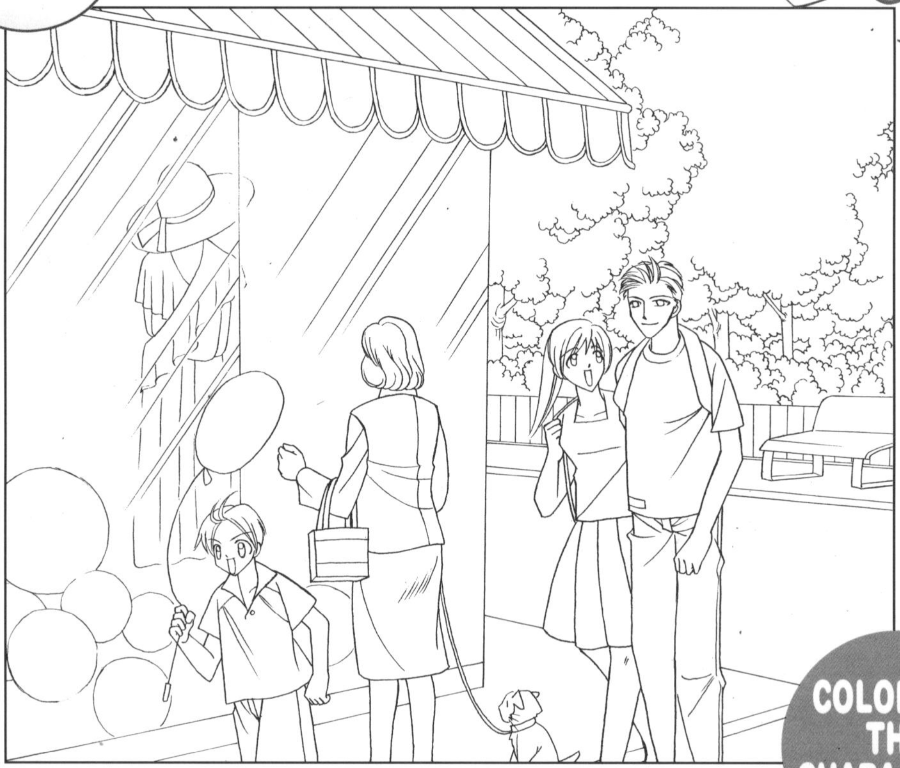

Use water resistant ink for the outlines.

Use colors other than black, as long as they're not too light! Try using brown or grey for outlines.

COLORING THE CHARACTERS

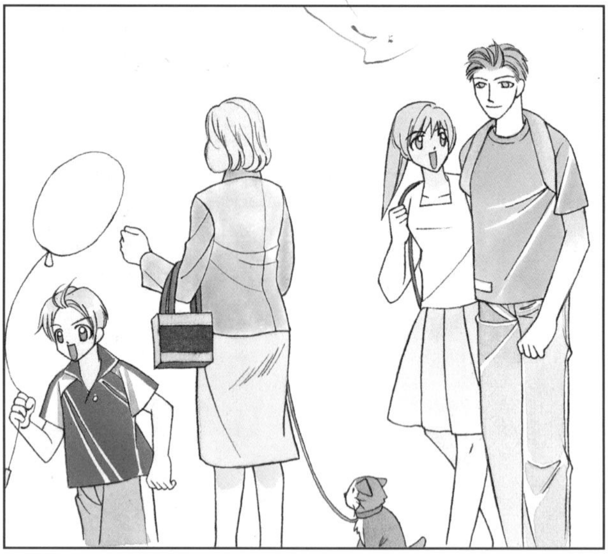

1. Paint water onto the area of paper you want to color, then paint a light color. Make sure the color doesn't bleed to other parts of the illustration.

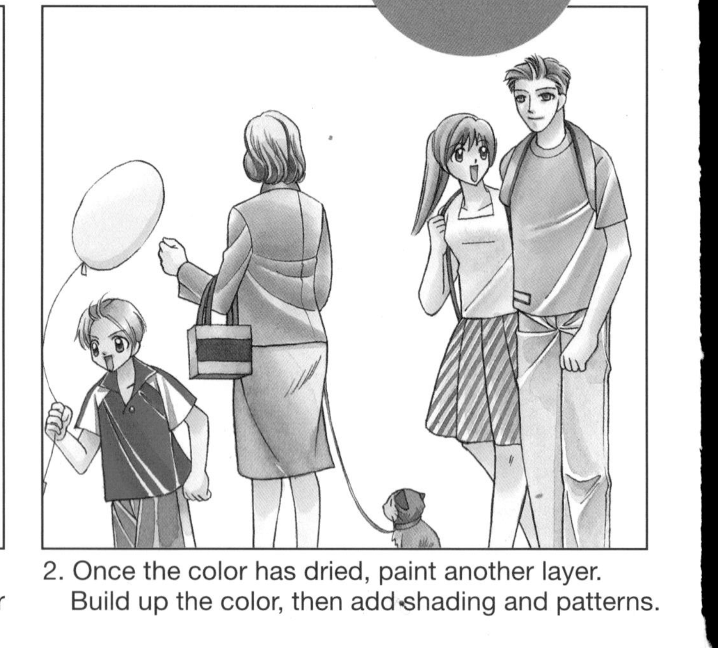

2. Once the color has dried, paint another layer. Build up the color, then add shading and patterns.

COLORING THE BACKGROUND

1. Just as with characters, first paint water over the area of paper you want to color. Before it dries, start painting with light colors.

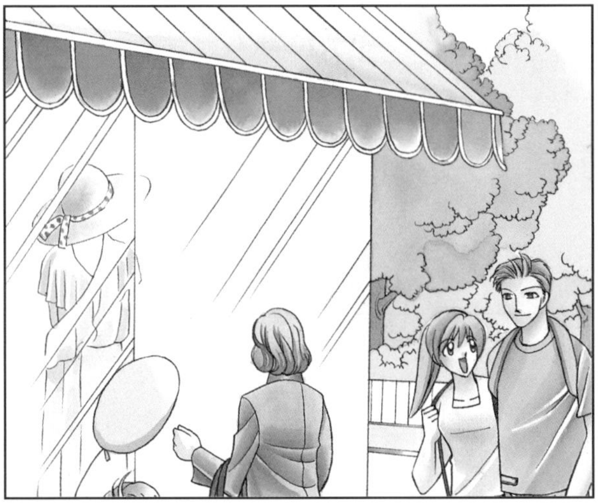

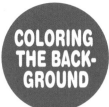

Protect the characters with masking!

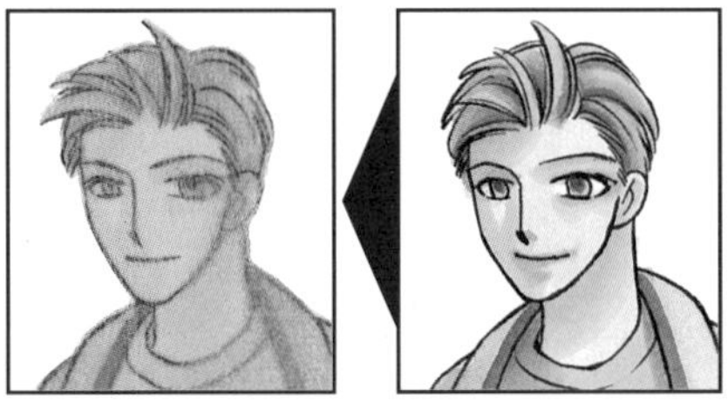

2. After the first layer of color has dried, start painting the next layer.

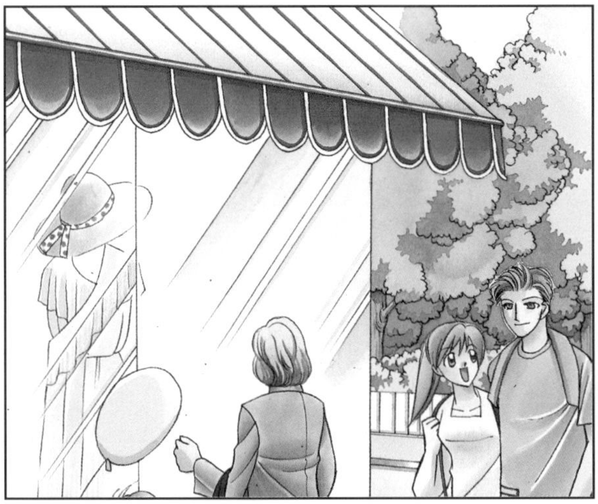

Trees **Window**

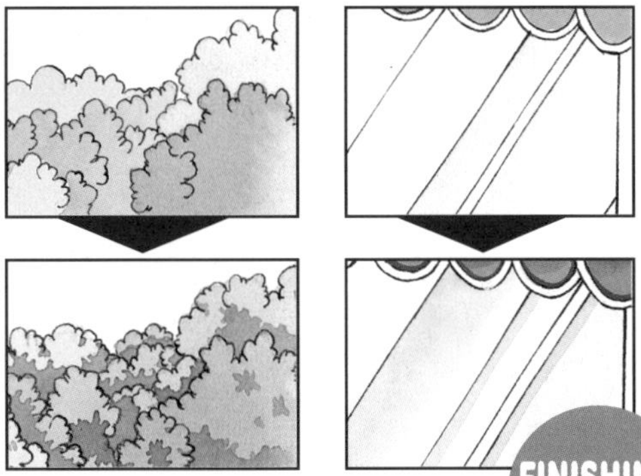

FINISHING TOUCHES

Add highlights with white ink.

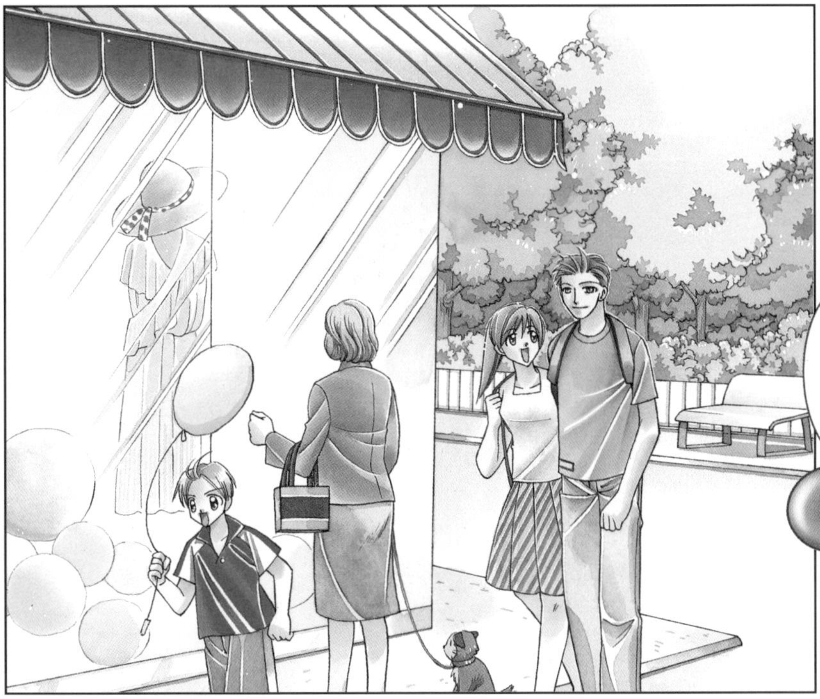

on trees

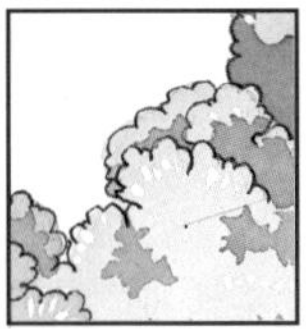

on clothing

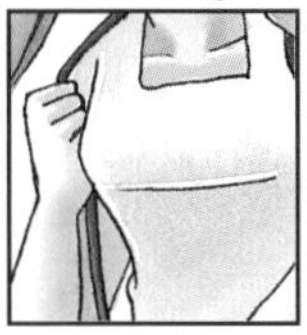

on hair

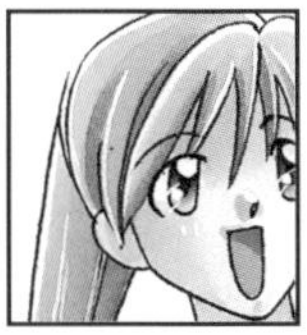

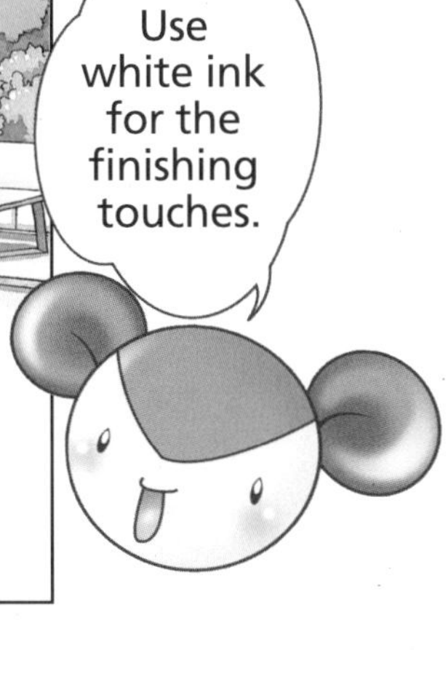
Use white ink for the finishing touches.

（英文版）漫画・イラストの描き方［中級編］
Draw Your Own Manga: Beyond the Basics

2005 年 4 月 25 日　第 1 刷発行

著　者　永友はる乃
発行者　畑野文夫
発行所　講談社インターナショナル株式会社
　　　　〒 112-8652 東京都文京区音羽 1-17-14
　　　　電話　03-3944-6493（編集部）
　　　　　　　03-3944-6492（営業部・業務部）
　　　　ホームページ　www.kodansha-intl.com

印刷・製本所 大日本印刷株式会社

落丁本・乱丁本は購入書店名を明記のうえ、小社業務部宛にお送りください。送料小社負担にてお取替えします。なお、この本についてのお問い合わせは、編集部宛にお願いいたします。本書の無断複写（コピー）、転載は著作権法の例外を除き、禁じられています。

定価はカバーに表示してあります。

© 2005 by I. C. Inc., Coade and Kodansha International Ltd.
Printed in Japan
ISBN 4-7700-2304-9